Apartheid: A Point to Cover

South African cricket 1948–1970 and the Stop The Seventy Tour

Arunabha Sengupta

APARTHEID: A POINT TO COVER

South African Cricket 1948–1970 and the Stop The Seventy Tour

by Arunabha Sengupta

Published by

CricketMASH,

Amstelveen, Netherlands

May 2020

Cover Design and Illustrations: Maha

ISBN: 978-94-92203-03-8

DEDICATION

To the idealistic young brigade of 1969–70, the 'long-haired trouble-makers', who went on to make a significant change in the world of inequality and injustice established and nurtured by the largely conventionally-haired, 'law'-abiding traditionalists.

CONTENTS

ACKNOWLEDGEMENTS

B Sreeram. I decided quite a few months ago that the book would have to begin with his name. Of course, we had to get the cover, dedication, and table of contents in place, but this acknowledgements section is where I truly start to express myself. And the acknowledgements could not be kicked off with any other name. To borrow a cricketing parlance, when Sreeram checks a book for facts, it stays checked. Besides, it does not end there; he is sure to unearth hidden histories underneath the established tales.

The value added by Sreeram in going deep into the layers of facts stretches from correcting clumsy chronological or clerical mistakes, to unearthing hitherto undiscovered gaps and errors in established sources to providing brand new angles, anecdotes, and insights. While I knew that I could expect all this for every cricketing passage in the book, Sreeram managed to provide the same degree of excellence as the action in this volume moved away from the cricket grounds to rugby fields, football pitches, and even distinctly non-sporting arenas like protest rallies, political gatherings, court cases, assassinations, and so on.

I have been collaborating with Maha for over three years now, and I have seldom come across a more brilliant and versatile artist. Her role in the book went beyond the splendid artwork as she doubled as a sounding board as well. No one was better equipped to produce artwork that encompassed the worlds of society, politics, and cricket.

I just about managed to meet Lord Hain before the world came to a standstill because of Coronavirus. It is said that one should never meet one's heroes because of the disappointment that invariably follows. In this case, the warning was quite ominous. After all, Peter was a hero to me because of something he had done 50 years earlier. Happily, this meeting was the exception that proverbially proves the rule. Peter was exactly as I had imagined him to be, felt as strongly about the movement that he had successfully led at the age of 20, and graciously agreed to write the foreword for the book within one week. He did it in one day.

The CricketMash research team of Abhishek Mukherjee, Mayukh Ghosh, Pradip Dhole, and Michael Jones were always ready with their inputs. Sumit Gangopadhyay was incredibly zealous and efficient in researching the obscurest of facts from the near-forgotten pages of history.

Considering the size of the book and the proliferation of cricketing terms, Amritorupa Kanjilal did a capital job of editing it.

Neil Robinson always had the doors of the MCC Library open with a welcoming smile whenever I needed to delve into obscure books and files.

My friend Pramathanath Sastry never hesitated to dip into his incredible reservoir of knowledge to come up with perceptive observations and recommendations.

Two of my favourite authors, Stephen Chalke and Tony Ring, were perpetually at hand with suggestions, encouragement and that elusive ingredient of genuine interest.

Finally, my daughter Meha was as proactive as ever in suggesting fonts, colour schemes, and design details.

A book of this extensive scope and subject matter would not have been possible without all these sterling contributions.

FOREWORD

by Peter Hain

For cricket and sports lovers, as well as those intrigued about the most institutionalised infestation ever of racist politics into sport, this book is a real treasure trove.

Historian and cricket lover Arunabha Sengupta has crafted a wonderful story of people who defied the odds and ultimately triumphed by ensuring that today sport in South Africa is organised according to the normal principle of selection and competition on merit – not race, as it was for nearly 50 years under apartheid, and for generations before going back to British colonial role in the nineteenth century.

Unusually he examines the sporting, social, and political history of South Africa through the prism of a cricket book.

His meticulous research and engaging photographs make this an even more compelling read. Fittingly, its appearance coincides with the fiftieth anniversary of the stopping of the 1970 all-white South African cricket tour to Britain, and also with the publication of my book Pitch Battles: Protest, Prejudice and Play (London, Rowman & Littlefield) co-authored with André Odendaal, South Africa's foremost sports historian and, like me, a sports apartheid struggle activist.

As chair of the Stop The Seventy Tour campaign in 1969–70, I led militant though non-violent invasions of cricket, rugby and tennis pitches to disrupt white tours representing apartheid South Africa. Arunabha Sengupta chronicles all that with care and diligence, as well as providing impressive depth and detail on cricket and society during the 1948–70 period.

From the novel vantage point of a cricket historian hailing from India and living in Amsterdam, he has woven a story of cricketing excitement amidst the harsh backdrop of South Africa's police state and apartheid's evil assault on human dignity and human rights.

House of Lords, London, March 2020

PROLOGUE: HULLE ENGELSE OF ONS ENGELSE

In retrospect, the most significant moment in the history of cricket was rather unremarkable. The ball was tickled down the leg side, the most basic of cricketing nudges.

The man with the bat could still be called athletic and powerful, but his lissom willowy form of the past had started hovering towards the thickset. A reflection of the enormous talent and ability that oozed there still, but perhaps with less than the youthful flamboyance, flash, and flair, now ensconced inside years and years of wisdom laced with experience and mortal flesh.

The relief as he took off for the elusive single was palpably etched across his face. From cosy armchairs, many will still cry themselves hoarse, coaxing us to believe that hundreds don't matter in a team sport. Ridiculous. They do. They will always matter. Overwhelmingly so. It is a function of our number system, of the way we count, a result of the eight fingers and two thumbs that close around the handle of the bat, pluck the beads of the abacus, click the buttons of a calculator, key digits into a computer spreadsheet, or just use the knuckle-brain coordination to arrive at sums and totals. It is imprinted in our consciousness.

A score of 87 not out in the first Test had not amounted to much, other than several weeks of harrowing tension. A century made all the difference. The moment two digits rolled on the scoreboard and a third appeared in the form of a '1' on the left, the efforts were recorded with special reverence. Every cricketer knew it. Especially the man who now acknowledged the cheers.

Later, in *The Basil D'Oliveira Affair*, he would write: "If I had scored a mere 99 I might have slid gently back into the obscurity into which I had drifted during a season when my skills had deserted me."

However, the scamper for a single at The Oval that afternoon did not really bear the mark of the colossally reverberating chain of events that it would kickstart.

Especially if one takes into account the pages of history among which that scurried run would stand out in the boldest of fonts.

The times were more than a changin', as Bob Dylan had insisted in his 1964 song. It looked as if the world had taken Harold Macmillan's Winds of Change speech at the start of the decade way too seriously and was trying its best to convert it into a tornado in every domain and direction.

The 1960s had started as a nightmare for human rights with the massacre at Sharpeville; the world had come to the brink of a nuclear disaster with the Cuban Missile Crisis. The Iron Curtain had been drawn firmly through the middle of the planet, turning the earth frigid with the chilly undercurrents of the Cold War.

John F Kennedy had been gunned down in 1963, Che Guevara in 1967. Vietnam and Czechoslovakia had been marauded by the two Superpowers. Fires had blazed all around for civil and other basic rights. Albert Luthuli's fight for the same had earned him the Nobel Peace Prize in 1960, Malcolm X had been rewarded with a bullet from a sawed-off shotgun in 1965, and Nelson Mandela's efforts had landed him in a cell in the infamous Robben Island in 1964.

1968 was perhaps the defining year when the world all but detonated.

Massacre continued in Vietnam, as did protests around the globe. At around six in the evening on 4 April, Martin Luther King Jr was fatally shot by James Earl Ray as he stood on the second-floor balcony of Lorraine Motel in Memphis. Less than a month later, students of the University of Paris were evacuated by the police from the Sorbonne Campus, resulting in perhaps the most powerful and riotous student rebellion in a decade defined by such.

On 5 June, US Presidential candidate Robert F Kennedy followed the fatal footsteps of his brother, as another assassination rocked the world. In the month that followed, violent protests kicked off in Mexico City, which would eventually culminate in the Tlatelolco massacre.

In the looking glass of the sporting arena, the explosive cocktail of political and social unrest surfaced in the form of unprecedented score-lines and demonstrations.

Cassius Clay boxed his way to the light-heavyweight gold in the 1960 Rome Olympics. Having changed his name to Muhammad Ali and having defended his heavyweight title against Sonny Liston, he refused to serve in the Vietnam War. "I ain't got no quarrel with them Viet Cong ... They never called me nigger." He was stripped of his title, and the resulting court case was eventually settled in 1971.

Sixteen days after that hastily run single at The Oval, at the West Side Tennis Club, Forest Hill, New York, Arthur Ashe served hard on match point and ran in to land a crisp backhand volley, thereby defeating Dutchman Tom Okker in a marathon five-set encounter 14-12, 5-7, 6-3, 3-6, 6-3. The very year the US National Championships went Open, it found a bespectacled Black man as the conqueror. It had not even been five months since President Lyndon Johnson had run his pen over the dotted line extending the Civil Rights Act to prohibit discrimination concerning the sale, rental, and financing of housing based on race, religion, or national origin.

The Black athletes had debated all along whether to participate in the 1968 Olympics in Mexico. Thankfully most of them did, and thereby found themselves on the most conspicuous of world stages. In October, Tommie Smith and John Carlos took their respective first and third positions on the victory podium for the 200-metre event, their feet shoeless, their black-gloved fists raised in the most famous sporting photograph of all time.

Even in cricket, a mere eight days after that Oval afternoon, Garry Sobers struck the hapless left-arm spin of Malcolm Nash for 6 sixes in one infamous over at Swansea, the last ball disappearing along King Edwards Road. While it was only incidental that Sobers also happened to be a Black man, it fitted snugly into the chronology of things.

That was the year when the world saw the dark side of the moon. History has its moments of symbolism.

It would also be the year in which Negroes would become Blacks.

Except, perhaps, in one part of the world. The curious country that would continue to walk backwards in time, in stubborn antithetical contrast to the rest of the world. Where the word 'apartheid' had been minted and had gradually found its way into the lexicon and national policy.

South Africa would take longer, way longer, to catch up with the rest of the modern world. It would take them 26 more years to end the vile system of apartheid.

And it will be several more decades from now, even as I write, before it attains anything approaching normalcy, such is the aftermath of the downright evil policy that had for long been the accepted way of life.

Basil D'Oliveira's tickle down the leg side was, in effect, a sturdy nail hammered into the coffin that was being painstakingly laid out, and that would take decades to be laid to rest. It was also a nail that pricked the apathetic White antiseptic bubble where it hurt the most.

We will come back to look at the Basil D'Oliveira innings in due course. For now, it suffices to limit ourselves to the moment.

He had gone in to lunch on the second day at 85, and was looking exceedingly nervous as he neared his hundred. A drive off Ashley Mallett had fallen just short of mid-off at 96. By now, he was keen to push singles. One such off Mallett took him to 99.

Bowling from the other end was the mystery spinner John Gleeson. The first three balls of the following over were good ones. Two of them took the edge as the batsman tried to work him to the on-side. And then there was a relatively innocuous one that was bowled straighter. D'Oliveira worked it to fine leg and—after 221 balls and 195 minutes—the hundred was his.

When he had got to 50, umpire Charlie Elliott had remarked, "Well played—my God, you're going to cause some problems." Now, the former Derbyshire opening batsman did not mince his words: "Oh Christ, you've put the cat among the pigeons now." Gleeson was a bit more reserved as he offered his hand, but he too was wondering along the same lines. "Well done, Bas, it'll be interesting to see what happens."

The man who raised his bat was 37. Well, officially he was 34, but we all know the story now. He had to lie about his age, out of fear of being considered too old to play for England.

By the laws of nature, he should have been recognised as one of the greatest batsmen of the world a decade earlier, alongside Everton Weekes, Peter May, and Neil Harvey. But he had made his Test debut just two years earlier. It was a testimony to his longevity as a great cricketer that he was still one of the very best batsmen of England.

In September 1953, at the Transvaal conference of the African National Congress, Nelson Mandela had borrowed the words of the Indian Prime Minister Jawaharlal Nehru to title his speech 'There is no easy walk to Freedom'. Years later, the title of the great man's autobiography would be *Long Walk to Freedom.*

There was no easy walk to freedom for D'Oliveira either. And freedom in his case was the freedom of self-expression as a magnificent cricketer, a display of his skill on the world stage. That freedom was denied to him, as it had been denied to too many of his people, fellow countrymen of Colour, fellow countrymen who were not White.

That he was in England, playing cricket, was a miracle in itself. He had already represented and also led what can logically be surmised to be the first truly representative South African national team ever. Way back in the 1950s.

But that team would never be blessed with the stamp of the establishment—an establishment that resembled an Old Boys' Club, where whims and anachronistic bigotry took the place of reason and logic as long as the colour of the tie was right.

The tale of D'Oliveira is oft-told—in some cases well-known—but more often than not sketchily. Nonetheless, it cannot be recounted as the story of an individual, a cricketer, a single sport, or even a lifetime. Those are ways to glimpse the facets of the story, without recognising the extraordinarily complicated structure that led to this fairy-tale finale.

Not quite the finale. There were to be complications, far removed from Dolly, the much-loved cricketer. Intrigue and complications, cloak-and-dagger in their intricacies, would dog every step. His participation at The Oval had been touch-and-go. Almost as soon as he reached his hundred, the phone rang in the office of Geoffrey Howard, the secretary of the Surrey County Cricket Club, supposedly from the Prime Minister's Office in Pretoria. The message was as loud as the transcontinental telephone lines of the late 1960s allowed, but it rang through clear as crystal. We will revisit this when we get back to this particular day in our story.

But where should we begin?

Perhaps we can begin in 1960, with D'Oliveira the young man in his late 20s. Just days after the Sharpeville massacre. As he stood confused on the platform waiting to board the train from London to Manchester, asking John Kay of *Manchester Evening News* where he could find the carriage for 'his people'.

Or perhaps in early 1963, with Papwa Sewgolum, the Natal-based Indian caddie catering to the needs of amateur White golfers. He won the Natal Open, beating 103 White participants, and yet had to accept the trophy in pouring rain because non-Whites were not allowed inside the clubhouse.

Or perhaps in September that same year, when Dennis Brutus, the President of the South African Non-Racial Olympic Committee (SAN-ROC) was shot in the back as he attempted to escape from police custody outside a Johannesburg Police Station. When an ambulance for the Whites arrived, it took one look, and then drove away on discovering that the man who lay bleeding was Black.

Or perhaps in 1965, when a 15-year-old White lad in South Africa called Peter Hain, clad in his school blazer, read out the address at the funeral of a dear family friend executed as a traitor. His parents could not attend because of banning orders served by the government.

Or perhaps we should look farther away, at New Zealand in 1960. The Wellington lawyer Rolland O'Regan collected 162,000 signatures for the petition 'No Maori, no Tour' to stop the Springbok-All Blacks contests. The encounter between the only two nations where rugby was not played but lived. When a constellation of stellar individuals from all walks of life assembled in a deputation to grace the Prime Minister's office in a protest, and the Bishop of Aotearoal, the Right Reverend WN Panapa, led the Maori members of the deputation in a haka.

South Africa is too complex. A melting pot turned vicious, it cannot be seen in black and white—literally or figuratively. Black has multiple hues. White has its problems of identity. And that is why this severe problem engulfed the land in a way encountered by few other nations.

We can perhaps try to exemplify the confusion with another Test match. This time at the Wanderers, Johannesburg, on 27 January 1965. The fourth Test of the series.

England under MJK Smith are up 1-0, having won the first Test at Durban. Perhaps buoyed by the unexpected presence of the great Wally Hammond in the dressing room, they have been bowled to an innings win by spinners David Allen and Fred Titmus.

But now, in the fourth Test, the hosts have attained a winning position thanks to the excellent ton by captain Trevor Goddard. The first and only one of his great career. Graeme Pollock and Colin Bland have thrashed 96 runs in an hour and a quarter.

Trevor Goddard completes his hundred with this hasty single at Johannesburg, 1965

With the ask of batting out two sessions for a draw, Smith sends Titmus in to open with Geoff Boycott, instead of the aggressive Bob Barber. This underlines his disinclination to go for the 314 runs.

Peter Pollock, young and fast, steams in, bowling his heart out. At 21, after 43 minutes of resistance, Titmus fends one and it is caught close in by skipper Peter van der Merwe. The normally majestic Ted Dexter cannot keep a nasty one down and is brilliantly taken by the bowler's younger brother Graeme at short leg. Ken Barrington, facing left-arm spinner Athol McKinnon, is caught in two minds, fatally late in drawing his bat away. Harry Bromfield pouches it up at gully. 33 for 3, with nearly three hours to play.

Peter Parfitt, who has hit an unbeaten 122 in the first innings, now joins Boycott.

After a while, the news is conveyed to nearby Pretoria that the English are struggling at 42 for 3. It is then that the curious question is voiced, that will generally be attributed to the then Minister of Justice BJ Vorster: "Hulle Engelse of ons Engelse?"

Translated from Afrikaans, this means: "Their English or our English?"

Yes, South Africa is complex. The identity as a nation is curious. Afrikaner nationalism, which formed the framework for the post-1948 policies of apartheid, was much more than *wit en swart*—black and white. It was a perplexing path through the 150-odd years of combustible coexistence between the British settlers and the descendants of the early Dutch pioneers, with the many-fangled mixtures of various people, the Germans and the Huguenots.

And then there were the Africans of various origins, the Xhosa from whom hailed Mandela, the Zulu from whom hailed Nobel Prize winner Luthuli, the nomadic pastoralist Khoekhoe who were plain lucky not to be massacred to extinction. There were the Indians in Natal. There was the mixed-race population, collectively called Coloured, often confusingly referred to as Malays, from whom hailed D'Oliveira.

So much so that at one point of time, there were as many as seven parallel national cricket boards in the country.

Back to the Test match.

Peter Pollock breaks down with a pulled thigh muscle after 11 scorching overs. He ends with 2 for 27, which is very nearly topped with a vital third wicket when the ball kisses the handle of Boycott's bat and flies just over the slips. McKinnon bowls 30 overs on the trot and ends with 3 for 44 from 35, but Pollock's firepower in cleaning up the tail is sorely missed. Boycott remains doggedly unbeaten on 76, having survived 247 deliveries. And Tom Cartwright, making the first and the minor of his two cameo appearances in our story, scores just 8 but bats through the last half-hour. England save the day at 153 for 6.

But it is more than cricket we need to look at if we want to understand one of the greatest social triumphs achieved through the game.

The complexities of the South African land are but a stepping-stone. That is why Mandela, imprisoned in Robben Island, spent days and years studying Afrikaner history, the grievances that the White Afrikaners nursed from the injustices suffered in the Boer War.

Hence, we need to begin our journey way, way back in time, at Green Point in Cape Town, a vast tract of waste land in the east of the city's commercial centre. The same Green Point where Basil D'Oliveira learnt the basics of the game, with matches organised among the Coloured people of the Cape.

We need to start in 1806, when we find the first mention of a cricket match in this part of the world.

Future Prime Minister Hendrik Verwoerd (seated on extreme left second row) watching MCC play in Pretoria 1956–57

SECTION 1
The Quest for a White Man's Country

1 ANGUISH FROM THE START

On 24 April 1806, Dr Huibert Nahuys van Burgst was travelling under Danish sails on a confidential government mission to Batavia on behalf of the Dutch.

As the ship approached Table Bay, the crew saw to their relieved surprise that the flags fluttering on the castle were Dutch and the uniforms of the soldiers were the welcome Dutch blue.

It was only when the ship was about to dock a "few cable lengths from the land" did the men on board realise that they had been conned. It had been the British flying the Dutch flags, wearing the blue uniforms over their red tunics, to lure the ship in.

Just a few months earlier, the British had taken over through a magnificent invasion.

Nahuys van Burgst was detained in Cape Town for two months. From his own account, it does seem that he enjoyed his stay immensely. And it is also in his account that we find the first mention of cricket in South Africa:

"With a number of [English officers] serving in the artillery and light dragoons I twice a week played a game of ball-casting, called cricket by the English, on level ground by the sea at Lion's Tail. Round twelve o'clock we started our sport, sometimes with more than thirty persons. A small cart carrying food and wine followed us and in a jovial spirit we usually had our midday meal."

That level ground by the sea at the Lion's Tail is Green Point Common, where Basil D'Oliveira learnt the basics of the game with his non-White, or even more specifically—Coloured—mates. It is the second oldest surviving cricket ground in the world outside England (the oldest being the Calcutta Maidans, where the Etonian Civilians played the Other Servants of the Company in 1804).

This is first known account of cricket in the Cape. The Fairest Cape. And as we can see, it was riddled with a tussle between the Dutch and the British right from the very beginning.

The Fairest Cape

When Francis Drake sailed past it during his circumnavigation of the world, he was enchanted. He called it 'a most stately thing, the fairest cape in the whole circumference of the earth.'

For long this Fairest Cape, and subsequently the entire subcontinent, remained a curious strategic chessboard. White pieces, powerful and not-so-powerful, tussled against each other, taking breaks to variously subjugate and massacre numerous Black pawns. They were worse than pawns. Very, very seldom were they allowed to advance through the squares for promotion, or to get anywhere close.

The ones who did, like Basil D'Oliveira, were miraculous exceptions. More often than not, the pawns were packed into their own dilapidated, matchbox zones, areas that became progressively smaller and more noxious. No game had worse rules.

For centuries the land had been home to the Khoisan and the Bantus, with various categories such as Zulus, Xhosa, Swazi, Ndebele, Basotho, Bapedi, Venda, Tswana, Tsonga, and many more.

Yes, all these names are complicated, too complicated to be mentioned in a cricket book.

Very few wanted them in those parts anyway. In 1652 arrived the first Dutch settlers. And it was their land no more.

In 1651, the Rump Parliament led by Oliver Cromwell had passed the so-called Navigation Act. The new law banned non-English ships from transporting goods from Asia, Africa, or America to England or its colonies. It was strategically targeted at the Dutch East India Company (Vereenigde Oostindische Compagnie or VOC), the first major multi-national company, with the first known corporate logo.

The resulting competition kickstarted a mini scramble. With the English setting their sights on St Helena, a strategic base in the Atlantic on the way to the Indian Ocean, the Dutch government decided to do everything in their power to offer resistance in European waters and overseas. The Cape was therefore considered a strategic location. And in 1652 arrived Jan van Riebeeck, the former head of the VOC trading post in Tonkin, Indochina. He set about occupying the Table Bay, founding a refreshment station on the way to the Dutch East Indies.

It did not take long. The Dutch burghers soon fell out with the Khoekhoe. The main bone of contention was the land that had, for all these centuries, belonged to the Africans and their cattle. The expanses were suddenly cordoned off for the White settlers. In 1660, van Riebeeck began the construction of a barrier stretching almost 14 kilometres to keep the Khoekhoe out of the VOC territory—the start of the various processes of segregation that we would see over almost three and a half centuries.

The Cape remained more of a victualing station rather than a lucrative colony. The indigenous Khoekhoe were gradually expropriated, hunted and killed like game. The chiefdoms disintegrated and many moved inland. A number of them became farm labourers.

Meanwhile, starting in 1658, slaves were brought in from the Dutch East Indies. As years wore on, the influx of slaves remained unabated. In strange contrast to the Americas, the slaves imported here were mostly not from Africa. Some were from Mozambique, a few from Madagascar, but mostly they came from Indonesia, India, and Ceylon, including a large proportion of Muslims. Hence the confusing and often wrongly interchanged term Malays.

Mixed race people emerged, giving rise to the Cape Coloured populace. Very, very few of the slaves were manumitted. On the other hand, use of *sjambok*, a rod made of animal hide and capable of inflicting severe pain, was found in every slave-owning household. Punishment at the stake and horrible deaths were common.

The White settlement, on the other hand, was not restricted to the Dutch. A handful of French Huguenots arrived in 1688 and later the German immigrants. These three White ethnic groups, with a tiny percentage of the Coloured mixing, gave rise to what was variously known as the Christians, Europeans, Cape Dutch. With time, they would eventually start to identify themselves as the Afrikaner people.

The Cape continued to function as a refreshment station on the way to the Far East and back. The major responsibility of the settlers was to produce food for themselves and the Dutch ships that passed by. Hence, they were classified as farmers—or to use the Dutch word, *Boer*. As a natural course of events, frontier wars between the Boers and the native population kept occurring in sporadic bursts.

A tale of anguish—cricketing and otherwise

By 1795, the number of burghers (White settlers) stood at 20,000 and the number of slaves at 25,000. *Gelijkstelling* (social levelling) in the form of inter-mingling between the slaves and the free people was denounced as acts undermining the very basis of a civilised society.

It was to this Cape that the first known First-Class cricketer arrived in 1797. His name, ironic or prophetic as one sees it, was Charles Anguish.

The complex commercial relations between the British and Dutch during the American War of Independence had turned the Cape of Good Hope into a major strategic location. It had become the Gibraltar of the Indian Ocean. Hence, General Sir James Craig was despatched to take over the Cape for the British. The invasion was easy. The fleet consisted of eight vessels, including three 74-gun warships. Within 48 hours, the Dutch proposed an armistice. The Union Jack was raised over the Castle and the colony capitulated to the British.

Charles Anguish arrived on 4 May 1797. He had been posted in the capacity of the Comptroller of Customs for the Cape region.

He was not much of a cricketer, although his family origins enabled him to play alongside the likes of Earl of Winchilsea, Charles Lennox, and 'Silver Billy' Beldham. His record was less than ordinary.

Neither is there any record of him playing in the Cape. Before Anguish could take part in cricket of the Cape, he killed himself. His suicide took place exactly three weeks from the day he arrived in this new land. Nevertheless, there have been several educated guesses that he might have swung a cricket bat after being appointed.

Just about a month after the death of Charles Anguish, Earl Macartney, the British Governor of the Cape, introduced the first of the infamous Pass Laws that would continue to dog the area for almost two centuries. The new internal passports, implemented on 27 June 1797, were meant to prevent native Africans from entering the Cape Colony.

The Brits and the game take root

The first British occupation of the Cape was quite short. Following the Treaty of Amiens, the territory was returned to the Dutch in 1802. However, barely a month or two had passed since the departure of the British garrison when Napoleon's desire to crush his foes across the channel became dangerously adamant.

The Dutch were caught in the power tussle without much of a choice. The Batavian Republic was virtually ordered to become a French department.

The result was inevitable. The first British warship returned to the Cape on Christmas Eve, 1805. By January 1806, the British were back at the helm.

This also kickstarted a century and a half of colonial rule, the great southern land administered from Whitehall in London. The second White dimension took its place alongside the Boers, creating a power struggle that would result in one of the most complex and troubled societies of all time.

Moreover, like most examples of imperialism, it would spread the other constants of avarice, cunning, conflict, bigotry, discrimination, evangelisation, Christianity, humanitarianism, xenophobia, syphilis, carnage ... and cricket.

It was at this British-occupied Cape that Nahuys van Burgst arrived in 1806.

The match described by Nahuys actually predates what was for long supposed to be the first reported game of cricket in the Cape. The *Cape Town Gazette* and *African Advertiser* published the following notice on 2 January 1808: "A grand match at cricket will be played for 1,000 dollars a side on Tuesday, 5 January 1808, between the officers of the artillery mess, having Colonel Austen of the 60th regiment, and the officers of the Colony, with General

Clavering. The wickets are to be pitched at 10 o'clock."

Two years later, on 13 January 1810, another notice on *Cape Town Gazette and African Advertiser* announced yet another match for a stake of 1,000 dollars between the Officers and the Rest of the Army.

Similarly, on 21 October 1814, at the Simonstown racecourse, a grand match was played between 22 gentlemen of the navy for a subscription purse.

It was the gentlemen officers of the army and the navy who really spread the game. From the Cape, the game reached Port Elizabeth, and then Durban—the ports where the soldiers docked as the colony expanded. Inland spread came much later.

What were these British gentlemen officers doing while they were not playing the 'Gentleman's Game'?

In October 1808, they were quelling a slave uprising led by Louis van Mauritius.

In 1811, Sir John Graham led a mixed force of British regulars, Boer commandos, and a newly formed regiment consisting of Khoekhoe soldiers in the fourth frontier war. Graham's order to his men was to destroy every Kaffir in sight.

The Xhosas were driven beyond the Fish River, thousands of them massacred. Graham, a Scottish aristocrat, whose grandson would later play in the first ever representative cricket tournament in South Africa, recounted: "[It was] detestable work. [We were] forced to hunt them like wild beasts." Colony, Christianity, cricket ... and carnage—they did go hand in hand.

It was in such a land that John Duffy arrived from Dublin in 1820; one of the five thousand '1820 settlers' who emigrated from Britain to the Eastern Cape to escape the post-Napoleonic War unemployment crisis back home. The Cape Colony government promised a better life.

At Port Arthur, later to become Port Alfred, he started his new life on land that had been made available for them when the 20,000 Xhosa had been driven away in 1811. There he met a girl, another of the '1820 settlers', who had arrived from England. The couple married and would form the maternal lineage of Adelaine Hain, and thereby her son Peter Hain.

The new immigrants were settled along the 'White' side of the Fish River, as a sort of bulwark against the Black chiefdoms which occupied most of the remaining parts of the country. This was an intriguing new White mix into the already complicated bits that composed the population.

2 LION'S RUMP BUT NO ELEPHANT'S MEMORY

Basil D'Oliveira nursed a bump on his head for long. He and his mates played their cricket on the cobblestoned streets of Signal Hill. When a police car was sighted, it was necessary to make a fast getaway. Perhaps he was too caught up in the game or perfecting a particular stroke when he was caught on the head by a truncheon of the law—or whatever passed as law in the 1940s South Africa.

He even woke up in a police cell once, detained for playing cricket on the streets. An uncle had to bail him out, using all his influence and powers of negotiation.

Signal Hill is the Lion's Rump, as opposed to the Lion's Tail that was the Green Point mentioned in Nhuys van Burgst's cricketing account. There is also the Lion's Head, not so obvious from the shape, a mountain flanked by the hill and the Table Mountain, completing the geographical anatomy

Signal Hill, which lies up the slopes on the east of commercial Cape Town, was so named because of the signal flags that used to communicate weather warnings and anchoring instructions to the visiting ships.

The very same year that Nhuys van Burgst was duped into landing in the Cape, the Noon Gun was set up in Signal Hill to fire time signals. The 18-pounder smooth-bore muzzle-loading guns designed by Captain Thomas Blomfield still fire every day at noon. It was also fired to notify the garrison that ships were sailing their way, and they could be called upon to defend the settlement.

A Time Ball was also set up—to relay the precise moment of 1 PM Cape Mean Time. It was still in operation in 1931 when Basil D'Oliveira was born there. Later, when he wrote *The D'Oliveira Affair* in 1969, he provided the same date of birth as he had given to the cricket authorities in England—4 October 1934. He was actually three years older.

It was on the cobblestoned streets of Signal Hill that D'Oliveira played his first cricket. Usually, one street played another. Living in a sort of maisonette at the top of a very steep slope, the young D'Oliveira did not belong to any of the streets. Hence, the other boys would toss to decide which team he played for.

Standing in front of the D'Oliveira house in the so-called Malay quarters, one saw to the right the huge expanse of the Table Mountain and the sprawling city of Cape Town below.

The Green Point lay a few kilometres down and a few years into the future. The first knack of the game was developed on those streets. As he would take strike in front of a tin can or a lamp post for the wicket, one of his playmates would stand on the top of a flight of stairs, making the tennis ball bounce accurately on the edge of the lowest step, so that it flew up to his ears. D'Oliveira had no choice but to swat it away. That is how he claimed to have learnt his favourite hook shot.

He was never coached. An aunt bought him Sir Donald Bradman's *Art of Cricket*, which he read in bed.

There was talent in those street games. D'Oliveira's assessment of one of his mates come across as a striking example of lost talent.

"There was [a] boy in those street games who used to keep wicket. I swear he would have been a Test player if he had ever had the chance. He would stand behind an oil can for hour after hour while the kids bowled to him. At that stage there would be no batsman. The ball would be hard […] the object of bowling out there was to be quicker than anybody else on view."

The defining phrase in the description of this unnamed champion is 'if he ever had the chance'. That is where the line was drawn. The colour line.

This unnamed champion in D'Oliveira's memoirs was Lobo Abed, one of the five famous Muslim brothers who emerged as extraordinary sportsmen from Cape Town.

Hampshire professional Jack Newman, the same man who was once ordered off the ground by captain Hon Lionel Tennyson for refusing to bowl while the crowd was barracking, later settled in Cape Town as a coach. According to his experienced eye, Lobo Abed was as brilliant as Godfrey Evans.

There were others as well—Cec Abrahams, Eric Petersen, and Ben Malamba to name just a few. We will come across them as we move forward with our tale.

However, even as D'Oliveira and his mates came through the ranks, graduating from Signal Hill and moving to Green Point, few contemplated playing Test cricket. It was a different world, beyond the dreams and ambitions of their people.

Not that D'Oliveira had the worst of the cards laid out by the hand of fate. He was born Cape-Coloured. From the point of view of social and political status, they traversed the uneasy middle path between the pampered White minority and the subjugated Black majority. Somewhat—although not entirely—like the Indian population that was concentrated mainly in Natal.

The colour of his skin was, to use his own words, 'oatmeal'. He could possibly be mistaken for a White. Later, when some of his English teammates browned easily in the sun, they joked: "Hey, Bas, who's the native now?" However, being born Coloured in South Africa was hardly a laughing matter.

The Blacks were hauled off into townships to live in despicable conditions, but it was not so for the Coloured population for the Cape as yet. D'Oliveira did manage to attend Roman Catholic schools, starting with St Josephs.

However, in his school, which he walked six miles to reach every day, he did not benefit from any cricket coaching facility and was left to learn the game on the streets of Signal Hill.

Three years before him, Cape Town had seen the birth of the future captain of the White South African national cricket team, Clive van Ryneveld. Van Ryneveld's father had played rugby for the Springboks in 1910, and he himself would represent England in Five Nations. His maternal uncle had played 18 Test matches for South Africa from 1913 to 1924. The young van Ryneveld attended the Diocesan College or Bishops, just a few miles away in Rondebosch. When van Ryneveld was admitted into the school as an eight-year-old, the master in charge of cricket was the future Test cricketer Pieter van der Bijl—who would score 460 runs at 51.11 in the 1938–39 Test series against Wally Hammond's Englishmen, including 125 and 97 at Durban in the infamous Timeless Test.

The beautifully curated wickets of the Bishops were tended to by the underpaid Black staff—the only way the non-Whites could dream of getting into the premises.

In 1947, Basil D'Oliveira had to forego his ambitions to become a doctor because of financial necessities. He started work as a platen pressman at the Cape Town branch of Croxley and Dickinson. It was more or less the same time that van Ryneveld left for Oxford, kickstarting a privileged sporting career which would see him emerge as a double international.

Making a living as a sportsman was way beyond the colour line. There were many more fundamental requirements one needed to struggle for as a non-White in South Africa. Requirements that came as a packaged deal with fundamental human rights in most countries. But human rights were far from given in that land. Especially after 1948.

Besides, the game itself was curiously segregated, mirroring the norms of that strange society. Cricket in South Africa was run by five parallel segregated cricket boards, with the plentiful abbreviations creating an alphabetical labyrinth as complex as the racial divide they stood on.

The South African Cricket Association (SACA) represented White South Africa, the only board that had the blessing of the Imperial Cricket Conference, the forerunner of the current day International Cricket Council. As the name implied, the international body was still coasting on the heydays of the empire. The memory of the dazzling sun that never set refused tally with the times when the actual sun was setting beyond the horizons of the erstwhile colonies and rising over newly independent nations. For the ICC, the SACA was all there was to South African cricket.

The South African Coloured Cricket Board (SACCB) was for the non-Whites, which further broke down into South African Independent Coloured Cricket Board (SAICCB) [which in turn became South African Coloured Cricket Association (SACCA)], South African Bantu Cricket Board (SABCB), and South African Indian Cricket Union (SAICU).

The alphabet soup seldom made for mixed offerings.

During the formative days of D'Oliveira, and before the 1950s, the non-Whites also played their own tournaments among their own fragmented groups. And it was very rare, if not unheard-of, for Whites and non-Whites to clash on a cricket field.

Faulty perceptions

Most of their cricket was contested in the shadows, on terrible grounds, without coverage, away from international eyes. It was after reaching England in 1960 that Basil D'Oliveira played on proper grass.

And even after he had fought his way into the county circuit, John Waite, the White South African wicketkeeper batsman, wrote in his 1961 book *Perchance to Bowl:* "One excellent reason we are not ready for [mixed race sport] is that there are no African, Indian or Cape Coloured rugby footballers, cricketers or athletes whose ability or exploits would justify their selection ahead of White candidates for South Africa."

He could not have been further from the truth.

In their seminal four-volume history of South African cricket, André Odendaal and his team assert that it is easy to imagine local slaves or free Black people preparing and serving the 'midday meal' referred to by Nahuys, or simply watching from outside the playing area. Indeed, one can also picture them as enthusiastic, often voluntary, ball boys.

However, the involvement of Black men in the sports of the supposed master race would be much more than peripheral.

November 1870. All of Queenstown turn out to watch the visiting St Mark's side, who have challenged the White Queenstown Club. It is quite a novelty, because the visitors are Black.

The Black men do quite well, holding on to a draw. Nathaniel Umhalla, the most promising batsman among the visitors, is the joint top scorer for them. J Benikazi, a former student of the Zonnebloem College, captures six wickets.

The Queenstown Free Press *notes: "Among the talk upon this unusual event we were surprised to hear some intelligent men, at least they call themselves such, shake their heads at it, and speak as though they thought they were demeaning themselves in playing such a game."*

This is the first reported match between Coloured and White sides in South Africa (we don't have written records other than a mention of the Hottentot-Africander [sic] match of 1854).

Although we need to note that Johnny Mullagh and the rest of the motley group of Aboriginal Australian cricketers had already undertaken their epochal tour of England two years earlier, the St Mark's-Queenstown game does precede the first ever Parsis vs Bombay Gymkhana match in India by seven years.

It was not a one-off game. In January 1871, a return fixture was arranged.

In 1980, Dawie de Villiers—rugby legend, Springbok captain, and later a cabinet minister in Nelson Mandela's government of national unity—declared: "Let's not forget that the Blacks have really known western sports for the last ten years."

Waite and de Villiers were perhaps not deliberately propagating untruths. Perhaps they were victims of a misconception spread through near-deliberate erasure of history.

The early history of South African sport was scrupulously documented by Maurice Luckin in his 1915 volume that ran 848 pages. However, it turned out to be the history which White South Africa wanted to read. In the 848 pages, there was only one mention of a cricket match involving non-White cricketers.

Luckin, still considered the authoritative text on the early history of South African cricket, completely ignores six Native Inter-town tournaments between 1884 and 1898 that ran parallel to the White Champion Bat tournaments, seven Malay Inter-Town tournaments between 1890 and 1898, as well as two extraneous native tournaments and a solitary extraneous Malay tournament.

And while Luckin is painstakingly accurate about the Currie Cup matches, he is silent about the Barnato Memorial Trophy for the non-Whites, which was often reported in even the major colonial papers of the day.

Reflecting on King Leopold II's Congo atrocities, Adam Hochschild says it is one long tale of the politics of forgetting. The history of non-White cricket in South Africa is comparable.

There are more striking remnants of non-white cricket in South Africa.

Zonnebloem College for the Kaffirs was set up by Sir George Grey, Governor of the Cape Colony. This seasoned administrator mixed humanitarian measures alongside abject disregard for justice—quite the exclusive domain of the British coloniser.

Riding on the tragedy of superstitious cattle-killing that had tragically affected the Xhosa people and broken the power of their chiefs, the British government sought to get many of the chiefs and their councillors out of the way to Robben Island—a prologue to the Nelson Mandela saga that took place almost exactly a century later.

However, Sir George also convinced several of the Xhosa chiefs and their councillors to allow their sons and daughters a chance to undergo British education at the Zonnebloem College. He promised to keep a personal eye on them and to return them on completion of their studies. The kids were, in effect, diplomatic hostages.

Initially located in Bishop's Court, Cape Town, which would eventually house Archbishop Desmond Tutu, the college kicked off in 1858; 33 princes and three princesses from the main

Xhosa clan and chiefdoms were escorted to the college by Grey. Grey also convinced Tswana, Sotho, and other chiefs to send their children.

Fitted in Western clothing and familiarised with every nuance of Western living, they were introduced to cricket in 1861. The boys continued their education, and their pursuit of cricket, in the years that followed.

Grey was succeeded by the Sir Philip Wodehouse, distant cousin of the legendary humourist PG Wodehouse. "Whereas parsimony was the usual practice at Zonnebloem, expenditure on cricket equipment featured in the accounts as a regular and rather extravagant outlay."

Nathaniel Umhalla, whom we have already come across playing for St Mark's in 1870, was the son of one of the Chiefs imprisoned in Robben Island. He would go on to become a teacher in a church, a journalist, a political activist, and the founder of the South African Native Congress in 1890 (which in 1912 would become the African National Congress). At the same time, he would have a parallel cricketing career as batsman, captain, and cricket administrator stretching over 30 years.

Alongside cricket, rugby and other White sports found their African manifestations—manifestations that remained hidden from the world.

In some ways, the Africans of 1850s and 1860s, at least the more privileged ones, had better cricketing facilities than D'Oliveira in the 1940s.

The Lovedale College cricket team dating from the late 1800s

3 NAME IS SMALL BUT DEEDS ARE GREAT

Piet Hein!, Piet Hein!, Piet Hein zijn naam is klein,
Zijn daden bennen groot, zijn daden bennen groot
Hij heeft gewonnen de zilveren vloot,
Die heeft gewonnen, gewonnen de Zilvervloot.

These are lines from the Dutch song *De Zilvervloot.* The legend describes a Dutch admiral, Piet Hein, who captured the *Zilvervloot*—a treasure fleet stocked with silver being transported from South America to Spain in 1628.

Here is the rough translation:

Piet Hein !, Piet Hein !, Piet Hein his name is small,
His deeds are great, his deeds are great
He has won the silver fleet,
He has won the Zilvervloot.

Holland being a small nation, the football fans sing about Piet Hein's deeds to remind the world that a small power can overcome a great one.

Much of the spirit of the song can be transferred seamlessly into the story of the approximate namesake of the Dutch admiral, Peter Hain. Not only is his name small, he himself was little more than a wisp of a boy during the tumultuous days of late 1960s and the climactic months of 1970. He celebrated his 20th birthday in the frenzy of the incredible youthful movement against the Springbok Rugby tour of 1969–70 and the proposed South African cricket tour of the summer of 1970. He was the lynchpin, the leader, the young man whose idealism was pure enough to blaze through centuries of apathy bred through robust trade relations and historic Old Boys' Clubs.

It would be fair to say that Peter Hain is the hero of our narrative alongside Basil D'Oliveira.

Peter was born in Nairobi on 16 February 1950. South Africa was going through a building slump, making it difficult for his father Walter to find work as an architect. The only job he found was in Nairobi, arranged for him by a partner in the firm for whom he had worked in his practical year. Hence, with his wife Adelaine, he travelled from Johannesburg to start a new life.

It was while stopping at the capital Salisbury (current day Harare) of Southern Rhodesia (current day Zimbabwe) that the young couple had an awakening. For the first time in their lives, they saw Black people sitting with White friends in the lounge of the same hotel where they stayed.

When they settled in Kenya, then a British colony with a White ruling elite, they came across a society in which racial divisions were a lot less formalised and extreme than in South Africa. True, the apartheid machinery was just about starting to be rolled out back home, and things were not yet as segregated as they were about to become. Nonetheless, the laxness of the boundaries made for a pleasant change.

Not that they were typical White South Africans anyway.

Adelaine Hain: Peter's Mother.

Ad, as we have seen, descended from the British settlers of 1820, who had come to the Cape looking for a new life during the unemployment that had followed the Napoleonic Wars.

She had grown up as Adelaine Stocks in the outskirts of Port Alfred, close to a Coloured family and with people of the Xhosa tribe passing by her door on their way to nearby towns.

Those were the days before rigid segregation. Although there was a historic colour bar, there were also some Black students attending the same school as she.

At school, Mrs Powell, a plump music teacher draped perpetually in a long cardigan, introduced her class to Paul Robeson through a gramophone recording.

Her students were more than surprised when she subtly explained that he was a 'native', and also a popular American film star. Later, studying at Victoria Girls High in Grahamstown, Ad came to know that the film *Sanders of the River* starring Paul Robeson was showing in Port Alfred's cinema. She urged her mother Edith to watch it for her. When the prospect of watching a Black man singing on the screen disturbed Edith, Ad had convinced her by stressing on the family's Christian Scientist faith: All were children of God. Edith had been impressed by Robeson.

And then there had been Miss Druce, Jewish, plain and stout, who invited the senior girls to listen to classical music in her study and quietly spoke about her belief in racial equality.

Adelaine was also the more politically conscious of young Peter's parents. Her father Gerald Stocks had been a prominent member of the English-speaking United Party, led by the Boer War hero and Prime Minister Jan Smuts. Adelaine had accompanied her father to public meetings, and on one occasion startled everyone by challenging the visiting United Party MP, Tom Bowker.

Walter Hain: Peter's father.

Wal's parents were Scottish immigrants from Glasgow. Like the ancestors of Adelaine, they had left for South Africa after another major war, the First World War.

His own exposure to politics had not really been as prominent as that of his wife, but neither was he a typical homegrown South African White man.

Joining the army, he had travelled far and wide during the Second World War. As a member of the 6th South African Armoured Division, he was wounded in action in Italy.

He was 19 at that time. When his 18-year-old comrade Lanky Brasler was shot, Wal saw Coloured stretcher-bearers ignore incoming fire to rush in and carry his friend to the regimental aid post nearby.

When Peter was six weeks old, Ad and Wal were invited by an Englishman to visit a settlement of *rondavels* with thatched roofs where the Kenyan Masai chiefs lived.

The enigmatic group of tall, thin, nomadic Masai people were captivated by the new baby. Water was sprinkled all over, which surprised the young parents.

Their English friend explained that the Masai were anointing the baby in their traditional custom of spitting. Far from being repulsed, Ad and Wal were delighted at this show of respect and intimacy.

Happy as their Kenyan days were, Wal was finding it difficult to adjust with colleagues at work. Hence, the young family decided to return home to South Africa. There was an opportunity to join the firm where Wal had worked in his final university year.

They came to a rather bizarrely brave decision—they would drive. That would be a great way to see the countries of Uganda, Belgian Congo, Northern Rhodesia (Zambia), and Southern Rhodesia (Zimbabwe). They packed the car, a 1936 Lancia Aprilia, with their stuff. With Peter just about a year old, the family started on this incredible tour.

During the four weeks of punctures, breakdowns, running out of petrol, curious African eyes, and dearth of food and drink, young Peter slept on the back seat amidst all their possessions and also made his parents proud by learning to walk. They finally made it into Pretoria thanks to the immense amount of help they received from the Africans and Indians along the way.

After a brief stint just outside Port Elizabeth, Wal was asked by his employers to move to Pietermaritzburg—the capital of the short-lived Boer republic of Natalia set up by the *Voortrekkers*, and subsequently the administrative capital of the British colony of Natal.

In a way, the Hain family completed a trek almost as adventurous, albeit not as bloody, as the ones undertaken by the *Voortrekkers* a bit more than a century ago and ended in the same area. However, they did it from the other side of the continent.

The Great Trek

After the arrival of the British settlers in 1820, the southern land continued along its troubled path, with complex dynamics between the different groups of people throughout the land.

From the beginning of the White settlement, the African agro-pastorialists were driven off their land in a series of brutally devastating wars, intermittently continuous over the years, the savagery hard to estimate.

The British settlers of 1820 had increased the ranks of the White population and engaged in property speculation with the confiscated lands. Alongside this, there were other changes. Slavery was abolished in the early 1830s. In 1838, as many as 38,000 slaves of the Cape Colony were set free. By mid-century, the freed slaves, Khoesan servants and their descendants had merged into the single underclass, now collectively grouped as Coloureds. The same coloured people from whom originated Basil D'Oliveira.

The Great Trek was a historical migration that started as a movement caused by grievances and discontent, and later developed legendary proportions through snowballing and mythical effect of history that is so natural in a closed society.

Disenchanted with British interference in a land that had become their home, the Dutch-speaking Boers gathered their families, ox-wagons, and guns, and started on their exodus away from the seat of authority in the Cape.

Much of the later Afrikaner nationalism, as we will see, harked back to the mythical images of the god-fearing bearded Dutch-speaking Boers with their kappie*-clad women, driving their ox-wagons across the Highveld, crossing the Orange River drifts, in protest against the British impositions of economy, culture and language. One of the major elements of this myth is also of South Africa as the God-given promised land meant for the Afrikaner Volk.*

The truth was a lot more prosaic. It was a speculative venture, more of a gamble, to occupy lands that did not quite belong to them. A lot of the voortrekkers *were men struggling in the Cape, plagued by debt and creditors, in whose priority list opposition to British imperialism came way lower than escape, and sensitivity against the English language did not even exist.*

Heavily armed with modern guns, and hitching their wagons together whenever under attack, the trekkers did fare well in the battles on the way. The biggest triumph was the Battle of the Blood River, in which around 460 Voortrekkers defeated between 10,000 and 15,000 Zulu warriors under King Dingane on the banks of the Ncome river in December 1838.

Eventually, the Boers formed their republic of Natal. However, in 1843 this was annexed by the British mainly because of the strategic location of the port which became Durban. Through a number of negotiations and treaties were formed the Boer Republics of South African Republic (later Transvaal) and the Orange Free State. They somewhat balanced the British colonies of Cape Colony and Natal.

During the late 1930s, the centenary celebrations of the Great Trek would result in a resurgence of Afrikaner nationalism.

4 SIXES IN SILENCE

1948–49. Basil D'Oliveira was just 17. His previous appearance in the David Harris Trophy for the SACCA as a 16-year-old had not been successful. He had disappointed. However, after 1,200 runs for St Augustine in the Cape Town Coloured club cricket scene that same season, the Western Province selectors decided to show faith in the tall lithe young man.

The match was against Griqualand West. To protect the youngster, he was sent in to bat at No 8. One of his colleagues at St Augustine, Alfred Amansure, sat watching the game. This is directly reproduced from his recollections:

"His first shot was struck over the long-off boundary for six. So, the captain moved a player to the offside boundary. Basil responded by hitting another huge six over mid-on. So, the Griqualand captain moved a player there too. Then Basil hit a straight six, cutting between both fielders."

He scored an unbeaten 48 that day, as Western Province won by 216 runs. More importantly, he was on his way. It was evident to every spectator that here was someone special, an uncut diamond in a country famous for that very thing.

D'Oliveira liked to hit sixes. He liked to dominate every sort of attack. It would be a very different D'Oliveira who would grace the international scene a decade and a half later—a great, great player still, but someone who had left the exciting genius of his early youth behind long ago. His late success did play a spectacular role in the socio-political landscape of his country and his people, but much of his most brilliant cricket was played in obscurity, a magnificent sundial shrouded by the shade of segregation.

However, someone was not quite enamoured of his six-hitting. And that someone was his father, Lewis D'Oliveira. Part of it was perhaps due to his having to reach in his pockets in his son's boyhood, to pay for all the windows shattered by his emerging bat. But more than that, he was a man who had certain strict views on the purity of cricket. A cricketer of fine abilities himself, Lewis D'Oliveira had for long been the captain of the prestigious St Augustine's Club that his son went on to represent, and eventually to lead. Lewis thought sixes were vulgar; they gave the bowlers a chance, a gamble that could be avoided. The reservations had very little effect on Basil. He continued to hit sixes, almost at will.

The desperate father offered to gift him a new bat if he managed a century without resorting to the crudeness of an over-boundary. A Canon bat with a red rubber handle. According to biographer Peter Oborne, the bat remained unclaimed, which is what D'Oliveira must have told him. In one of D'Oliveira's own accounts, however, he did manage to get it and when it bounced on the handle it went '*boing, boing, boing*'. Memories are always fallible.

Starting for Croxley's at the age of 15, the young lad worked from eight to five. Every hour other than that was devoted to his development as a sportsman. He played football in the winter and was mighty good at it. In the long summer, he played cricket.

Croxley's did have a cricket team as well, and D'Oliveira represented them in the corporate tournaments. At the age of 19, he amassed 225 against the local Mariedhal Club. The entire innings lasted just 70 minutes, his first century coming up in 25 minutes and the next in 40. Of these runs, 208 were made through 10 fours and 28 sixes. That must have given Lewis

D'Oliveira nightmares. What made it even more remarkable was that the total score of the side was 236.

The six-hitting remained unabated through the next half-decade. In 1950–51, D'Oliveira took over the captaincy of St Augustine's from his father. In 1954, playing against Trafalgar, he hit 46 in an eight-ball over. The sequence was 6,6,6,6,6,6,4,6.

However, the big hitting did not really reflect a lack of seriousness. D'Oliveira's training regimen was exacting to the point of being obsessive. He would call his team for meetings at his home in Bo Kaap and then they would run up the Signal Hill together. Often D'Oliveira would run up to the top on his own. In a conversation with Oborne in 2003, he said that he often felt a kind of freedom at the top of Signal Hill. The boom of the midday gun could be heard, and the infamous Robben Island could be viewed from the peak. D'Oliveira somehow felt that here, at the top of the Hill, apartheid could not extend its ugly tentacles. Here he was just a citizen of the world.

The preparation of the wicket was also an elaborate affair. There was no club-house, no groundsman, not even a proper cricket pitch. It was the same Green Point where Dr Huibert Nahuys van Burgst had indulged in cricketing in 1806. Now it was a vast tract of wasteland, frequented by dogs, tramps, beggars, and rodents. A stretch of gravel and dirt, interspersed with thick grass, made for the playing surface and was home to some 20 cricket clubs including St Augustine's.

There was just one hut where a solitary roller was stationed for use. It was here that members of the clubs arrived early on weekend mornings, to transform the desolate premises into a patchy approximation of a cricket ground. When there was an important match scheduled on Saturday, D'Oliveira and his mates walked all the way to the ground on Friday evening and set about clearing stones and debris from the pitch, bringing buckets of sea water from the nearby beach to create the surface.

The following morning D'Oliveira and his men would bring the mat, spread over two bicycles, pushed from the captain's home to the literal version of the poor man's cricket ground. The pitch and playing area had to be cleared yet again, to undo any overnight damage that might have taken place. Finally, after all the elaborate preparations, the game could begin.

At the end of the day's play, the mat had to be wheeled back home; this time, the cumbersome bicycle bearing the unwieldy apparatus had to be pushed uphill.

This was the grind that he had to put in week after week in order to play his bit of cricket. Perhaps the daily drudgery necessitated maximum self-expression through the sixes he struck. He bowled as well, as he would do on several occasions for England later on—both medium pace and off-breaks. His best bowling figures for St Augustine was 9 for 2. Yes, that is nine wickets for two runs, against Heatherley in 1949–50.

Everyone who saw him could vouch that there was no other cricketer remotely of his class in the country.

Yet, in spite of all his talent, D'Oliveira could not really contemplate being in the official arena himself. Playing alongside White men happened once in a while, perhaps when one or two of them were liberal or condescending enough to indulge the natives. But playing at the highest level? That was unthinkable.

Krom Hendricks had almost made it, having dazzled WW Read's side with his pace in 1891–92. Born of a Dutch father and a St Helena mother, he was rather incorrectly called a Malay bowler. Read strongly advised the South Africans to take him along on their tour of 1894.

However, he was not selected. There were suggestions of his being employed as a baggage master, but there was no question of his being a regular member of the side.

And there was the curious case of Charlie 'Buck' Llewellyn. The immensely gifted all-rounder slipped through the colour bar and played 15 Tests for South Africa during a 16-year period, due in part to light skin and part to exceptional talent.

But those were exceptions.

Charlie Llewellyn

5 ROOTS OF SEGREGATION

It was a few months before the launch of Basil D'Oliveira in the David Harris Trophy with those three towering sixes that the changeover occurred.

On 28 May 1948, the Invincibles played out a draw in a characteristically rain-shortened match against Lancashire at Old Trafford. Don Bradman scored a sedate 43. He was beaten by three successive deliveries from the 19-year-old left-arm spinner Malcolm Hilton before he tried an over-ambitious pull stroke, over-balanced, and was stumped.

Several South Africans also woke up stumped to the rather astonishing news that the National Party had clawed its way to power, in alliance with the small Afrikaner Party. DF Malan, the Prime Minister-elect, could say with some degree of relish, "Now we feel at home again in our country."

It was the Prime Minister in office, the Boer War hero Jan Smuts, who was blamed by most. Too preoccupied with the Second World War, too eager to side with the Allies, too quick to have made peace with the British after the Anglo-Boer War, too busy being an international figure, a 'handyman of the Empire'. Afrikaner unity was now a fact, and the destiny of South Africa would finally be the one that the first *voortrekkers* more than a century ago had intended it to be.

It is often assumed that apartheid kickstarted on that very date.

However, it was hardly an overnight transformation. The roots went far deeper.

The infamous Glen Grey Act dated back to 1894, the Franchise and Ballot Act even earlier to 1892.

The notorious Native Lands Act was established in 1913.

Even very recently, in 1946, the Asian Land Tenure Act had confined Asian ownership and occupation of land to defined areas of the town.

However, with the 1948 elections, a dam opened up. Social segregation, job reservation, economy, education, marriage and sex, land ownership, political representation, geographical confinement—all came down to playing around with colour. Alongside these, there were increasingly oppressive laws of banning, detention without trial, and imprisonment for state security.

But again, it did not happen overnight. And all of that was not Afrikaner conspiracy.

The British-Boer conflicts were always there throughout the 19th century. The huge number of Africans and the lesser number of Coloured and Indians were caught in the middle. The cracks that made this complex surface of endless tussles and vicious policies started with a curious-looking pebble.

At least, Erasmus Stephanus Jacobs thought it was a pebble. Looked unusual, though. The little boy with the big name standing on the De Kalk farm near Hopetown in Cape Colony could not figure out what it really was.

The Boer farmer's son used it to play the children's game of 'five-stones'. It was good fortune, in multiple senses, that a neighbour, a farmer called Schalk van Niekerk, saw it and was curious enough to offer to buy it from the Jacobs family. The boy's mother laughed at the suggestion of buying a stone and offered it for free. Van Niekerk promised that if it turned out to be a diamond, he would share the proceeds with her.

The stone was passed on to John O'Reilly, a travelling trader. O'Reilly was certain that it was a diamond. It was shortly thereafter that Dr Atherton, the official Cape Colony mineralogist at Grahamstown, confirmed the good news. The stone was eventually valued at £500 in London. In 1946, by then named the Eureka Diamond, it would be sold in London for £5,700.

The first diamond in South Africa had been discovered. It was 1866.

13 year earlier, in 1853, James Stephen, a long-serving senior colonial official, had described the Cape Interior as "the most sterile and worthless in the whole Empire." In retrospect, that statement deserves an elite place—in the same category as Maurice Tate's 1929 pronouncement that the young upstart named Don Bradman would not get a run in England.

The discovery of diamonds kick-started the rush to Africa. Hordes of British speculators and diggers flocked to the Cape, to Natal, and then to the Boer republics, seeking to make their fortunes.

A shy, sickly 17-year-old called Cecil Rhodes arrived in 1871, seeking warmer climate for his health. It possibly did not quite help—he died young, in 1902, at the age of 48. But in the intervening years, he made a fortune in diamond and gold, became the Prime Minister of the Cape, lit the flames of what would become the Boer War, and founded his own country called Rhodesia.

He also played a leading role in preventing Coloured fast bowler Krom Hendricks from touring England in 1894.

In the mid-1880s, gold was also discovered on Witwatersrand. It doubled the rush. Towns mushroomed around the mines, almost overnight. Johannesburg accelerated from a mine-township to one of the richest cities of the world within a decade. Cricket followed dutifully in imperial footsteps.

Of course, there was more.

More frontier wars followed, with the natives massacred under the guise of empire-building and spread of civilisation.

1879 saw the terrible invasion of Zululand. The Zulus were defeated by the superior British firepower, but not before they had surprised the invaders in the battle of Isandlwana. Cricket pads were discovered among the 2,000 dead bodies strewn around the battlefield.

Moreover, with the richest deposits of diamond and gold discovered in the Boer Republics, the tussle between the British and the Boers intensified.

In 1877, the British annexed Transvaal, supposedly because the Boer Republic was bankrupt and was having a difficult time subjugating the African chiefdoms. According to the missive, diamond rush and Imperialist expansion had nothing to do with it. The Boers surprised the British in 1881 when they fought back to regain their land, celebrating their victory in the Battle of Majuba—the first Boer War or the first War of Independence.

The gold rush attracted even more speculators and diggers. Cricket followed on their heels. The first Test matches were played in 1888–89.

Monty Bowden played in the first ever Test in South Africa in 1888–89 and led the team in the second. He stayed back in South Africa and turned speculator, and subsequently a member of the Pioneer Column of Cecil Rhodes, on a vanguard expedition to 'open up' and secure the mineral resources of Rhodesia.

During the expedition, Bowden suffered from fever and the after-effects of having been thrown from his cart, added to epileptic seizures and the problems caused by alcohol. He died in hospital, which was in reality a mud hut, and was buried in a coffin made out of whiskey cases. He was 26, and never got to know that he had been England's youngest Test captain.

Alfred Milner: Arch Imperialist

With the diamond and gold proving too great an attraction, and the unsophisticated farming nations of the Afrikaners standing in the way, something had to give. In 1899, the unabashed warmongering of the arch-imperialist Alfred Milner, governor of the Cape Colony, resulted in the second Anglo-Boer War.

The British believed the Anglo-Boer War would be a short one. In reality, the scorecard of the Boer War shows it to be one of the bloodiest, longest, costliest, and most humiliating war indulged in by the Empire in the hundred years between 1815 and 1914. According to Rudyard Kipling, it taught the British 'no end of a lesson'.

The casualties in the two-year-seven-month war numbered more than 30,000 killed and 100,000 wounded or missing in action. The conflict cost the British taxpayers £200 million.

JJ Ferris, the magnificent bowler from Australia, one-half of the dreaded Turner-Ferris combination. He also bowled for England and took 13 wickets in the 1891–92 Test he played in South Africa. He was one of the cricketers who died in the war. Frank Milligan, the Yorkshire batsman who played both the Tests when Lord Hawke's side visited South Africa just before the war, was killed during the campaign to relieve Mafeking. Eleven other first-class cricketers perished, the most unfortunate of elevens in cricket.

When Lord Hawke's first side visited in 1895–96, they were stopped by Boer commandos as the train entered the Afrikaner heartland. It was the time of the infamous Jameson Raid. During that tour, CB Fry played for the English side, touring on the recommendation of his friend KS Ranjitsinhji.

Various sources say that the original choice was Ranji himself. According to André Odendaal's Cricket and Conquest *Ranji was discouraged to tour based on a quiet diplomatic word.*

What hurt perhaps even more was Lord Kitchener's measures of scorched-earth policy and concentration camps. The burning of the cleared farms and moving of civilians into atrocious concentration camps was one of the most notorious measures taken by the British.

The Boer internees were placed in tents—45 tents for women and children. Meat was at first not part of the provisions for the women and children in the camps. Even after revisions, basic requirements such as vegetables, jam, or fresh milk for babies were not provided. Finally, there was a total lack of basic sanitation and only rudimentary medical facilities. The results were measles, typhoid, dysentery, and severe malnutrition.

In all, 26,370 Boer women and children died in the concentration camps—the most shamefully ignominious entry in the scorecard of the Empire's wars.

This left a scar on the Afrikaner identity and went a long way to construct the disfigured shape of the society thereafter. That is why, sitting in his prison cell, Nelson Mandela read *Commando,* the Boer War classic by Deneyz Reitz.

Boer woman with dead child in one of the British-run concentration camps

Perhaps as sundries, there were 64 other internment tents set up for the Africans in which some 20,000 died. That, however, was just a statistic.

It was not just collateral damage for the non-Whites. While ostensibly it was a war between two White factions, Africans, Coloured, and Indians were caught up in the conflict, both actively and passively, as participants and victims. Boer commandos employed 7,000 to 9,000 African and Coloured servants to ride with them, known in Afrikaans as agterryers. *The British used unarmed Africans and Coloureds for all sorts of chores. Apart from this, 30,000 armed blacks were used in the war towards the later stages.*

Armed black soldiers did participate in the Boer War for both the sides However, their involvement and contributions were generally ignored.

Apartheid cannot be really understood without taking into account the Boer War and its aftermath, the horrific deaths of the Boer women and children. The hellish tragedy of concentration camps was not kicked off by Nazi Germany. The British had beaten them to it.

When the Peace of Vereeniging was brokered, to ensure the grudging collaboration of the two White communities, the natives were placed on the sacrificial altar.

Alfred Milner's prescription for the role of Blacks in South Africa was simple: "A political equality of White and Black is impossible. The White man must rule, because he is elevated by many, many steps above the Black man."

In 1905, the Milner-appointed Lagden Commission legalised theft of dignity, land, and freedom of movement from millions of people. This in effect laid the framework for apartheid, including General Pass Regulations, Special Regulations for Labour Districts, and the rest of the Labour Control details.

A year later, the Asian Registration Act was passed, requiring all Indians to register and carry passes.

That same northern winter, 1906–07.

The South African rugby side tours Britain. Worried that the London press may quickly tag a nickname to their team, they choose the emblem of a small antelope typical of Africa. The press swallows the bait. The South Africans become the Springboks.

They conquer. They are victorious in 26 of their 29 matches. They win two, lose one, and draw one of their internationals.

Captain Paul Roos, with his trademark black ribbon around his forehead and over his ears instead of a scrum cap, speaks at Church meetings on the tour with a deep voice and pronounced Dutch accent. After all, rugby is the soul of the Afrikaner.

During the Devon game of 17 October, with 18,000 watching at the Plymouth County Ground, the visitors refuse to take field. The reason is that the opposition half-back Jimmy

Peters, local club favourite, is born to a West Indian father at Salford.

The Springboks gingerly agree to play only when the South African High Commissioner and the Town Mayor hint at possible riots if the fixture is cancelled.

The 1906–07 Springboks in England

By the time South Africa became a Union in 1910, the non-Whites had lost most of their rights of citizenship. A small number of Blacks from the Cape were the only ones to retain their rights to vote, but even they were not allowed to contest elections.

The overly racial constitution of the newly formed Union was alarming enough for African activists and intellectuals to come together in Bloemfontein in January 1912. With the call 'we are one people', the South African Native National Congress was formed, which would later become African National Congress (ANC).

A year and a half down the line, in July 1913, the Africans were hit with the nuke equivalent of legislation.

The Native Land Act virtually legitimised forcible evacuation—92.7% of the land in the country became marked for White ownership only. The four times larger population of the Africans had to squeeze themselves into 7.3% of the country's area.

Not only would they have to give up their lands, the Blacks living on the White farms as tenants and shared croppers were now compelled to become wage labourers.

In the famous words of African intellectual Sol Plaatje, the Blacks had been turned *pariahs in the land of their birth.* It was the middle of the winter when this law was passed. Some people were turned out of their land in mid-winter, and sympathetic Whites were threatened with fines and jails if they continued to shelter them.

Sol Plaatje

Two years after the formation of the South African Native National Congress, another political body was formed that would have supreme influence on the destiny of the land.

Minister of Justice JBM Hertzog, Boer general in the war, had grown worried about the increasing affinity for the British he detected in both Prime Minister Louis Botha and his deputy Jan Smuts. Botha had been so seduced by London that he had even donated the magnificent Cullinan diamond to King Edward VII.

In 1914, at Bloemfontein, Hertzog formed the National Party, with an Afrikaner ideology, in opposition to Botha and Smut's South African Party. The motto was 'South Africa first'.

One of the co-founders was Charlie Fichardt, captain of Free State, who played against the visiting MCC in tour matches in 1905–06 and 1909–10.

In this environment of racial chasm, and the doors of representative cricket only open to Whites, the non-Whites did carry on competing in their own Barnato Trophy. The SACCB had been set up in 1903. Away from the eyes of the world, often in spite of ridiculous facilities, the non-White cricketers were batting on.

But both White and Black cricket had to take a break when a 19-year-old Bosnian Serb shot Archduke Franz Ferdinand in the neck and his wife Sophie in the abdomen as their car stood outside a café in Sarajevo.

Europe seemed to be on the verge of cracking into two, and South Africa was not to remain far from the fray.

Before the First World War, South Africa played 40 Tests, winning eight and losing 27. How many Krom Hendricks remained uncapped? Would the results have been better if the teams had been more representative than White?

We can only speculate.

6 GREAT WAR, GREATER BOUNDARIES

Reggie Schwarz and Gordon White, two of the famous googly quartet, architects of South Africa's first successes in Test cricket, died in the First World War. The former succumbed to the Spanish flu epidemic, the latter killed in action.

Googly-bowling all-round great Aubrey Faulkner was decorated in Gallipoli, but it was also at Gallipoli that his fellow all-round cricketer Frederick Cook lost his life.

Claude Newbury had looked likely to be a promising weapon in the bowling line-up during the days before the Great War. His first Test wicket was of Jack Hobbs and his tally of 24 had Frank Woolley appearing four times. He was killed on the Western Front.

Entering the war with a military that was just two years old, and facing vehement Afrikaner protests by German-allied voices, South Africa, the most minor Test-playing nation, topped the score board in terms of Test cricketing fatalities. The others who perished were Reginald Hands, Arthur Osche, and Bill Lundie.

Lundie's final victim was the England and Yorkshire medium pace bowling all-rounder Major Booth. Booth died as Second Lieutenant in France—according to historian Michael Jones, "not managing to reach the rank his name implied."

Of the four other Test cricketers who met their ends in the atrocities were three who played against South Africa—Colin Blythe, Tibby Cotter, and Leonard Moon. The only exception was Kenneth Hutchings.

South Africa also lost five rugby internationals.

"If a cricketer has a straight eye let him look along the barrel of a rifle, if a footballer has strength of limb, let him serve and march in the field of battle," voiced Sir Arthur Conan Doyle, urging young men to die for a battle fought due to differences between old men. He reminded them that there is a time for games, a time for business, and a time for domestic life. South African sportsmen, like others around the world, responded. And died for their pains.

Conan Doyle never took a Jezail bullet in his shoulder as did Dr John Watson in Afghanistan. However, during the Boer War, he had lobbied with the decision-makers to get close to the action.

Sent in as a doctor, he set up a hospital in the Ramblers Cricket Club ground, Bloemfontein. The pavilion was used as the main ward. In the midst of battling severe attacks of typhoid and receiving flak from the journalists and ministers for insufficient medical facilities, Conan Doyle had the time to arrange inter-hospital football matches.

All this resulted in his own account of the war, titled *The Great Boer War*. Later, his pamphlet *The War in South Africa: Its Cause and Conduct* went a long way in earning him knighthood in 1902, much more than the enthralling adventures of Sherlock Holmes.

Perhaps, later, he combined his interests together and tried to capture the departed spirits of the fallen cricketers on photographic films or in the movement of the ectoplasm. Who knows? One does know that the great writer was an arch imperialist.

Around 85,000 South African Blacks participated in the war, mostly in unarmed labour services. Segregation, insisted upon by President General Botha, ensured unknown graves, unsung valour, and ineligibility for medals of honour.

CJ Nichols, the Coloured net bowler who impressed Plum Warner and Colin Blythe during the 1905–06 MCC tour, performed the role of a batman to Western Province cricketer Lieutenant-Colonel Vollie van der Bijl. Nichols was engaged to coach the French troops in cricket and organise cricket matches in France.

Albert Christopher, who represented Natal in the Barnato Trophy, led the stretcher-bearers of the South African Indian Bearers Corps in East Africa. He was one of the few non-White servicemen to receive the Distinguished Conduct Medal.

The end of the war sees hastily arranged cricket and rugby matches in England between servicemen, with the standard of play remaining uniformly high. It is essential to boost the morale of a war-ravaged nation.

While Herby Taylor, BG Melle, and MA Bell play for the Dominions against England at The Oval, peace is celebrated by the rugby-playing soldiers by contesting an international inter-services King's Cup. Springbok captain Billy Millar leads his men against New Zealand, Australian, Canadian, British (playing as Mother Country), and the Royal Air Force.

'Ranji' Wilson

The New Zealanders win this proto-World Cup, defeating Mother Country at Twickenham. This is followed by a visit to South Africa by the New Zealand team on their way home. They play 15 matches in the country and essentially kickstart the most incredible rivalry in the rugby world.

The tour is sponsored out of their own pockets and is partially paid for by a New Zealand jockey. These are the days when, freed from the clutches of war, sportsmen can go miles out of their way to revive normalcy and spirit.

One line however cannot be crossed. Among the New Zealand Army stars who win the King's Cup in England is Nathaniel Arthur Wilson.

Partly West Indian, this dusky star has won 10 caps for New Zealand and is called 'Ranji' Wilson because of his colour. He is not taken to South Africa.

The Australian Imperial Forces side led by Herbie Collins visited South Africa after the war. They played Western Province, Transvaal, Natal, Natal Colleges, and two matches against a representative South African side.

CJ Nichols, the Cape Town bowler who had impressed Warner and Blythe and had organised cricket in France, was appointed baggage master by the Australians. That is as close as a Black man got to White cricket. In war and peace, some boundaries remained impenetrable.

7 INTER-BELLUM RACE-LINES

It can qualify as the mother of all comparative statements, but Basil D'Oliveira did grow up enjoying relative privilege.

He could not access some exclusive spheres of life cordoned off for the Whites. He could not continue his studies as he wanted to and become a doctor. He could not play for the official cricket teams of his state or country. He could not even hone his skills on a proper cricket pitch.

However, he did attend Roman Catholic schools, he did obtain a decent job, and he could concentrate on cricket without having to worry about his next meal. Unlike urban Blacks, he and his family had not been herded into ghetto-like townships with terrible living conditions. They would be moved from time to time whenever forced relocation reared its ugly head. But they were not segregated to suffocation.

D'Oliveira grew up with White, Black, Muslim, Indian, and Chinese neighbours.

Like everyone else in South Africa, D'Oliveira accepted his lot—that he was Coloured. In *Time to Declare*, he remembers: "I vaguely had the impression that we were different from the Whites, that we did not see much of each other. On rare occasions when my club played a White team, it was under conditions of secrecy."

For practice, he made his own bats out of pieces of wood, shaped by hand, smoothed so that there would be no splinters. They did have to play in an enormous open area belonging to the City Council where 25 pitches held 25 simultaneous matches, often bumping into each other as they changed over in the field or chased balls to the boundary. All the clubs did have to share one solitary hut for storing their cricketing equipment.

But he still had it better than the Indians, and definitely much better than the Africans.

As he wrote in *The Basil D'Oliveira Affair*: "I am not certain of the sociology of our past, and when asked what is a Cape-Coloured, I can only repeat what we grew up to understand it to be. A Cape-coloured is someone not Indian, not African, but a combination of either Indian and White or African and White. Out of this mixing a new race was born. In South Africa, if you are mixed you are Coloured, and that's the end of it."

The Coloured people had it a shade better than the other discriminated classes. They were few in number and therefore not a direct threat to the Whites. Way less in number than the Africans—the Blacks. And then, there was also the question of racial intermixing. By definition, the Coloured had White blood.

While they did have to carry passes in Free State, there were rights in other parts, especially in the Cape where 80% of them lived. The Glasgow-educated Dr Abdulla Abdurrahman, the Cape's first Coloured councillor, had lobbied heavily. A series of secondary schools had been set up in Cape Town. Dr Abdurrahman was also a proponent of equal rights for all races.

However, the relative privileges stemmed further from a different, less-than-ideal direction—as an offshoot of the developing Afrikaner nationalism, channelled through the policies of the increasingly powerful National Party.

The plight of the White Afrikaner had less to do with the basic human necessities with which the marginalised races of the nation wrestled. But their specific troubles were palpable enough.

On one side was the memory of the Boer War, the humiliation and the tragedy of the concentration camps, and—in spite of self-government and eventually a Union—the yoke of being the conquered people.

They were culturally confused, a largely agrarian community shaped by principles of the Dutch Reformed Church, trying to perform painful contortions to fit into a capitalistic corner of the Empire.

Economically, they struggled, with practically no presence among the major companies. The high-end, technical jobs were all dominated by English-speakers, as was most of civil service.

The Afrikaners lagged far behind in education, a very low proportion reaching a decent level of schooling. And while there was a focused movement to promote the Afrikaans language as a means to discover national identity, it was a new language developed in 1880 to enable the local, unschooled Afrikaners to read the Bible. A modified, simplified version of Dutch, it lagged way behind in terms of esteem, intelligentsia, literature, and strength when compared to English.

The Afrikaners were depicted as uncouth, uncultured rustic brutes during the publicity and propaganda phase of the Boer War. Not only had that image stuck, the condescension with which they were viewed was rather conspicuous.

Afrikaans was also vilified, even in the *Cape Times*, as 'mongrel', 'hotch-potch' or 'degenerate'.

Accepting English was not an option. As former Orange Free State President Martinus Steyn said in a letter to National Party founder JBM Hertzog, "The language of the conqueror in the mouth of the conquered is the language of slaves."

Hertzog's National Party promoted Afrikaner nationalism with an immense emphasis on language. Nationalism was the counter to the 'jingo Imperialism' of the English-speaking South Africans.

On the evening of 15 June 1918, was born the Afrikaner Broederbond. From an idealistic open society for the Afrikaner with members professing financial independence and commitment to the Afrikaner cause, it soon became a secret and elite Afrikaner society, with every important Afrikaner in the rolls—a body that would go on to play a decisive role in the fate of the nation.

By the time D'Oliveira scored his 158 at The Oval, the number of members of the Broederbond stood at 8,154, the number of cells 560. Among the members were Prime Ministers and the pillars of apartheid—DF Malan, JG Strijdom, Hendrik Verwoerd, and Johannes Balthazar Vorster. And of course, the most notoriously feared man in South Africa, Hendrik van den Bergh, the head of South African state security during the apartheid regime.

It was in 1924 that the National Party, forming a coalition with the Labour Party, came to power for the first time. The following year, DF Malan, Minister for the Interior, made Afrikaans an official language. It was later categorised as one of the three great gambles of the Afrikaners, alongside the Great Trek of the 1830s and the Boer War at the turn of the century.

Being a small, non-threatening, but significant community, the Coloured were converted into a vote bank. Hertzog promised the Coloured community access to rights that were not extended to the Africans.

To combat the 'poor White' fears of the Afrikaners, a difference was created between 'civilised labour' and 'uncivilised (Black) labour' segments. The New Deal promised the Coloured voters inclusion in the 'civilised labour' category.

Most Coloured folk were poor, employed as unskilled labourers or domestic help. They had hardly any presence in senior administrative positions in the civil service or technical professions.

JBM Hertzog

If they somehow got into those positions, they suffered discrimination in salary, treatment, and pension.

However, they could own property in the Cape. In Western Cape in particular, from where D'Oliveira hailed, all the towns had a mixed area where the Coloured and the poorer White lived together.

After the election, the National Party government did increase spending on Coloured education by 60%.

The relative privileges took a hit when the enfranchisement of the White women took place in 1930. The resulting increase in the number of voters reduced the percentage of the Coloured votes to negligible. Their support was not deemed that important anymore.

However, compared to the Africans, the Coloured population were in a virtual heaven.

Segregated in huge numbers into reserves that covered a miniscule geographical proportion of the country, the Blacks lived a horrid life.

The reserves were most often not connected by railway lines. Those employed as cheap labour in the cities lived in dismal conditions, in hostels in the form of match-box shacks.

The colour bar excluded them from skilled jobs. They were hardly ever allowed in trade unions and, even if they were, their voices did not reach the wage negotiations. Colour bar also meant much lower income than a White man doing the same job.

The movement from the preserves to the urban locations and back was regulated by the pass laws. The Urban Areas Act of 1923 required all Black men in White areas to carry passes at all times. The Colour Bar Act of 1926 amended the Mine and Works Act to prevent Black mine workers from practising skilled trades. The Native Administration Act in the following year made the British Crown the head of their native affairs in their own settlements.

The Great Depression that hit the world did not spare South Africa either. And of course, as the nation tried to rally by leaving the gold standard by 1932, raising taxes on import, petrol, postage, and so on, more marginalisation of Africans was invariably seen as a quick win to balance the losses of the Whites.

1935. Joe Louis bounces back from some early pounding and overcomes Primo Carnera in six rounds at the Madison Square Garden. It puts the Coloured boxer in international spotlight

Taking literary liberties to create a composite of this fight along with an unspecified bout against a White 'contender', Maya Angelou draws a strikingly evocative portrait of what Louis meant for the Negro population in Stamps, Arkansas.

In her autobiography I Know Why the Caged Bird Sings, *she describes the radio commentary and the reaction of the crowd who gathered to listen to it:*

"'...It looks like Louis is going down.' My race groaned. It was our people falling. It was another lynching, yet another Black man hanging on a tree. One more woman ambushed and raped. A Black boy whipped and maimed. It was hounds on the trail of a man running through slimy swamps. It was a White woman slapping her maid for being forgetful."

Louis recovers. Angelou describes the elation of such wins in captivating prose: "Then the voice, husky and familiar, came to wash over us—'The winnah, and still heavyweight champeen of the world . . . Joe Louis.'

"Champion of the world. A Black boy. Some Black mother's son. He was the strongest man in the world. People drank Coca-Colas like ambrosia and ate candy bars like Christmas. Some of the men went behind the Store and poured white lightning in their soft-drink bottles, and a few of the bigger boys followed them. Those who were not chased away came back blowing their breath in front of themselves like proud smokers."

Finally, she ends with this telling paragraph:

"It would take an hour or more before the people would leave the Store and head for home. Those who lived too far had made arrangements to stay in town. It wouldn't be fit for a Black man and his family to be caught on a lonely country road on a night when Joe Louis had proved that we were the strongest people in the world."

Joe Louis

A year later, there was another supreme triumph, on the world stage.

In Berlin, on 3 August 1936, Jesse Owens, getting off the mark in the innermost lane, perhaps takes his coach's instructions too literally.

"Imagine you are running on coal," he has been told. As this 22-year-old, another sporting pearl from Alabama, takes off, his feet hardly seem to touch the ground. He crosses the finishing line at 10.3 seconds, with fellow American Ralph Metcalfe arriving a tenth of a second later.

The stop-motion camera system developed by the Zeiss Ikon and the Agfa companies are not required after all. Certainly not for Erich Borchmeyer, the 32-year-old German on whom the Führer had pinned his hopes.

Owens wins gold in the 200m, long jump and the 4 x 100m relay as well.

Adolf Hitler, however, has his own explanation: "People whose forefathers came from the jungle are primitive—more athletically built than civilised White people."

In a contrasting parallel to the success of the Black people in these two iconic sporting events, on 10 July 1936 the lot of the Black people in South Africa got even worse. The Representation of Natives Act removed the Black voters from the Cape electoral roll and restricted their rights to electing three Whites to Parliament.

Apart from the Whites, Blacks, and Coloureds, there was of course a fourth group of South Africans.

The Indians were primarily centred in Natal, and a few in Transvaal, having been recruited as coolie labour from India in the 1860s. A large percentage became tradesmen and shop owners. Curiously, they were not granted citizenship till 1961, having been variously labelled as an 'Asiatic Curse' and a 'strange and foreign element that is not assimilable'.

Alongside the White criminals, these Asiatics were initially banned from entering Orange Free State. Later they were given passes valid for 24 hours to carry out goods deliveries.

The segregation and the changes did manage to restore some amount of parity to the White Afrikaners.

Cultural nationalism developed and thrived. Economic awakening of the Afrikaner led to a greater corporate share of the national economy. The *Dertigers* or Generation of the Thirties, produced commendable contemporary poetry and literature in Afrikaans. Afrikaner academics, such as historian PJ van der Merwe, published outstanding work. Guided largely by the Broederbond, a strong body of Afrikaner entrepreneurs also emerged by the late 1930s.

While the Afrikaner insecurities were indeed disappearing, it was at the cost of creating an increasingly troubled society around them. The curious and segregated situation of the other races went ahead to form one of the most convoluted cricketing structures in the world.

8 FIVE TIMES CRICKET EQUALS LESS

The legendary Transvaal and Nottinghamshire all-rounder Clive Rice is apprehensive. He has just landed at the Dumdum Airport of Calcutta, in charge of the first-ever South African side on an official tour post-apartheid.

It is November 1991. Nelson Mandela has finally been released from prison, and the Rainbow Nation has turned over a new page. India is their first port of visit after the 21-year isolation.

Rice fears the worst. The city has a history of rioting, especially when cricket is concerned. And some of the riots are connected with politics as well. In 1969, a mob smashed the windows and doors of the hotel where the Australian team was put up, on the spurious suspicion that Doug Walters had served in the Vietnam War.

Will they erupt now that the South Africans are here, emerging from a long history of exploitation and suppression of their non-White people?

India has always had an anti-apartheid policy. In 1974, the tennis side refused to travel to South Africa to compete in the Davis Cup final, awarding the trophy by default. MK Gandhi, before he became the Mahatma, was one of the major activists against discrimination during his two decades in South Africa.

What the South African skipper witnesses as the team bus hits the road is beyond his wildest dreams. From the airport to the hotel, streets are lined with people who have turned up to welcome the touring team.

Years later, Rice tells the author in an interview: "I don't think even Obama would get that reception."

When he steps into the field for the opening match of the series, the atmosphere is unbelievable in the steaming cauldron of Eden Gardens with nearly hundred thousand fans assembled for the historic match. The noise is deafening.

The picture of Rice demonstrating his appreciation by joining his hands together remains a touching sporting photograph.

However, unlike widely believed till this day, that was not the first time South African cricketers played in India.

Way back in November 1921, a team of soccer and cricket players comprising South African Indians from Durban had visited the country on a two-month tour. They called themselves Christopher's Contingent, after the chief organiser Albert Christopher, influential advocate, war hero, and a former Barnato Trophy cricketer.

Sailing on board the *Kargola,* this contingent arrived in India in late November 1921 and played 14 games of football across Bombay, Banaras, Allahabad, Ahmedabad, Agra, Delhi, Madras, Calcutta, and Poona, along with two games of cricket in Calcutta. A letter that they carried from Fleming Johnson, Mayor of Durban, stated that they were "well-known residents of Natal, respected not just by their fellow Indians in the field of sport, but also by the European community."

The visitors did not quite represent the cream of South African Indian cricket, partly because the focus was on football and partly because several of the best cricketers could not get four months leave from their jobs.

In the cricket matches, they drew against Presidency College at the college ground on 14 January 1922. The following Sunday, 21 January, they lost a game to the historic Mohun Bagan Club by eight wickets, Moni Das compiling an unbeaten century and the footballing great

Gostha Pal hitting an unbeaten 64. For the Natal side, captain Billy Subban scored 22 and vice-captain Baboolal Maharaj struck 51 with eight boundaries. Calcutta's *The Statesman* described Maharaj's innings as "very sound, especially on the leg."

The 1921–22 team of South African Indians to India

After the second match, skipper Billy Subban and vice-captain Baboolal Maharaj were requested by the Mohun Bagan side to turn out for them in a club game against Balligunge. This actually disproves another long-held view that the traditional Mohun Bagan club did not recruit any foreign player till the Nigerian footballer Chima Okerie played for them in 1991.

The 1991 connection of the two historical misconceptions is purely coincidental.

The South African Indian side also met Mahatma Gandhi at Ahmedabad and were supported and assisted by the Indian Olympic Association.

Maharaj, hailing from Pretoria, had often played for the Transvaal Coloureds because of the lack of organised cricket for Indians in the state. Apart from football and cricket, he captained Pretoria Standard 15 at rugby for 11 years, and excelled at swimming, cycling, boxing, and weightlifting.

Subban, the skipper, was another fantastic all-round sportsman, who played for Natal in the 1913 Barnato Trophy and was often referred to as the Indian Dave Nourse. In the football match against the superb Mohun Bagan side, and against the European Combined XI, his goalkeeping supposedly reminded the crowd of Summerfield who had played there a few seasons earlier.

In Durban, Subban played as goalkeeper for Pirates of India and later Greyville. He was also a champion cyclist. But when he returned from the epochal tour of India, he paid a steep price for his sporting adventure—he was sacked from his job at the Durban bakery where he had been employed for 20 years.

There were serious attempts on the part of the Natal Indian organisers to get the Natal side into the Indian Quadrangular on a regular basis. Unfortunately, that did not materialise.

There was another tour that has all but fallen off the record books with time. In 1934, the Indian Football Association XI crossed the Indian Ocean to play 19 matches in South Africa, most of them in Natal. They won 18 of the games, mostly by big margins, losing one solitary match. The visitors showed exceptional skill in playing barefoot, but the White soccer bodies were not interested in taking them on.

With segregation deep-rooted by the end of the 1930s, the South African Indian Cricket Union (SAICU) was formed in 1940. It was mainly the Natal and Transvaal sides that contested for the Christopher Trophy. This was the last segregated cricket board to be formed.

The other communities had already found it practically impossible to continue playing integrated cricket.

The Barnato Memorial Trophy had been resumed in 1921–22 after the Great War, championed by the SACCB. For this board, the word 'Coloured' implied anyone from the non-White cricketing population. However, with segregation in the society creating increasing logistic and relational divides, it became difficult to get all the races to play together.

With the formation of the separate South African Bantu Cricket Board (SABCB) for the Africans, the Barnato Memorial Trophy went into hibernation from 1932.

The Coloured cricketers had formed the South African Independent Coloured Cricket Board (SAICCB) in 1926—restricted to the Coloured cricketers in the more exclusive interpretation of the term. They contested the David Harris Trophy.

It was in the David Harris Trophy that Basil D'Oliveira started making waves in the late 1940s.

The Coloured cricketers regularly played a high standard of cricket. This was testified by the liberal South African White cricketing legend Dave Nourse, who regularly coached and played with them. AJ 'Dol' Freeman of Western Province, for example, was often called the 'Malay Wally Hammond.'

Taliep Salie, the Coloured leg-spin googly bowling all-rounder, was magnificent. He once captured all 10 wickets in an innings when a Malay XI played one of those rarest of rare matches against a White South African side—a team that included Test players Dave Nourse, Xen Balaskas, and AW Palm. Salie was apparently offered a slot in the Kent side by Frank Woolley, which he refused. Later, Brian Crowley attributed his refusal to 'the absence of a mosque in and near Canterbury'. Clarrie Grimmett was impressed enough by his bowling to remark that Salie would win a berth in any international side. After his death in 1969, Gesant Toffar stated in his obituary that Salie was rated by knowledgeable critics as a greater all-round cricketer than Basil D'Oliveira.

The SABCB was formed in 1932. That the Black Africans managed to play the game in spite of the litany of legalised and extra-legal oppression is in itself a testimony to the resilience of mankind and the appeal of the game.

A lot of them came from the mines. Frank Roro of Transvaal, who became a major star, emerged from Kimberley. Some said he was perhaps better than both the two major batting pillars of the official White South African side—Eric Rowan and Bruce Mitchell.

Black cricketers were popular enough to feature in advertisements. 'T. Chiepe' of Free State was even called Hutton of the side.

In Natal, cricket among Africans was majorly championed at Adams College. Jackie Grant, the West Indian captain of the 1930s, became the principal of Adams in the 1950s and regularly turned out in the matches himself. Herby Taylor was one White cricketer who coached the

Natal Africans before they left for their provincial tournament.

Eric Rowan

Frank Roro

We can see which picture is clearer. However, the comparative quality of the two cricketers remains unclear.

SACA, SACCB, SABCB, SAICCB, SAICU. Not really helping matters, SAICCB renamed themselves SACCA or the South African Coloured Cricket Association.

It was definitely easier for some to score a century or take five wickets in an innings than to remember the abbreviations and the full forms of the different cricket boards.

In other sports, the segregation and separate development mirrored cricket.

Springbok legend Danie Craven reckoned that the rows upon rows of the fezzes, the Cape Town Malays in the stands at Newlands, were the most knowledgeable supporters of the world. However, fez-wearing players were not really welcome.

In 1937, the Progress Club accused Thistles of playing Gustav Ferreira, a player rumoured to have been seen wearing a fez. The Union spent a lot of time and energy trying to get to the bottom of it. Ferreira turned out to be T. Coosium, indeed a fez-wearing Muslim, and he was banned.

Everard Jackson, who played in all three Tests against the White Springboks during the latter's 1937 tour of New Zealand, did not even make the preliminary trials as the team prepared for the 1940 tour. Nor did any other Maori star.

The series was eventually cancelled due to the Second World War.

By the time the 1938 Rhodes Cup was held, however, the Coloured Board had surmounted every obstacle in their way to piece together a representative non-White South African team. The intention was to play the visiting All-Black side of 1940. However, with German tanks rolling into Poland, the painstaking preparations fell through.

And all the while, White South Africa played Test cricket. White cricketers of the land against cricketers of the White countries.

What difference would a Baboolal Maharaj, Frank Roro, or 'Dol' Freeman have made to the destiny of the official South African cricket side had they been given a chance? One can only speculate. What one does know is that White South Africa played 50 Tests between the First and Second World Wars, won 7 and lost 20.

They were devastated in Australia in 1931–32, coming up against a youthful run-making monster called Don Bradman. When Bradman failed to recuperate from illness in time for the 1935–36 tour of South Africa, Jack Fingleton and Stan McCabe with the bat and the leg-spinning pair of Clarrie Grimmett and Bill O'Reilly made rather short work of them.

Chuck Fleetwood-Smith explains the intricacies of the chinaman

There is a picture of Chuck Fleetwood-Smith explaining the intricacies of chinaman to a Zulu boy.

There is another photograph of Arthur Mailey, who covered the tour as journalist, bargaining with a Black vendor. Taliep Salie's net bowling fascinated Clarrie Grimmett.

But no cricket took place between the Australians and the non-Whites.

Failures against Australia notwithstanding, the South Africans ran England close, playing six series against them, winning two and losing three. The high point was when another leg-spinner, Xenophon Balaskas, bowled them to a memorable Test win at Lord's on a wicket that had been ravaged by *leatherjackets*. That win also clinched the series—their first series win in England. They also won the first series they contested against the new Test cricketing nation New Zealand.

They discovered a classy left-arm spinner in Cyril Vincent, were carried forward till 1932 by the greatness of Herby Taylor, welcomed the solid Bruce Mitchell in the interim, and ended the inter-bellum period with splendid shows of brilliance by Dudley Nourse and the cultured batsmanship of Alan Melville. Jock Cameron died young but flashed briefly and brilliantly in front of and behind the stumps.

The cricketing journey between the World Wars ended with the infamous Timeless Test.

Arthur Mailey with a local vendor

West Indies started playing Tests in 1928. India opened their Test cricketing account in 1932. South Africa chose not to notice.

The brilliant KS Duleepsinhji managed to play one Test for England against the visiting South Africans in 1929. After that he was not picked in the series, or even for the Gentlemen. It led his coach, the former South African great Aubrey Faulkner, to remark scathingly about the blemish on English cricket.

The following summer, with over 400 runs in the Ashes series, including a superlative 173 at Lord's, Duleep was a virtual certainty in the English side. However, it was Maurice Turnbull who batted in the middle-order spot Duleep should have occupied when England toured South Africa that 1930–31 summer. Duleep was side-lined with supposed 'illness'.

In many ways, the Indian prince was a precursor of Basil D'Oliveira.

However, there were some quaint exceptions.

Denijs Morkel was a decent Western Province all-rounder hailing from the famous Morkel family of cricket and rugby stars. He played 16 Tests for South Africa during the late 1920s and early 1930s. He produced some fine performances on the 1929 tour of England. However, soon his health started failing and the tour of Australia in 1931–32 was quite forgettable.

Settling in England, Morkel was recruited by Julien Cahn—the eccentric, millionaire entrepreneur, an amateur magician and cricket crazy with his own travelling team and pneumatic pads.

After the South African had scored 251 on his debut for the curious team, Cahn set Morkel up with a motor trade business in Nottingham. In return, the mild-mannered all-rounder turned in some fantastic performances.

When the Indians visited in 1932, Morkel did play against the dark-skinned cricketers, scoring 49 and picking up four wickets in an innings win. It pleased Cahn no end.

The following year, he played West Indies; Learie Constantine and Morkel dismissed each other in the match. He also played for Cahn's team against the West Indians in 1939, when he caught both the great Black cricketers in the side—George Headley and Learie Constantine.

Another South African recruited by Cahn was the incredibly multi-dimensional character Bob Crisp, who will play another cameo role in our story. Both Crisp and Morkel toured with Cahn's side to play Ceylon and Malaya in 1937.

Of course, Morkel had more important things than colour to think about.

A look at the scorecards tells us that this must have taken place during the 1935 season. Morkel was going through an unusually rough patch, and was apprehensive that Cahn would not engage him the following season. It was the custom of Cahn to go through the scorebook at the end of the season and decide who was to stay and who was to part ways with his team. And Morkel's motor business was linked to the decision if not totally dependent on it. It was Cahn who supplied Morkel most of his customers.

Hence, he hatched a plan with friend and teammate, the Nottinghamshire medium-pacer John Hall. At 2 AM one night, Morkel and Hall left the luxurious hotel where the team was put up, made for the cricket ground, and broke into the pavilion. Having retrieved the Cahn XI scorebook, the two ran out on to the shorefront and flung it into the sea. The records destroyed, Morkel continued in the side the following season.

This is not to imply that he was otherwise racially biased. It is simply that as far as anecdotes go, this one is irresistibly juicy and the author could not help himself. It also shows that there were too many things weighing down on Morkel's mind to think of colour even if he wanted to.

Denijs Morkel

9 GREATER WAR AND GREATER GAME

March 1939. Basil D'Oliveira is seven. His day starts early, at five thirty or so. By seven he is already walking. Downhill all the way, not too difficult, but the distance is about six miles. That is how far the St Joseph's School is.

Returning will be literally uphill. That will be the routine for several more years. Even in the late 1960s, when D'Oliveira revisits the place, there is no bus that goes up Signal Hill. It is too steep.

The ongoing Test series has moved to Durban and, after four Tests, it is 1-0 in favour of Wally Hammond's Englishmen. The interest is unprecedented, especially after the excellent showing of the home side in the fourth Test at Johannesburg.

Trains are packed as fans stream in from the rest of the country. The conversations are rife with cricket. Edrich has hit 150 against Natal. But will he play? He does not seem to be cut out for Test cricket.

The match is slated to be timeless.

The centenary celebrations of the Great Trek

The previous year, the Great Trek of the 1830s was brought back into Afrikaner consciousness with heavy dollops of mythification. The centenary of the epic journey of the *voortrekkers*, along with the hagiographic retelling of the Battle of the Blood River, saw symbolic ox wagons passing through hamlets and assembling on a hill outside Pretoria.

The foundation stone of a *voortrekker* monument was laid. Huge crowds gathered to cheer the wagons as they passed through the towns, with participants dressed in traditional Boer attire.

That was also the time when *braaivleis* (barbecue) became a fashionable party fare. Not too many South Africans know it now, but braai essentially re-enacts the way the Voortrekkers cooked their meals on the veld.

With all eternity stretching out ahead, skipper Alan Melville and Pieter van der Bijl bat with utmost care and caution. They go on and on. It is three hours and 20 minutes before Melville, while pulling Doug Wright to the boundary, brushes the stumps with a pad strap and a bail falls off. 131 for one. It sets the tone of the match.

Predictably, the frenzy that developed during the centenary of the Great Trek was vehemently anti-British. Thousands of Afrikaners were swayed by the feelings for their *volk*. At a mass meeting on 16 December at Blood River, DF Malan spoke in vivid historical images, singling out the problem of urban poor Afrikaners as the greatest challenge to Afrikaner survival.

The South Africans bat well into the third day, amassing 530. Van der Bijl hits 125 in seven and a quarter hours. Dudley Nourse, a superb stroke-player, gets sucked into the timelessness of things and spends six hours over 103. Debutant Reggie Perks picks up five for 100.

Among the 250,000 who gathered to attend the ceremony was Alan Paton, the writer who later gained fame for his novel *Cry, the Beloved Country*. In later life, he became a staunch opponent of apartheid.

However, at that time, he was caught up in the celebrations and also grew a Boer-like beard according to the fashion. But when a young Afrikaner in the crowd jovially remarked, "Now we'll knock the hell into the English," Paton left, losing both his sympathy for Afrikaner nationalism and also, on reaching home, his beard.

After a modest England first innings, Melville eschews the follow on. He follows up his first innings show with a hundred batting at No 6. Van der Bijl scores 97. England are set 696 to win. Paul Gibb spends seven and a half hours at the wicket for 120. Edrich is relatively quicker, amassing 219 in seven-and-a-quarter hours.

Rain washes out Day 8. By the end of Day 9, not including the two rest days, Hammond is on 58, Paynter 24. England 496 for 3. Another 200 to win. Most of the men who had arrived for the Test have left on outgoing trains.

Hertzog, coming to the end of his third term as Prime Minister, was now in an experimental coalition with Jan Smuts and his South African Party (SAP). He advocated neutrality in case the European situation worsened. Smuts agreed at first.

On the morning of the 10th day, SACA announces that MCC will have to catch the evening boat. This day will be the last, timelessness be damned. Pieter van der Bijl, the master in charge of cricket at Bishops who coached the young Clive van Ryneveld, has already had two haircuts during the Test.

At 611, the pitch finally shows signs of dormant life. A ball from Norman Gordon kicks and Paynter is caught behind for 75. Rain interrupts play at 631 for 4. Hammond has batted more than five hours already.

An England supporter from Umkomaas, 30 miles down the coast, sends a message through the broadcasting company: "It's raining hard here, will Mr Hammond hurry up?"

Hammond brings up the 650, then stretches out to Eric Dalton. His right leg is raised as he misses the ball. A smart stumping.

At 654 for 5, the rain gods have had enough and send down their disapproval in torrents. The *Athlone Castle* is about to depart. After a brief discussion between the captains and the management, the Englishmen leave in a hurry. They have just enough time to take the train to the vessel.

The Test calls time on Timeless Tests.

The world almost called time on itself.

The original South African decision to remain neutral during the Second World War was overturned with the Germans invading Czechoslovakia. Jan Smuts, the brilliant English-educated lawyer, ex-Boer commandant, and suave statesman, changed his mind. Regardless of political costs, he considered it a moral duty to stop Adolf Hitler—not only for western civilisation, but also for humanity.

He managed to cobble together a majority of 80–67 to enter the conflict, siding with the Allies. Hertzog resigned and Smuts formed a new government, beginning his second term as Prime Minister. South Africa entered a second bloody war with the rest of the world.

Smuts, unmistakably Afrikaans in accent and use of idioms, had all along been detached from the movement around the Afrikaans language. At the same time, he had remained a captivating figure for the English-speaking South Africans, a champion of the reconciliation between the two White factions. A deep thinker, one of the founding members of the League of Nations, and author of an internationally acclaimed philosophical treatise, he was accepted worldwide as one of the greatest intellects of his generation.

Not surprisingly, Smuts was soon accused by the Afrikaners of playing along Anglophilic colonial lines.

While Hertzog and moderate Afrikaners opposed the involvement in the war by resigning, there were others who believed in siding with the Axis powers.

The Amsterdam-born sociologist Hendrik Verwoerd, a champion of the poor-Whites, used his position as the editor of *Die Transvaler* to promote Afrikaner nationalism. He also became a mouthpiece of Nazism for which he was convicted in 1943. He was to become Prime Minister of South Africa and would be known as the *Architect of Apartheid.*

His successor as Prime Minister, BJ Vorster, was actually a general in the neo-fascist extra-parliamentary mass movement called Ossewa-Brandwag (ox wagon), with an ostensibly independent para-military wing Die Stormjaers. Vorster was interned because of his militant operations. One of the lasting bonds he formed during the internment was with Hendrik van den Bergh, who later became the infamous head of state security, often called the Tall Assassin.

Ben Schoeman later became Vorster's Minister of Transport. At the National Party Congress in November 1940, he voiced: "The whole future of Afrikanerdom is dependent on a German victory."

The Ossewa-Brandwag quickly gained 400,000 supporters. It was obvious that neither the Boer War nor the concentration camps had been forgotten.

However, with the tide of World War II turning by 1943, the pro-Allies South African Party (SAP) romped through the elections—'Khaki election' as it was called—to win Smuts a second successive term as Prime Minister. But the rising Afrikaner nationalism was palpable everywhere.

Afrikaner sportsmen reflected some of these sentiments.

Boxer Robey Leibbrant, who came fourth in the light heavyweight class in the Berlin Olympics, received sabotage training in Germany and landed in a German U-Boat just off the coast of South Africa. He was caught and sentenced to death for treason. Smuts converted the sentence to life imprisonment.

Wrestler Johannes van der Walt joined the Ossewa Brandwag and was shot in the back while trying to escape from an internment camp.

Cricket, as can be expected, had fundamentally pro-British vibes.

In the War, General Montgomery called on the Eighth Army to hit Rommel for six out of Africa. During an Army vs RAF XI encounter, the game at Lord's was halted for a few minutes when a flying bomb exploded 200 yards from the ground in Albert Road.

Wartime cricket was played in every battalion—Allied army-men from cricket-playing nations took breaks from the fighting to engage in memorable matches.

It was during one such game in Cairo that the headline Laker skittles Australia *ominously appeared for the first time.*

Dudley Nourse hit 9 sixes off nine balls for South African XI against the Military Police in Cairo. In Greece and North Africa, South African fast bowler Bob Crisp had six tanks blasted from under him within a month but carried on fighting.

Bob Crisp

In England, a coded message in April 1945 revealed that Benito Mussolini was dead, but Hitler was still at large. It read: '*Ponsford is out but Bradman is still batting.*'

Once again 123,000 Black South Africans volunteered for the Cape Corps and Native Military Corps. Dol Freeman, the Malay Wally Hammond, rose to become sergeant major, the highest rank allowed to non-Europeans.

The end of the war is celebrated with the glorious series of Victory Tests between the English Test cricketers and Australian Servicemen. However, perhaps the most poignant encounter is played in August 1945, when the England side take on the Dominions.

Wally Hammond leads the Englishmen, featuring stars like Bill Edrich, Doug Wright, Eric Hollies, and Harold Gimblett. Facing them are eight Australians, a South African, a New Zealander and a West Indian.

Australian Test cricketer Lindsay Hassett, supposed to lead the Dominions, develops an illness. The choice of the replacement captain is not easy.

But ultimately all apprehensions of racism-related complications are overcome. Deservingly, days from his 44th birthday, the great West Indian all-rounder Learie Constantine walks out to toss with Hammond.

It is judged by Plum Warner as one of the finest matches played at Lord's, something Wisden *readily agrees to.*

In three days, 1,241 runs are scored, and 16 sixes are struck. One of the seven hit by Keith Miller in his 189-ball 185 rattles the guttering of the main stand by the press box. One of the 4 sixes struck by Hammond during his two hundreds in the match bounces through the Long Room and clatters against a display case.

In the crunch moment with the game in balance, 48 runs required with three wickets in hand, Constantine 'with a prehensile bound and lethal throw' runs out Phillipson. In the end, Dominions triumph by 45 runs, and Constantine's masterly strategy and fielding has a telling effect on the result.

'Cricket in excelsis', *writes Warner.*

One of the openers for the Dominions is Desmond Fell, the Natal batsman. It remains the curious case of a White South African playing under the captaincy of a Black cricketer during the segregation-apartheid period.

Rugby too had its moments. Whenever New Zealander soldiers and South African army-men came together, impromptu scrummages were formed, in Cairo streets, Italian farms or London pubs. South African Services won a tri-nation against Australian Air Force and New Zealand Forces.

In 1945, a South African Sixth Division side, including future captain Stephen Fry, toured nine countries in four months, losing just twice.

Of course, all the brightness and light brought about in the dark days of war did not make sportsmen immune to the shelling and the bullets.

Transvaal Test cricketer Dooley Briscoe served alongside Bruce Mitchell in East Africa and was awarded Military Cross for his exploits in Italian Somaliland. He was killed in Ethiopia.

Chud Langton, who bowled 91 overs in the Timeless Test, died in Nigeria while serving as a flight lieutenant.

Also in the fatalities list was Maurice Turnbull, the England cricketer who played in South Africa in 1930–31, the tour that Duleepsinhji did not manage to make. Turnbull was also a rugby international for Wales.

In all, nine Test cricketers died in action, Hedley Verity being the greatest of them all.

Something else was taking place during these years of the Second World War.

In 1942, in the Transkei Native Reserve, a 23-year-old Xhosa lad born with the name Rolihlahla was facing a perplexing problem. He had grown up as a village boy, much of his childhood spent under the care of Jongintaba, chief of the Madiba clan. Sent to Fort Hare College, he was expelled for leading a protest against the terrible food served there. Back in his village, he was now informed by his foster father that his marriage had been arranged and was to take place right away.

Rohihlahla and Justice, the regent's son staring at a similar fate of forced marriage, had no alternative but to sell the prize oxen of their guardian and board a train, making for distant Johannesburg.

In the big city with dazzling lights and innumerable diversions, Rohihlahla made important connections, such as meeting Walter Sisulu. Obtaining his BA, he enrolled at the Witwatersrand University for a Law degree.

In 1944, Nelson 'Rohihlahla' Mandela joined the African National Congress.

SECTION 2
Celebrating a National Party

10 APARTHEID BEGINS

Summer 1947. The summer of Denis Compton. An enthralled John Arlott writes, "It was a dream that passed across English cricket in a summer of amazing sun and lit the furthest corner of every field in the land."

At Nottingham, South African Post-War cricket starts with elegance and promise.

Alan Melville bats through the day, almost as if he has taken over the mantle of timelessness from Test cricket. He does not hit the ball—he coaxes it to go where he wills. Dudley Nourse seems to start with a bat made entirely of edges as he starts. However, soon it is all middle.

The two add 319 in just four hours. Melville flicks a full toss from poor debutant Cecil 'Sam' Cook into the crowd beyond square leg. Nourse drives Bedser straight back and it ricochets off the pavilion rails. Only towards the end of the day, Nourse loses his stump trying to hit Eric Hollies into the Trent.

The scoreboard reads 376 for 3. Nourse 149. Melville 183 not out.

Just about a year ago, on 18 April 1946, at the Roosevelt Stadium, Jersey City, Warren Sandell of the Giants threw a letter-high fast ball. There was an explosive crack as Jackie Robinson's bat swung hard. The ball glistened brilliantly in the afternoon sun and went hurtling hard and high far over the left-field fence 300 feet away. The three-run home run meant that Jackie Robinson had successfully broken the colour barrier in the Minor League.

In the Cape, Basil D'Oliveira dressed in his spotless whites and approached the Ottoman's Cricket Club. The impeccable dress code was an integral part of the Coloured cricketers. Whatever the facilities and the conditions of the ground, however limited their opportunity, they strived to maintain a level of etiquette that would make most of the conservative White cricket clubs envious.

Ottoman's, named after the old Ottoman Empire, was as old as the Birth of The Ashes. Founded in 1882, it had not moved from its address at 23 Pentz Street, Bo Kaap. However, D'Oliveira's intentions of joining the club were different. He did not want to play for the great St Augustine's because his father Lewis was the captain there.

South Africa total 533 and with Lindsay Tuckett capturing 5 for 68, England follow on. But not before Edrich and Compton, the two splendid knights of the summer, provide a glimpse of what is to follow, adding 106 of the 208.

D'Oliveira was turned down by Ottoman's—the first of the many, many rejections he would face. Ottoman's was a Muslim club and they did not want a Roman Catholic cricketer. In the complicated Cape society, the reason was just one of the many that could be cited. Yes, the segregated South African nation was hurtling quickly towards government-approved apartheid, but the complicated divisions within its own sectors were aplenty.

D'Oliveira was rebuffed, but still did not want to play under his father. With the help of his two close friends Willie and Alex Bell he set up the club Belgiums. It would be a couple of years before he would finally opt for St Augustine's.

In the second knock, Compton keeps his boyish pranks in check. It is his annus mirabilis, but he bats sensibly keeping the rules of cricket and logic in consideration. The result is a blemish-free 163. The match heads for a draw. In the second innings, Melville limps while he bats, but still strokes his way to his second hundred of the match. "To give flavour to an epilogue whose light notes were like chamber music coming after Beethoven's Ninth," writes John Arlott. Three centuries in three successive innings in Tests, the first and second eight years apart.

In 1946, the Indian Representative Act was repealed, and the Asiatic Land Tenure Act essentially stopped Asians from owning or occupying new property without a permit. The act struck at the heart of Indian commercial and economic life. Apart from affecting trade and property matters, it also made it virtually impossible for the Indian people to earn a decent living.

They were also condemned to live in increasingly over-crowded slums and locations, much like the Africans had been forced to do for years now.

As a result, the Indian government ended trade relations with South Africa and recalled its High Commissioner. In June, in a prayer meeting in New Delhi, Mahatma Gandhi called for South Africa to stop hooliganism of the Whites. Ironically, the very next day, a group of White men attacked a gathering of Indians participating in passive resistance in Durban. Hundreds of Indians were arrested in July.

South Africa spend the summer without defeat in the tour matches, but after the splendid showing at Nottingham, the rest of the Tests are disappointing. The second Test is at Lord's, the haunt of Compton and Edrich—the terrible twins of the summer. One day they will have stands named after them, shoulder to shoulder, staring eye to eye at the pavilion and at the corresponding stands named after the diametrically opposite pro-establishment duo Plum Warner and Gubby Allen.

By the end of the first day, it is 312 for 2, Compton 110, Edrich 109.

When India had toured England as the first visiting side after the war in 1946, they had been similarly outplayed in the Tests but had performed creditably in the tour matches. According to *Wisden* they "raised the status and the dignity of their country's sport."

Vijay Merchant, Vijay Hazare, and Vinoo Mankad had to munch on rice and potatoes at the residence of John Arlott as the ace commentator realised much too late that the men he had graciously invited were vegetarians.

Now, as Compton and Edrich end their association at 466, Arlott knows it is a record without being told by anyone wielding a *Wisden.* They have added 370. Edrich scores 189, Compton 208. England 554.

And now Compton with his left-arm chinaman gets the limpet-like Mitchell stumped for 46. Melville's fourth Test century in a row cannot save the follow-on. Edrich runs in to pick up three wickets in the second innings. Doug Wright finds the pitch to his liking and spins out five men in each innings. Hutton and Washbrook have only 26 to get and they do their job like trusted salarymen without being in a tearing hurry to close their ledgers and leave for the day.

On 10 July, between the second and third Tests, the visitors go up to Dublin to contest an innocuous two-day match against Ireland. The poor Irishmen find the off-breaks of Athol Rowan too difficult to negotiate and are bundled out for 102.

On the same evening, in the Muslim Hall of Johannesburg, wrapped in thick coats against the bitterly cold Highveld winter, delegates from the SAICCB, SABCB, and SAICU got together in a landmark meeting.

Segregation in every domain had forged working solidarity among the marginalised people. In 1946, the Doctors' Pact, signed by Dr Xuma of ANC, Dr Dadoo of Transvaal Indian Congress and Dr Naicker of the Natal Indian Congress, promised cross-racial unity among the new generation of leaders. There was a reflection of the same in the cricketing domain.

Presided over by Rev BLE Sigamoney, the discussion that day centred around forming a non-racial cricket organisation.

The South African Cricket Board of Control (SACBOC) that emerged added a fresh string of letters to the already complicated abbreviation mix.

The SACBOC promised to bring about a strong unity, arrange tournaments between the various unions, and—a final goal which seemed far-fetched at that time—"invite teams or arrange to send a team from South Africa to an overseas country."

They intended to base their template on the Indian Quadrangular and Pentangular. In India, the communities of Hindus, Muslims, Parsees, Europeans, and a loosely defined Rest side contested some of the most fondly remembered tournaments—something which may seem shocking now but was only practical in the days when the communities stayed apart.

SACBOC wanted to start Inter-Race National Tournaments, between the Africans, the Coloureds, and the Indians.

It would take a while for the SACBOC to be formally launched. The momentous day arrived on 30 September 1950. Six months later, in March 1951, the first SACBOC Inter-Race National Tournament was contested at the Natalspruits Ground, Johannesburg.

Old Trafford. Compton and Edrich together again. "A circumstance which by now [has] become something of a nightmare to South Africa," writes Arlott.

The terrible twins add 228 this time, in three and a quarter hours—Edrich 191, Compton 115.

South Africa trail by 139 in spite of a solid first innings score. In the second essay, Nourse hits out with a ferocity that compensates for the lack of grace that many writers mourn in his play. Compton's left-arm googlies are dispatched over long on twice. Guess who bowls him at 115. The other half of the twins, Edrich. This season, whatever they do continue to come off.

England require 129 in 165 minutes. They get there with seven wickets and an hour to spare.

On 15 April, a month and a half before the Nottingham Test, Jackie Robinson made his major league debut. At Ebbets Field a crowd of 26,623 spectators witnessed the event, more than 14,000 of whom were Black. Robinson became the first player since 1884 to openly break the major league baseball colour line.

At Headingley, South Africa bat on a wet wicket and are dismissed for 175. Compton and Edrich both fall under 50. But it is the home ground of the greatest English batsman of the era. Crowds stand six, eight, even twelve deep in great queues to the turnstiles—for was not *Lenoott'n* not out and threatening a century? Hutton is run out for exactly 100.

Nourse duly completes his second 50 of the match, but with the lower order trying to bat out time with six wickets down, Lancashire's amateur captain Ken Cranston comes on to bowl. Just eight weeks after his first-class debut, his seventh over in the innings reads [w.w.ww]

Hutton and Washbrook ensure a 10-wicket win.

The British Royal family reached Cape Town on 17 February 1947. They left on 24 April. Jan Smuts, now 78, was way too detached from the problems at home. He was an international figure, spending time abroad, drafting the United Nations Charter. He met the King, the Queen, Princess Elizabeth and Princess Margaret aboard the *HMS Vanguard* and entertained them through the 35-day visit. In November, he would be one of the major guests at the wedding of Princess Elizabeth.

The Afrikaners did not quite like it and Smuts paid the price the following year, with a poor campaign.

Jan Smuts, seen here with Mr and Mrs Winston Churchill and son Captain 'Japie Smuts. By this stage of his career, he was an international figure way detached from home.

In the final Test at The Oval, Bruce Mitchell spends all but 15 minutes of the match on the field. He moves as sedately as ever to 120 in the first innings, before saving the match—almost winning it—with another big hundred in the second.

South Africa need 451 to win. Mitchell and Nourse add 184 for the third wicket before Nourse (97) leaves at 232. They slump to 266 for 6. Mitchell guides the side to 423 for 7, ending 28 runs short of victory.

So focussed is he on his batting that he loses sight of whatever else is happening around him. From 266 to 314 his partner is Tufty Mann. At five o'clock, Mann is caught by Hutton off Wright and Tuckett comes in. At half past five, Mitchell hits a four. Tuckett and Mitchell stop running when the ball reaches the boundary and meet in the middle of the pitch. Mitchell has a puzzled look on his face. "When did Tufty get out, Lindsay?" he asks. He ends unbeaten on 189, having transformed the Test from dead to epic. The series ends 3-0 in favour of England.

Bruce Mitchell and Dudley Nourse

The experience of Jackie Robinson in America and of Merchant, Hazare, Mankad, and the others in England should not lead us to believe that the racial demarcations existed only in South Africa.

Across the Atlantic, as the Black American soldiers demanded the rights for which they had fought the Second World War, White mobs assassinated as many as six Negro war veterans in a single three-week period that summer.

In Georgia, one of those veterans died when a group of hooded men pulled him, his wife, and another Negro couple out of a car near Monroe, lined the four of them in front of a ditch, and fired a barrage that left 180 holes in one of the four corpses.

When state investigators and the FBI compiled enough evidence to take before a grand jury, the latter declined to return an indictment. "My God, I had no idea it was as terrible as that," exclaimed President Harry S Truman.

In 1946, a 17-year-old Martin Luther King Jr quit his job at the Atlanta Railway Express Company because the foreman insisted on calling him a nigger.

In Belgian Congo, atrocities kickstarted by King Leopold II more than half a century ago continued as human rights seeped through in sluggish, often stagnant, trickles.

As Don Bradman continued to pile runs in his post-War avatar, and as Ray Lindwall and Keith Miller terrorised opposition batsmen, the relatively small population in Australia led to the frenzied slogan 'populate or perish'. It was an ethnocentric call for filling the country with Europeans to prevent it from being overrun by 'yellow races', paraphrased by Minister of Immigration Arthur Calwell's infamous witticism: "Two Wongs don't make a White."

Through the 1950s and 1960s, West Indian and Asian immigrants faced problems in every walk of life in Britain as well.

It was only in South Africa, camouflaged in the garb of 'separate growth', that apartheid became a radical White survival plan and eventually a mandated government policy.

However, for the 1948 elections, apartheid was not the primary driver.

Living costs had increased sharply, wages had fallen for the White workers, and the influx of the Black workers had continued. Unemployment was a problem as well. Besides, the participation in the War had not gone down well with the Afrikaners. There were also allegations of discrimination against them.'

When DF Malan's Nationalists, in alliance with the Afrikaner Party, came to power in May, the new Prime Minister elect rejoiced with the words, "Today South Africa belongs to us once more." He had in mind not the Black-White struggle, but the rivalry between the Afrikaners and the English community.

South Africa was indeed complex. It was eventually the Blacks, Coloureds, and the Indians who suffered the consequences of this tussle for power between the two White factions.

Not that Smuts himself had been a champion of the non-Whites. Far from it. All his life he had been obsessed with defending western civilisation. For a major portion of his career, it had been South Africa where western civilisation was confronted with Black barbarism. Yes, for Smuts, the Africans, and even the Coloureds, were synonymous to barbaric. At times, he could be humanely paternal and was not entirely deaf to the pleas of the Africans for a reasonable standard of life. But segregation had been in his scheme of things as well and he was quite unwilling to compromise on White unity by responding to African needs. The 'native question' was low on his priority list, which started with Afrikaner and English unity in South Africa during his earlier years and ended with grander goals of western unity in face of the new barbarism of powerful nations like Nazi Germany and Bolshevik Russia.

But Malan's and the subsequent National Party governments would soon carry forward the legacy of segregation into the darkest morass of White utopia.

The Cabinet in 1948. Broeders to a man.

1947 also saw Nelson Mandela assume the role of secretary of the ANC Youth League.

11 FIRST VOICES OF PROTEST

Durban. 20 December 1948.

England need 128 to win in 135 minutes. A rain delay eats up 10 minutes. In pursuit of quick runs, they slip to 70 for 6. Compton and Jenkins add 45 but they both depart with 12 more to get.

Cliff Gladwin reaches the crease with a grin on his face. South African captain Dudley Nourse enquires, "What are you looking so cheerful about?"

"Well, cometh the hour, cometh the man," replies the coal miner from Derbyshire.

One eight-ball over. Eight to get. Tuckett stands at the end of his run up. "Just bowl straight and let them get themselves out," murmurs Nourse.

Alec Bedser and Cliff Gladwin at the wicket. As Mayukh Ghosh will put it years later: "*The bright prospect from the much-fancied Surrey [...] The foul mouthed, hardworking coal miner from the unfancied Derbyshire.*"

In the commentary box, the man billed as the 'Voice of the MCC Tour' by the local papers is getting fidgety. "If this goes another five balls, there will be no commentator left," says John Arlott.

Arlott in South Africa

Arlott had an eventful tour. He once sneaked on to the field during one of the early matches, taking the drinks tray from the twelfth man.

There were newspapers inventing humorous stories around him. For example, the one about the pregnant Afrikaner cricket fan Maria Paapenpoel, eager to call her babies after 'de MCC speelers'. Expecting twins, she has no difficulty in choosing 'Eric' and 'Alec' as the two names, obviously after the Bedsers. But she has triplets. "I will call him Yon Arlott after de famous broadkastinger," she says.

A misjudgement from Eric Rowan at the deep midwicket boundary gives Gladwin and England four.

Dark and drizzling. "The hills of North Durban completely hidden by rain," informs Arlott.

Then Bedser misses one.

"Two to win [...] that hit him in the stomach, it was passing a foot over and 5000 people appealed and not one came off," Arlott describes.

Nourse and Mann toss at Durban

In the midst of the cricket, Arlott went on a trip to the Black township with the England wicketkeeper and future MCC Secretary Billy Griffith. "A trickle of stream ran through the middle; they peed into one end and drank from the other." Both Arlott and Griffith were horrified.

A single stolen, bringing the scores at par.

"127 for 8, neither of them tried the overthrow, I don't think either of them have sufficient nerve or sufficient wind, and I certainly have no wind at all."

It comes down to one off the final ball.

"Don't worry, my young champion," Gladwin assures himself and Bedser.

Dead straight on middle and leg. Gladwin swings, misses, the ball whacks him painfully inside the right thigh.

"Run!" shouts Bedser.

"They've run," screams Arlott, his Hampshire drawl coming out thicker than ever, carried through by the deepest of emotions. The stumps are broken but Bedser makes it by a whisker.

"England have won [...] it belongs to a novel, not *Wisden*." And even as the players run from the ground the crowd are on it. "This wicket now looks even worse that it did a minute ago with half Durban running on it."

Denis Compton signs autographs during the tour of 1948–49

January 1949. Cape Town Test. Denis Compton is bowled by Athol Rowan for one. Later, he soaks in the bath.

The boxer Freddie Mills has beaten Johnny Ralph in Johannesburg in an eliminator for the Empire heavyweight title. He served in India with Compton during the War. Now, at the latter's invitation, he comes to meet Compton in the pavilion. At the entrance, a club official stops him. The world light heavyweight champion is asked to wait while the official contacts the chairman.

Wally Mars, the QC, is the chairman of the Western Province Cricket Club. There is a reason WPCC is said to be the MCC of Cape Town. When the official informs him that Freddie Mills wants to come in to see Compton, Mars asks, "Who's Freddie Mills?"

"The boxer," replies the official.

"Boxer? No, we don't want any boxer in the clubhouse," Mars grunts.

Since Compton is in the bath, captain George Mann explains who Mills is and that he is there at the invitation of the Middlesex and England legend.

Mars is simply bemused that MCC can be associated with Mills and the boxing profession. He refuses again: "I don't think a prize fighter will be at home with the members of the WPCC."

The media seizes the remarks. Even Western Province members are shocked. Mars is forced into a public apology.

On 4 December 1948, however, Compton was not soaking in the bath. He was scoring 300 against North Eastern Transvaal at Benoni. On that same evening, Arlott, walking along Commissioner Street in Johannesburg, was greeted by the sight of a rather inoffensive Black man being kicked into the gutter by a White Afrikaner. The victim got up and, apparently apologetically, walked away. Arlott's stomach turned.

His train journeys had shown him luxurious apartments on one side, and tar-barrel hovels on the other.

South African cricket commentator Charles Fortune had invited him for dinner. On his way back from Fortune's place in Grahamstown, Arlott had offered to drive his native cook back to her quarters. They drove through a thunderstorm, and when they got to the squalid accommodation of the African woman, Arlott never forgot the sight. "Shame, hesitation, doubt, guilt struggled in the mind."

The day he was leaving South Africa, he had to fill a departure form. He left the section marked 'race' blank. The immigration officer was not satisfied. "What race are you?"

Arlott looked at him. "Human," he answered.

"What do you mean?"

"I am a member of the human race," Arlott's voice was decisive and his eyes were locked in a staring match, but an inner guardian angel told him that he was not out of the South African jurisdiction yet. A tremor of fear ran through him.

Through his gritted teeth, the officer said, "Get out."

Arlott was most happy to oblige.

On returning to Britain, Arlott recounted his impressions of South Africa for *Meet the Commonwealth* on the General Overseas Service. His talk was measured and politically correct for those times, reflecting only on the bright spots. However, in March 1950, on the *Any Questions?* radio programme, he lost all restraint:

"Well, rather to my horror—I speak from personal observation in this matter, of course—the existing government in South Africa is predominantly a Nazi one, and most of the present cabinet there, under Dr Malan, supported Hitler during the past war and objected to anybody who had served in the English forces." He went on to recount how the Zulus had been shot by the South African police during a riot and how in the conservative north "a man who had a car with no brakes ran down and killed a Bantu and his wife was fined, I think, 25 shillings—but it may have been 27 shillings and a sixpence."

"Anything can happen to a native in South Africa—any form of violence, carrying through as far as murder," Arlott continued. "And you may rest assured that the person who kills him or ill-treats him won't suffer in any real way at all."

A month later, on 21 April 1950, Dr Malan's government announced that BBC news relays via the South African Broadcasting Corporation were to be banned by 1 July. The ostensible reason provided was 'politics', and the example given was John Arlott's recent 'Nazi' comment.

A number of England cricketers, including Denis Compton and Godfrey Evans, condemned Arlott for this 'tactless' broadcast. According to Compton, it was 'hypocritical' to accept hospitality and criticise the hosts.

The cheerleaders of apartheid were aplenty among the cricketing establishment, influenced by the White bubble of privilege inside which they romped around in the luxuries of South Africa during tours. And, of course, the faithful adherence to the tenets of the Old Boys' Club.

However, Arlott remained a confirmed opponent of apartheid. And he will go on to play a vital role in our story.

By the time Arlott voiced his opinion about the situation in South Africa, things had nosedived.

12 STEALING WITH THE EYES

Late 1949. Lindsay Hassett and his men reach Durban on board the *Nestor* and are greeted by South African dignitaries, the Australian High Commissioner Alfred Stirling, and the 38-year-old skipper of South Africa Dudley Nourse. "How are you, Dudley? I hope you're not feeling too well," greets Hassett.

It is a leisurely tour. 76 days will elapse before they play the first Test. While returning to Durban from a match in Richards Bay, Hassett lays a wreath on the grave of JJ Ferris, the great Australian bowler and Boer War casualty.

Ken Archer recalls seeing "as soon as you arrived, on the docks hundreds of Coloured working effectively in a chain gang, as slaves. Being a good little Australian boy, I'd never seen people treated like that before." That is no doubt true, but there is a trace of naivete in the words. Australia is no heaven for the non-White either.

When touring countries visited South Africa to play official Test matches, they contested against the White South Africa. Sometimes the likes of D'Oliveira did visit the Newlands to watch the White stars in action. There were separate entry and seating arrangements for the non-Whites.

The seating area, according to Oborne's book on Basil D'Oliveira, was known as *The Cage*, and was the worst position for viewing, insulated from the side and the rest of the crowd by wire fences. Van Ryneveld remembered it slightly differently. The south-western corner of the ground was a good viewing area, closer to the ground than any other, partially bounded on one side by a low railway stand and from 1956 partially bounded on the other side by the main public stand and the cordoned-off area in front of the sight screen, enclosed for 'obvious reasons'.

Whatever be the case, young Black cricketers went there to 'steal with their eyes.' To pick up the techniques and the finer points from the White cricketers of home and away by watching.

Neil Harvey hits 178 so casually at Newlands that D'Oliveira perhaps feels that he is watching one of his cronies in action on the cobblestoned streets of Signal Hill. His mastery is so effortless that partner Sam Loxton, who contributes 35 in a stand of 140, later complains: "Never mind singles, he was taking three off the last ball of every over. When I finally got to face the bowling, I hadn't seen one for ages, and got out." Of course, *the sixes get longer in the bar*. If we look at the ball-by-ball records as extracted by Charles Davis, we will find Loxton stretching the facts quite a bit.

Even accounting for the romanticism associated with the reminiscences glorifying comrades-in-arms, that is some innings. D'Oliveira sees it from the 'cage', and he 'steals with his eye'.

Legal stealing is the privilege of the Whites.

Neil Harvey launches into a drive at Newlands

The tour is eventful. Keith Miller joins mid-way, Bill Johnston almost dies in a car accident on his way to meet a girl, and Neil Harvey follows his 178 at Cape Town with 56 not out and 100 at Johannesburg, 116 at Port Elizabeth and, above all, a magnificent unbeaten 151 at Durban to manufacture a five-wicket win after trailing by 236 in the first innings.

However, they never play any Coloured cricketer. There are African and Indian bell-boys, caddies and waiters. The Australian cricketers tip them well and treat them with courtesy. At Durban, they are entertained by a native dance troupe and are presented with shields, assegais, and knobkerries at the Dunlop factory.

While visiting a Durban preparatory school, Hassett encourages the students to attend tour matches. "You can learn more from watching good cricketers play than you can from the average coach or from reading books," he advises before adding, "When I come to the wicket, then you can have a snooze."

D'Oliveira does not hear the advice but follows it nonetheless. He never snoozes, regardless of who is at the wicket.

The Australians, the comment of Archer notwithstanding, enjoy the tour thoroughly. Ensconced in the White bubble, subsequent touring teams will also have the times of their lives here.

It was outside the bubble that legalisation of barbarism continued.

The Prohibition of Mixed Marriages Act of 1949 made marriages between Europeans and non-Europeans illegal. People suspected of flouting the law were often followed around by the police and subjected to surprise law-approved break-ins.

The following year, the Immorality Act was amended to prohibit extra-marital sex between Europeans and non-Europeans.

Curiously, had this law been around earlier, Basil D'Oliveira would not have had come into the world.

That summer the great rugby rivalry had been restarted with the All Blacks visiting the shores. Even before the tour of MCC in 1948–49, the New Zealand Rugby Football Union had received an invitation to visit South Africa. The NZRFU accepted, after consulting the Maori Advisory Board, releasing a statement that read: "In view of the domestic policy of South Africa [...] much as it is regretted, the players cannot be other than wholly European."

Loud protests ran through the peaceful islands, and ET Tirikatene, MP for the Southern Maori, called for NZFRU to do the obvious thing and turn down the invitation. The ridiculousness of sending an all-White All Blacks team was discussed even in the budget debate.

Amidst dissenting voices from wide-ranging organisations, including Members of Parliament to war veterans to workers organisations, writer OE Middleton was the first to point towards a new direction.

"Must we agree to the 'Maori grandmother' Gestapo witch hunt because South Africans are afraid of the effect on their submerged thousands when they see a native race living in dignity on equal terms with White men?" he wrote, before continuing. "No All Blacks team should play in or visit South Africa until that country revises its policy of racial discrimination."

Thus, the first public suggestion was made to call off a tour because of the way South Africa treated its own Black population.

The tour went ahead. The Springboks won 4-0.

As a consolation to the Maori stars—Johnny Smith, Ben Couch, and Vincent Bevan—who had missed the tour, the NZRFU hosted the Wallabies while the all-White All Blacks were busy in South Africa. The international matches were granted full Test status by the NZRFU even though most of their main stars were away. The Maori stars thus did not really miss much in terms of Test caps, but the rugby nation as a whole paid the price for supporting apartheid with simultaneous series losses.

Others were paying a more serious price for resisting apartheid. On May Day 1950, ANC organised a one-day stoppage of work. More than half the workforce stayed at home. However, ferocious police attacks and shootings caused 18 African deaths and left many more injured.

Another law unleashed in 1950 was the Group Areas Act, which assigned racial groups to different residential and business sections in urban areas. Essentially, this law ensured that the most developed areas would be reserved for the Whites.

And of course, there was the infamous Population Registration Act, formally classifying South Africans by race. This classification was based on physical appearance as well as reputation, often through ridiculous and humiliating processes such as the 'pencil test for hair'. The application of this law led to breaking up of homes, with siblings and other family members classified differently as Whites and Coloureds.

One cricketer who suffered from this Act was SACCA left-arm spinner Owen Williams. Part of his family was declared White and the rest Coloured. This resulted in furtive visits, denials, 'playing White', and eventual alienation. Williams migrated to Australia where he settled with a tinge of sadness.

In 1950, yet another landmark development took place in the growth of apartheid. Dr Hendrik Verwoerd was appointed senator and minister of native affairs.

Amidst all this turmoil, Basil D'Oliveira was launched with his spate of sixes in the David Harris Trophy. By 1950–51, Lewis D'Oliveira was leading the St Augustine Club for the last time. His son was considered the best man to take over. At 19, he was already a splendid leader of men and also an iron disciplinarian.

13 REACHING OUT

"The South Wales express sped through the Severn Tunnel and on into Glamorgan. I sat, chin cupped in palm, and brooded … and listened. The wheels clattered on:

'You'll never get a run. You'll never get a run. You'll never get a run.' I heard them. And, I suppose, I hated them."

Jackie McGlew's words at the very beginning of his autobiography *Cricket for South Africa* perhaps constitute the most beautiful start to a cricket book. The 22-year-old, on his first assignment for South Africa, had made three outings to the crease. At Maidstone, Bill Edrich had knocked back his middle stump before he had taken guard; at least that's how it had seemed to him. The beautiful backdrop of the cathedral at New Road, Worcester, had rung out with the appeal of the 40-year-old Reg Perks, and McGlew had been declared leg before for nought. At the Fenners, the young man had tried to rush across for a single, and Eric Rowan at the other end—approximately double his age—had not been interested. Three outings, three blobs.

Thankfully, the streak was broken. At Cardiff, McGlew finally got off the mark and managed to bat through to the following day, his five hour and 10-minute effort bringing him 110. One of the illustrious careers of South Africa was on its way.

If things had followed the realm of logic and justice, McGlew's experiences, sentiments, frustrations, and runs could have been D'Oliveira's. He was a year younger than McGlew. And with every bit of respect for McGlew the diligent performer, we can say that D'Oliveira was several times more talented.

It was the summer of 1951. Alongside McGlew there would be others making their debut during the first Test match at Trent Bridge. One of them was Clive van Ryneveld, the same all-round sportsman who grew up a few miles from D'Oliveira, went to Bishops and was awarded a Rhodes Scholarship to Oxford University. In 1949, he had played rugby for England in the Five Nations.

McGlew and van Ryneveld would both become captains of South Africa, and later both would join politics. McGlew, a defender of apartheid, would gun for the National Party. Van Ryneveld, liberal and a supporter of non-White cricketers, would be one of the 12 MPs to form the Progressive Party.

Also making his debut would be the wicketkeeper-batsman John Waite, who would insist, 10 years down the line, that there was no non-White sportsman in South Africa who could replace a White counterpart in a representative side.

By the time the tourists played Glamorgan again, it was early August and the Test series was proving to be a keenly contested one. On board the *Arundel Castle,* the 15 South African cricketers, the baggage master Bill Ferguson, and the five-member press contingent had decided on forming a Club. Athol Rowan had suggested they call it the *Noursemen,* after their skipper Dudley Nourse. Rules had been drafted and a tie had been designed, with the head of a Viking on a green background. The tie was to be worn every Monday. Anyone forgetting to do so would have to buy a round of drinks.

It was at Swansea, during the second match against Glamorgan, that the tie was worn for the first time. Charles Fortune, the commentator, had completely forgotten about it. He desperately tried to convince CO Medworth of the *Natal Mercury* that his need was greater but to no avail. Even the good natured 'Fergie' did not fall for Fortune's entreaties. Finally,

Fortune went into the dressing room. With the South Africans on the field, he deduced that the cricketers would not require their ties for a while. Out he came with an uncomfortable knot on his neck.

The *Noursemen* greeted each other with a raised left thumb, a tribute to their captain. After having broken his thumb while stopping a Tom Graveney drive at Bristol early in the tour, the great Dudley Nourse batted over nine painful hours to compile a magnificent 208 at Trent Bridge. The knock put South Africa 1-0 up in the series. England came back to clinch a hard-fought rubber 3-1, but with a bit of luck the result could have been reversed.

Dudley Nourse

Just before the side had left for their England tour, the South African team had been entertained by Prime Minister DF Malan. During the evening's festivities, the 76-year-old leader had surprised them by asking whether they had enjoyed their stay in South Africa. The Prime Minister had been under the impression that they were English cricketers. Cricket was somewhat impregnable to some of the older Afrikaners. Shades of "Hulle Engelse of ons Engelse."

Of course, all this happened miles away from the small microcosm of cricket in which the likes of Basil D'Oliveira continued their own brand of the game amongst their own people. The new captain of St Augustine's went about his duties with utmost seriousness. He also played football at a remarkably high level of proficiency.

While it was a rarity to see Charles Fortune in a tie, curiously the Black and the Coloured cricketers, as well as the cricket officials, were meticulous about their dress code. The players were expected to dress in spotless whites and keep their kit clean. Dirty shoes or flannels landed one in front of a disciplinary committee. Members of the cricket associations could be turned away from meetings if they were not clad in proper suit and tie.

Some of the etiquettes of the elite White clubs were followed with great ritualistic imitation. Whether that is good or bad is debatable, but it does underline a very characteristic pattern among the subjugated people. A club tie formed on a whim was a pleasant diversion for White cricketers and journalists. For the Black cricketers and administrators, it was a symbol of pride, identity, and a quest for equality.

DF Malan

Under the Malan government, more apartheid laws were making their appearance. The Native Building Workers Act of 1951 legalised the training of Blacks in skilled labour in the construction industry but prohibited their using those skills outside their own homelands. It was very much in line with the 'separate growth' tenet of apartheid.

Segregation was enhanced by the Prevention of Illegal Squatting Act. There was also an attempt to remove Coloured voters from the common electoral rolls, but this was declared invalid by the Appellate Court. This move had to wait till 1956 to be finally implemented.

The demonstration held by the Coloured protesters against this Act in Cape Town in March 1951 fascinated Mandela and Sisulu. The latter suggested starting a nation-wide civil disobedience movement coordinating all the races. The roots of the Defiance Campaign were sown.

The newly formed SACBOC, however, went forward full throttle. In March 1951, the first SACBOC Inter-Racial Tournament was arranged.

In the tournament, 43-year-old Frank Roro led the SABCB side and scored 116 against the SAICU and 66 against the SACCA. Roro, a small man with quick eyes and feet, was named one of South Africa's 10 cricketers of the 20th Century by the United Cricket Board of South Africa at Newlands in January 2000, during the Test match between England and South Africa. Late recognition but a poignant one, contradicting the views of the John Waites and the Dawie de Villiers over the years.

Three of the Abed brothers can be seen in this photograph of the SAICU team. Tiny and Lobo Abed standing at the extreme right. Goolam seated second from left in the middle row.

However, the champions that year were the SAICU, Tiny Abed's eight wickets against the SACCA proving to be vital. It underlined the strong cricket culture of the South African Indians, quite like the parallel development that produced the Ramadhins, the Kanhais, the Kallicharrans, the Chanderpauls, and the Sarwans in the Caribbean.

The SACBOC was not content with just the tournament.

In January 1951, the secretary Rashid Varachia left for India carrying a shipload of ambitious dreams. In Madras he met Anthony de Mello, the president of the Board of Control for Cricket in India (BCCI). He followed it up by visiting KR Collector, the secretary of the Cricket Board of the newly formed Pakistan.

Varachia outlined the plans. An Indian tour to South Africa, leveraging on the Indian connections of the land and the constant scathing attacks on segregation and apartheid that the Indians had led over the years. Varachia proposed a 12-match schedule, including three 'Tests' at Johannesburg, Cape Town, and Pretoria. SACBOC offered to cover all the expenses.

De Mello was noncommittal. He said he would have to consult with the Indian government.

Varachia approached Pakistan. The costs of a Pakistan visit would be considerably less, estimated at £7,500 against an Indian visit of £13,000. The SACBOC hoped the Pakistan board would cooperate.

Ultimately, neither materialised. India was committed to the schedules mandated by the Imperial Cricket Conference. SACBOC did not have membership in the official international body, which would definitely complicate matters. And while Pakistan was not bound by any such terms when Varachia approached them, they received Test status in 1952, which readjusted the priorities for them.

It did not demoralise Varachia, Sigamoney, and the others. They just plunged in another direction.

Other sporting bodies were following suit.

In the White rugby world, the Springboks ruled, beating all four home nations in their epochal tour in 1951–52, adding France for good measure. The 44-0 drubbing of Scotland became stuff of legend.

Closer to home, the African vs Coloured 'test' matches kicked off and the boards started looking for opportunities to play the New Zealand Maoris and Fiji.

The South African Soccer Federation also started inter-race matches between African, Indian, and the Coloured national teams.

The idea of non-White people seeking out other non-White people to engage in sporting activities was looked askance by the White world. They chose to ignore that they had done exactly the same within their own race all through the ages.

14 BRILLIANT UNITS, COMMONPLACE WHOLE

"I doubt whether any international cricket team has begun an overseas tour in such an atmosphere of gloom and pessimism as the 1952–53 South African side to Australia," writes Johnnie Moyes.

With the retirement of Dudley Nourse, the unavailability of the Rowans, and the untimely death of Tufty Mann, the inexperienced South Africans look real pushovers. As it generally happens in such cases, the Australian Board turn snooty. Like they did prior to the 1910–11 series, they ask South African Cricket Association to cover all the costs of the tour. It is considered too great a financial risk for the hosts to sponsor what will clearly be a mismatch. After all, the South Africans have won just one of the 33 Tests they have played against the Australians.

By the time the series ends, however, Jack Fingleton writes: "South Africa may become the cock of the cricketing walk."

Skipper Jack Cheetham, veteran of the battlefield, analytical as befits his profession as an engineer, hatches up plans to bridge the gap of experience and talent with tactics.

Danie Craven, the Springbok rugby great, is engaged to draw up a fitness regimen, and the routines are diligently implemented during the voyage on the *Dominion Monarch* and almost immediately in the WACA Ground on landing.

The captain astutely mixes rigid army discipline with light-hearted implementation for the benefit of the side. There is a 'bounce committee' which levy fines for certain misdemeanours—2/6 for being late for a shipboard function, 1/- for being unshaven, 1/6 for missing church, 2/6 for making a move on the girlfriend of a colleague. Curfew is at 11 PM.

Danie Craven

Moreover, the available technology is used to the hilt. John Watkins and Headley Keith even have cine shots taken of their batting and bowling at the nets to study and work on the faults. McGlew and Roy McLean bat on concrete wickets, arranging for the fastest bowlers of the locality to hurl down short-pitched balls in order to perfect their hook shots.

During late evenings, Cheetham and manager Ken Viljoen spend their time studying the scoring charts prepared by Bill Ferguson.

Back home, apartheid, now championed by Native Affairs Minister Hendrik Verwoerd, was charging ahead full steam.

The first Test at Brisbane sees Harvey at it again, helping himself to 109. As Hassett comes in to bat, the crowd take him to task. "You're too old Hassett, you need a bath chair." Undaunted, the captain scores 55, adding 155 with Harvey.

In the hotel, Cheetham, who has just become a father, uses his war-time smattering of Italian to help out the Davis Cup team. The tennis players from that country find it difficult to order in the restaurant. He comes across Dr Haas Haas, a marine photographer, whose theory is that when confronted with a shark under water, a shout can distract it and save one's life.

On Sunday, the Springboks Watkins and Murray caddy for Lindwall and Miller as the fast-bowling duo tee off against a pair of local golfers.

In the hotel, Cheetham also comes across Indian Davis Cuppers Ramanathan Krishnan and Sumant Misra, in Australia to play Belgium. He makes passing reference about them in his account of the tour. One wonders whether he is aware of the deeds of the Abed brothers—South Africa's own Indian cricketers—playing in the Christopher Trophy. In his later years as administrator, he will have to become aware of the sporting world in all hues.

The young South Africans fight hard. They are set 337 to win and end Day Four at 150 for 2. However, they lose their way to Ray Lindwall and Ian Johnson on the final day.

In January 1952, Mandela helped draft a letter to Prime Minister DF Malan demanding the repeal of six unjust laws that imposed pass laws and institutionalised apartheid. If the suggestion did not meet the desired outcome, ANC would embark on the Defiance Campaign. Malan's response was dismissive—the laws, according to him, were not degrading or oppressive, but protective.

This was taken as a declaration of war. Mandela became the volunteer-in-chief for the Defiance Campaign and spoke in a rally in Durban to ten thousand people. It was also the first time that he openly urged for unity among the non-Whites.

The margin of defeat in the first Test is just 96 runs, but Queensland umpire Col Hoy is informed that he has not been selected to stand in the second Test at Melbourne. "The gates have been so bad, the board didn't think they could afford to bring you down here," he is informed.

But Australia are in for a shock.

Hugh Tayfield, the tall, suave off-spinner in only his second Test series. Morris drives him uppishly on the first day. At silly mid-off, Cheetham leaps up and parries it up. Tayfield does an about-turn, runs a couple of yards, and dives full length to hold the catch. He ends up with 6 for 84 in the first innings. The fifth wicket is of Keith Miller. The all-rounder drives him hard and high, and onward it sails, destined for the crowds. Russel Endean runs along the fence, times his leap perfectly, and clutches it in his extended right hand. "Good God! He's caught the bloody thing!" exclaims Miller. The fitness drills have come off. Endean adds 162 serene runs in the second innings alongside his fantastic fielding effort. In only his third Test match, he bats over seven and a half hours with virtually no back-lift. Just nine boundaries—one hook, four sweeps, and four cuts—all horizontal bat strokes. There are 69 singles, many of them dabbed to third man with his wide, well-taped bat. Playing on his name, RS Whitington describes his innings as Endless. No wonder Endean considers Bruce Mitchell as his model.

Tayfield does even better in the second innings with 7 for 81. South Africa win by 82 runs.

Morris c and b Tayfield after the ball is deflected by Cheetham at silly mid-off

In the dressing room, the South Africans receive Australia's cricket-crazy Prime Minister Robert Menzies. He compares Endean's catch with that of "Uncle" Dave Nourse to dismiss Bill Whitty off Aubrey Faulkner. He says when a ball landed in those 'frying pans' Nourse called hands, it never escaped.

Later, the tourists receive a congratulatory cable from their own not-so-cricket-crazy Prime Minister DF Malan.

On 26 June 1952, Mandela tasted a prison cell for the first time, arrested for breaking the 11 PM curfew for Blacks. The Defiance Campaign was in motion. In three months, some 8,000 people would be jailed. In late July, the offices of ANC were raided, and Mandela was arrested under the Suppression of Communism Act.

Ian Craig, the 'new Bradman', is not selected. The men on Sydney's infamous Hill are not amused. "You beat Craig in only one thing, Hassett, and that's years," they holler.

Predictably, Australia go 2-1 up. Harvey hammers 190, delighting the 30,000-strong Saturday crowd, and the crushing win is by an innings.

At Adelaide, just before the match, Don Bradman pads up to join the Springboks at the nets. A 20,000-strong crowd gathers early and most of them ask whether Craig is going to play. They are not amused when informed he will be the 12th man. As the spun coin lands, Hassett tells Cheetham: "You've a little trouble ahead when you tell the boys that you've lost the toss." One wicket falls on the first day—McDonald 154, Hassett 163, Harvey 84. It is beastly hot. McGlew will remember scraping the flies off his forehead.

Bradman with the South Africans at Adelaide

Leading by 143, Australia go for quick runs in the second innings. Harvey completes the century he missed in the first knock at a run-a-minute.

South African journalist Charles Fortune must freshen up after the day's play to attend a dinner and does not feel like going all the way to the Glenelg Hotel. He requests Cheetham for the use of the dressing room. The rules are strict and, fearing a precedent, the South African captain refuses. Dejected, Fortune repeats his request to Hassett. "Certainly Charles, you can do what you like to," the Australian skipper responds. "Fill the ruddy tub with beer if you wish."

Hassett declares setting a target of 377—more realistically the task is to bat out 257 minutes. When the visitors survive to end with 177 for 6, Endean spending two hours over

17, Don Bradman pokes his head in and says: "Well done chaps."

The unfancied team is the first post-war side to go into the final Test in an Australian series with the rubber still undecided. The final Test is therefore contested over six days.

On being released on a suspended sentence, Mandela and Oliver Tambo established the first African law firm in the country, 'Mandela & Tambo'.

In October 1952, Mandela was elected president of the Transvaal ANC. Two months later, along with 51 other ANC leaders, he was banned from attending any meeting or gathering, from talking to more than one person, and from leaving Johannesburg without permission.

The indomitable Harvey is at it again when the series returns to Melbourne for the final Test. He bats just under five hours, ending with 205. The 17-year-old Ian Craig finally makes his debut and beautifully drives the fourth ball he faces to the cover boundary. The youngster gets 53 and Australia amass 520. In *Sydney Morning Herald,* Tom Goodman writes, "Australia cannot lose the match. The only question now is whether South Africa can fight out a draw."

The young South Africans keep at it. Lindwall and Miller are not playing the Test, and a string of solid contributions against the slightly lesser attack take them to 435. Waite 64, Watkins 92, McLean 81, Cheetham 66.

Eddie Fuller of Western Province will never do anything worthwhile in Test cricket again, but here, in his second Test, he captures five wickets. That includes Harvey for seven. Tayfield picks up three. 30 wickets in the series for him. Cheetham's policy of placing attacking fields in spite of the big deficit works superbly. Australia are 209 all out in the second innings.

At the end of Day 5, South Africa requiring 295 to win are on 94 for 1.

The pendulum swings on the final day. Endean falls for 70, with just three boundaries. Watkins hits 50. Tension builds when Benaud bowls Funston to make it 191 for 4. Young Roy McLean tugs at his cap and informs Cheetham, "Don't worry Pop, I'll get them for you." He proceeds to play an ugly wild swipe against the turn and is dropped by Arthur Morris first ball. And then, he blasts his way to 76 in 80 minutes with flashing cuts, drives and hooks.

The series is tied 2-2. This is the first team to hold Australia in their backyard since Jardine had unleashed Bodyline in 1932–33.

Bryan O'Brien, a Melbourne man who backed the Springboks at 3 to 1, throws a party for the team at Claridge's Night Club. Glamorous women are there to entertain them.

1952 ended with ANC becoming a more direct organisation; the Zulu chief Albert Luthuli was appointed president and Mandela his deputy.

The happy cricketing Springboks stop over in New Zealand to win the two-Test rubber 1-0. At Basin Reserve, Jackie McGlew bats eight hours and 54 minutes for 255, a South African record that will stand for 17 years.

The final Test at Auckland draws to a close on March 17. Two weeks later, at Johannesburg, the second Inter-Racial cricket tournament organised by SACBOC kicks off on Easter weekend.

Roy McLean drives Hassett for the winning runs

Basil D'Oliveira opened the innings of the SACCA and posted two century partnerships with 'Chong' Meyer. In the side was the fast bowling all-rounder Cecil Abrahams.

A South African Malay Team participated, the first such combined side since 1891–92, when Krom Hendricks had bowled to WW Read's Englishmen. Playing for the Malays, somewhat controversially since he was more readily categorizable as Coloured, was Eric Petersen. This excellent fast bowler captured 19 wickets in the tournament. Also representing the Malay side were the supremely talented brothers Goolam Abed and Lobo Abed.

At the top of the wicket-takers' list, alongside Petersen, was the SAICU off-break bowler with the curious run-up, Mohamed Garda. The Africans were led by the veteran Dol Freeman and had Ben Malamba as their fast bowling spearhead.

Cec Abrahams was a fantastic bowler who could bat in the middle order. He followed D'Oliveira into English league cricket.

'Lobo' Abed—that superb wicketkeeper with breath-taking leg-side stumpings whom we have come across at Green Point. 'Tiny' Abed was 6'3", tiny compared to Lobo, who was 6'5". An attacking batsman, a fast swing bowler, and brilliant close to the wicket, Tiny was described as a debonair all-rounder in the mould of Keith Miller. He went on to play professional rugby in England. Another brother, Dik Abed, was to play professional cricket in England and the

Netherlands.

Eric Petersen was a fast bowler who specialised in cutting both ways.

The Coloured side SACCA proved too strong for the others, winning the brand-new jug-eared silver trophy made in London. It was specifically built for the tournament by the cricket-loving Dadabhay brothers from Transvaal, major players in the textile industry.

At the end of the tournament, the captain of the SABCU side, Dol Freeman, remarked: "Our side can be compared favourably in the international arena, let alone the best European side." He was talking about a representative SACBOC side chosen from the best players of the tournament.

Basil D'Oliveira stands fourth from left in the Western Province side with the David Harris Trophy

It certainly begs the question and at the risk of repetition, we must ask it again.

The side playing in Australia and New Zealand were in transition. With the departure of men like Bruce Mitchell, Dudley Nourse, Eric Rowan, Athol Rowan and, earlier, Alan Melville, there were gaping holes to be plugged.

Apart from Tayfield there was no current or future great in the bowling department. And while McGlew, Endean, McLean, and Waite would serve the country for long, none of them apart from McGlew could be called distinctly classy.

With superb tactics and passion, they did square the series against Australia. But what could have they achieved if they had a young D'Oliveira in the top order, Goolam Abed and Cec Abrahams bringing in all-round strength, Lobo Abed behind the wicket, Eric Petersen opening the bowling with Ben Malamba?

People do speak of the outstanding South African side just before the isolation—how they were arguably the best in the world when they were forced to walk into the premature sunset. But for all the brilliant non-White cricketers other than D'Oliveira, the sun did not rise at all.

As we will repeat so often in these pages, we will never know.

Of course, in 1952–53, even entertaining such thoughts could land one in the bad books of the secret police of South Africa.

Meanwhile, Charles Fortune remained quite confident that Endean and Tayfield would walk into any World XI. Well, not that they were not deserving—at least Tayfield definitely was. But the world, as seen by Fortune, was quite monochrome.

The South African Cricket Association, pleasantly surprised by the success of the team, asked Cheetham, McGlew, Endean, and the manager Viljoen to document the secret of their success for future South African sides. Viljoen called it *The Vilcheet Plan.*

All the while, the apartheid legislation continued unabated.

The Bantu Laws Amendment Act limited the category of Blacks who had the right to permanent residence in urban areas.

The deceptively named Natives Abolition of Passes and Co-ordination of Documents Act of 1952 did repeal the many regional pass laws, but in their place instituted one nationwide pass law. It was made compulsory for all Black South Africans over the age of 16 to carry a 96-page passbook when in White areas. The law stipulated where, when, and for how long a person could remain in such areas.

Amidst all this turmoil, the potentially brilliant units that could be combined into one magnificent South African side remained disjointed entities, many of whom did not even know that the others existed.

The exception is one individual who got lucky, much like Charlie Llewellyn had done long, long ago.

Athlone born all-rounder Denis Foreman from Cape Town managed to play three matches for Western Province in the Currie Cup of 1951. No one really made a fuss, apart from a couple of comments about the touch of a tar brush. The following year, he was in England, his football skills earning him a contract with Brighton and Hove Albion. From 1952 to 1967, he played 125 first-class matches for Sussex.

However, for the rest, things were about to get worse, much worse. Yes, there was still room for conditions to turn worse.

15 SEPARATE 'DEVELOPMENT'

26 December 1953. Ellis Park.

For the first time, the South Africans are hosting the Kiwi cricketers. In rugby, the rivalry defines life for the two nations. But the cricketing equivalent of the Springbok-All Blacks encounters promises to be benign. South Africa is not yet that big a force in the cricket world, and New Zealand is not considered a force at all.

The two teams lodge in the same Johannesburg Hotel. The players mingle, laugh and eat together. On the first morning itself, Roy McLean races up the stairs at desperate speed, with John Reid in hot pursuit, seeking vengeance for some bit of tom-foolery. Hardly ever has a Test series been played in better spirits.

However, the second day dawns with sombre news. The Wellington-Auckland overnight express has plunged into the flooded Whangaehu River near Tangiwai on Christmas Eve, the same day the Test began. Among the many who have perished is Nerissa Love, the young fiancée of 21-year-old Kiwi fast bowler Bob Blair. The speedster remains grieving in the hotel as the rest of the team leave for the game. At the ground that morning, the South African and New Zealand flags droop dejectedly in the sunshine as they fly half-mast.

Disaster strikes on the field as well. Neil Adcock generates frightening pace off the wicket, the balls fly venomously from length. Murray Chapple is bowled off his glove and chest to make it 9 for 2. And then, Bert Sutcliffe plays three balls and wafts at a fourth that climbs into his face. The thud as it hits him on the side of the head is sickening. He drops in a heap. Dead silence. Ambulance men rush out with a stretcher. However, the classy batsman staggers to his feet and somehow manages to trudge out of the ground, captain Geoff Rabone and some of the South Africans helping him along.

Sutcliffe goes down

In the hospital he collapses for a second time. His left ear has been split, behind which there is a ghastly gash.

While Sutcliffe is at the hospital, Adcock bowls to Lawrie Miller. The ball strikes him on the chest. He bravely tries to continue batting, but when he coughs blood Cheetham walks up and persuades him to retire.

Both Sutcliffe and Miller are advised not to play any further.

Both do.

With the score 41 for 4 at lunch, they cannot afford not to.

Miller falls at 81. And with his head swathed in bandage, Sutcliffe emerges in the hard white light to tremendous applause. The Springboks join in without restraint. It is Dave Ironside who has the ball. The second delivery is a bouncer. Sutcliffe steps back and hooks. Over square leg. A six.

At 108, Adcock is back. Fast and furious as ever. Sutcliffe cuts him delectably to the point fence. At the other end Tayfield is wheeling along. Sutcliffe steps forward and drives high and straight, into the crowd. The total is 123. Follow-on is averted, something which looked impossible at lunch. Two balls later, Sutcliffe repeats the stroke with the same result.

But Adcock is at it again. Wicketkeeper Frank Mooney is struck a damaging blow on his left hand.

After tea, wickets fall in a hurry. 138 for 7. 146 for 8. Sutcliffe strikes Tayfield for another six. The score is 154 for 9 when Guy Overton is caught at slip off Ironside.

The players have already started walking off the ground when out of the gloomy tunnel beneath the stand there emerges Blair. Slow, fumbling with his gloves, but sure.

The entire stand rise for him, in silence. Between the New Zealanders in the dressing room and the South Africans in the field there is not a single dry eye. Sutcliffe meets him in the middle, his arm goes around the fast bowler. One hit on the head, the other recipient of a deathly blow to his heart. Both out to do battle.

As he faces his first ball, Blair hurriedly passes a hand across his eyes. He plays out the Ironside over.

The next over by Tayfield. Eight balls of drama. The field spreads far and wide as Sutcliffe takes strike, but not as far as they need to be. The stroke is made off the leg stump, the ball soars over mid-wicket. The silence around the ground turns into a synchronised roar. And it continues. South Africans in the stands applauding the brave Kiwi cricketer. They have not stopped roaring when Sutcliffe on-drives Tayfield sweet and clean over long-on for yet another six. Two balls later the stroke is repeated, as are the motions of the scorers. The ball drops into the raucous crowd next to the sight screen.

The fifth ball comes up and Sutcliffe taps it away for a single to keep the strike next over. Blair takes guard. Tayfield runs in. A ball is blocked. And then the fast bowler puts his foot firmly down the pitch and swings it over mid-wicket. Blessed are the crazy lot among whom the ball lands that day. The Tayfield over costs 25, "a counter-attack on a Hollywood scale," writes Dick Brittenden.

Ironside runs in and Sutcliffe hits him for a graceful boundary. But he cannot retain the strike. Cheetham wisely keeps Tayfield on. Blair comes down the track and is stumped. In 10 minutes, the two have added 33. Sutcliffe, 80 not out, has hit 7 sixes. In 66 years of Test cricket only Hammond has hit more.

Sutcliffe and Blair return to tremendous applause. The left hander has played one of the greatest innings ever. And now he stands at the gate, allowing Blair to pass through first. In the words of Dick Brittenden: "Through they went, arms about each other, into the darkness of the tunnel, but behind them they left a light and an inspiration which several thousand lectures on how to play a forward defensive stroke will never kindle."

The applause continues long after the two disappear into the tunnel.

Dudley Nourse would later say that this was the most enthralling day's play he had ever seen. The most evocative of cricketing action, the poetry, the ethos, the odes and the epics that the game conjures up. In the stands and in the field, they were normal South Africans who were party to this fascinating action, imbibing the emotions and spouting forth their own, every single soul moved by the heroism and tragedy, the bravado and the anguish.

These were the same South Africans who were largely apathetic and often condoning towards apartheid, to the evils of subjugation and discrimination, to the violation of the most basic human rights; not unsupportive of the ridiculously brutal and barbaric legislations handed out to the vast majority of their people.

It is always curious how perfectly normal souls, possessing values of decency and fellow-feeling like any other group of human beings, with ability to feel and profess empathy, become vocal supporters of atrocious regimes.

In 1953, South Africa did turn atrocious, even more than it had been.

The African's 'inherent character' conceptualized by Verwoerd had profound policy implication for education. The Commission on Native Education 1949–51, laid the ideological basis and the administrative framework for the Bantu Education Act. Essentially, this was racial segregation of schools, enforcing the Mission-operated schools to come under government control. Even universities were made 'tribal', and all but three missionary schools chose to close down when the government would no longer support them.

"It is in the interest of the Bantu that he be educated in his own circle," Verwoerd explained. "He must not be a Black Englishman in order to be used against the Afrikaner." His argument was: "What is the use of teaching a Bantu child mathematics when it cannot use it in practice? [...] It is the policy of my department that education should have its roots entirely in the Native areas and in the Native environment and Native community. There Bantu education must be able to give itself complete expression and there to perform its real service. The Bantu must be guided to serve his own community in all respects. There is no place for him in the European community above the levels of certain forms of labour. Up till now he has been subjected to a school system which drew him away from his own community and partially misled him by showing him green pastures of the European but still did not allow him to graze there."

Through all this and other sparks of spectacular nonsense, Verwoerd was backed by extreme confidence. According to him, he had never suffered from self-doubt.

The ANC attempted to counter this by trying to create schools of their own, while asking the students to boycott the schools run by the government. However, this was not a fair fight, since they lacked the funding and infrastructure, and the police stepped in to harass the parents who dissented against the Act.

There were other Acts as well. The Reservation of Separate Amenities Act legalized the racial segregation of public premises, vehicles and services. The Act clearly made it legal not only to adhere to segregated facilities, but also to completely exclude people, based on their race, from public premises, vehicles, or services.

Whites-only areas, parks, benches, beaches and seats appeared very soon.

And to ensure that the indispensable work went on in spite of these policies, Native Labour Settlement of Disputes Act prohibited the Africans from indulging in strike actions.

The South Africans win the series 4-0. In the final Test at Port Elizabeth, they need to make 212 in 225 minutes. They fall behind the clock and find themselves on 81 for 3. Endean, the chartered accountant who still lives with his parents and is considered the most eligible bachelor of South Africa, now sheds his 'Endless' tag. With Watkins, he adds 107 in 70 minutes. His 87 is studded with 14 boundaries. South Africa get there with 40 minutes to spare.

The marginalisation encroached even into the segregated world of South African sports. In 1951, the South African Soccer Federation had been formed, merging the African, Coloured, and Indian football bodies. In the 1952 inter-race soccer tournament, the Coloured XI played the Bantu XI in front of 15,000 people.

A South African Indian team was selected to tour India in 1953, following the footsteps of the 1922 tour of the Christopher Contingent. Bob Pavadai, the SACBOC president, was appointed manager of the side. However, just as the team was about to board the ship in the Durban harbour, it was announced on the radio that their passports had been revoked by Eben Dönges, Minister of the Interior, a major stalwart among the mighty architects of apartheid.

Segregation

In the midst of all this discrimination, two Indian journalists from Port Elizabeth performed a minor miracle. Syd Reddy and Damoo Bansda had already brought out the first issue of a new cricket newspaper called *Cricket Souvenir,* focussing on the SACBOC non-White cricket but also covering news from the international arena.

At the end of the 1953–54 season, Reddy and Bansda published the first *South African Non-European Cricket Almanack.* This 147-page volume is filled with historical narratives of the different racial cricket organisations that went into forming the SACBOC.

In June 1953, Nelson Mandela's six-month ban, which prevented him from attending meetings and leaving Johannesburg, came to an end. He drove to a small town in Orange Free State to represent a client. He had hardly stepped into a local courthouse when waiting policemen handed him a fresh banning order. The new ban required him to resign from all organisations, including ANC, and again forbade him from leaving Johannesburg.

On 21 September, in an ANC presidential address delivered in his absence as a banned person, he insisted: "Never surrender."

Linking the freedom movement of South Africa with other revolutionary eruptions in Tunisia, Kenya, and Rhodesia, he ended the speech with the words: "You can see that there is no easy walk to freedom anywhere, and many of us will have to pass through the valley of the shadow (of death) again and again before we reach the mountain tops of our desires."

In Pretoria, Peter Hain was just three years old when his parents received an invitation through an old Nairobi friend to join a new non-racial Liberal Party. With the memories of the more relaxed racial structure of Kenya still fresh in mind, alongside the images of the friendly native faces they had come across on their long road trip back to South Africa, the couple thought this was a good idea.

When they moved to Ladysmith, where Wal opened an office for his firm, an architectural student called Annette Cockburn joined them to gain work experience. She had recently joined the Liberal Party, and this offered further encouragement.

When a new local branch of the Party was set up in Ladysmith, there was no place to hold the inaugural meeting but in Ad and Wal's modest rented home.

The meeting was attended by Alan Paton, the party's national president, the author of *Cry, the Beloved Country*, whom we came across during the *Voortrekker* centenary celebrations. It was here that Elliot Mngadi, later the national treasurer of the party, popped up and told his hosts, "This is the first time I've come through the front door of a White man's house."

1953 saw the end of a 34-year career for Gasant Ederoos Behardien as baggage master and ball boy. The Black tailor and businessmen, also known as Gamat, served both the Western Province and the Springbok rugby teams. He was considered their lucky charm.

Curious that a Black man from the most sordidly subjugated section of society could be considered a lucky charm by privileged White rugby stars.

16 ROCK AROUND THE CLOCK

145 runs required in 135 minutes. To keep the series alive.

They could have drawn level at Lord's after taking a 171-run first innings lead, but a Peter May hundred and a Compton half-century had refused to put out the white flag. John Woodcock summarised it as "some of the best batting that has come from an English pair in adversity since the War." After that Brian Statham had blown them away with a spell of 7 for 39.

At Old Trafford, Jackie McGlew, leading the side for the first time in the absence of an injured Cheetham, grudgingly remarked that for luck with the toss alone Peter May was well worth his place in the England side.

McGlew took blows from Frank Tyson in the first innings, retired hurt when no longer able to grip the bat properly and came back to hit a hundred. This time they led by a humongous 237 in the first innings in spite of a big hundred by Compton.

But May braved the assault of the terrifying bowling duo of Neil Adcock and Peter Heine, along with the metronomic accuracy of Trevor Goddard and Hugh Tayfield. Yet another hundred for this great post-War batsman.

Things are incredibly tense now; the tension is relieved only when Neil Adcock volunteers to bat up the order if really quick runs are needed. His partner in crime, Peter Heine, chuckles. He is proud not because he has made the vaunted English line-up hop with his searing pace, but because he remains the only member of the team yet to score a duck on the tour. That has been his brag for a while now.

Now the limpet-like McGlew cuts the first ball from Tyson for four. The second ball goes through to the keeper, Graveney substituting for the injured Evans. Goddard, that amazing all-rounder at home whether running in with the new ball or facing it, charges down the wicket and makes his ground with time to spare. The tone is set. The chase is on.

They score 14 off the first two overs, singles being stolen off the pitch. May positions Lock four yards from the bat to stop them.

Goddard perishes, mistiming a drive off Bedser. The great Surrey medium pacer bowls Keith with a ball that moves off the pitch past the drive. 23 for 2. The clock is ticking away.

It is July 1955.

The previous year, the Bantu Resettlement Act was enacted. Administered by the Minister of Native Affairs, Hendrik Verwoerd, it legalised the removal of Blacks from any area within and next to the magisterial district of Johannesburg.

Sophiatown. A rare place where nobody—almost nobody—looked at the colour of the skin. It was who you were that counted. Sophiatown was not a slum—it was an idea, an ethic.

When plans were unfurled to uproot natives from this vibrant Sophiatown, residents united to protest against the forced removals. They chanted the slogan "Ons dak nie, ons phola hier" (we won't move, we're staying put).

Roy McLean—a man who can turn the match around. Like he did at Melbourne. Bedser's first ball comes up and he pushes his left leg up the wicket and aims a vicious slog. Bedser and Graveney appeal as it hits the pad. Dai Davies shakes his head. Cheetham in the dressing room checks to see whether his heart is still beating.

Tyson oversteps and McLean crashes the no-ball into the square leg boundary. Off Bedser, he slams one into the crowd beyond square leg. A drive wide of mid-on gets him three, and they have caught up with the clock.

Sophiatown

The English Anglican Bishop, Father Trevor Huddleston, joined the Sophiatown resistance. "Sophiatown was a remarkable and vitally vigorous community," he said later. "It's extraordinary how many gifted people came out of the place."

Anti-apartheid activists Sussex-born Helen Joseph and Johannesburg scholar Ruth First were among others who joined the resistance as well.

And of course, there was Mandela. On 13 December 1954, he addressed the crowd at Soweto, even voicing that nonviolent resistance was becoming useless.

ANC issued a statement: "The African people have rejected the removal scheme as a brutal and wicked plot to rob the African people of freehold rights and to resettle them in specified areas in tribal groups [...] If the Nationalists implement the removal scheme an extremely dangerous and explosive situation will arise."

McGlew continues in his role, which will become known as sheet-anchor. And then Tyson's delivery flies at him and crashes into his chest. From the distance of four yards, Tony Lock hears the dull thud. But even as the concerned Surrey spinner approaches the diminutive batsman, he is waved away. McGlew does not even rub the spot.

The following over sees the defining moment. McGlew steers Bedser for a single. McLean swings thrice but hits nothing but thin air. And then he spoons one back to the bowler. Big Alec tries to accept it with his left hand even though both palms are at his disposal. The catch is spilled.

McLean celebrates the life, scoring with abandon. The score rises quickly. Tyson is hooked to the boundary, twice. And then there is the short-arm pull which sends the ball speeding past mid-on. The score is into the seventies.

Trevor Huddleston in Sophiatown

On 9 February 1955, around 2,000 policemen, armed with handguns, rifles and clubs known as knobkerries, forcefully moved the black families of Sophiatown out into Meadowlands, Soweto. Mandela ruefully reflected: "In the end, Sophiatown died not to the sound of gunfire, but to the sound of rumbling trucks and sledgehammers." Sophiatown, renamed *Triomf*, was rezoned for Whites.

An hour to go, just 50 to get. The England players gather around the trays as the drinks are brought out. They take their time. The two batsmen remain at the wicket, willing the fielders to get on with the game. Both glance nervously at the pavilion clock. The waiter seems to take ages to walk off the ground.

McLean brings up his half-century at run-a-minute. And then he cuts Tyson blisteringly. At point, Parkhouse, substituting for Evans, pulls off a spectacular save. McGlew is halfway down the track. Caught on the backfoot, McLean has hardly moved. Now, desperate to respond to his captain's call, he rushes down frantically. May comes up from mid-on to take the throw. McLean run out by some 10 yards. 95 for 3.

McGlew is unsettled and upset. He defends dourly. But there is Paul Winslow. 108 in the first innings with three sixes, one of which landed into the practice ground at the Stretford end and took him from 96 to 102. It was an innings of rare savagery, especially for the era. Now he pushes a few balls back and then drives Bedser hard and high into the crowd. 100 up. The Surrey man lumbers back for the next delivery, and Winslow drives again. The result is the same.

It has been a very eventful tour for Winslow. In East Midlands, 11 actresses invited 11 Springboks to the Derby Playhouse to watch their play *Women of Twilight.* At the drinks party after the show, Winslow fell for one of the cast, 23-year-old Moira Gray. Ten days later they were engaged. They would be married in October.

Now he has hit two sixes. The Springboks are ahead of the clock. 107 on the board.

The Group Access Development Act received Royal Assent just a couple of weeks before the Manchester Test match. The purpose of this one—administered by the fertile brain of Eben Dönges—was to exclude non-Whites from living in the most developed areas.

The same month, June 1955, the ANC, along with the allies South African Indian Congress and South African Congress of Democrats, stated the core principles of the South African Congress Alliance. This 'Freedom Charter' stated unequivocally: "We, the people of South Africa, declare for all our country and the world to know that South Africa belongs to all who live in it, Black and White, and that no government can justly claim authority unless it is based on the will of all the people; that our people have been robbed of their birth-right to land, liberty and peace by a form of government founded on injustice and inequality; that our country will never be prosperous or free until all our people live in brotherhood, enjoying equal rights and opportunities; that only a democratic state, based on the will of all the people, can secure to all their birth-right without distinction of colour, race, sex or belief; And therefore, we, the people of South Africa, Black and White together—equals, countrymen and brothers—adopt this Freedom Charter. And we pledge ourselves to strive together, sparing neither strength nor courage, until the democratic changes here set out have been won."

It was criticised in South Africa as 'a typical communist ploy'.

In 1955 SACBOC, the non-White body, gathered up the guts to ask Imperial Cricket Conference, ICC, for affiliation. Obviously, they didn't get a response.

Paul Winslow had an eventful tour

38 runs to get, 50 minutes left. It is all over bar the shouting.

However, there is Tyson. The man who is fresh from knocking over Australia. The man who chants Wordsworth as he walks back to his bowling mark. He continues to bowl at phenomenal pace.

McGlew manages yet another glide to the leg for a single. Winslow whips him away, using the scorching pace to send it to the square leg boundary. The next ball dips in—one can almost see the venom flying off it as it accelerates. Winslow tries to repeat the stroke, it goes under his bat and the stumps come down crashing. 112 for 4.

The Rhodesian Mansell is in now. Bespectacled, cautious. The South Africans are still ahead of the clock. Tyson steams in, putting everything into the ball. Mansell defends as if his life depends on it.

Bedser at the other end. McGlew has run out of the really hard-hitting stroke-makers among his partners. Unless he is desperate enough to take the offer of Adcock and the brags of Heine seriously. He turns the second delivery off his toes, past mid-on. The batsmen take two. The next is punched through the covers. May sprints behind it—it is touch and go—but the ball pips him to the fence.

Three quick singles are run. And then Lock whips one in sharply, almost getting another run out.

Another single, another four.

16 required, the clock shows three minutes to six. 33 minutes remain.

In the David Harris Trophy for the Coloured, held at Natal from December 1954 to January 1955, Basil D'Oliveira hit a majestic unbeaten 155 against Transvaal, and then followed it up with 112 against Natal. Western Province won the tournament, and the SACCA selectors named D'Oliveira the captain of the national Coloured team to contest in the third SACBOC Inter-Racial tournament.

D'Oliveira's teammate and long-time rival Cec Abrahams, one of the foremost all-rounders in non-White cricket, decided to take a different stand. This magnificent cricketer informed the selectors that he would not be available for selection of the national Coloured team. He opposed in principle to SACBOC's racially structured biennial tournament. He had voiced the same reservations that Mahatma Gandhi had about the Quadrangular (later Pentangular) cricket tournaments in India.

Tyson is far from giving up. The ball is too fast for Mansell to get his bat down in time. There is a dreadful thud. Up go the Englishmen. Frank Lee, that stodgy Middlesex all-rounder, raises his finger. 129 for 5. Is there another twist?

Waite is the new man in, tugging nervously at his gloves. Fresh from 113 in the first innings, only the third Test hundred by a South African wicketkeeper. But the conditions are drastically different here. The first ball he faces is lightning quick. He is late in bringing down the bat. The dressing room heaves a sigh of relief as it misses the stumps and thuds into Graveney's gloves.

His bat is late on the next one as well. The ball crashes into his thigh and trickles to the leg. As Graveney runs across to field, the batsmen steal a leg-bye.

McGlew, in his first Test as captain. A pair in the Lord's Test. That must have reminded him of the nightmarish start of his previous tour. And now 104 in the first innings 46 in the second, yet to be dismissed in the match. Fortunes can really fluctuate.

Tyson pitches up and the skipper drives him past mid-on. The batsmen run hard for the first and turn for the second. Only 13 remain.

In runs Tyson again, fast and furious. A similar ball, a similar stroke. Only this time, the ball beats the bat and crashes into the stumps. The crowd rises as McGlew returns. 132 for 6.

Russell Endean comes in and his nervousness almost radiates across to the stands. May looks at his options. Bedser has gone for 61 in 10 overs. The last Test match for this great cricketer. There is Titmus, there is the scrooge-like Bailey who had drawn a Test against Australia two summers ago by bowling down the leg. But for some reason, he opts for Lock.

Endean plays him nervously. Lock draws him forward, beats him with turn, and throws his arm up in despair as it misses the edge and the stumps. A maiden over. Quite a miracle under the circumstances.

From the other end, Tyson charges into Waite. Another six tension-filled deliveries with nothing to show for them. Yet another maiden. The clock is catching up.

Back in Natalspruit, Johannesburg, the absence of Cec Abrahams did play a role in the Inter-Racial Dadabhay Trophy of April 1955. It started predictably enough, with the SACCA

Coloured side winning against the Malay team by eight wickets, Basil D'Oliveira hitting a blitzkrieg 153 in just 98 minutes. But in the deciding match, they surprisingly lost against the South African Indians on first innings. Facing a first innings total of 326, openers Herman and Meyer added 158, but then SACCA fell away for 297.

The tournament was high-scoring, but it saw a remarkable bowling feat. W 'Steve' Stephens of the SAICU Indians, captured all 10 wickets in the second innings of the match against the Africans. The 10/57 was rendered more remarkable because the first four wickets were captured with medium pace and the remaining six with leg breaks and googlies. There were some remarkable players among the non-Whites.

The tournament also received proper coverage in the press. Apart from Syd Reddy and Damoo Bansda, *The Leader* and *The Graphic* in Durban and *The Sun* in Cape Town reported the matches as did the *Drum* magazine.

Endean leans forward to negotiate Lock, misses, and just manages to push his backfoot into the crease before Graveney can break the stumps. What if Evans was fit?

At the other end Waite ducks under a Tyson bouncer. Ten minutes have passed and only two runs have been added. This is getting too close for comfort.

And then Lock makes one kick up. It touches Endean's gloves and Titmus at second slip grabs it. 135 for 7. Endean has enjoyed the England tour—the theatres, the ballets—but he will have sorry memories of this innings. Ten runs required, 17 minutes remain on the clock.

Tayfield is at the wicket. He is a handy batsman. More importantly, he is level-headed. Waite and Tayfield are calm, much calmer than some of the middle-order men. Psychologically however, England are down to the wicketkeeper and the tail, no matter how vehemently Tayfield's record as batsman disputes the claim. Only Adcock and Heine remain. Heine sometimes claims that being an Afrikaner in an English-speaking side pushes him two positions down in the batting order. Now he fidgets in the dressing room, perhaps grateful that he is not there in the middle with just Adcock, brandishing a batting average of around 5, to follow.

Tayfield plays off the rest of the Lock deliveries. The batsmen get together in the middle of the pitch. Louis Duffus, taking several leaves out of the Cardus handbook, will later write the dialogue between the two as if he was there. Cheetham, feet way more firmly on the ground, will make no such pretension—he will later summarise what was relayed back to the dressing room. Waite is to take the fast stuff. Tayfield is to get the runs off Lock.

Let us remember that Lock can often be faster than Bedser.

Still 10 runs to win.

Drum. The Johannesburg magazine for Black readers with a major cricketing connection. It had been founded by Bob Crisp, the Springbok fast bowler, tank commander, broadcaster, and a member of Julian Cahn's cricket side.

He had dreams of selling his magazine across the continent, but the dreams were slightly skewed. Crisp was no apartheid proponent. However, he was a romantic at the other end of the spectrum—imbued with the idea of the noble savage. His idea of a great copy was a series called *Know Yourselves,* a history of the various tribes. There would be articles on tribal music, features on religion, farming and famous men, and cartoon strips about Gulliver and St Paul. He even serialised Alan Paton's *Cry, the Beloved Country.*

Soon, however, the finances were taken over by Jim Bailey, the son of the cricket-financier Abe Bailey who had orchestrated the 1912 Triangular Test Tournament.

Bailey knew *Drum* needed something else: "Hot dames, jazz, pin-ups, sport." Crisp had to go. A group of charismatic young Black reporters joined. Henry Nxumalo worked there till he was killed in 1957, Todd Matshikiza, Arthur Maimane, Can Themba, Casey Motisi, and others till they were exiled or, in the rarest of rare cases, retired at the end of their term.

Last Days of Sophiatown ran the headline of *Drum*'s photographic feature, filled with pictures of people being evicted from their homes, their possessions strewn around the street. Beneath it, in bold type: "*Big machines and men with picks are beating down the last walls of Sof'town. Take a last look and say goodbye.*"

And *Drum* reported cricket. Non-White cricket. It's a pity that Crisp had to go. His editorials on Dadabhay Trophy would have been fascinating.

The second ball of a new over from Tyson. Fast as ever. Chopped by Waite to the slips. Denis Compton does not take it cleanly. For all their serious dialogue about who will face whom, the batsmen cross over.

Tayfield pushes the next ball. Lock is just a couple of yards from him at silly point. No run.

Tyson walks back, murmuring to himself. From the passing trains, passengers crane their necks to catch a glimpse of the action. The next ball is down the leg side, Tayfield glances it fine. It beats Graveney. The dressing room is all up on their feet, thinking it is a boundary. But Bailey comes tearing around from fine leg, picks it up in one action, and whips it back to the keeper. Just a single.

Tyson runs in to Waite, and off the last ball of the over, Waite latches on to a short ball. Is Tyson getting tired? Perhaps. The ball pitches in his half, and Waite cuts it for four.

The target is halved with one stroke. Four to win. Six minutes remain on the clock.

Lock and Graveney appeal for a leg before decision as Tayfield swings mightily and misses. No, says the umpire. The next ball, another lusty swing, another muffled appeal. Heine cannot take it anymore. He picks up his bat, gloves, and cap and goes down the steps, making for the players' gate. The idea is not to waste a moment if he has to go in.

Halfway down the steps he trips and falls, crashing in a heap to the bottom of the stairs.

The over is bowled. Tayfield has not been able to get bat on ball. Lock has sent down his second maiden. Now he inches even closer as Waite faces Tyson.

The first ball is played with a dead bat. Lock snatches it up on the bounce, prepared to throw down the stumps at either end if anyone shows inclination to venture out.

The third ball of the over. Pitched up. Waite goes forward, drives, past Lock, uppish but out of reach—plenty of open spaces there. Parkhouse the substitute chases it, the batsmen sprint. One run is taken, two, the ball makes its way slowly across the turf. Parkhouse closes in. The batsmen cross a third time—and finally the ball wins. It has crossed the ropes. Four minutes remain on the clock and the match is won. The batsmen, prepared to turn back for the fourth run, meet each other in a dancing embrace.

Peter Heine is still lying in a heap at the bottom of the stairs, not able to summon the nerve to get up. The roar of the crowd is ominous. To his frenzied mind, it means a wicket has fallen. He is now reassured by the kindly hand of an elderly member of the Lancashire County Cricket Club. "It's all right lad, you can stop praying—your team has won."

The series is alive. Before the tour, Jack Cheetham made the boldest of pronouncements: "This could be South Africa's greatest tour." Ambitious words those, while taking on a team that had just conquered Australia and retained The Ashes in the most emphatic style. He can breathe easy that it is not all over just yet.

The triumphant team song in the dressing room is surprisingly Afrikaans. *Wat maak Oom Kalie daar?*

Congratulatory messages come in from all corners, the Governor General, the Members of the Cabinet, The Leader of the Opposition ... even one from the Prime Minister.

It is not from Malan, who has stepped down a few months earlier. The man at the helm is

Hans Strijdom, *The Lion of the North.*

South Africa had changed hands, and the ones guiding the destiny now belonged to yet another uncompromising Afrikaner Nationalist.

In fact, Malan had preferred the more moderate Minister of Finance, Havenga; but the NP leadership tilted towards Strijdom, as the NP sentiments themselves turned towards the more conservative North. Verwoerd was a strong supporter. Strijdom was a firm believer in White minority rule. Apartheid had already become a way of life. Diplomatic ties with other nations were becoming less important with time.

At Headingley, Cheetham sits with his arm on a sling as McGlew leads the side again. Once again, he leads from the front. The South Africans trail by 20 after low scores in the first innings. McGlew bats 400 minutes for 133. Endean ekes out 116 not out in four hours, a dour innings, full of common sense, efficiency and judiciousness, as befits a chartered accountant.

500 in the third innings. On a scorching final day, Tayfield kisses his cap before handing it to the umpire and runs through the England side with 5 for 94. Goddard has incredible figures of 5 for 69 from 62 overs. The last six wickets fall away for 46. The series is 2-2. At the corner of the main street in Johannesburg, traffic is held up for a while by a crowd of about 500 people who spread across the pavement and into the roadway while listening to commentary outside a radio shop.

A week before the decider at The Oval, the British Lions won a cliff-hanger at Ellis Park. In front of a world record crowd of 95,000, they triumphed 23-22. They ended the series tied 2-2, the only break in a 70-year pattern of British failure in the southern hemisphere.

When the Lions played Junior Springboks at Free State Stadium, Bloemfontein, non-White spectators were refused entry.

Before the final Test at The Oval, Cheetham receives a telegram from Ben Schoeman, the Minister of Railways. It is in Afrikaans: "Last month I laid a big African elephant low in Bechuanaland. All railway men join with me in hoping that you and your team will at least fell eleven little Lions at The Oval. Good luck."

Cheetham is back to lead the side. The weather is cooler after a couple of months of heat wave. Tayfield once again has magnificent figures. 19-7-39-3 in the first innings and incredible second innings analysis of 53.4-29-60-5. But the wicket is taking turn, and the 244-run target set by another gem of an unbeaten 89 by Peter May proves too much. Especially on the famous Oval turner with the Surrey pros Jim Laker and Tony Lock hovering like a couple of birds of prey. Three of the four leg before decisions, given by the trilby-hatted Tom Bartley, look rather harsh. The ball turning square and Keith, Endean and McLean sweeping off the front foot. Not the best calls.

The series ends 3-2. Manager Ken Viljoen, Cheetham, May and Gubby Allen speak in an interview on television. This is quite a novelty for the South Africans. The country is still without this not-so-new-fangled contraption and will remain that way till the mid-1970s.

At the end of the Test, another Springbok is caught by a maiden. Two young women somehow manage to make their way from the Oval stands to the party to celebrate the end of the series. One of them is the strikingly beautiful 27-year-old Muriel Tredwell. A year later she will save up enough to travel to South Africa. Two years later she will become Mrs Russell Endean.

Endean is more circumspect as a batsman. Perhaps it reflects in life as well. He takes way more time to marry than Winslow. *Die Vaderland* will report *Endean Eindelik Geboul* (Endean finally bowled)

Action at Ellis Park, 1955. Non-white spectators were refused entry for this match

On the eve of the first Test at Trent Bridge, sportswriter Sy Mogapi formed an All-South African 'fantasy' team who could have taken on England.

The team list had read [in batting order] : Jackie McGlew (captain), Chong Meyer (coloured), John Waite, Russell Endean, Basil D'Oliveira (vice-captain, coloured), Tiny Abed (Malay), George Langa (African), Hugh Tayfield, Neil Adcock, E Jeeva (Indian), M Anthony (Indian).

Perhaps this team would have won the series.

Eleven days after the final Test was over, Emmett Till, a 14-year-old African American, was lynched in Mississippi, after allegedly offending a white woman in her family's grocery store. In November, the grand jury refused to indict his killers.

On the first day of the last month of the year, 1 December 1955, in Montgomery, Alabama, 42-year-old Rosa Parks refused to follow the bus driver James F. Blake's order to relinquish her seat in the "Coloured section" to a White passenger.

Those were exciting—or frightening—times to be alive, depending pretty much on the colour of your skin.

17 THROWN INTO THE SEA OF FORGETFULNESS

Johannesburg, December 1956. It is the dismissal of Denis Compton that queers the pitch. Jim Laker will maintain that it is on the bounce that Tayfield catches it. "It looked to pitch two feet in front of the bowler, who picked it up on the bounce. He threw it up in the air and danced around."

Can we put it down to the rivalry between the two greatest off-spinners of the world? After all, Tayfield's 37 wickets at 17.18 in the series will continue to read incredible. Laker, 46 in the 1956 Ashes, 19 at Old Trafford alone, will have to remain content with 11 at 29.45. Laker will never write a kindly word about Tayfield.

However, there does seem something wrong with the catch. With McGlew injured, Clive van Ryneveld is the skipper. He speaks to the bowler and then the umpire, and then makes his way to Compton. But the Middlesex maestro does not want to be recalled. "Strong South African connections, including a South African wife," is how Laker will explain Compton's behaviour later. South Africa claw their way back into the match. 84 for 4. England 127 ahead.

But does Compton really deserve to be there? His inclusion seems more of a sympathy gesture after the kneecap was removed and eventually found its way into the Lord's museum. The circumspect nudges and pushes, with the ball hardly turning and no one in the outfield, is not the Compton we are familiar with. The previous summer, his 705 runs have come at 35.25, scored with a miserably tentative replica of the flashing blade of the gallant knight of 1947 who had ushered in the sparkling happiness of peace time. The 94 and 35 not out in the final Test of the season were more of an exception.

However, the English selectors did not really have too many options. Rev. David Sheppard, 670 runs at 41.87, an authoritative century in the same Ashes Test which saw Laker pick up 19 wickets, has refused to tour.

Returning to England in 1955 after the Sophiatown protests, Archbishop Trevor Huddleston published his seminal work in 1956—*Naught for your Comfort.* It dealt with his experiences in Johannesburg—the extremes of racial discrimination, the ghetto conditions where intimidation and fear rivalled totalitarianism at its worst. It was loaded with a full barrage of evidence—discriminatory legislation, antiquated justice, restrictions on speech, gathering and movement, housing issues beyond imagination, squatter camps, reserves that were virtually controlled concentration camps, the Bantu Education Act aimed towards downgrading all native Blacks, brutality, contempt, economic blocks.

Huddleston spoke in a meeting in the House of Lords in London, to ask the worlds of sports and arts to boycott South Africa. David Sheppard heard him speak. After the talk, the two men of cloth walked up and down the Terrace of the House of Lords by the river. Huddleston suggested that nothing would jolt people of South Africa more than if MCC refused to send a team there.

Perhaps it was this discussion that influenced Sheppard or perhaps it was his job as the curate of Islington. In any case, he made himself unavailable. Crawford White of *News Chronicle* wrote a piece with the headline: "I Won't Play in Africa", which coloured the decision in the public mind.

Peter Heine has been nicknamed, not very charitably, 'The Bloody Dutchman' by the English cricketers. Black hair straggling over his eyes and a great red streak across the front of his shirt, where he polishes the ball with palpable viciousness, he cuts a ferocious figure. He bowls as much at the batsman as at the wicket. Sometimes, he allegedly tells batsmen, "I want to hit you."

Peter May is all class as he drives Heine, the stroke emitting a crack like gunshot. Tayfield is placed effortlessly into the vacant mid-wicket area. At the other end, Trevor Goddard comes back and Doug Insole forgets about the leg-slip. But the fielder stationed there does not have to catch it as Waite dives across and holds it with his outstretched gloved hand.

Trevor Huddleston's idea of boycotting South African tours would take another 12 years to come to fruition. But copies of *Naught for your Comfort* did reach the *Edinburgh Castle* as the England team sailed. However, manager Freddie Brown ensured that the side was kept away from 'political issues' at all cost. He flung the entire set of books into the Bay of Biscay.

In the introduction to his account of the tour, Charles Fortune begins with the words: "Cricket is a glorious game. It is also one of England's minor industries—and South Africa is its best overseas customer." One does not allow minor issues to impact relationship with one's best customer.

Captains: Lt Col Stanyforth, Freddie Brown, Wally Hammond, Arthur Gilligan, and Peter May
South Africa was always a good place to catch up.

May flicks Heine off his toes, and Endean flings himself to his left and clutches the ball even as his body thuds on the ground. Heine pummels Colin Cowdrey like a mattress. The batsman is still in a daze as Adcock runs in and the tame edge is snapped up by Goddard. More than an hour of struggle for six measly runs. 126 for 7. Evans lashes at the bowling and swings Adcock into the crowd over fine leg. But the rest of them fall in a heap. 150 all out.

Before they left England, the visiting cricketers had been given their usual preliminary briefing by the President of MCC, Walter Monckton, the first Viscount Monckton of Brenchley. Having worked in the propaganda and information department during World War II, this former Solicitor General in Winston Churchill's 1945 caretaker government was the ideal person to address such a sensitive issue. The players had been categorically told that colour, as a topic of conversation, was forbidden, never to be mentioned. The safest thing to talk about was the 1955 visit of the British Lions.

As the sun flashes on the corrugated roofs of the far hills, Goddard comes out with Scotch Taylor, to gun for the 204 to win.

But the rousing cheers that greet the two opening batsmen turn into a stunned hush soon after the innings starts.

May, defensive to the realms of pessimism, gives Statham and Bailey just one slip each. Hutton would never have imagined such conservative measures. However, Hutton was the professional. May is a gentleman amateur, supposed to play with romantic adventure of the supposed Golden Age. Misconceptions about cricket are aplenty.

However, Goddard snicks a Bailey outswinger to that solitary man at slip. Insole takes it coolly.

Keith shuffles across, twice coming close to being leg before. Then Bailey moves one away and he flashes. Insole is ready but Evans soars across him to come up with the catch.

Waite, promoted in the batting order to stem the rot, defends with hard hands. The Statham delivery rolls back, ever so gently, into the stumps, and the bail gently topples over.

Bailey seems to bowl past, over, through Taylor's bat, before he finds the edge. Insole takes it again.

Endean goes back to force a Statham delivery that proves too quick and loses his off-stump.

A drizzle and bad light provide some relief to the hosts at 36 for 5 before they come back on. McLean casually flirts with a shortish Bailey delivery and Insole takes the easiest of his three catches. And in the last over of the day, the three short-legs make Watkins delay his forward stroke and he is bowled by Laker.

40 for 7.

A dramatic day that has seen 14 wickets tumble, half of which took South Africa soaring high with hope and half that brought them down to their knees.

The following morning, Wardle's chinamen and googlies confound batsmen, but May asks him to stick to conventional finger spin. Amateur at the helm, rejoice all. It takes an hour and 20 minutes—longer than it should have, but England eventually mop things up. The tourists are 1-0 in the series.

The Test started on 24 December, and Christmas was naturally the rest day. Laker spent it with a friend, a mine manager near Johannesburg.

He recounted his experience with the natives who worked in the mine. They lived in a compound nearby and "were allowed to run a compound cricket team, which played against similar sides in the district." Laker was not really one to hint at the White supremacy. In fact, he makes several unusually strong statements in his *Over to Me.* However, whether satirically or not, he hints at the 'were allowed' bit. Even the minimum privileges of life had to be permitted by the White *baas.* Cricket among the mines was a major circuit of the African game. In a rare stroke of luck, Laker had just come across it.

Laker's host asked him whether he would mind paying a visit to the compound nets. The off-spinning legend welcomed the idea.

He describes it thus:

"It was an astonishing sight. They had put up a special net for me, and at least 200 Coloured men, all neatly dressed in whites, stood in a line, waiting. They didn't know me, but they saw and recognised the MCC touring blazer [...] I was greeted like an Oriental prince.

"I watched the nets for a while and then picked a batsman who seemed to have a little more talent than the rest. But he was playing the most tempting stuff from the safety of the crease. I suggested to him that he used his feet a bit. One of those bowling tossed a ball up for me, and I showed the batsman what I meant.

"This was something he had never seen before [...] even before I left the nets that day, he was hammering his colleagues all over the place."

A few days later, Laker got a letter from his friend stating that his 'protégé' had scored 140-odd in an inter-compound game.

Laker concludes that there was talent aplenty among the Coloured of the country and a keenness of for cricket could be seen among the Test match crowds of Black spectators. Given some decent coaching, he thought they were good enough to raise a side to play a worthwhile game against a touring team.

Brave words to pen, but Laker had his feet planted firmly enough on the ground to know that it was an impossibility in the circumstances.

Cape Town. The task is to bat out the day. Winning is out of the question, but it will be terrible to lose both the first Tests.

But Wardle is proving difficult to negotiate. The pitch has deteriorated as well. Last evening, his googly bowled McGlew round the legs in a cloud of dust. Keith danced down the wicket and the ball beat him and Evans as it turned and rose. And then the batsman hit one down the throat of May at extra cover.

Now, it is 42 for 2 on the fifth morning and Goddard is attempting to bat all day. But the chinaman induces an edge and Bailey holds it at slip. May frowns, but with the wickets falling, he doesn't voice his disapproval at the unorthodox spin. The breeze makes the ball drift away and the usual wrist spin brings it in. Sometimes, the googly turns it away. Wardle is using the footmarks of Goddard with masterly precision.

After McLean drives Wardle straight and through the covers for two boundaries, Endean faces Laker. Spin from both ends with the pitch crumbling. He plays as much with the pad as possible, having, according to Alan Ross, "as much regard for his bat of one who fancies it to be made of porcelain." One ball pops up vertically from the pad and is about to drop on the stumps. Endean swats at it with a gloved hand, as if banishing a fly. Evans and Laker ask the question. Endean walks back, out handling the ball, the first ever to be so dismissed in Test cricket. "I thought of heading it away, but it seemed too theatrical," Endean will say some years later.

Laker did not mince his words in his 1960 book. He had already retired, and hence did not quite need to. "I can't see [a match against a Coloured side] happening. The South Africa Government's view on so revolutionary an idea as a cricket match between Blacks and Whites can be guessed. MCC, for their part, would never suggest such a thing."

He goes on to lament that "South Africans have never seen Worrell, Weekes, and Walcott [...] As far as cricket is concerned [their] racial policies have worked for the disadvantage of all."

Laker does not stop at that. The next passage makes for the most revealing of all the accounts of South Africa written by English, Australian, and New Zealand cricketers during the apartheid era.

Raman Subba Row, the classy Northamptonshire and England batsman, was at the peak of his powers as Laker was completing the book in 1960. He had amassed 1810 runs at 46.41 in 1958, 1917 at 46.75 in 1959, and 1503 at 55.66 in 1960. He was just back from a century in Georgetown in West Indies, against Wes Hall, Chester Watson, and Garry Sobers.

Hence, Laker turns to the next scheduled MCC tour of South Africa in 1964–65. "Chances must be on Raman Subba Row being in the form which demands selection. Yet, I cannot imagine Raman—Cambridge Blue, county captain, Test batsman—being picked. He is of

Indian extraction; after a quiet word with MCC I imagine he would tactfully find himself unable to go [due to] business commitments."

The South African policies were evil. But this paragraph of Laker lays bare the extraordinary amount of nudge-nudge wink-wink condoning of criminal government policies indulged in by the White cricketing countries.

Endean handles the ball. Laker is the bowler with his back to us. However, he did not turn his back on what he saw on the tour.

At 67, McLean tries a clever little scoop towards leg off Laker and finds the ball hurrying into his pad. He is leg before.

And then, Wardle fools Waite into snicking a googly to slip. Watkins is completely foxed as he misreads the turn and the attempted pull lobs back into the Yorkshire spinner's hands. Heine misses a straighter faster one. Four wickets fall at 67. No one has the foggiest idea about Wardle.

Five runs later it is over: 72 all out—the same score as at the end of the first Test. England 2-0 up in the series. Wardle 7 for 36, 12 for 88 in the match.

There is a reason why Laker was so scathing. It had to do with his other brush outside the White bubble during the tour. It took place during the Cape Town sojourn. He was with Alan Oakman, who had rented a car to go out for the evening. Driving back, late in the evening, Oakman was too late on the brakes as a Coloured man on a bicycle shot out of the corner.

The man lay on the ground, leg broken, and Oakman, visibly shaken, got out of the car wondering what to do. A crowd gathered around him, mostly White. No one was really interested in what happened to the black man. "Hello, Mr Oakman, will you sign my book?" … "You played a bad stroke today, Mr Oakman."

A policeman came along and started by asking, "He was drunk wasn't he, Mr Oakman?" The Sussex all-rounder had no answer. So, the policeman picked on a Black man in the crowd. "You live near this nigger … he's always drunk, isn't he?" The scared Black fellow nodded. That was all the evidence required to close the case. "Once this 'justice' was done, the injured man was taken to the hospital."

Another batsman falls to Wardle

That was 1956—the year of the Coloured vote constitutional crisis.

The removal of the Coloured voters from the common voters' roll in the Cape Province had been stalled so far because two-thirds majority backing was not forthcoming. With the restructuring of the Senate in 1955, the upper house was now packed with National Party members. The South Africa Amendment Act was now passed.

There was also the Natives Prohibition of Interdicts Act, which denied Blacks the right of appeal against enforced removal.

The Black Sash organisation of white women protest against the removal of the coloured voters from the voter's roll in the Cape Province

The Industrial Conciliation Act with its almost corporate nomenclature provided clauses for segregation in the various industrial unions. It prohibited registration of any new 'mixed' unions and imposed racially separate branches and all-White executive committees on existing 'mixed' unions. Strikes were prohibited in 'essential industries' for both Black and White workers. Political affiliations for unions was yet another nicety done away with.

And perhaps the most telling of them all was the Riotous Assemblies Act. The Act prohibited gatherings in open-air public places if the Minister of Justice considered it could endanger the public peace. Banishing was also included as a form of punishment—a direct result of the Freedom Charter.

In the 1950s, Tom Sharpe, the Cambridge-educated novelist, worked as a social worker and teacher in Johannesburg. In 1961 he was deported for sedition. In 1971 was published his brilliant satire based in the country, aptly titled *Riotous Assembly.*

18 HEADLINES ABROAD

Durban. Day 3. The Saturday evening has seen a wild party for the players and the press at the home of Denis and Valerie Compton.

Now, on Monday, South Africa are 163 for 4, in response to England's not-so-impressive 218. May is intent on defence. Statham beats McLean several times outside the off, but the captain does not bring in a second slip. The previous hour has seen 22 runs, mostly off the edge, for one wicket.

Now the Lancashire pacer is taken off. McLean heaves a sigh of relief. Laker comes on. McLean pulls a four, drives another past mid-off, and tickles one fine for three. Funston now sweeps him, and Compton, hot from the recent chase, cannot get around in time at long leg. 15 runs off the over. Laker is banished to the outfield by May, "with such predictable speed as do Soviet executives remove deviationists to Siberian salt mines," writes Alan Ross.

It is 1956. In October, Soviet tanks have rolled into Budapest. Russian metaphors are aplenty in every report.

Early in the year, Ad and Wal Hain, with their three young children Peter, Tom, and Joanne, moved to England. They were themselves young, and it was a good idea to see the world before the kids were old enough to incur substantial travel costs. Wal arranged a job in Easton and Robertson, an established UK architectural firm. The family car was sold to pay the fare of the ocean liner. From Cape Town they sailed to Southampton, and took the 'boat train' to Waterloo.

It was a bitterly cold winter, with the washing freezing on the line. They moved into a rented first floor flat in the London suburb of Ealing. Cold, smoggy over the coal fires, still rebuilding after the destruction of the war, London seemed unfriendly.

Wal's salary was meagre, and rent was high. They were so broke as to make stew out of the shin of beef, cutting the best bits out and keeping the rest for a main meal of soup the following day. Ad's sister Jo was working in London at that time. She helped out with the kids, who found her rather too strict.

Wardle is on at the other end and McLean pulls three boundaries off one over. May frowns, deliberates, toys with the idea of Siberian banishment following the footsteps of Laker. But he keeps the Yorkshireman on. There is one sanction—he has to bowl the orthodox stuff and stay away from the back of the hand chinaman nonsense. Wardle is not happy, but he mixes the regular slow left arm fare with one that comes in with the arm. Funston tries to steer it and plays on. 199 for 5.

Bailey is on now, entrusted with keeping McLean quiet. At the other end, Waite plays back to a Statham delivery that is almost a half-volley and is bowled.

McLean carries on, hooks Loader, and audaciously carves him through cover. Bailey runs in, tidy as ever, but the batsman spoons him over short mid-wicket for a boundary, and then glides him to the leg for another. At five minutes to two, he pushes to cover to bring up his century—the first one against a touring England side since Arthur Morris and Neil Harvey at Brisbane three years ago. A friend has promised him £50 for the three-figure mark. Perhaps blissful in the pecuniary delight, he edges the second ball after the landmark. Bailey's delivery seams a bit from the pitch and Insole holds a fine catch low down at slip.

The McLean hundred notwithstanding, the lead managed is just 65.

The Hains moved to Kent, to a tiny cottage on a farm in Ruckinge, overlooking Romney Marsh. The rent was a lot less. They were lucky to learn about it from a friend they had met on the ship from the Cape.

As summer approached, things became tolerable. Peter and his brother Tom played in the farm. During a spell of hot weather, they took their beddings and slept in the front lawn. The milkmaid surprised them in the morning.

During the summer, in spite of the fatigue of the long drive to work each day, Wal taught the boys cricket and football.

The forward defensive blade of Bailey irritates Heine no end, more so now that the South Africans have a bit of an edge in the game. He pitches them short and Bailey is hit on the knuckles.

Pieter Heine

The next morning Insole accompanies Compton to the middle. Bailey has fractured a bone at the base of his little finger.

England look like they are coasting to safety at 77 for 1. But then Compton checks his pull off Tayfield and is caught at silly mid-on. May tries to pull as well, misses, and is leg before. Cowdrey comes in and Tayfield bowls with two silly mid-ons and a leg slip.

But Cowdrey stays for over two hours. And when Tayfield gets Evans caught at the wicket, Bailey lumbers in again, scorning an injection. Tayfield, 14 maidens on the trot in the first innings, bowls a nagging length and line. Bailey, who has spent an hour on 4 in the first innings, is not bothered. Alan Ross writes, "hypnotic maiden had become as soothing and necessary to Bailey as opium to a Mandarin."

Off the last delivery of the day, the ball pops up. 'Catch it,' cries Tayfield, and van Ryneveld obliges at short leg. It seems that Bailey has lifted his bat out of danger and the ball has bounced off the pad. But Tayfield's passionate appeal bears fruit. Bailey cannot believe it. He leans on his bat and walks in circles even as the other players go in. He cuts a sorry figure alone on the pitch.

144 runs in the day, the score 192 for 6. The lead 127. It can go either way.

In August, Ad, Wal, and young Peter learnt of the women's march. Over 20,000 women of all races descended in Pretoria. Arranged on a Thursday, the traditional day when Black domestic workers had a day off, it was against the Pass Laws being extended to African women. There were 14,000 petitions for Prime Minister Strijdom. The one prepared by the Federation of South African Women started thus:

"We, the women of South Africa, have come here today. We African women know too well the effect this law upon our homes, our children. We, who are not African women know how our sisters suffer. For to us, an insult to African women is an insult to all women."

A headline in *Drum* read: *Will our women carry passes?* "We will never carry passes under any conditions," said Lillian Ngoyi, president of the ANC's women's league. "We know what these passes are doing to our males. We have seen them bundled into vans and sent to farm labour camps. Passes will place us at the mercy of the police."

On his 29th birthday, Tayfield ends with 8 for 69. But Insole remains unconquered, six hours and three minutes for 110, his first fifty-plus score in Test cricket. Later, he will say this about Tayfield: "I did not like the man, so I was determined not to get out to him."

Tayfield: One of the greatest off-spinners ever

Wardle spends 73 minutes over his eight. Laker, Loader, and Statham all prove difficult to budge. May has little intention of setting a target. The innings has to die a natural death, which it does when Statham is caught at short-leg.

190 to win in 250 minutes. It does seem unlikely when Pithey's off-stump is knocked back by Statham with his second ball.

Goddard and Keith add 39 but take far too much time.

Wardle is into the act now. Goddard, aware of the urgency, comes down the pitch, swinging hard. The ball turns away, and the edge is taken by Cowdrey at slip.

McLean, the centurion, enters. A long hop is dispatched for four. The next ball is a flighted chinaman. McLean is beaten in the air. The ball comes back a foot and bowls him. 49 for 4.

By tea, Endean and Funston take the score to 60. 130 required in two hours.

After the break Wardle drops a hard, low return catch off Funston. The very next ball sees the batsman edging to the slip that has been taken away. In desperation perhaps, the batsman pulls twice, off the middle-stump, to the mid-wicket fence. The next ball is driven through the covers for three. The score stands at 82. And May steps in, removing the chinaman license. Back to orthodox stuff from Wardle. A pity. South Africa going for runs was England's chance to get them out. The defensive ploy encourages a stalemate.

Statham from one end. Loader from the other as Wardle is taken off. When Laker replaces Statham, he turns a ball sharply. Spin can win the game, but May opts for safety first.

1956. In Suez, the British, French, and Israelis attacked Egypt. The liberal newspapers *The Guardian* and *The Observer* covered it widely. A stark contrast to the parochial and conservative South African media. Ad and Wal read voraciously and formed a much better understanding of world affairs.

83 required in 55 minutes. Endean begins to walk out as the ball is delivered and lobs it over the bowler's head. When Funston pulls Laker to mid-wicket for four, it is down to 66 in 40.

The match virtually ends at this score.

Funston, head in air, tries to drive Loader and loses his stump. The next over, Laker intercepts the strange walking lob of Endean, runs back and holds it. For all his improvisations, Endean's 26 has taken two hours and a quarter.

124 for 6, and May finally feels secure enough to bring both spinners on. Van Ryneveld and Waite play out time. 142 for 6. The series remains 2-0.

In December, yet another sibling was added to the Hain family. Sally was born on Christmas Day.

19 TREASON AND TAYFIELD

Johannesburg again. Is it Mrs Verity Ann van Ryneveld, the young skipper's bride, who brings luck to the captain? McLean wonders. It is only the third time in 14 Test matches that May loses the toss.

McLean is full of quaint contemplations that day. Bailey yorks Goddard to make it 151 for 3. The progress has been drab and slow, and McLean, much like the other scribes, attributes the robustness of the South African score to May's conviction that Test match fields should be set defensive from the start.

Bailey is past 100 wickets. He is nearing 2,000 runs as well, hovering on the threshold of the elite club of all-rounders who have scored 2,000 runs and captured 100 scalps. He will soon sit alongside Keith Miller and Wilfred Rhodes. Handshakes all around. It is McLean who walks in now. Later he will muse "Just imagine the difference in spectator value between a Keith Miller and a Trevor Bailey either as bowler or batsman." He has never seen Rhodes of course, but he adds, "Yorkshire's Wilfred Rhodes, who started as No. 11 batsman for England and ended by opening, was much before my time, but I'm quite sure he could, despite the county of his birth, never have been as dour as Bailey."

At that particular point in time, Vinoo Mankad has 2,084 runs and 158 wickets in Tests. But he does not feature in McLean's White world of cricket.

As if to drive home his point, McLean starts injecting excitement into the game. Left foot away to the leg, head up, bat horizontal, he slashes Loader to Insole at slip. The offer is grassed. He mixes glorious strokes with chancy ones. Evans fumbles a return and he gets home when he should have been running back to the pavilion. He is dropped again off Loader and then hits a no-ball from the same bowler for six. At the end of the day he is 56 not out, South Africa on 234 for 4. "Don't let anyone tell you a batsman does not need luck in making a decent score," he writes at the end of the day.

Jim Laker's charitable comments about native talent was after seeing an unnamed batsman in compound cricket in the mines. However, in December 1956 and January 1957, as SABCB's Native Recruitment Council (NRC) tournament was played at Port Elizabeth, another Black cricketer sparkled away from sight.

Eric Majola of Eastern Province hit 51 and captured 5 for 22 against Natal. Against Transvaal he hammered 67 and took 5 for 14. When he played Orange Free State it was an unbeaten 46 and 5 for 22. Against Midlands he ended with 56 and 4 wickets for just one run. He happened to be a top-class fly half as well.

There were extraordinary sportsmen among the non-Whites.

Over 30,000 people flock to the ground on the second morning. McLean shows Bailey how it is done, carting half volleys outside the off-stump to the long-on boundary. Van Ryneveld is steady at the other end. He has gotten married on the second of February, between the third and fourth Tests. His honeymoon in Plettenberg Bay has been cut short so that he can be ready for the Test. His wife Verity has been flown to Johannesburg at the expense of SACA, but she has not been allowed to stay in the team hotel. Van Ryneveld holds one end up as McLean sweeps Wardle off the middle stump to square leg to bring up the 50 of the partnership. The score is past 300, for the loss of six wickets.

But then, McLean pushes one to square leg wide of Laker and runs, without really calling. Halfway down the track, he looks up to see his captain has not moved. His luck finally deserts him. Tragically he has to walk back for 93. The innings comes to a quick end after that, amounting to 340.

Now Bailey endeavours to suck the life out of the game. Heine hits him on the chest, raps him on the knuckles, bruises his hands. But the Essex man braves him and his frustrations and lasts 102 minutes for a measly 13. Insole, batting ahead of Compton at No 3, looks solid. May comes in at No 4 and bats bareheaded for the first time in the series. Along with the cap he also seems to have left his rustiness behind, hooking Heine for six. England end the day at 87 for 2.

Majola was not the only all-round athlete. Malamba, the destructive fast bowler, was a fantastic rugby player as well. The star striker of the Coloured XI who won the 1956 inter-race soccer tournament was Basil D'Oliveira himself. In the lines of Wally Hammond, CB Fry, Denis Compton, and Willie Watson, D'Oliveira excelled at both football and cricket.

But all this took place far away from the White bubble.

The non-White sportsmen were seeking opportunities through international contacts. To counter the efforts with their own legislation, Minister of Interior Dr Eben Dönges and his team came up with specific policies in 1956.

Whites and non-Whites had to organise sport separately.

No mixed sport within the borders of South Africa.

No mixed team to compete abroad.

International teams competing in South Africa against white South African teams needed to be all-White, according to South African custom.

Non-White sportsmen from overseas could compete against non-White South Africans in South Africa.

However:

Non-White organisations seeking international recognition had to do so through the already recognised white organisations in their code of sport.

The government could refuse travel visas to 'subversive' non-White sportsmen who sought to discredit South Africa's image abroad or contest the government's racial policies.

It rains on Sunday. But by the time the teams are back in the ground, the sky is a clear blue and it is hot with a light breeze. At long last, May shows glimpses of his usual mastery. Heine is cut away twice for four, and then driven with the sound of thunderclap when he changes ends. Van Ryneveld is driven and pulled.

Goddard and Tayfield come on, choking the runs to the point of coma. It is they who combine to get rid of Insole. Tayfield raps him on the pads, the umpire says no, the ball trickles to Goddard at slip. Insole thinks it is past him, and darts across for a leg bye. Goddard obligingly breaks the stumps. Run out for 47.

May follows soon, his woodwork disturbed by Adcock.

Before and after lunch, wickets fall in a flurry. But Compton, unsure, scratching around, dropped before scoring, hangs on. Wardle hits Tayfield for two sixes in a bright cameo against the run of play. Laker sticks around to aid Compton in saving the follow on. When Heine is put back on Compton runs down the wicket to the fast man, as if he is the Compton of yore. He is caught at slip for 42. England 227 for 9.

But Statham and Loader stand up manfully against the much delayed second new ball. They bat 50 minutes to add 24 before, at the stroke of stumps, Loader turns Goddard round the corner into the hands of the leg-slip. The lead is 89. Just 164 runs on another dreary day of Test cricket.

1956 was the last time during the apartheid era that a Springbok-All Blacks tour went ahead devoid of any controversy. Even the New Zealand Communist Party did not object to the visit of the South Africans, their only grievance being that broadcasts were delayed instead of live.

In all 686,760 spectators attended the four-match series won by the All Blacks 3-1. It was South Africa's first series defeat since 1903. Large numbers slept outside the grounds to guarantee admission.

During the visit, *New Zealand Herald* published 55 cartoons by Gordon Minhinnick, 25 of which featured the Springbok tour. An advertisement in the *Christchurch Star* read: "Refined gentleman wishes to meet cultured widow, view matrimony. Must have independent means and tickets to the third test."

The only opposition to the tour came from the Maori Women's Welfare League.

Charles Davis will estimate Bailey's career strike rate to be 26.5 runs per hundred balls. Tony Pithey, the South African opener for this Test, will end up with exactly the same numbers at the end of his career. Trevor Goddard is no Victor Trumper either. South Africa, in this must win game, manage 51 for no loss at lunch.

When Laker spins one between the bat and pad of Pithey to bowl him, the batsman departs for a 145-minute crawl amounting to 18. Waite is pushed down the order as South Africa intend to go for quick runs. But as often happens, they have batted slowly enough to dig themselves into a hole.

Promoted in the order, Funston sweeps Laker for a four and a six. May immediately removes the wicket-taker. At 91 for 1, Goddard edges Bailey to the keeper. McLean mistimes a hook; it shoots up like spray and comes obligingly down into Cowdrey's hands at gully. Funston is stranded in the middle of the pitch as Endean does not run. Endean himself slashes Bailey and Insole grabs it in front of his midriff. 97 for 5. The match has turned much faster than the batsmen have scored.

Waite tries to block his way out of the hole, employing the same methods that have landed them there in the first place. Only Tayfield shows some valour and gets just returns, cracking two drives off Statham. But then he sees Adcock charging down for a run that has neither been contemplated and nor called, and the innings folds for 142. England need 232 to win on a wicket that is still playing true.

There are 45 minutes left in the day, and the Adcock-Heine duo spend 25 of them buzzing deliveries over the heads of Bailey and Richardson. With the score on 10, Tayfield comes on. The second ball sees Bailey go forward. It pops up and is taken by Endean at short leg. Umpire says out. Bailey cannot believe it. It cannot happen twice in a row.

England finish the fourth day at 19 for 1. 213 to get. The match hangs on a knife's edge.

In 1956, the South African Soccer Federation, the non-racial non-White organisation, applied to FIFA for international recognition. Of course, it was not entertained.

The same year, South Africa, Ethiopia, Egypt and Sudan founded the Confederation of African Football. Fred Fell, the South African representative, made it clear that they could only send either an all-White side or an all-Black side to the planned 1957 African Cup of Nations. This was unacceptable to the other members of the Confederation, and South Africa were disqualified.

There was some encouraging development in a lower-profile sport. The non-racial South African Table Tennis Board was recognised by the International Table Tennis Federation. The non-White team was invited to participate in the Stockholm world championships, 1957. Immediately, their passports were refused or revoked.

Apartheid sports was not smooth sailing, but it would take years for the South African government to realise this.

If South Africa go on to win, it will have to be Tayfield. He has to bowl all day. As Ross writes: "Should van Ryneveld at any time have to take him off it would be tacit surrender."

He starts with three short legs, all with long arms almost within reach of the batsman's pockets. Insole sweeps him through the three fielders. Ross, the great exponent of the English language, seems to have exhausted his endless facility for description. He ends up describing the direction of the stroke as "to the stand reserved for Non-Europeans." Is it a political gaffe?

During the trip, Ross drove through Transkei. "The trader's stores, every thirty miles or so, bear the familiar advertisements for Joko tea, and on adjacent shed the words 'Kwa Teba', the slogan of the Native Mine Recruiting Corporation. Kwa means 'here' and Teba is a native simplification of Taberer. The first man to recruit native labour for the mines."

He was referring to Henry Taberer, the fast bowler who played a Test against Australia in 1902–03 and then became manager of the Native Labour Bureau and adviser to the Native Recruiting Corporation for the Chamber of Mines.

Richardson is looking good. He is driving, sweeping, and pulling with ease—46 runs in the first hour. Things start to look bleak for the South Africans. Tayfield wheels on but at the other end Heine bowls too short. Richardson now cuts Tayfield, delaying the stroke, almost taking the ball from Waite's gloves.

At noon it is 65 for 1. The pitch has not really revealed any demon. Tayfield now pitches outside the left-handed Richardson's leg stump. The opener tries to sweep and is bowled around the legs.

It is Cowdrey who comes in to join him. Ahead of May and Compton. Perhaps this is a thoughtful move, but he keeps pushing his pad forward. Tayfield flights one up in response. Cowdrey comes out and deposits him over long on.

The stroke rejuvenates him. He bats like a dream. Only once is he a bit lucky. Funston is off the field and Arthur Tayfield, the off-spinner's brother, is substituting for him. He loses sight of a lofted stroke in the outfield. Otherwise Cowdrey plays without blemish.

Insole keeps sweeping Tayfield. The deep square leg becomes essential. By lunch 100 is up with eight wickets still in the bank.

The South African non-White cricket authorities had not been idle either. India and Pakistan had not responded, and hence they turned their sights elsewhere. This time they looked closer to home.

In September 1956, Checker Jassat of SACBOC flew to Nairobi. The target was Kenyan Asian Sports Association. The Kenya Asian side had players with experience of first-class cricket in India and Pakistan. They played regularly in Tanganyika and Uganda. Ambitious and enterprising, they were seeking international connections themselves. Soon, MCC would be visiting them as well.

Arrangements were finalised. The Kenyan Asians would arrive in Johannesburg in early November 1956. The seven-week tour would include three 'Test' matches against the SACBOC South African non-Europeans.

The South African government approved the visas of the visitors. The organisers had been wise enough to step along all the lines stipulated by apartheid legislation. It was a South African non-White team playing another non-White team visiting the country.

Basil D'Oliveira was named captain of the first representative non-White South African side.

After lunch, Insole reaches his half century with yet another sweep off Tayfield, and then hits Goddard through the covers. Heine bowls short yet again and Cowdrey hooks him for two boundaries.

At 147 for 2, England is on top. Goddard runs in, keeping it tight. Insole tries to force him off the backfoot, edges, and is magnificently caught left-handed at slip. The catcher? That man again—Tayfield.

Insole walks back for 68. The last two Tests have brought him 238 runs for thrice out. Strangely, he will play only four more Test innings and score 32 more runs.

About the tour, Insole would comment that the Afrikaans radio commentary on South African Broadcasting Corporation boosted the game's popularity no end. The 1955 England tour had recently resulted in the first tour book in Afrikaans—*Amper Kriieketkampioene* by Werner Bernard.

Just 85 runs to get, Cowdrey going strong, May walking out, and Compton yet to bat. England are still in the driver's seat. But eight minutes later, it becomes a tense battle. May plays what Charles Fortune calls 'Zulu hoick' and we will give the commentator the benefit of doubt. He times the ball well enough, but it goes straight into his pad. Endean, retreating in evasive action, stops, staggers and dives forward to catch it. 148 for 4.

Compton looks weary. For the past several innings, his only scoring option against Tayfield has been a chop past the slips. Now he tries to drive to the on-side and deposits it straight into the hands of Goddard at short mid-wicket.156 for 5. The end of specialist batsmen.

Compton caught Goddard bowled Tayfield

The *Cape Times* wrote: "The appointment of Basil D'Oliveira as captain was expected and is a most popular choice. He has experience and ability and his forceful batting should be a big asset to the side." Other papers were not so encouraging. *Golden City Post* was not at all optimistic about the chances of the South African non-White side against the experienced Kenyan Asians.

Even now, when discussions turn to the non-White side led by D'Oliveira, there remains the sense of acknowledgement with a caveat. Not many are convinced that it is a landmark achievement. After all, it is a non-White side, only part-representative, and more importantly, without the blessing of the ICC.

Only if one pauses for a while will the irrefutable truth be apparent. The team led by Owen Dunnell in 1889 was a side of White minorities, in no way representative of the entire South African population. Even in 1956–57, the side playing Test cricket consisted of the White minority. The Old Boys' Club was still strong, even if somewhat shaken in the foundations with Len Hutton becoming the first professional captain of England—a couple of decades after Lord Hawke's infamous pronouncement: "Pray God, no professional shall ever captain England." But White South Africa was not only welcome, it was the best destination for many a White cricketer.

On the other hand, D'Oliveira led a side that represented more than 80% of South Africa. Van Ryneveld, who grew up in virtually the same neighbourhood, was still leading a side representing less than 20% of the land.

May, who has been defensive throughout, suddenly turns the gambler. It is not Evans who walks in, but Johnny Wardle. The man who has been repeatedly asked to stick to the orthodox version of his spin is now given license to swing his bat.

Or is it the advice of manager Freddie Brown? Having been a wrist-spinner who enjoyed giving the ball a whack, perhaps he identifies with the Wardle approach?

In any case, Wardle finds four men patrolling the long boundaries and sweeps Tayfield five times in one over. On four occasions it results in couples, and on the fifth it reaches the fence. The score rattles along.

Van Ryneveld keeps Tayfield on but brings Adcock back at the other end. Cowdrey scampers across to ensure Wardle takes Tayfield while he negotiates the fast man. The Kent batsman brings up his fifty.

Now Tayfield changes his line and bowls outside the off. Wardle slashes hard. Waite throws the ball up. The decision is out, but not all the Englishmen are convinced. 30 runs added between Wardle and Cowdrey in 36 minutes, the former's share is 22.

It is tea with England on 186 for 6. 46 runs required. Cowdrey still at the wicket.

The White cricket authorities were ready to offer Newlands, Cape Town, as the venue for the first 'Test' against the Kenyan Asians. However, some in the SACBOC felt that it would be like doing a deal with apartheid. Ultimately Hartleyvale was chosen. Headquarters of the Western Province soccer team. According to Lobo Abed, it was a gravel pitch with a carpet over it. There are clumps of grass. Boundaries were too short on the side.

D'Oliveira did not complain.

Evans and Cowdrey start after tea. Tayfield is tireless. Before each over he takes off his cap and kisses it before handing it to the umpire. He digs his toe into the ground. And then he ambles in. Runs come in singles and the occasional two. And then Evans goes back to dab Tayfield to third man once too often. The canny spinner outwits him. The ball touches the angled bat and goes on to the stumps.

It is Laker at the wicket now. 36 needed. A run comes, then another, then yet another. Cowdrey faces Tayfield. The off-spinner sends down a half-volley. The match has gotten too close for this to be let go. The batsman jumps out and drives. The ball travels fast and the bowler hugs it to his stomach. "Tayfield took that stinging catch with the eagerness of a starving hawk snatching a long-sought meal," jots down Charles Fortune. 199 for 8 and England's last specialist batsman makes his way back to the pavilion.

Laker and Loader fight hard. For fifteen minutes they keep Tayfield at bay. But the ploy of pressure with four men near the wicket and cover with two men deep on the long boundary is difficult to overcome. Laker lofts Tayfield and is caught fifteen yards inside the fence. The sun is in Duckworth's eyes, but he manages to hold it. 208 for 9.

Loader and Statham push and swing for six more runs. And then the former takes the oft-failed aerial route. Still no Funston on the field. The substitute is still Tayfield's brother Arthur. And he holds the catch in the attitude of prayer.

Loader is caught in the outfield and South Africa win

Victory by 17 runs, thanks to the incredible Hugh Tayfield. He has bowled unchanged all day. 37-11-113-9. Eight ball overs. On a pitch that has not helped at all. Nine wickets with the magic of the fingers of his right hand and the 10th caught with his left. He is carried on shoulders to the dressing room. No South African has ever taken 9 in an innings, nor has any South African taken 13 in a match.

Five days later Ross writes in his notebook: "[Tayfield] has become a national hero, at a moment when a thrilling Test match has miraculously squeezed some of the poison out of South African life."

No, Ross could not keep toeing the politically correct line all through.

It was difficult. The country was burning. On December 5, 1956, Nelson Mandela was woken up early in the morning by the police. His house was searched and subsequently he was arrested for high treason.

Over the next 10 days, another 155 leaders within the congress of the people—mostly Black, but also with some Coloured, Indian and even White among them, virtually the whole ANC leadership—were arrested on the same charge. It was a massive country-wide operation, the victims brought to the Fort, the infamous prison of Johannesburg, by bus or flight.

A laconic Albert Luthuli commented, "It was rather like a joint executive of the Congress [...] Distance, other occupations, lack of funds and police interference had made frequent meetings difficult. [Now] delegates from the remotest areas were never more than a cell away."

Albert Luthuli with Anthony Sampson

20 TIE, TRIMUPH, AND TEE

Port Elizabeth fills up with farmers, all there to attend the final Test of the series. Many of them are Afrikaners.

The Afrikaans commentary has really proved successful. With the Afrikaner Nationalists coming to power, there has been a conscious effort to alter the balance in sports long dominated by the English-speaking community. Rugby has, of course, long been the Afrikaner domain. Even there, Sandy Sanderson, the English-speaking head of Transvaal rugby, has been ousted by a Broederbond-managed coup. Jannie le Roux and Louis Luyt will be at the helm for a very long time.

Shakoor Ahmed—a good enough cricketer to tour England as wicketkeeper-batsman with the Pakistan side in 1954. He represented Punjab, Lahore, Multan, and Central Zone in first-class cricket. He batted number four for the Kenyan Asians.

Lobo Abed brought off a brilliant catch to dismiss one Kenyan opener. Cecil Abrahams sent back the other one. Ben Malamba ran through the middle order. But the experienced Shakoor shepherded the innings with exceptional skill on that difficult wicket, scoring 101 before being run out in a desperate bid to keep the strike with the No 11 at the other end. That was a serious percentage of runs. The Kenyans score was just 149. But on a wicket such as Hartleyvale, it could easily be a match-winning one.

The SACBOC Team against Kenyan Non-Asians, December 1956
Standing: EI Jeewa, S Raziet, Ben Malamba, Cec Abrahams, S Abed
Seated: MR Varachia (secretary), Chong Meyer, D'Oliveira, AM Jassat (manager), Armien Variawa,
A Bell, BD Pavadai (President)
Front: AS Bulbulia, E Lakay, H Abrahams

When the South African non-Whites lost two quick wickets, including D'Oliveira's teammate the consistent Chong Meyer, it seemed that the pronouncements of the press would come true. The Kenyan team was a lot more experienced. But the 25-year-old skipper forsook his attacking instincts, put his head down and batted calmly. There was an early chance, but the 70 he got that day was otherwise flawless. Salamodein 'Laam' Raziet, Amien Variawa, Cec Abrahams, Alex Bell, all pitched in with useful scores. The total stretched to 258 on the second morning.

Abrahams and Bell fell among the Kenyan batting at the start of the second innings—four wickets going down for just five runs. A partial recovery was halted with Malamba getting Shakoor—the centurion of the first innings—caught for 16. At 46 for 5, the end seemed near. But skipper Chandrakant Patel and late order batsman Arvind Patel, both experienced men, put on a century partnership. Malamba accounted for most of the latter batsmen, but there were decent knocks down the order. A score of 218 meant a non-trivial target of 110.

D'Oliveira guided them again, coming in at 42 for 2, seeing through till the end with 36 not out. The victory margin was six wickets.

The South African non-Whites had won their first ever international match. It had taken their White counterparts 17 years.

More surprisingly, the cricketers from the several racially distinct communities had welded into a cohesive unit.

Johnny Wardle greets the South Africans on the morning of the Port Elizabeth Test with his usual, "Good morning, fellow workers." His smile is wider than usual. He is off duty. Of all possible ways of getting injured, he has slipped a cartilage while playing snooker. Statham has a bruised toe, and hence Tyson is back in the side. The usual problems of a long tour.

The wicket is green. The groundsman has supposedly been advised by an Indian expert from Kingsmead. Expertise trumps segregation. But the rumour is that the groundsman would have liked several more weeks for the new turf to settle in. Every Saturday and public holiday, rugby matches are held on the ground, which do not help matters.

The conditions are difficult. The light is poor and May squints at the coin to find that he has lost the toss second time in succession. In the field, he hands Bailey the new ball instead of Tyson. "The Typhoon seems to have blown itself out," says McLean.

However, when Bailey cuts the ball disconcertingly and traps Goddard leg before, many among the English scribes voice that they have been harping on the Essex man's potency with the new ball for years. Waite looks unhappy back so high up in the order. He scratches around for 20 minutes before edging one from Loader. Evans scoops it up in front of first slip. Funston stretches his left leg outside the line of the leg stump, padding up to a typical negative Bailey delivery, but it ricochets off his pads on to the stumps. 21 for 3 in the first hour, 40 for 3 at lunch. Endean, promoted to No 5, holds one end up. Pithey looks, according to Ross, "stiff as if a taxidermist has been at him."

He departs in the first over after lunch. Bailey makes it move away, and Evans catches the edge in front of slip even as it dies. His string of five maidens is snapped when McLean on-drives him. It is mid-afternoon when spin is re-introduced after three Laker overs of the morning session. Four wickets are down, but the field set by May remains defensive. McLean strikes Lock so hard that it rebounds back 12 yards from the picket fence behind square leg. Even over this dreadfully slow outfield. A lofted on-drive follows.

But Lock cramps him for room. He bowls over the wicket and dead on the off-stump. McLean fidgets and tries to steer a shorter one too close to his body. Evans snaps it up.

Endean and van Ryneveld bat with a curiously detached sense of ennui. "Like vessels with no navigational aid," writes Ross. At tea, it is 88 for 5. Analysis of 14-7-11-3 for Bailey. At twenty minutes to six, when van Ryneveld successfully appeals for light, the score is 138 for 5.

The Natalspruit Indian Sports Ground, Johannesburg, was a very familiar territory for D'Oliveira's men. The SACBOC tournaments were held there. Laam Raziet thrived on the much better wicket, scoring 109. 'Tiny' Abed struck 54. Hassim Abrahams 63 and Cec Abrahams 55. Even an uncharacteristically low score of 9 by D'Oliveira did not stop the home team from amassing 377. Blaise D'Cunha, the leg-break googly bowler who played a first-class match for Sind and also represented Kenya in table tennis, picked up five wickets.

Cec Abrahams, Bell, and Malamba soon had the visitors in all sorts of trouble, four wickets tumbled for 14, the fifth after a small recovery at 67. But Shakoor Ahmed, batting lower down the order at No 7, demonstrated his class yet again, striking a superb 120.

Trailing by 120, the Kenyan bowlers forced their way back in the game. Four wickets went down for 27. But D'Oliveira and Cec Abrahams steadied the ship, adding 47. D'Oliveira top-scored with 44, Raziet, wisely held back down the order, contributed 40. The 165-run second-innings score meant 286 to win for the Kenyan Asians.

The start was disastrous yet again. The first four wickets fell for next to nothing. But Gafoor Ahmed hit 63, VV Bhandari kept them in the hunt with 91. In the end, when Tiny Abed bowled Bhandari to end the match, they were 39 short.

A fascinating match, and in their first ever international series, the South African non-Whites had emerged triumphant.

The White South Africans add just 26 runs on the second morning. The wicket proves far more difficult after the rain in the early hours. The pitch has a honeycomb of cracks. Endean goes back to a Tyson delivery that keeps low and traps him leg before. Laker gets some to turn in the 'Manchester' manner. It is not going to be easy playing on this surface.

That is borne out almost immediately as England commence their innings. Heine sprints in and hurls it down with all his might; it almost shoots along the ground and just misses Richardson's off-stump. Bailey's defensive instincts save him from a shooter early on and after that he eschews the very idea of backfoot play.

Richardson does not. He goes back to an Adcock delivery that strikes him plumb in front. Compton goes forward to the first ball with conviction and is tentative to the second which takes the inside edge of his crooked bat and hits the leg-stump. England 4 for 2 at lunch.

Basil D'Oliveira pulled out of the third 'Test' at the last minute due to injury. It was played at Kingsmead, Durban, the first time the non-White cricketers were allowed on a Test venue.

Vice-captain Amien Variawa took over. It could have been a low-scoring thriller, but rain ensured a draw. The visitors were skittled for 71, Tiny Abed capturing 4 for 9. Rasik Patel, the left-arm medium pacer who would cross swords with D'Oliveira years later, proceeded to blow the hosts away for 88, with only Cec Abrahams with 39 standing up against his 6 for 36. Kenyan Asians were 111 for 8 when the match came to an end.

The South African non-Whites, uncoached, till then without a yardstick to measure how good they were, had taken on an international side and proved to be the better team. Checker Jassat was justifiably proud: "This is a vital lesson that we have learnt from the tour, and one can genuinely hope that its inestimable value to the future well-being of cricket is not lost in the maze of technicalities and self-interest."

Bailey proceeds to bat in that dogged manner that only he knows and breaks the tedium of the dead bat with two drives off Adcock. May survives a shooter, turns Heine to the mid-wicket boundary, and produces two vintage off-drives off Adcock. Then Tayfield kisses his cap and hands it over to the umpire. A shooter turns almost square and it misses everything, including Waite, as it disappears for four byes.

Tayfield kisses his cap before bowling to Compton

Bailey presents a dead bat to the good length offering from Tayfield. Anything with air he lofts back over the bowler's head. Goddard chokes up the other end. May tries to force him square. The ball comes straight on to him and shoots up into the air off the edge. May turns his head in disappointment. A roar from the crowd tells him that the catch has been taken at cover.

There is no bounce on the wicket. Loader, Tyson, Adcock, Heine—no one has been able to get lift. Heine is forced to bowl fuller. He gets Insole with one that whips sharply back to catch him plumb in front. He bowls a straight and fast one to Bailey and this rather simple plot seems to be the only one that the Barnacle has not taken into consideration. It rearranges his stumps. He follows it up with yet another which moves a shade back, and Evans is not up to it. 86 for 6. In four overs, Heine has taken 3 for 7.

Cowdrey struggles all along a 42-minute stay and then gropes for one from Adcock outside the off-stump. Waite throws the ball up. 88 for 7.

Tyson and Lock, forced into the role of making their bats count, base their game on forward defensive pushes. The rare ones in the gap get singles, the ones which are edged sometimes count for two. Tayfield limps off after an unusually unsuccessful 22 overs.

After 48 minutes of grim struggle, Tyson pushes a bit too hard, and the ball lobs back to Heine. 48 minutes with only a solitary run against his name. 97 for 8. The day ends at 110 for 9, but not before Lock and Loader are hit on their toes with telling effect. The culprit is the Bloody Dutchman.

"One does not mind a turning wicket, but the shooting pitch has reduced the match to a farce," writes McLean.

Oil of Olay is a pink fluid, rather than a cream. Perhaps that is one of the major reasons for its success. The name, a clever spin on a key ingredient, lanolin, was chosen by the inventor Graham Wulff, a former Unilever Chemist from Durban. He and business partner Jack Lowe actually tested the product on their wives and friends before launching it.

It was a success. Wulff rode on the uniquely packaged bottled product. And he was a golf fanatic.

At the Beachwood Golf Club, Durban, he was playing with partner Lowe, Edmund Anderson, a chemical engineer at their plant, and the crazy golf addict David Andrews.

That day the caddie of the volatile Andrews was a local Indian man.

At the fifth hole, Andrews played a poor drive. The heat was getting to all of them, especially Andrews who had a habit of throwing his clubs if a stroke went wrong. He turned to his Indian caddie and asked him for advice on selecting a club for the approaching green.

The Indian man sniffed the breeze, saw the 145-metre distance, and selected a six-iron. The following stroke of Andrews was decent but short.

"You call yourself a first-class caddie?" he turned, face flushed, and barked at the Indian guy.

The man bent his head, put down the kit and started walking towards the clubhouse.

"Hey man, where do you think you're going?"

"To the clubhouse, Sir, to get you a first-class caddie."

Andrews was shocked, but restrained his frustrations. He summoned the man back.

"What's your name?"

"Papwa."

"What made you so sure that a six-iron was the club for that shot?"

Papwa hung his head for a bit and then replied slowly, "I play a bit, Sir."

Andrews picked up a six-iron from the bag and thrust it challengingly in the direction of the caddie.

Papwa took the club, looked at the distant flag, and practiced his swing. Andrews and the others burst outs laughing. Left hand below the right, and yet a right hander's stance. This man was hilarious.

Papwa swung the six-iron back, and with the smoothest motion of his hips, he arched through. His arms followed, and his wrists flicked like a whip. The ball rose, soared to its zenith some four metres beyond the flag, bit into the ground, and spun back within a foot of the hole. Andrews gaped, and then his stern features broke into a smile. Soon, the Indian caddie's hand was being shaken by all the four White golfers.

There is only one wicket to be picked up. That is done without the addition of a run. But there are two victims. Before Adcock bowls Lock with a near shooter, Heine sprays his stuff down the leg. Waite sprawls around to collect. His shoulder needs attention.

He is not alone. After a spirited half hour, the injection to dull the pain in his foot wears off and Loader has to come off. In the hotel Compton has fallen down the stairs and bruised some ribs. He does not field all day. A dismal way to spend time during the final Test of a great career.

Tyson bowls off just five paces. Bailey is nagging as ever. An hour and a quarter passes with Goddard and Pithey not really indicating that scoring runs is part of the game.

Laker comes on after an hour and a quarter. Pithey tries to sweep and is bowled off the pads. With Waite temporarily out of action, Endean is promoted even further up the order. A ball from Tyson swings in, hits his pad and then his wicket.

South Africa crawl to 28 for 2 at lunch.

After the break Laker finds turn if he gives it air. But he often pitches short and Funston pulls him with absolute abandon, relieved from the constant medium pace rendered mysterious by the wicket.

The casualty list continues. Goddard sweeps Lock into his chin. Van Ryneveld appears after a considerable delay while the players fidget and umpires look at their watches.

Funston plays Lock on to his body and the ball trickles on to the stumps. McLean shows some intent, stepping out and hitting Bailey to midwicket. But he departs at 98, trying to repeat the stroke to one shooter that hugs the pitch. Bailey retires to try on a heel pad, and Tyson nips one back off a crack to get van Ryneveld leg before. Goddard returns, chin strapped and plastered, but touches a Tyson ball to Evans. Tayfield comes in now, and Waite appears only when Duckworth, after having kept several shooters out, falls to one that cuts back and bounces.

The wicketkeeper and off-spinner, both carrying injuries, see through till the end, the runs added with painstaking tardiness. 122 in the full day. The match is close, but the cricket, including the pitch, is at its worst.

As they went around the course, Wulff asked about Papwa. It turned out that as a child Papwa Sewgolum had been gifted a Syringa stick by his father, a municipal grasscutter in Durban. He had imitated golfers in the nearby course ever since, and had become a caddie as it was the closest he could get to proper facilities. He had won non-White tournaments contested between the caddies. Wulff, listening with lips pressed under his handle-bar moustache, was fascinated.

They discussed the various inequalities and laws that prevented him from playing. There was a conviction growing in Wulff that Papwa should be given proper opportunity.

By 1956, Wulff and Lowe had employed Papwa in their company. His job was to place caps on the bottles of Oil of Olay. Officially, his salary was £10 per month; unofficially, it was doubled. His workload was light. He was given plenty of time off and access to facilities to hone his golfing skills.

The roller bumps over the cracks on the fourth morning; speed-breakers would have been smoother.

The three remaining South African wickets fall for just 12, two to Tyson to give him 6 for 40. Waite has laboured 84 minutes for an unbeaten 7, grimacing after practically every delivery. But he bravely dons the big gloves again.

189 to win. The wicket is as treacherous as when the match started. It has not really deteriorated. The vagaries are more predictable. Some in the South African camp think that they have set 50 runs too few.

Adcock steams in and spends the first over spraying it everywhere, making Waite move gingerly. And then he fires in three yorkers in succession. Richardson digs out two. The third one is too quick for him.

May comes in, eager to lead from the front. No 3 is in any case his justifiable position. Waite hands over the gloves to Endean and withdraws. The shoulder dislocation is too painful.

Heine bowls something akin to a fast off-break. It almost bowls the England captain. But he soon sends Heine to the distant mid-wicket pastures. Van Ryneveld hares after it, dives, and pulls it in, saving the fourth run. Every one of them is vital.

Heine and Adcock strike the pads several times, Goddard gets one to break back a lot and almost hits the stumps. Tayfield also bowls an over. But England go into lunch at 27 for 1.

After the break, May tries to hit Tayfield out of the firing line. A firmly driven two, a pick off the toes that is smartly caught by a gentleman reclining high on the grass bank to the left of the scoreboard. And then one crashed first bounce to the right of the scoreboard. In the next over, Goddard pitches one in a crack and it deviates drastically from outside off to bowl the skipper. 21 runs. 153 runs for May in the series at 15.30.

Cowdrey comes in. Tayfield and Goddard—will there ever be another pair of such pinch-fist bowlers? A painful hit to Bailey's knee induces the Barnacle to break the shackles of maidens. He drives Goddard for four.

Now Cowdrey tries to hit his way out of trouble and is dropped twice in successive balls off Tayfield, once by the bowler and once at cover. But May has set the tone. Tayfield in the groove is dangerous. He must be hit out of the attack. Bailey times the hit well, and it soars towards wide mid-wicket. McLean sprints across to his right and holds it ankle-high, while running full tilt. 53 for 3.

Cowdrey, now reversing into ultra-cautious, puts his bat and pad together. Tayfield gets his edge, it flies off the pad and van Ryneveld at short leg dives to take a scintillating catch. 57 for 4.

Cowdrey c van Ryneveld b Tayfield

After fifty minutes of painful struggle, Compton, playing what will turn out to be his last Test innings, prods forward. It goes up off bat and pad and Endean steps around the stumps to take it. "Rather like a butler from behind the bar," writes Ross. It is certain that he will never play a Test in South Africa again. The crowd gives him a generous round of applause as he walks back. 71 for 5.

Insole swings at Tayfield and is taken at the deep square leg. It is all but over. Evans hits Tayfield twice, the ball landing among the Indian crowd behind long off. But a waft at Heine ends in the gloves of Endean, who is doing a magnificent job.

Lock drives Heine. The stroke, according to Ross, is "so old-fashioned that he looks like a cartoon by Spy." Tyson swings Tayfield for six and drives him for four. 28 runs added for the eighth wicket at a run-a-minute. Is there some hope?

At 127, Lock swings Tayfield and Goddard at short-midwicket swoops to his right to embrace the ball. Then the roles are reversed, as Tyson slashes at Goddard and Tayfield takes him near his boots at slip. Loader, professing by death or glory, lofts Tayfield hard and high. McLean is there, his body arched beyond the pickets, holding on.

South Africa win by 58 runs. Tayfield breaks Vogler's record of 36 wickets set in 1910. The series is tied 2-2.

"To obtain a calmer reflection of one of the most exciting days in our cricket history, I give myself 24 hours' notice before attempting any comment," writes McLean. He has no choice really. The team celebration dinner takes up most of those 24 hours.

Compton c Endean b Tayfield

A series with the bowling attacks more or less equally matched, with Tayfield providing the telling edge. With the big guns of English batting, Compton, May and Cowdrey, ending with spluttering and muffled reports, the limited but spirited batting of South Africa managed to match their combined firepower.

Yes, that was the problem with South African cricket of the mid-1950s. Plenty of very good and even great bowlers. Superb fielders. But a definite lack of class in the batting.

Once again, the D'Oliveira question. What if they had the services of this great batsman during those days?

Of course, there were far more serious questions asked in South Africa those days. From January to June 1957, the Alexandra Bus Boycott raged—70,000 township residents refused to ride the local buses to and from work—and the boycott soon spread to other areas.

SECTION 3
Uncompromising Toughness and Consistency

21 TRIAL AND ERROR

1957–58. Ian Craig is the Australian captain, having jumped the queue according to many a teammate and pressman. The boy wonder, measured against the closest physical manifestation of the infinite, Don Bradman, has thus far not really blazed the turf, or even set it simmering. Six Tests have brought him 255 runs at 23.18. That 53 on debut remains his only half-century.

Besides, the team has no Lindwall, no Miller, no Morris, no Hassett, and no Archer. The South African pressmen dub them the weakest to visit the shores. To add to the woes, Harvey breaks a finger and misses the first Test.

When Hassett's men were here in 1949–50, they had seen the British flag and heard '*God Save the King*'. Now, everywhere Craig and his team go, they see the South African Union flag and hear *'Die Stem van Suid Afrika.'*

The start is also ominous. Goddard and McGlew add 176 for the first wicket. By the third afternoon, Australia are 177 for 6, facing a first innings total of 470.

Only a young debutant called Robert Simpson drives delectably and uses his feet with finesse. His 60 gives slight respectability to the score. Down the years, he will be called Bobby.

The troubles for the tourists continue. Alan Davidson struggles with his eye. A piece of hot coal lodged there on Christmas eve, and on Christmas Day the eye had to be operated. Now, as Heine charges at him, four wickets in the bag, his eye waters. Signalling to the dressing room, he lies on his back. Ian Craig comes running out and administers eye drops. For his living, Craig sells pharmaceutical drugs for *Boots* behind the counter, on a dusk-to-dawn shift, at London's Piccadilly Circus. He is an expert in first aid.

Heine has problems with his ankle. He bowls half-throttle. Davidson swings him down the throat of fine leg at 244. But Benaud carries on batting. Wally Grout has been uncharitably called 'long-stop' by Dick Whitington. Before the match, a journalist showed him his pen sketch of the wicketkeeper, and Grout told him: "You've left out my team function, I'm a long-stop." Now he keeps Benaud company and the score progresses beyond 300.

Ian Craig meets Clive van Ryneveld

1957. The year started with 60 Black pastors and civil rights leaders from several southern states in the USA meeting in Atlanta, Georgia. Amongst them was Martin Luther King Jr. Their aim was to coordinate nonviolent protests against racial discrimination and segregation.

In South Africa, the 'Church Clause' of the Native Laws Amendment Act expelled Blacks from the White church services.

That same year, a beautiful 22-year-old social worker arrived to work at the Baragwanath Hospital in Soweto. She was from the home area of Oliver Tambo in the Transkei.

Mandela saw her waiting for a bus while driving by. After a few days, she visited a law court with a friend and saw Mandela conducting a court case. Tambo's future wife Adelaide introduced Winnie Nomzano Madikizela to Mandela. For the 39-year-old, going through divorce proceedings with his first wife, it was love at first sight.

Enjoying South Africa. Neil Harvey points out the attractions to Ian Craig

After the third day, the Australian players want to relax but the manager Jack Norton has imposed a 10 PM curfew. South Africans are also under curfew, but for them it is 11:30 PM.

Davidson has had enough of Norton. He and Favell decide to "bugger the curfew."

Coming out of a show nearby, they bump into Funston.

"You guys are supposed to be tucked up," the Springbok says.

"We had to get out, we were going crazy," explains Davidson.

Funston hands them the keys to his Peugeot. The two drive 35 miles towards Pretoria for a look-see. Their innocent excursion ends at 1 AM.

When they check with the concierge for their room-key, all they get is a note: *Report to me. I've got your keys. Norton.*

After some unprintable discussion, they get a bed at the home of the Rosenbergs, local cricket lovers.

Next morning, they are warned: 'You two are in trouble. You're on the first plane home.'

That day, Australia cut the lead down to 102 runs. Before the series Benaud averaged 20.66; after this series he will score at 23.90. But in this series, he wields the willow like a bona fide master batsman. He even tames Tayfield, employing the use of his feet, which seems to be the general Australian strategy against the spinner. The 122 he gets will remain his career-best. In response, South Africa slip to 19 for 4 against the two left-arm fast bowlers Davidson and Meckiff.

Davidson ends the innings with 6 for 34 from 17.4 overs. Norton overlooks the indiscretion and repeals the curfew.

Van Ryneveld had an eventful 1957. After leading the side to 2-2 tie against England, he became a father. Subsequently, he was persuaded by close friend, the young Union Party leader Zach de Beer, and leader of opposition Sir de Villers Graaff, to stand in a parliamentary by-election at East London.

A few months before the 1958 general election was due, Herman Malcomess, the United Party MP for East London, died. At de Beer's suggestion, Sir de Villers Graaf, recently elected leader of Union Party, convinced van Ryneveld to stand. This would be the last election till 1994 in which Coloured voters would vote in the same roll as the Whites. Van Ryneveld soon found himself canvassing their votes.

He was also invited to lead South Africa in the first two Tests. But within 24 hours of the announcement of the team, he was out of action. It was Benaud with the bat again. While chasing 55 in 39 minutes against Western Province, Benaud opened with McDonald and drove hard. Van Ryneveld split the webbing below his left thumb.

McGlew took over the captaincy and Endean was named deputy. This was surprising, because Endean played under Waite's captaincy for Transvaal.

Now Waite and Endean add 129 to rescue South Africa. They end at 176 for 5. A crowd of 19,992 assembles on the final day, full of anticipation of yet another exciting climax. But injuries to Heine and Goddard make McGlew a bit apprehensive. They crawl to make 25 additional runs in 80 minutes before the innings dies a natural death. Meanwhile, Waite is offended by the off-breaks of Jim Burke. "He was a blatant thrower," he declares later.

Australia are not interested in chasing the 300-plus total after Burke damages his finger to Heine. Craig bats 109 minutes for 17 and is roundly booed. The end is anti-climactic.

Cricket has stepped into the modern age. The teams fly to Cape Town for the second Test.

In 1957, Walter Hain received a phone call from Chips Sive, from his previous architectural firm in Pretoria. There was an open position, and if he wanted, he could return in late 1957.

All these months in England had not been easy. The news from South Africa, of the Treason Trial, of the apartheid laws, of the violent clampdowns to protests—all these had made Ad and Wal restive and concerned. The salary was also not really significant in England. From their Kent house, the daily journey to London was tiring. When he resigned his London job and joined the Kent City Council's architectural department in Maidstone, that came with its own challenges.

Borrowing money from the Pretoria firm for the ticket, Wal flew back in December. Seven-year-old Peter Hain stood up and said, "Well, I'd better cut the bread then."

Ad and her four children took the ship back. The local farmer drove them to the station from where they took the boat train to Southampton. In the ocean liner, the children played in the nursery while Ad enjoyed a brief respite from her chores.

Wal was waiting with both sets of grandparents when the ship docked in Port Elizabeth.

Newlands is reputed to be the most beautiful cricket ground in the world with a tomb in the middle. Win the toss and you are unlikely to lose the match.

Additionally, the selectors do not want to risk Heine's ankle. When Craig wins the toss, a sense of despondency sets in among the hosts. It is 190 by the time the first wicket falls. Burke bats for nine and a half hours for 189. Even a three-ball duck by Craig does not help. Australia amass 449.

It is Benaud who wins them the match, this time with the ball. In New Zealand, a Timaru chemist has prescribed him a calamine boracic lotion for the wear and tear of the skin on his first and third fingers. He applies it diligently and spins, according to a Ray Robinson estimate, more than 1,000 deliveries before the first ball in a tour match.

All the preparation does bear fruit. He picks up 4 for 95 and South Africa follow on. His 5 for 49 in the second innings take the fight out of them. Endean is bowled by his flipper, painstakingly learnt from Bruce Dooland.

Alongside this, he takes the captain's permission to crouch closer at gully to Davidson's bowling and catches a stinging square drive by Waite parallel to the ground.

The end of the match, however, is a fairy-tale for chinaman bowler Lindsay Kline. Craig introduces him for a second spell, with the score 99 for 7. Off the second ball, Fuller slices one which Benaud dives to hold on the leg side. Off the third, Tayfield swings his bat but the ball thuds into his pad plumb in front. The following ball has Kline changing his mind while running in and bowling a googly to Adcock. The snick is brilliantly held at slip by Simpson. Hattrick to end the match. Australia 1-0 up.

Simpson catches Adcock and it is hat-trick for Lindsay Kline.

While South African batting struggled in the Tests, Basil D'Oliveira was going through one of his several purple patches. The next edition of the SACBOC Inter-Race tournament had been planned for 1957. Because of the visit of the Kenyan Asians, it had been pushed back by a year.

In early 1958, the tournament was eventually held at the Princeton grounds in Wynberg. Against the fiery Eric Petersen bowling for the Malay team, D'Oliveira scored 84. Against the SABCB, he amassed 102 and captured 4 for 20. SACCA was the champion side yet again.

This was the last time the tournament would be held by dividing the teams according to races. Voices would become stronger for provincial—rather than racial—make-up of the sides. On 27 January 1958, the unanimous decision was reached by the four affiliates of SACBOC to banish racial divides. Race would be superseded by geography.

D'Oliveira finished with the highest aggregate among the participants of the four Inter-Racial tournaments, with exactly 600 runs at 60. He figured in five of the 12 century partnerships witnessed in the competition. Eric Petersen headed the wickets tally with 58 scalps at 12.75. What if?

Sometime in 1958, D'Oliveira penned the first of his now-famous letters, in green ink on cheap, lined notepaper. They were addressed to the man behind the voice that had brought English Test and county cricket to him through the magic of wireless. He hung on to every word he heard on the radio when John Arlott was on air. The voice he heard convinced him that the man behind it was 'nice and compassionate.'

D'Oliveira wrote to ask whether there was a chance of playing cricket in England for a living.

While they are outplayed at Cape Town, at Durban the hosts bat themselves to stupor and stalemate. "One of the most boring games of cricket in which I have played at paddock, school, club, first-class or Test level," Benaud will say.

With Heine and Goddard back in action, the Australians find it difficult to get going. It is Craig who holds the innings together, but he takes his time doing so. 52 from 190 balls. Adcock blasts out the top order. The second morning, Australia lose four wickets, two apiece to Adcock and Heine, for just eight runs. 163 all out. South Africa again look like coasting on their habit of coming back from behind in the series.

But when they lose two wickets for 28, they opt for safety first. McGlew and Waite start crawling through the second day and are glacial on the third. By the third morning the bowlers are tired and the sun beats down mercilessly. Yet, only 40 runs are scored in the first two hours. McLean counts 10 half-volleys and full-tosses pushed back to the bowlers.

Waite beats McGlew to the century in the second session. The opening batsman gets there in 545 minutes, 'bettering' Peter Richardson's existing record for the slowest by a full hour.

When they pass Nourse and Rowan's record of 167 for the third wicket against Australia, set on the same ground in 1950, a few statistically nerdy spectators are still awake enough to clap. At 196 for 2, the reason for the applause is lost to the players on the ground.

Grout asks, "What are they clapping for?"

"A record," ventures Waite.

"Long playing?" asks Grout.

258 for 2 after 122 eight-ball overs. Craig takes the new ball. A run later, McGlew is dismissed. 572 minutes and 499 balls for 105. Debutant Ron Gaunt is too tired to exult. Waite is bowled by Davidson at the same score, 134 from 513 minutes in 462 balls. They are all out the next day for 384, compiled in 13 hours and five minutes. Benaud has effectively lulled them into run-lessness with 50.7 overs that have fetched him 5 for 114.

Another of Benaud's victims

Ad and Wal Hain joined the small but active branch of the Liberal Party that had strangely remained active in Pretoria. Pretoria—the bastion of parochial Afrikanerdom, a veritable citadel of apartheid.

Shortly after their registration, a peaceful women's demonstration against the pass laws in the nearby township of Lady Selborne was broken up by baton-wielding police. John Brink, the local Liberal Party chairman, drove down to restrain the police. Late in the day, when he had not returned, Wal joined a search party that drove off to look for Brink.

Ad and the kids were waiting anxiously when Wal returned. According to him, he had met Brink returning bloodied, in a windowless car. The vehicle had been stoned by the residents, who did not know that the White man in the car was on their side. Brink had been saved by the local ANC organiser, Peter Magano, who had recognised him and jumped on the bonnet to drive the crowd back.

Ad and Wal woke up fast to the dangerous realities of South African activism.

On the final day, Harvey and Mackay are fighting to save the match. Tayfield is at them, scrupulously accurate, canny, scheming. At the end of the over he goes and stands at slip.

Mackay turns Goddard fine, very fine, and the batsmen run. Tayfield, in spite of the long spell, sets off after the ball at full pace. The batsmen think it is boundary and stop. Tayfield stops the ball with his boot at the edge of the boundary and hurls it back. It reaches Waite with Mackay out of ground, but he lobs it to van Ryneveld who has come up to the bowling end. Harvey is also out of the crease. On some urging by Funston, van Ryneveld gently lifts the bails. Dazed, Harvey mumbles, "You can't do that."

Umpire Marais at the bowler's end, walks across to check where Tayfield has stopped the ball. It is inside the fence. If there is an appeal, Harvey will have to go. Van Ryneveld says there will be no appeal.

Harvey bats another hour. Australia finish the Test at 292 for 7.

Perhaps with a bit of gamesmanship, the South African captain could have won the game. But van Ryneveld is a sterling character.

The Hains lived in a rented house in Hilda Street, in the Arcadia suburb of Pretoria. Walter Hain allowed a Black boy, Tatius, to stay in the servant's quarter with his mother.

Tatius, in his early teens, was walking along the pavement when two White men took exception to him penny-whistling. They beat him mercilessly, to 'teach him a lesson'.

Peter and his family saw him return home, crying, face bloody with gashes and bruises, legs and arms raw with welts.

Wal went to lodge a complaint at the local police station. The officer in charge just smirked at him. Rebuffed, he sent a letter to the *Pretoria News.* It was published, and thus Walter Hain made it to the watch list of the Special Branch.

Johannesburg. It reads like a casualty list. Adcock retires after six fast and furious overs with a temperature of 101. Heine pulls up with an old heel injury and bowls at a much-reduced pace. Goddard, with a sore finger, has to bowl more. And at the other end, Burke, with a sore throat, bats all day to remain unbeaten on 79.

When Harvey is the second out before lunch, instead of the out-of-form Craig it is Benaud who comes in at No 4. The fastest century of the series is worth £100 and Benaud has already hit it in the first Test. Now he slams another, bettering it by 19 minutes. Three hours of sheer joy, totalling exactly 100.

He is not done though. When South Africa bat, he polishes the tail, 4 for 70, and the hosts follow on. In the second session of the fourth day, he gets Endean and Goddard, the first two wickets, both spectacularly caught at slip by Simpson. 119 runs in the whole day, and they will say 50 years later that Test cricket has lost its charm.

On the final morning, Benaud gets McGlew for a six-hour marathon amounting to 70. Simpson takes the catch again. The rest of them fall away. Victory by 10 wickets. Benaud 5 for 84. It seems like he has taken over from Miller.

Australia win the series. Robert Menzies sends in a cable: *Congratulations on a remarkable team success.*

Arranging it with the help of Menzies, Jack Fingleton, accompanying the team as a scribe, has a 75-minute interview with Minister of Native Affairs Hendrik Verwoerd. He asks about the detention laws. "In a most pleasant talk [...] I had the temerity to tell Dr Verwoerd that no democratic country could tolerate his detention laws. He claimed that desperate ills needed desperate remedies; that his government was certain that anybody 'put inside' under the detention act was a communist, was a possible saboteur."

The SACBOC officials were hard at work, seeking opportunities for the non-White game. Talks were being finalised with neighbouring African countries.

Basil D'Oliveira was preparing to take his team across Serengeti. A team of labourers, artisans, craftsmen and technicians. Bantu, Indian, Coloured, Malay.

Craig offers to drop himself for the final Test. He wants to play Les Favell. Burge thinks it is a good idea, but Harvey doesn't. He is not too happy at being passed for captaincy, but now he tells Burge, "I've been playing Tests for ten years and I know that there's never been an Australian captain dropped on tour in cricket history. As far as I'm concerned it won't happen this time." Craig plays.

On the Rest Day, Ray Robinson takes Ian Meckiff, Barry Jarman, John Drennan, and Lindsay Kline to a match played between two Coloured sides. The pavilion is fashioned from two old tramcars. The ground on which they play can hardly be called a surface. However, the greeting they receive is extraordinary. "These little Black kids knew everything about the players," remembered Kline. One of the kids says he is Harvey. Another calls himself Davo. The Australians stay all day, the enthusiasm of the Africans rubbing off on them.

The next day, a local newspaper publishes a story about the visit. Manager Jack Norton is fuming. He has received a complaint from the SACA that the players are fraternising with the natives. If they do anything like that again, they will be heading home.

Craig makes just 17. Endean catches him off a stinging on-drive at silly mid-on. That is one of the three miracle catches Endean takes in the innings. Burke is caught low down at full stretch off Adcock in the slips. Grout is caught left-handed after a full-length dive from leg-slip off a perfect leg-glance.

But Davidson takes 4 for 44 and 5 for 38. Only Tayfield's 66 rescues the hosts from 105 for 7 and stretches them to 214 in the first innings. Benaud scores 43 as Australia take a 77-run lead, and captures 5 for 82 in the second innings. Simpson keeps holding those catches at slip, 13 in the series. Australia make it 3-0 with an 8-wicket win. Not before Adcock produces a barrage of bumpers and some of the fastest bowling seen in the 1950s.

A delighted Don Bradman is there to welcome the team as the *Dominion Monarch* returns with the Australians in April 1958.

On 16 April, the South African general elections were held.

The National Party were victorious again.

In East London, however, Clive van Ryneveld won against National Party candidate Robbie de Lange by a comfortable margin.

22 SUCCESS IN SERENGETI

On 30 July 1958, the South African Non-European cricket team leave the Jan Smuts airport for a two-month tour of Kenya, Uganda, Tanganyika, Zanzibar, and Southern Rhodesia. Around 200 well-wishers assemble and there are plenty of flashes of camera bulbs. The team is to play 15 matches, including three 'Tests'.

The side is led by D'Oliveira. The vice-captain is Tiny Abed. Among the others are all-rounder Cecil Abrahams, fast bowler Eric Petersen, wicketkeeper Lobo Abed, top order batsman Laam Raziet, and left-arm spinner Owen Williams.

SACBOC side for the tour to East Africa. D'Oliveira standing third from right.

In June 1958, Mandela and Winnie got married. Mandela was given a relief from his bans to travel down to the Transkei for wedding celebrations.

The South African Non-Europeans get off to a horrid start on the tour. Kenya is in the grip of the Mau Mau rebellion. And the Kenyan Asians rout them as the members take a while to find their feet.

D'Oliveira stands among the ruins, hitting 59 out of 131 all out. Tiny Abed picks up four wickets and Lobo Abed holds some scintillating catches. But the match is a disappointment.

However, they do not lose any other match on the tour. Adjusted to the conditions, gelling as a team, they conquer as they move through East Africa.

Eric Petersen thrives on the fast pitches of East Africa. His off-cutters are so vicious that D'Oliveira does away with slips and places four short legs.

In front of his furious pace, Moshi XI falls away for 107, Mombasa for 41 and Tango XI for 80 and 37. Against Zanzibar, the South Africans allow just 85 and 29 as Tiny Abed picks up 8 for 23.

They return to Nairobi to contest the first of the three unofficial 'Tests'. Their opponent is Kenya.

On 1 August 1958, the Treason Trial opened. Defending the accused was, among others, Bram Fischer. Scion of an elite Afrikaner family, he was a communist who had become a close friend of Mandela and a hero of the ANC.

The trial would go on for two and a half years.

Plagued by the pace of Petersen, the Kenyans hatch a ploy. They know the fast bowler has feet of clay. The man, a carpenter by profession, is susceptible to drink, dope, and other vices. It puts him in direct conflict with D'Oliveira, a stickler for discipline, who cannot understand how a cricketer can have such inclination for self-destruction.

The Kenyans arrange for him to stay at a rather sordid downtown hotel, which in reality is a brothel. The ploy works to a great extent. The South Africans bat first, and Petersen comes in smelling of drink—sleepless and in no state for presentation, let alone play.

D'Oliveira is furious. He threatens to send him home on the next flight and has to be dissuaded by the rest of the team. Whether because of that or not, he himself falls for a duck. The visitors totter at 24 for 3 before a patient 41 by Cecil Abrahams and a handy 31 by Tiny Abed help them to 196. Petersen himself somehow scores an unbeaten 13.

After this however, Petersen produces one of his fastest and most lethal spells of bowling. He captures 6 for 51. With the other bowlers not quite effective, D'Oliveira brings himself on and takes 2 for 30. The hosts score 190. The match is tantalisingly poised with just six runs separating the sides.

The lead has inched along to just 11 when D'Oliveira walks in at 5 for 2. Both the openers gone.

"No one will hesitate to applaud the magnificent performance of the young South African captain," writes a local Nairobi paper. The same piece compares some of his on-drives to Wally Hammond (surprising because Hammond's famous drives generally blazed through the off-side). There are also reports about late cuts and cover drives. The partnership with Ahmed Deedat yields 112. With John Neethling he adds 141. He scores 139. Cecil Abrahams hits an unbeaten 50. D'Oliveira closes the innings at 314 for 7.

The Kenyans never look like getting the 321 for victory. D'Oliveira picks up three second innings wickets to complete a fantastic all-round performance. Kenya succumb to a 165-run defeat.

The tour proceeds along these lines.

On 24 August 1958, Hans Strijdom died in office. In September, National Party selected Hendrik Verwoerd as his successor.

His motto was kragdaadigheid and konsekwentheid—uncompromising toughness and consistency. "I don't believe in a policy of conciliation," he said. "I believe in a policy of conviction."

Bold, decisive, driven by iron-will and a complete lack of self-doubt—he was the chief architect of apartheid.

The worse of apartheid was yet to come.

East Africa is beaten by seven wickets at Nairobi. Eric Petersen picks up five, Tiny Abed eight, D'Oliveira two. The captain scores 96, Deedat 66, Neethling 53, Cecil Abrahams 77 and 31 not out.

At Mombasa, they face the Kenyans again. D'Oliveira is run out for three in the first innings and the team totals an unimpressive 193. However, Eric Petersen again routs the hosts, with 5 for 14. Abrahams captures 4 for 20. The total is just 49.

D'Oliveira is back among runs in the second innings with 50. He declares at 183 for 6. Abrahams takes three and Petersen four as the Kenyans manage just 72 in the final innings.

Triumph by 255 runs. All three 'Tests' are won by handsome margins.

It is quite a feat.

Hendrik Verwoerd: Architect of Apartheid

Before the visit of the South African non-Europeans, East Africa and Kenya had been visited by international-quality teams.

There had been the Sunder CC of India with Test cricketers Pankaj Roy, Nari Contractor, Vinoo Mankad, Mushtaq Ali, Jasu Patel, Prakash Bhandari, and Naren Tamhane. There had been the Pakistan Writers XI with Hanif Mohammad, Waqar Hasan, Alimuddin, Imtiaz Ahmed, Wallis Mathias, Abdul Hafeez Kardar, Anwar Hussain, Mahmood Hussain, and Zulfiqar Ahmed. Finally, there had been an MCC side with amateur cricketers led by Freddie Brown and including the likes of Peter Richardson, MJK Smith, Colin Ingleby-McKenzie, and others.

The local sides had given a fairly good account of themselves in these matches.

Basil D'Oliveira's side now had a proper yardstick to know exactly how good they were.

In August 1958, the Liberal Party launched a weekly news and comment magazine, *Contact*, covering the anti-apartheid struggle. Adelaine and Walter Hain subscribed, and within a month Ad became the Pretoria correspondent. Asking her children to play quietly, she clattered away on her small Olivetti typewriter covering the Treason Trial in town. In August 1958 itself, Ad and Wal met and talked to Nelson Mandela, Walter Sisulu, and the other defendants of the Treason Trial. When the trial held in the Old Synagogue broke for lunch,

Mandela and the others were provided lunch by sympathisers from the local Indian community. Ad and Wal remembered Mandela as 'a large, imposing, smiling man.'

By now the skipper is not on speaking terms with his spearhead. Eric Petersen has developed a friendship with one of the girls of the brothel and insists on taking her everywhere. He even brings her to official functions.

Sir Evelyn Baring, Governor of Kenya, invites the team to his residence in Nairobi. Petersen takes his girl with him to the Governor House. Luckily, Sir Baring, who has fallen off a horse and is injured, cannot attend the evening.

The cricketers return to Cape Town as superstars. The victory banquet is held at the Woodstock Restaurant and then there is a mayoral reception at the City Hall. D'Oliveira is voted Sportsman of the Year by the readers of the *Golden City Post.* MPs, clergymen, councillors, and socialites attend a dance during which Col Billingham, Mayor of Cape Town, presents the skipper with a trophy.

The proud captain with the Mayor

In October 1958, South African Sports Association (SASA) was formed at the Milner

Hotel, East London. A body that would eventually amount to 70,000 non-White sportsmen among its members. The founder was activist, educator, journalist, and poet Dennis Brutus. The purpose of SASA was to give South Africa's non-White sportsmen the chance to compete on the international stage. Running on small donations, using the photocopier of a local liberal NGO, no office, and no staff, Brutus took on the deeply embedded racially discriminatory South African sports establishment.

The new organisation sought to undermine racist sports structures on three fronts:

The SASA appealed to the white organisations to reject discrimination and to select sides on merit.

The SASA appealed to international sports organisations to insist that South African sides were representative (International Olympic Committee, FIFA, ICC all received appeals from Dennis Brutus, and flagrantly ignored them).

The SASA appealed to the population of countries involved in competition with South Africa to campaign against racial sport.

23 IF GANDHI FAILED, HOW WILL WORRELL SUCCEED?

"I always supported the visiting country—after all, they weren't denying me the chance to play in such a magnificent stadium [Newlands]," wrote Basil D'Oliveira in *Time to Declare.* He however, added, "But I never had a hatred for the White man. I knew about the laws of the land, about the separate development policy [...] and we would have been foolish at that time if we had tried to buck the system ... I had no desire to exchange my cricket bat and soccer boots for a gun."

However, with the exposure of Serengeti, fissures appeared on the veneer of placid acceptance, and hope trickled in.

The SACBOC had become more ambitious and they were canny operators as well. The arrangements of the international tours, home and away, had been based on using the obtuse apartheid rules to their benefit. Nothing in the legislation prevented non-Whites from playing other non-Whites. In fact, it was in line with 'separate development'. The Board literally reached for the stars.

The stars in this case were the West Indians. Frank Worrell was invited to lead a team of Black West Indian cricketers on a tour of South Africa in November and December 1959. The schedule was drawn up and funds were arranged. Rashid Varachia, Checker Jassat, and Bree Bulbulia were the main progenitors of the idea. In fact, during the West Indian tour of England in 1957, Bulbulia, a textile merchant, had showed up in the London hotel of the cricketers and suggested the idea to Everton Weekes and Sonny Ramadhin.

Varachia even contacted the Minister of Interior, Dr Eben Dönges, to obtain permission. In early January he was able to announce that he had received a letter from the minister stating that he had agreed in principle to the admission of the West Indian cricket team. Newlands, Wanderers, and Kingsmead were secured for the matches, £5000 was raised to guarantee expenses. Travel details, accommodation, and even sight-seeing trips including a game reserve, were planned with meticulous detail. The SACBOC were also contemplating separate seats for the Whites to attend the matches.

Among the cricketers, the developments were greeted with tremendous excitement. The West Indians were one of the strongest teams in the world. And although they had not yet had a regular Black captain apart from one single Test match in 1948 when George Headley had led the team, Frank Worrell was all but ready to take over from Gerry Alexander. There was heavy lobbying for the elevation of Worrell, mainly by the Marxist cricket-writer CLR James.

The team was to be a constellation of most brilliant stars. Garry Sobers had just broken the world record score of Len Hutton. Conrad Hunte and Collie Smith were the other young talents. Sonny Ramadhin, Alf Valentine, and Everton Weekes, apart from Worrell himself, were legends. There were also Frank King, Chester Watson, Ralph Legall, Ivan Madray, and Donald Ramsamooj. Although only scheduled to play the SACBOC affiliated sides, they were considered strong enough to beat the White South African team.

As tour brochures were being distributed and blazers for the non-White Springboks were being designed, D'Oliveira and the other cricketers could hardly contain their excitement. Their imaginations ran wild. D'Oliveira later said that there were even suggestions among the players to request Worrell to throw a match so that the world sat up and took notice of the non-White cricketers in the land.

Worrell would perhaps have never considered the option. But for now, studying for a BA at Manchester University, he vehemently supported the tour. He even had ties made for the team—in mauve, green and blue.

It was now that opposition came—not from the usual embargos implemented by the apartheid legislation, but from a diametrically opposite direction, from one of the most vocal anti-apartheid activists.

Dennis Brutus, the poet heading SASA, had been canvassing for proper international opportunities for Black cricketers. By general logic, he should have been one of the major supporters of the tour. However, his argument was that for a Black international side like West Indies to visit South Africa was as good as colluding with apartheid. It was tacit acceptance of the regime and its policies.

1959 was business as usual for apartheid South Africa. This image is from Cato Manor, Durban. A woman's march is being broken up

If the South African non-Whites played only Black countries like Kenya, Uganda, and

Black cricketers of West Indies, it essentially meant toeing the apartheid line. Why, di not the SACBOC themselves decide to do away with racially organised cricket and give precedence to geography? Brutus and his organisation were fighting for non-White sportsmen and sportswomen to be chosen in proper race-blind Springbok sides. Non-White cricketers from a high-profile cricketing power visiting the land to play non-White cricketers was against this fight. It would be a backward step. Instead, they should be targeting proper Test cricket.

The first letter in a series of communications aimed at the cancellation of the tour was written, in fact, by Alan Paton.

Paton, a patron of SASA and a friend of Jackie Grant, even used a channel to convey his reservations to the legendary Sir Learie Constantine. Canon John Collins of St Paul's Cathedral wrote to Constantine saying that Paton thought a tour by West Indies would be seen as an acceptance of apartheid by both the South African government and the ANC.

Brutus used all his organisational talent to champion the cancellation of the tour. He managed to form an alliance between ANC, the trade union movement, and a variety of Coloured and Indian organisations. They together wrote to Worrell suggesting that the tour would be a "conspiracy between colour bar sportsmen and the South African government to persuade—by fair means or foul—non-colour bar sportsmen to accept apartheid and an inferior status in the sporting world." There were also threats that the anti-tour protesters would disrupt the games.

There are schools of thought that argue that Brutus was looking for an issue to establish his authority as an important activist. There are others who think that he did have a genuine concern.

Whatever be the actual reason, the protests bore fruit. There was growing consternation that it was way more than a cricket tour and the cricketers were being placed in a cauldron of conflict that would take much more than cricketing skills to overcome. One important voice even exclaimed: "If Gandhi failed in South Africa, I cannot see how Worrell will succeed." West Indies withdrew.

The tour was cancelled. From the soaring hopes of playing Frank Worrell and Garry Sobers at Newlands, Wanderers, and Kingsmead, it was back to the segregated hell-hole of ghastly conditions, unprepared grounds and non-White cricket away from the eyes of the world.

The fissures of hope had been welded shut. D'Oliveira had given 28 years of his life to cricket. He knew he was extraordinary at his craft. After all these years, his modest dreams and anticipations had been crushed by agencies beyond his control.

He decided that his cricketing days were over.

In the beginning of 1960, he took an important step. He had known Naomi for many, many years. They had always known they would be married one day. However, during the courtship D'Oliveira always seemed to be training or playing.

Now, with cricketing roads practically hitting a series of dead ends, they could get concentrate on the relationship.

In January 1960, Basil D'Oliveira and Naomi got married.

24 'PUTTING' APARTHEID TO SHAME IN THE VOORTREKKERS LAND

27 May 1959. The Piper Twin Comanche privately owned by Graham Wulff ensures that much of petty apartheid bureaucracy associated with foreign travel can be circumvented. Dressed neatly in the Durban Indian Golf Club blazer and tie, Papwa kisses his family goodbye at the Stamford Hill aerodrome. The plane takes off towards Johannesburg.

At the Johannesburg airport, Wulff and Papwa wait on tenterhooks as the South African customs and emigration officers look at Papwa's passport. They consult a list of names, walk away to confer with one another, make phone calls. Wulff's handlebar moustache bristles.

In April, opposed to the ANC's multi-racial stance, Robert Sobukwe and other Africanists broke away to form their own party—the Pan Africanist Congress (PAC). To them, Whites and Indians were foreign minorities, and ANC was not militant enough. The conservatives in Europe and America welcomed Sobukwe. He seemed a promising alternative to ANC, which was closely linked to the communists through thick Cold War lenses.

The officers return, look at the letter with an official letterhead, and ask Papwa some pointed questions. They radiate annoyance. The wait lingers on. In the plane, Mavis, Wulff's second wife, waits nervously.

Finally, an officer returns alone and stamps the passport. Wulff smiles widely and thanks him in broken Afrikaans. Within minutes they are airborne.

The adventure starts, past Beira, Dar-es-Salaam, Entebbe, Juba, Khartoum, Cairo, Benghazi, Tripoli, Tunis, Rome, and London. Papwa mumbles a Hindu prayer as he sees Wulff and Mavis engage in animated conversation in the cockpit as the plane circles above London. In the cloud and mist, Wulff has not been able to locate Gatwick and the radio is crackling with static. Papwa even summons the western gods ... mumbling 'Jesus Christ'. However, Wulff manages to land in Biggin Hill, the famous fighter base. The adventure continues. It will end at the Koninklijke Haagsche Golf en Country Club, Wassenaar, Netherlands.

Papwa had temporarily flown away from even greater problems in South Africa. That same month, May 1959, the Verwoerd government abolished the system of African political representation in the parliament through their four White representatives. According to the Prime Minister, the four representatives kept alive the Black hope that they would be represented in the common political system.

In the following month, June 1959, the Extension of University Education Act made it a criminal offence for a non-White student to register at a formerly open university without the written permission of the Minister of Internal Affairs. Non-White universities were established and there was a blanket refusal to any non-White student from pursuing a course in a white university if that same course was also offered in a non-White university.

In Scotland, Papwa comes across the South African golfing great Gary Player. They hit it off, practicing together for the British Open at the Muirfield Course. Player even picks Papwa up from his hotel and drives him to the course.

At his North Berwick Hotel, Papwa receives a telegram from the ladies of the Beachwood Golf Club where he caddies. The receptionist reads it out to him: "Good wishes and good golfing." Papwa cannot read, he has never been to school.

June 1959 also saw growing tension in other parts of the world due to the apartheid policies. In spite of vociferous protests across the country, the New Zealand Rugby Football Union insisted on choosing an all-White All Blacks side for the 1960 tour of South Africa. The Maori All-Black great George Nepia telegrammed: *"Best of luck. Let me know if you need a fullback."*

On 18 June, the first street demonstration against New Zealand's sporting contact with South Africa took place in Wellington.

For the 77-year-old Prime Minister Walter Nash, it was perhaps too late to realise the escalating issue racism in sport was turning into. However, he did make a couple of statements bordering on support for the protests. "I cannot conceive God created certain sections of people to be on higher or lower levels than others … But that does not permit me to be the judge of members of the Rugby Union" and "I wish I could see a way of sending Maoris without incidents and troubles. I have tried but I cannot see a way."

The Citizen All Black Tour Association (CABTA) was formed in June, to combat racial discrimination in the selection of the 1960 rugby team. By October the issue had reached the parliament.

In the British Open, Papwa cannot qualify for the final two rounds by two strokes. Gary Player emerges champion.

An error in communicating the date by the Professional Golfers' Association prevents him from arriving in time for the Paris Open. The press reports that Papwa Sewgolum is the most disappointed man in Europe.

However, he steadfastly moves to The Hague for the Dutch open.

Progressive Party in January 1960. Clive van Ryneveld second from left in the rear row. Helen Suzman is third from right in the front row.

Verwoerd's grand design for the country continued. According to him, Africans had to exercise their voting rights separately, in the reserves set aside for them. There were to be separate homelands for each of the eight separate language groups of African people, full-fledged independent Bantustans. This was the Promotion of Bantu Self-Government Act.

Reactions to this Act were various and led to disagreements within the United Party as well. Twelve members of parliament resigned from the United Party after the Bloemfontein congress in July, among them the East London MP Clive van Ryneveld. The 12 members formed their own Progressive Party in November 1959.

One of the key members of the party was Helen Suzman, who would be the party's only Member of Parliament for the next 13 years and would unequivocally protest all the apartheid legislation all through.

It is one of the most beautiful courses of Europe. The list of past winners of the Dutch Open include the great Aubrey Boomer, who was victorious from 1924 to 1927. South Africans have triumphed as well, Sid Brews in 1934 and 1935, Bobby Locke in 1939.

Papwa's start is excellent. At the end of the first round, he leads the field with 67. The second is 69, four strokes below par. Five ahead of Dutch champion Gerard de Wit at the fourth hole of the last 18, Papwa decides to play safe.

De Wit rallies. Four birdies and an eagle at holes five to nine. Papwa trails by a stroke. But steeling himself, he birdies 12th, 13th, and 14th, while de Wit manages par. Two strokes ahead now, that is how things stand at the last hole.

David Rathswaffo visited the Hain home often. A storehouse of stories, this Black clerk at the Pretoria Supreme Court was a great favourite of the young Peter Hain. He often passed confidential information to Adelaine Hain, with peculiar malapropisms and idiosyncrasies. "Can I see you in camera?" was his code for confidential information, and Peter could never determine whether it was a code, or he really thought he was making sense. When informed that the phone could be tapped, he changed his voice to a whisper.

In 1959, the government decided that Blacks could not carry out such responsible tasks. David Rathswaffo trained his White replacement before being made redundant.

That same year, prominent Pretoria Liberal and local doctor Colin Lang contested the Pretoria East by-election to the Provincial Council. The Hain residence became the virtual campaign headquarters. As Ad typed a monthly newspaper called *Liberta*, Peter was asked to perform the tasks of collating the sheets and stapling. He was nine.

Papwa puts. The ball trickles towards the 18th hole and shows slight signs of holding up before it disappears. De Wit clasps his hand warmly. The man who is not allowed to compete in Open tournaments in his own country has travelled to the land of the forefathers of the Afrikaners and has won the Dutch Open.

An editorial in the *Leader* hints at the political significance: "With the success of Papwa in international golf, the Colour Bar in sport has received another severe jolt. Papwa's success in the 'home country' of the original *Voortrekker*, the birthplace of Dr Verwoerd, makes the embarrassment even more unbearable for the apostles of apartheid."

The *Golden City Post* observes mournfully: "Back home the winner of the Dutch Open wouldn't be allowed to take part in a White tournament except in a menial capacity." The same article quotes Sid Brews, former Dutch Open champion and president of the South African Golfer's Association, saying it was unlikely that Papwa would be allowed to compete in the South African Golf Open.

Papwa Sewgolum, with his curious reverse grip

By February 1960, Naomi was pregnant with their first child. Basil D'Oliveira had already reconciled himself to a life without cricket, the life of the normal Coloured South African man, trying to forge a semblance of respectability on the morass of discrimination.

That was when the letter reached him.

SECTION 4
Trials and Tribulations

25 FLYING THROUGH FIRE

The letter was from John Arlott. After almost two years of knocking on doors, he had achieved what is virtually impossible—a contract in the Central Lancashire League for Middleton. For just one season and the pay was only £450.

"Dear Basil D'Oliviera [sic], Now I have an offer for you to play as a professional in England this summer. But it is imperative that you cable me your decision about it at once. It is with Middleton who for the last two seasons have won the Central Lancashire League. I cannot pretend that this job would be an easy one. You would be expected to bear a fairly heavy share of the bowling through these long afternoon matches, and the professional is normally expected to carry the main weight of the batting too."

After Roy Gilchrist announced his departure, Wes Hall was deputed to be the replacement professional for Middleton. Just three months before the start of the season, he was forced to pull out by his long-term employer Cable and Wireless. All big-name cricketers were contracted with other clubs. Middleton needed a professional.

D'Oliveira's jubilation was tempered by mundane concerns. £450. Of that, about £200 would be spent in the air fare. Besides, Naomi was pregnant. She would be left alone back home.

But looking at him, Naomi said with conviction, "Bas, you'll never forgive yourself if you give up now."

Damoo Bansda was an Indian sportswriter and part-time barman. He was part of the duo that produced the first South African non-White Cricket Almanack. He was the one who had sent D'Oliveira's list of performances to the *World Sports* magazine. He had relentlessly pushed D'Oliveira's case to the wider world.

He was D'Oliveira's first port of call.

Bansda worked in a Whites-only bar. D'Oliveira crossed the Buitengracht Street, into the domain of the Whites. He walked along the cobbled streets of Greenmarket Square, past the Micheales Museum, to Adderley Street. There stood the Grand Hotel where Bansda polished glasses and poured out drinks. D'Oliveira slipped through the back door to avoid attention, especially police attention.

In the backroom of the bar, he talked to Bansda. About the letter, about the dream, about the £450 pay and passage money.

"Don't worry Bas, we'll get you there," said Bansda, and added: "Don't worry about Naomi's pregnancy. My family will take care of her." They composed a telegram of acceptance to be sent to Arlott.

Bansda's brother-in-law was Frank Brache, one of D'Oliveira's oldest friends. Ishmail Adams was a Muslim friend, a businessman. Bansda, Brache, and Adams formed a three-man fund-raising committee.

In the next few weeks, raffles were arranged and money was raised in bars. Cricket unions up and down the land were contacted.

Along came Gerald Innes, the Western Province cricketer, who had toured Australia with Jack Cheetham's team in 1952–53. In a friendly match between the Western Province XI captained by Cheetham and a Western Province Malay Cricketers XI in 1951–52, he had been dismissed by Eric Petersen.

Now he told D'Oliveira: "Never mind the laws, Bas. We'll get you to England."

Innes whipped up a team of White cricketers and Peter van der Merwe, the future South African captain, led the players against a non-White side led by D'Oliveira. The White cricketers walked along the boundary, alongside Bansda and his men, as buckets filled with coins from the crowd. That match alone raised £150.

The total money raised was £450.

But was D'Oliveira good enough to succeed on the soft English wickets?

For help, he turned to Tom Reddick—a former Lancashire cricketer and a member of the Julien Cahn travelling team. Once, Reddick claims, he had caught George Headley's fierce hook shot off Cahn's lollypop bowling at short leg while merely trying to protect himself from fatal injury. Unfortunately, like many grand tales, this cannot be verified by the scorebooks.

Reddick ended his career playing a season for Western Province. Now he coached in Cape Town. For four nights every week for a month, Reddick coached D'Oliveira in his backyard. Before that, D'Oliveira had never been coached for even five minutes.

"League cricket is the hardest school of cricket possible," Reddick told him. "The pitches aren't particularly good. They play in all types of weather, sometimes when it's half dark and almost always without a sightscreen. You'll be up against some of the best players of the world, who have to earn their money as professionals. You'll be judged by only two standards—your own success and your club's success."

Reddick often ended the coaching sessions by inviting D'Oliveira inside for a drink. This was the first time the cricketer had ever been inside a White man's home.

1960. The Union of South Africa turned 50. British Prime Minister Harold Macmillan travelled to the land as "they celebrated the golden wedding of the Union." He was at the tail end of a visit to several of the African states.

On 3 February he addressed the Parliament in Cape Town.

"The wind of change is blowing through this continent, and whether we like it or not, this growth of national consciousness is a political fact. We must all accept it as a fact, and our national policies must take account of it."

The powerful speech would ring out through the pages of history for years to come. In essence he meant that the storm of African nationalism was rising as a process of European decolonisation. And Britain, acting in terms of both moral commitments and material interests, was now siding with the forces of African nationalism against apartheid.

This was a surprising deviation from the usual platitudes, and an embarrassing one for the South African government. Verwoerd, however, insisted that apartheid was a process of decolonisation.

Buoyed by the shot in the arm from the Winds of Change speech, the ANC called for an economic boycott in protest against the Pass Laws. But the Pan African Congress beat them to the major demonstration.

On 21 March, Sobukwe and 150 other activists went to the Orlando police station without passes. In Cape Town, over 1,500 people did the same.

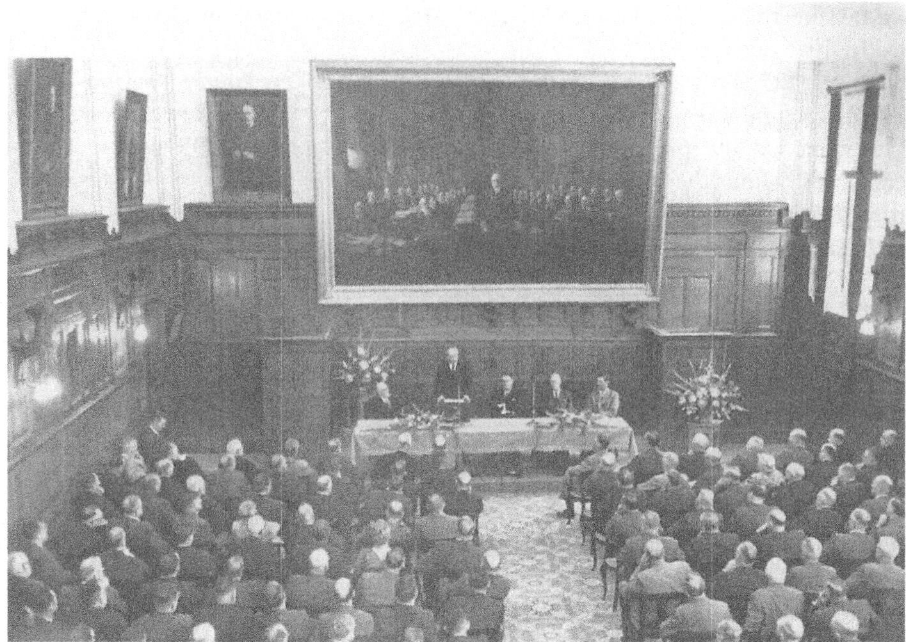

Harold Macmillan's Winds of Chamge Speech

Sharpeville, the small township outside Vereeniging, saw between 5,000 and 10,000 people surrounding the police station fence. Unarmed and peaceful, they offered themselves for arrest for not carrying passbooks.

The sheer size of the crowd unnerved the policemen. They later said stones were thrown when F-86 Sabre jets and Harvard Trainers flew low in an attempt to disperse the crowd. Supposedly three policemen were struck. The young, inexperienced officers, armed with Sten submachine guns and Lee-Enfield rifles, panicked. They opened fire, shooting randomly. Many among the crowd were shot in the backs as they turned and fled.

In all, 69 people were killed, including eight women and 10 children, while 180 were injured.

The Sharpeville massacre

In 1994, 21 March would be made The Human Rights Day in South Africa.

On 10 December 1996, President Nelson Mandela would choose Sharpeville as the place to sign the Constitution of South Africa into law.

Later, UNESCO would mark 21 March as the yearly International Day for the Elimination of Racial Discrimination.

For the time being, in 1960, the United Nations Security Council condemned the South African government—Britain and France abstaining. The South African stock market crashed through the floor.

Nelson Mandela and Albert Luthuli burnt their passes in public.

The reactions of the South African Government were fast and predictable.

The following day, Hendrik Verwoerd informed the Parliament that the Anti-Pass Resistance in Sharpeville had not been targeted at the Government. Perhaps by now he believed himself while mouthing statements as ridiculous as these. Absolute power often leads one to delusion.

On 23 March, Robert Sobukwe, leader of the Pan Africanist Congress, Albert Luthuli, and 11 others were arrested for incitement of riots.

On 24 March, all public meetings of more than 12 people were banned.

On 28 March, Cape Town was shut down as they mourned the deaths.

On 30 March, a general strike paralysed Cape Town. With the police brutally attacking townships, 30,000 Black workers marched into the city, demanding that their leaders be released from the prison. Over 2,000 people were detained as the government declared a state of emergency.

Mandela burns his pass

In the midst of all this mayhem, on 29 March 1960, Basil D'Oliveira said farewell to Naomi and the other members of his family at the Cape Town International Airport and flew to London.

26 MAKING MERRY IN THE MIDLANDS

John Kay, the cricket correspondent of *Manchester Evening News,* was there to meet D'Oliveira as he cleared immigration. He had taken a day off work to travel down to London.

At the immigration, the wide-eyed young man from the Cape looked for the queue marked for Blacks and Coloureds. They spent the night at Arlott's London flat.

The next day, as they were walking down the platform to board the train to Manchester, D'Oliveira looked apprehensive. "Which is the separate carriage for my people?" he asked.

"Basil, you're in a different country," Kay replied. "Things are not done that way here."

Kay informed Arlott later that his protégé had dined on the train. He could not get over being allowed to eat and travel with White people.

Middleton had arranged a dinner for their new professional at the local golf club. D'Oliveira could not quite fathom that the White men were celebrating his being in their midst. Awkward, shy, and inwardly terrified, he spent the evening glued to the television set in the corner. A football match was being telecast. South Africa was still without any television.

Clarence and Mary Lord warmly welcomed him at 53 Rochdale Road. They would be his landlord and landlady. They tucked him up in bed with a hot water bottle and "seemingly hundreds of blankets" telling him to sleep as long as he wanted.

As days went by, D'Oliveira took his time to adjust to the new world. Living as a first-class citizen was new, very new—something he had never experienced before. But at the same time, he missed Naomi terribly and missed the familiar world of Cape Town.

The English summer was wet and miserable. To him the conditions were more than difficult, they were totally alien. He had never played on grass, never experienced this dampness, never seen the ball swing this way.

He was in exalted company. Hedley Verity had played for Middleton as professional. Roy Gilchrist had played there very recently. Garry Sobers played for Radcliffe. The history of the league was filled with extraordinary cricketers. He was supposed to guide the side as a professional; to not only perform better than everyone else but also coach them in the intricacies of the game. But the moment he went out for his first nets, it was evident that all the other cricketers of the club knew more about the game than him.

For a while, he could not make any sense of the cricket or its social dimension. He did not drink. He sipped orange juice at the pub as the rest downed their beers. He walked a yard behind the rest of the group on their walk to the pub and back. At first, he even asked teammate Paul Rocca where the Coloured dressing room was.

His first opponents were Heywood with West Indian wicket-keeper batsman Clairmonte Depeiaza the professional. Depeiaza tore into the bowling scoring 110 out of 196 for six. D'Oliveira was impressive with 3 for 45 from 19 overs. He batted decently as well, scoring 27 before being caught on the boundary.

But the second game got him just eight with the bat. The teammates were patient, even helpful. Some of them advised him on facing the moving ball, when it was D'Oliveira who was supposed to do all the coaching.

A 70 against Werneth was encouraging, but then he fell for 13 against Rochdale and 9 against Littleborough. Against Radcliffe he managed 45 unconvincing runs while the rampaging Garry Sobers picked up 7 wickets. The following match saw him get only 3.

175 runs with the bat in 7 innings. Middleton had lost four of them. No one said so, but D'Oliveira knew he was miserably failing to match normal expectations. He was also facing problems at his day job as a printer at the *Middleton Advertiser.* The machinery was more

advanced than Croxley's. Moreover, the weeks were spent in trying to forget the disappointments of Saturday.

He wanted to go home.

Arlott and Kay discussed his fortunes during their weekly phone calls with increasing apprehension.

It was Eric Price who provided the watershed moment. A 42-year-old veteran, he had played two seasons for Lancashire and two more for Essex just after the war. He was the most experienced cricketer of Middleton.

"Bazz, your method is wrong," he informed the confused young man. Price explained that in England the batsman let the ball come to him. He had to play the balls later—much later than he did in Cape Town. D'Oliveira later remembered that there was no jealousy or scorn in Price, just interest.

As Oborne says, "If Price had been a different sort of person, or Middleton a different type of club, there is a reason to believe that by the end of the 1960 season Basil D'Oliveira would have packed his bags, returned to South Africa and never been heard of again."

D'Oliveira did as Price said. He watched the others as well, just as he had done all those years from the 'cage'. The change was astounding.

From 24 June, his scores for the rest of the season were 91, 48, 28, 72, 53 not out, 72, 88 not out, 5, 21, 55, 47, 55 not out, 6, 93 not out, 7, and 14.

Poor start notwithstanding, he topped the Central Lancashire League batting averages, his 930 runs at 48.95 pipping Garry Sobers and his 1,113 runs at 48.39.

He also picked up 71 wickets at 11.72.

Wisden appreciated the performance, noting: "Middleton had every reason to be satisfied with their gamble in signing the non-European, Basil D'Oliveira, from South Africa."

His non-European South African origins were still difficult to get used to.

However, the White composition of the South African Test side was so axiomatic that D'Oliveira's performance was not produced as a contrast to the rather prolonged struggle that the Springboks had encountered during the English summer.

D'Oliveira returned home in triumph, his contract extended for two years by Middleton, his return airfare, the passage money, and the accommodation of Naomi and the expected baby already paid for. On his return to Cape Town, he was driven in an open blue American car up Adderley Street to the City Hall to be received by the Mayor. The streets were lined with cheering crowds, the procession led by a pipe band. D'Oliveira wrote to Arlott, "Naturally the Boere (I hope you can pronounce the Afrikaner word Mr Arlott) were aghast that a darkie could get such an ovation."

Tom Reddick had to get a permit to attend the function held in D'Oliveira's honour. Being a White man, he could make a speech, but he could not eat, drink, or sit with them. He arrived after they had all eaten, murmured 'Thank you' in way of speech, and sat. No one cared.

His son was born a month after his return. D'Oliveira named him Damian, after his enormous benefactor and fund-raiser, the reporter and barman Damoo Bansda.

27 WE HAVE TO WAITE FOR BLACK AND WHITE TO PLAY TOGETHER

Saturday, 9 April 1960, was blessed with a clear sunny afternoon. In Johannesburg, it was time for the Rand Easter Show, the most important agricultural and industrial showcase in South Africa, held every year since 1907.

Hendrik Verwoerd was attending the event. Just before viewing the prize-winning cattle in the arena, he made a speech, concluding in his high-pitched voice: "We shall become nobody's corpse, we shall fight for our existence and we shall survive."

After a while, he turned from the prize bull he had been admiring and made his way up to the President's Box to sit and watch the animals parade around the arena.

Sitting near the box was David Pratt, a rich White English businessman and farmer from the Magaliesberg, near Pretoria. As the Prime Minister resumed his seat, Pratt took out a .22 pistol fired two shots at point-blank range. One bullet perforated Verwoerd's right cheek and the second his right ear.

Pratt was soon overpowered and taken into custody. Rushed to the hospital, Verwoerd recovered without serious injury. In his hearing Pratt claimed he had been shooting 'the epitome of apartheid' but to injure, not kill. On examination, he was found to be of unsound mind. He was admitted to a mental hospital in Bloemfontein, where he committed suicide on 1 October 1961.

The day before the attack on Verwoerd, both ANC and PAC had been declared illegal by the government. On 4 May, Robert Sobukwe was sentenced to three years of imprisonment.

The attempted assassination had no link to all that, it was the work of a deranged man.

However, even some of the National Party leaders maintained that the attempt exacerbated Verwoerd's despotic tendencies. The Prime Minister was always considered headstrong. And now, even his colleagues had trouble convincing him to change some of the stances. There had been efforts to convince him to abolish the pass-book system after Sharpeville. However, the Prime Minister's complete faith in his policies were forged stronger by the firing from point-blank range.

It is Jackie McGlew at the helm again as the South Africans tour England. As they land at London via Amsterdam on 17 April, protesters gather. One placard says *Apartheid isn't Cricket.* Another declares *Sharpeville wasn't Cricket.* Yet another says *Ban Racism in Sport.* One is pretty damning: *Sharpeville Was Murder.* Chants and slogans are hurled at the cricketers as they make their way through the airport.

Charles Fortune dismisses the protesters in his account as a "tattered and bleak little conglomeration of chilly looking adolescents."

Fortune is not amused by the motley gathering. "For weeks before the South African team set off, our newspapers in the Union carried stories of the opposition rife in England to the visit of the Springboks. Priests and politicians, scholars and undergraduates had, it seemed, gone on record and into action to stop the cricket tour."

Now, seeing lukewarm dissent in the airport, he is scathing in his criticism of the protesters. MCC, he says, has rightly discerned that England *en masse* will have none of it. "These demonstrators were no more than the cats-paws of certain churchmen who had seized on the visit of the cricketers as an opportunity to gain for themselves some public notice."

However, at Cambridge University, students and others hand out pamphlets at the entrance to Fenners.

At a press conference, manager Dudley Nourse asserts that the team is there to play cricket and politics should not be linked to them in any way.

Charles Fortune

Fortune's diatribe against the churchmen had its reasons. Rev Trevor Huddleston's *Naught for Your Comfort* and his 1956 views of stopping sporting contact with South Africa were well known. Rev Nicholas Stacey had refused to preach the traditional 'Sportsmen's Service' before the Edgbaston Test.

Besides, there was David Sheppard.

The Duke of Norfolk had approached him, asking whether he would captain his team in the opening match of the tour. By 1960, Sheppard was convinced that he would not turn out against an all-White South African side. He refused. However, he was still plagued by the question of whether he should make his refusal public.

Sheppard wrote to Joost de Blank, his former bishop. At the current moment, de Blank was the Archbishop of Cape Town. De Blank wrote back: "It would do a tremendous amount for our cause here."

As a member of the MCC Committee, Sheppard informed MCC President Harry Altham about his decision. Altham asked him to reconsider. Sheppard says that he sat on the embankment, reading the Scripture, wondering what to do. Isaiah 58:1 convinced him. When Sheppard told Altham that his mind was made up, the MCC President arranged for him to disclose his intention of going public to the MCC Committee.

There was an immediate explosion from Lt Col RT Stanyforth, who protested the "political and religious statement." However, Altham stood by Sheppard. The former England captain made a brief statement of his decision to BBC News.

Not everyone had Fortune's capacity for casual dismissal of protests in the aftermath of Sharpeville.

However, all through the decade, Sheppard would fall out over his views with some of his teammates—the principal antagonist being Peter May.

The South Africans are plagued with troubles from the beginning. Russell Endean has stayed behind, unwilling to leave his wife alone in a country to which she is still unaccustomed. The management has a strict 'no wives' rule this time.

And then Geoff Griffin's action is called by Frank Lee and John Langridge in the match against MCC.

Proceeding to Edgbaston for the first Test, they keep things tight as England crawl to 175 for 3 on a painstaking first day. Neil Adcock, bowling persistently on the stumps, picks up five wickets as England suffer a lower middle order collapse. A total of 292 is hardly satisfactory.

But the visiting batsmen are brittle against the famed pairing of Trueman and Statham. The ageing bowling powerhouse of Adcock and Tayfield try to get South Africa back into the game, but the 310 runs required to win prove too much, especially after veteran McLean falls leg before to Trueman second ball of the fifth morning.

Cowdrey, Dexter, Subba Row, MJK Smith. Waite writes: "Four of the main English batsmen are non-professionals, a fact that must have made Lord Hawke swivel merrily in his grave."

D'Oliveira perhaps wonders how it is that the Springboks have no problem playing against Subba Row in England, and yet cannot contemplate reinforcing their tottering unit with a non-white South African plundering runs a few miles away.

Adelaine Hain was by now the person for all non-Whites to contact whenever they fell afoul of the police. With PAC and ANC becoming illegal, Liberal Party remained the only legal Anti-Apartheid body in Pretoria. Black membership swelled. Branch meetings were held in the living room. Wal and some like-minded friends collected Black members from their townships and ferried them to the gatherings.

At Lord's, Charles Fortune has more reasons to be upset. A section of the press box bursts out in cheers when Griffin is called by Umpire Lee. Fortune compares the cheers to the jubilation of a mob when a young lad is sent to the gallows for a minor crime.

Griffin is called 11 times in all, but he ends the innings in sensational fashion. MJK Smith, on 99, looks for a dabbed single with the field closing in. The resulting snick is held by Waite. That is the last ball of Griffin's over.

The next over brings 13 runs and the half-century of Peter Walker. In comes Griffin again and flicks Walker's bails with a full-length ball. Trueman walks in and heaves the first ball. His leg stump goes flying—a hat-trick split in two overs. Griffin bowls only four more balls in his Test career. Cowdrey declares at that score, 362 for 8. Statham uses the Lord's slope to capture 6 for 63 in the first innings, and 5 for 34 in the second.

Waite, a Capricorn, reads in the forecasts that he will be affected by a mystery. When he is given out leg before padding up to a Statham delivery on the final day, he has no doubt that the curious decision is the mystery hinted at in the astrology columns.

As the Test finishes at 2.30, an exhibition match takes place from 3.30. Griffin is called again, this time by Umpire Syd Buller. He bowls under arm which is again called by Buller because he has not informed the batsman. Somehow the over is finished.

Griffin plays the next match against Lancashire as a specialist batsman, scoring 65 not out. He does not bowl another ball on the tour.

In February 1960, a constellation of stellar individuals from all walks of life assembled in a deputation to grace the Prime Minister's office as protests against the all-White All Blacks tour of South Africa continued. As Rolland O'Regan, the founder of Citizen All Black Tour Association (CABTA), accused the New Zealand Rugby Football Union of indefensible racial discrimination against the Maori people, the Bishop of Aotearoal, the Right Reverend WN Panapa, led the Maori members of the deputation in a haka. Supporters of the movement included New Zealand cricket captain Walter Hadlee, Maori rugby union star George Nepia and mystery writer Ngaio Marsh.

After the Sharpeville massacre, the protests gained further momentum. In mid-April, the All Black trials in Wellington were disrupted by about 15 protesters walking on to the ground and sitting on the grass near the halfway line.

On the eve of the departure of the teams thousands demonstrated in both Wellington and Auckland. As the TEAL Electra airliner took off from Whenuapai with the All Black team on board, a group of student demonstrators caught the security by surprise by rushing across the tarmac and shaking their fists. The aircraft passed just a plane's width from them.

At the other extreme, backrower Red Conway was so keen to tour South Africa that he amputated the injured third finger of his right hand rather than risk medical delays.

At Trent Bridge South African woes continue. After a moderate score of 287 by England, Trueman and Statham rout the visitors for 88. When they follow on, McGlew tries a rescue act with a dogged innings. But as O'Linn calls for a single after a push to the cover, bowler Moss moves across to field and the South African skipper is obstructed. He is run out as Statham's throw shatters the wicket. Just 24 runs remain to be scored on the final day, all 10 wickets standing. Rain pelts down and play cannot start till 3. Mindful of the threatening skies, the Springboks bowl with great purpose. England make it with eight wickets to spare. The series is done and dusted. The batting is as brittle as they come. D'Oliveira is just a train ride away, but no one thinks of calling him.

Prominent liberals and anti-apartheid activists were detained in Pretoria and the rest of South Africa in the aftermath of Sharpeville. This included a number of people close to the Hains, many on first name terms. For the first time, the Hain house phones were tapped, mails were anticipated, and Security Police cars stood outside their premises all day.

In June, Adelaine Hain was informed that her name was in a list of people to be arrested and that she should leave immediately to a home unconnected to the Liberals. The children arrived home from school to learn that an impromptu holiday had been planned and were duly exhilarated. But Peter, being the oldest, was told the reason. They drove 14 hours to arrive in Port Alfred, their grandparents' place.

While in Port Alfred, Peter accompanied Wal to Eastern Cape and Natal to meet Alan Paton. The 10-year-old did not really know of the writer's stature. However, he remembered something that Paton said that day, "I am an all-or-something person."

Later, this was to become the watchword for his own political activities.

A traditionally wet Manchester means two days are lost. At last one of the batting pillars finds his touch. McLean scores 109, but the match cannot be brought to life in spite of the best efforts.

On the fourth day of the Test, Brian Chapman of *Daily Mirror* suggests that the South Africans take on an International XI drawn from the non-White cricketers of the Northern cricket leagues at The Oval. The side he recommends comprises Frank Worrell, Conrad Hunte, Hanif Mohammad, Garry Sobers, Stanley Jayasinghe, Ralph Legall, Dattu Phadkar, Chandu Borde, Wes Hall, Basil D'Oliveira, Sonny Ramadhin, and Tom Dewdney.

Such a match, of course, does not take place. But one cannot help but wonder about the international issue that would have exploded if the South Africans had come face-to-face with D'Oliveira in 1960 rather than 1968–69.

D'Oliveira did play alongside some of the South Africans on that tour, during a benefit game on a Sunday for Eddie Fuller, the former South African seam bowler then playing for Cumberland. Fuller himself invited D'Oliveira. This was the first time the Coloured South African cricketer came across some of the White Springboks. One of them, Trevor Goddard, became a close friend.

D'Oliveira top scored that day with 50-odd. At one stage, he batted with Peter Carlstein, the South African batsman. Later he confessed that whatever Carlstein did in that innings, he tried to do better.

In August 1960, the emergency was lifted and the Hains returned home from their 'holiday'. Soon after that, the house was raided by the Security Police for the first of many times.

Neil Adcock

Finally, at The Oval, the South African unit comes together. Adcock takes six and the England batting manages 155 through bad light and regular interruptions.

None of the Springbok batsmen hit a ton. Goddard comes closest but falls a run short, snicking Statham to slip. But they end 264 runs ahead with two days to go.

However, Pullar and Cowdrey add 290 for the first wicket and England finish the fourth day at 380 for 4.

South Africa are set 216 to win in three hours. Goddard scores 28 in two. They end at 97 for 4.

The series finishes 3-0 in favour of England.

"This has been a punishing summer," writes Jackie McGlew.

"Trumanised and Stathamised," summarises John Waite. While some young South Africans do pick up other bits of grand experience that comes with an England tour, others don't. As Waite puts it: "Two youngest batsmen in the 1960s Springbok side, Colin Wesley and Peter Carlstein, were discussing where they would go on leave after one of their matches in the west of England. 'Think I will take a look at Stratford-on-Avon', said one of them, I shan't tell you which. 'What's there—an aircraft factory?' asked the other."

1960. At Eindhovensche Golfclub, Valkenswaard, Papwa Sewgolum won the Dutch Open for the second year running.

Returning from the England tour, John Waite writes his account of the visit in a book curiously named *Perchance to Bowl.*

Chapter 3 is titled *Why White Cricketers Do Not Play Non-White Cricketers in South Africa*

Waite questions David Sheppard's stance a little curiously. "*We did wonder whether he had forgotten the attitude Jesus Christ adopted in regard to Mary Magdalene on the occasion of their original meeting."*

Referring to the pamphlets at Cambridge, Waite mentions Dick Whitington turning to one of the students who offered him a pamphlet saying: "No, thank you. I'm becoming a little bored with all this. Just what do you think you're achieving?" And then Waite goes on to say that he considers MCC Assistant Secretary Billy Griffith's gesture of sharing the bus trip from London Airport to Park Lane Hotel as more Christian than the 1960 David Sheppard. *"It sprang from a far more enlightened mind, from a mind and heart that had shared in the agony of Arnhem, from a mind and heart that is completely devoted to 'playing cricket' in every sense of the term."*

Sharing the battlefield and fighting on the same side as the South African Whites and therefore standing beside them while the world lambasted them for apartheid. This feeling of camaraderie was also confessed and voiced by JBG Thomas, the rugby reporter of the *Western Mail,* who documented the torrid demonstration-ridden Springbok visit of 1969–70 in his book *Springbok Invasion.* We will come across that later.

The premises of the Old Boys' Club, with Coloured men facelessly flitting about serving chhota pegs of whiskey, is too precious and nostalgic a corner of the world to abandon.

John Waite

Having criticised Sheppard, Waite turns to the policy: "*We will be delighted to make a cricket tour of the West Indies, Pakistan and India, provided we would be judged upon our actions on such a tour.*

"No South African sportsman [...] has any objection to competing with or against a Coloured man outside South Africa. From a purely personal viewpoint no South African sportsman has any objection to competing with, or against, a Coloured man inside South Africa [...] The real reason why White and Black or Coloured South Africans do not normally play with or against each other is not a personal reason, it is a political reason. It is the Black and Coloured people who have been most prone to mix politics with sports."

Alluding to the Black organisations who prevented the visit of the West Indian team the previous year, Waite explains: "*The real reason why White and Black and Coloured do not compete against each other in South Africa springs from a belief, right or wrong, that the Black and Coloured public of South Africa is not equipped or ready for multi-racial sport any more than the Black and Coloured public of the Union is ready to govern South Africa or to manage its industries.*

"If a White boxer were to batter a Negro boxer in a bloody battle at Johannesburg's Rand Stadium before a multi-racial crowd there could be savage repercussions which might result in severe loss of both Black and White lives. If a Black boxer were to batter a White boxer before such an attendance, I for one would not wish to have my wife along. It is the Black and Coloured people of South Africa who must prove that they can take a victory and a licking before inter-racial and multi-racial sport can be safely conducted in South Africa."

After a lengthy discourse, he concludes: *"No, I do not believe that the time is quite ripe yet for inter- or multi-racial sport on a big scale in South Africa. Many of us Whites only wish that it were."*

And of course, he goes on to say that there was no non-White sportsman in South Africa who could replace any White sportsman in any sporting side. Rich indeed, given Lobo Abed was generally accepted to be a far better wicketkeeper batsman than Waite himself.

The lines are repeated here only to summarise the parochial, patronising, supremacist, and myopic view that the White bubble continued to proudly profess and project during those times. And this is 1961 we are talking about, not 1861.

It is also pertinent that Waite did not write the full book himself. It was ghost-written—officially termed 'edited'—by Dick Whitington, the biographer of Keith Miller, Lindsay Hassett, and a prolific writer of cricket books. While Whitington is notorious for his cavalier approach towards facts, this collaboration also symbolises the attitude of condoning camaraderie that existed between a large part of the White cricketing nations.

Elsewhere, things were not ideal either.

In February 1960, four African American college students in Greensboro, North Carolina refused to leave a Woolworth's "Whites only" lunch counter without being served.

Nine months later, in November, six-year-old Ruby Bridges had to be escorted by four armed federal marshals as she became the first student to integrate William Frantz Elementary School in New Orleans.

In the South African summer, D'Oliveira celebrated his triumphant return from the Central Lancashire League by leading a Western Province Invitation side, called Baslings after his own name, on a triumphant tour of Natal. He hit 117 and captured 5 for 23 against Northern District at Ladysmith.

28 DETENTION TIME

In October 1960, the referendum organised by National Party asked whether the Union of South Africa should become a Republic. Of course, the question and the votes were restricted to the Whites.

"You need friends. Don't let Verwoerd lose them all," campaigned the United Party. However, only in Natal was there an overwhelmingly negative response. Orange Free State more or less clinched the issue with 76.72% voting in favour. Overall, there were 52.29% who voted for.

In March 1961, South Africa announced its intention of withdrawing from the Commonwealth on becoming a republic.

On 31 May, the shift took place.

The 1961 Republic of South Africa Constitution Act states: *"God is credited with having given South Africa, 'this their own' land, to a specific people."*

Yes, South Africa was an anachronism.

This queered the cricketing pitch.

Rule 5 of the ICC regulations provided that membership of an organisation would cease if a country was no longer part of the British Commonwealth. Under the constitution of ICC, there could no longer be official Test matches contested by the country. Forget the international outcry against the apartheid policies, the rules of the governing body of cricket themselves were against South Africa playing Test cricket. In fact, South Africa's invitation to the Empire Games at Perth was withdrawn a month after leaving the Commonwealth.

Dennis Brutus pressed home the point by saying that South Africa should never have had Test status, as they never represented the whole country.

SACA requested a change in the ICC regulations. This was met with a resolution to defer the decision for a year, following a vote in which England, Australia, and New Zealand were pitted against the non-White country boards—West Indies, India, and Pakistan. The vote was split along colour lines. The decision was to continue the existing relations unofficially, the Test matches to be decreed unofficial.

However, the White countries, Australia, England and New Zealand, would continue to consider the representative matches played against South Africa as regular Test matches. CO Medworth of *Natal Mercury* was one of the cricket commentators of the country who condemned the non-White cricket boards of West Indies, India, and Pakistan for "allowing politics to encroach on the noble game of cricket."

In those days, cricket could be used to promote civilisation in only one direction.

In South Africa, February 1961 saw the first instance of non-White cricket on a provincial basis when a combined team of Coloured, African, and Indians from Eastern Province travelled to Cape Town to play a similar combined team of Western Province.

SACBOC had turned over a new non-racial leaf.

In the midst of all this, one Coloured and one White South African family underwent experiences that were generally reserved for the other group.

Basil D'Oliveira returned to Middleton with Naomi and baby Damian. As it had been in the case of Basil, the reality of being a first-class citizen came as a shock to Naomi. She was overwhelmed by simple gestures of appreciation and kindness on the part of White people.

In cinema halls, she felt everyone was looking at her during the interval, wondering what right she had to be there among the privileged. She gripped Basil's arm so hard that there would be bruises the next day.

When fellow cricketers visited him at home, Basil sat with them in the living room. Naomi withdrew into the kitchen, unsure how to react. When a lady behind the counter in a shop wished her well as she was "the wife of our pro", she cried all the way home.

The D'Oliveiras moved to their own house, 13 Radcliffe Street, close to the cricket ground. The other Middleton cricketers ganged up to help. It was a simple place, but Naomi could not believe her turn of fortune.

Eventually, she did fit in.

All the while, D'Oliveira was scoring runs and taking wickets.

In March 1961, the four-and-a-half-year Treason Trial came to an end. The accused were found not guilty.

Oliver Tambo left the country to ensure that ANC survived outside South Africa. Nelson Mandela went underground before he could be predictably rearrested. He travelled the country disguised as chauffeur, gardener, or chef, popping up in ANC meetings and giving interviews to White journalists. He was soon nicknamed the Black Pimpernel.

Robert Resha, Patrick Molaoa, and Nelson Mandela arrive for yet another session of the mammoth Treason Trial

In May 1961, a caring hand shook 11-year-old Peter Hain awake in the wee hours of the morning. As he opened his eyes expecting one of his parents, he saw the middle-aged family friend Nan van Reenen.

"Peter, your parents have been put in jail," she said.

Drowsy, confused, Peter tried to grasp what had taken place. From the deep recesses, perhaps from a combination of the experiences of his few tender years and his genes, something whispered: "Stay calm. Carry on."

Nan informed him that with fellow Liberal Party activists Maritz van der Berg and her son

Colyn, Ad and Wal had been putting up posters of the 'Stay-at-Home' protest called by Nelson Mandela. The Security Police had turned up and detained them.

It was not unexpected. For the last several months there had been constant vigilance of the security police, and the phones had been tapped. Nevertheless, it was a shock.

Soon, his grandmother arrived. The Black maid of the family, Eva Matjeka, took charge with her able hands. A fellow activist lady baked a huge meringue cake to cheer the kids up. Peter and the rest of the kids went to school as usual. However, he had grown up overnight. His little sister Jo-anne cut holes through her mom's petticoat, putting her arms through them, so that she could feel her presence.

Ad and Wal were among the first people to be detained under the new 12-Day Law. Wal, Maritz and Colyn were put in a cell in the Pretoria Local jail in relatively tolerable conditions. Ad was locked up alone in a large echoing hall in Pretoria Central Prison. The wardress made her flesh creep, especially when she came up to watch her take a bath. She decided on using the more private wash basin. Through the stairwell, she heard the screams of Black woman prisoners being assaulted.

Ad had also secretly chewed up and spat out a leaflet urging people to go on strike and stay at home—the one piece of incriminating evidence that could have led to charges. Having recently watched *From Russia with Love,* Peter was fascinated by this cool cloak-and-dagger manoeuvre.

It was a relief for the kids to come back from school and find their parents back home, Wal with a newly grown beard. However, their struggle was to continue. Wal was forced into unemployment. For a while they had to get by on donation from an unnamed Liberal Party member and on account from sympathetic shopkeepers.

July 1961. The Verwoerd government imposed the Indemnity Act. It was no longer permitted for the courts to hear any criminal charges or civil claims against the government, its leaders or its employees for actions taken between 21 March 1960 and 5 July 1961. The 224 civil claims for damages served against the Minister of Justice by the victims of Sharpeville and their families amounted to Rand 800,000. The act ensured that all but a very few of the claims were nullified.

D'Oliveira completed his second league season with 1,073 runs at a colossal 59.61. With the ball he was not as successful, with only 31 wickets at 23.67. Towards the end of the season, he met cricket writer, broadcaster, and the mixed-tour impresario Ron Roberts. Actually, it was his old benefactor John Kay who introduced them.

The meeting would go on to have a huge bearing on his story.

On 13 to 15 September 1961 a meeting of the Australian Cricket Board was held at the Cricket House. In the meeting a piece of correspondence was discussed. Dr Yusuf Dadoo, the South African Marxist, had written on behalf of the South African United Front. An unsuccessful body, this was formed for a brief while with the intention of reconciling ANC and PAC. Dadoo's letter requested Australia to take no action on the proposed move for the continuation of SACA's ICC membership.

The meeting was attended by the new Board member Clem Jones, a science major in geology and the Lord Mayor of Brisbane. For the next decade and more, he would be the most vocal anti-apartheid conscience in the Australian Cricket Board.

In October 1961, ANC President Albert Luthuli was awarded the Nobel Peace Prize—the first person of African heritage and nationality to be so awarded (Ralph J Bunche, who won the Prize in 1950, was African American). Luthuli's ban was temporarily revoked to allow him and his wife to travel to Oslo to accept the award. Nationalist publication *Die Transvaler* described the award as "an inexplicable pathological phenomenon." In his acceptance speech, Luthuli said, "South African Minister of Interior announced that [...] I did not deserve the Nobel Peace Prize for 1960. Such is the magic of a peace prize, that it has even managed to produce an issue on which I agree with the Government of South Africa."

In November, Nelson Mandela became the leader of the armed ANC wing, *Umkhonto we Sizwe* (Spear of the Nation). Apartheid had not really been affected by more than a decade of non-violent protests. It was time for a different tack.

There were firm opponents to the new direction—even among the staunch anti-apartheid activists like Walter Hain. Mandela clarified his stance. *Umkhonto* intended to perform sabotage with strict instructions not to harm individuals.

On 27 December, the first inter-provincial SACBOC tournament for non-Whites was held in Johannesburg. The president, Harrison Butshingi, wrote in the tournament brochure: "We have shown the world that we, Non-White sportsmen of South Africa, are a unified group, and that we entertain no racial barriers in our ranks."

In December 1961, *Umkhonto* began a campaign of placing bombs in government offices, post offices, electric substations, and similar locations, carrying out some 200 attacks in 18 months.

The Hains were amazed that they were able to place some of the bombs in Pretoria offices where all government workers were White. Peter Magano explained with a smile: "Don't forget, the messenger boys are still Black."

On 9 December, a tall 16-year-old left-handed batsman made his debut in the Currie Cup, scoring 54 for Eastern Province against Border. By the end of the next month, Graeme Pollock would have scored his first century against Transvaal B.

On 12 December 1961, Graeme's elder brother Peter captured 6 for 38 on his Test debut at Kingsmead, Durban, clinching a close 30-run win against New Zealand.

29 SABOTAGE AND SANCTIONS

It is Peter Pollock who opens the bowling with Neil Adcock in the final Test at Port Elizabeth. The combination of youth and experience soon removes both the Kiwi openers with just 20 runs on the board.

Paul Barton has dislocated his shoulder trying to go for a catch in the Johannesburg Test. At practice he has tried to convince everyone that he is all right. But he has not been able to drive full tosses beyond silly mid-off. Captain John Reid has included him in the side as a giant gamble. He plays a gem—109 with 20 boundaries, most of them beautiful drives. Highpoint of a career with a Test average of 20 and first-class numbers just a little better.

The tail wags. The score registered is 275.

1962. Nelson Mandela left the country to be trained in military operations in Algeria. At the pan-African conference in Addis Ababa, his speech was sparkling: "The freedom movement in South Africa believes that hard and swift blows should be delivered with the full weight of the masses of the people, who alone furnish us with one absolute guarantee that the freedom flames now burning in the country shall never be extinguished."

On 5 August, back in South Africa, he was driving through the Natal countryside dressed in a chauffeur's uniform when he was arrested at Howick. His life on the run ended after 17 months.

Dick Motz captures two quick wickets but has to leave the field with a pulled muscle between the ribs. Jack Alabaster and John Reid bowl spin from both ends, the latter switching to off-spin because of a bad knee. But the wicket helps them. It is 115 for 6, and the hosts are in trouble. Captain Jackie McGlew enters at No 8. Injuries—the perennial tale of a long series. McGlew has an injured thumb and a troubled shoulder. Alabaster and Reid bowl their spin. McGlew sticks around. The faster bowlers come on, but they pitch the ball up. Reid says he does not want McGlew to suffer more injury—more like charity than courtesy. The Springbok captain remains not out with 28. The innings ends at 190.

However, things heat up during the last hour and a half of the second day. Sparling is caught off what seems to be a bump ball, but not before having his ribs broken by a ball from Pollock. The South Africans don't reciprocate the fellow feeling of the New Zealanders. Adcock and Pollock make the ball whistle around the heads of the batsmen. In the first innings, they had bowled bouncers at tail enders Alabaster and Bartlett. At the end of the day, Gordon Leggat, the New Zealand manager, issues a statement saying that the hosts, including McGlew, could not expect that sort of chivalry the second time.

The Sabotage Act widened the definition of sabotage to include strikes, trade union activities and writing slogans on walls. The maximum penalty was hanging, the minimum five years of imprisonment. The burden of proof was reversed—the accused was assumed to be guilty until proven innocent. Publications opposing the Government could be fined R20,000.

This Act extended the powers of the Minister of Justice, John Vorster, enabling him to ban any individual or organisation. Suspected saboteurs could be put under house arrest without trial and prohibited from attending social gatherings.

Dowling and Reid come together at 50 for 3. Reid is cheered when he opens his account after a long vigil. But the South Africans are bowling short and rather wide. They don't use the spinner Bromfield even though the wicket is taking definite turn. Too bad Tayfield is no longer there to win such matches.

Adcock bowls with a long-on. South Africa want to play for a draw and win the series 2-1. This is not impossible in the four-day Test in spite of smallish first innings scores.

Dowling has to battle almost five hours for his 78. Reid makes 69 in 201 minutes. Goofey Lawrence cleans up the tail and New Zealand total 228.

314 to win. Catches go down and the hosts end the day at 38 for no loss.

That was the year that the United Nations called for political and economic sanctions against South Africa. In a combined effort, Martin Luther King and Chief Albert Luthuli launched a Human Rights Campaign in which they appealed for Action against Apartheid.

"If I lived in South Africa today, I would join Chief Luthuli as he says to his people, 'Break this law'. Don't take this unjust pass system where you must have passes. Take them and tear them and throw them away," voiced King.

Eddie Barlow, the young bespectacled opening batsman resembling Billy Bunter, plays a solid and attractive knock. Farrer scores just 10 but stays long enough with him to add 57.

McGlew walks out in his final Test innings, cheered by the crowd and applauded by the New Zealanders. Motz even sends him a no-ball. 100 comes up with Barlow and McGlew together. Just before lunch Reid—mixing spinners with off-cutters now—gets one past Barlow's blade and bowls him.

The match, however, is decided after the break. Noel McGregor, fielding some 60 yards from the bat at square leg, hits the stumps at the bowler's end to catch McGlew short. 26 in his final innings. Waite is taken brilliantly at leg gully by Dowling off one of Reid's off-cutters. McLean is bowled by an Alabaster leg-break while defending. Tiger Lance is snapped up behind the wicket. 142 for 6.

But there are young guns among the Springboks who want to win. Rhodesian Colin Bland is a fantastic batsman and great fielder. His 32, including a six, takes the hosts to 193 before Reid catches him plumb. Lawrence falls after a dogged 17, foxed by Alabaster. 199 for 8.

In 1962, after years of making clear that separate White and Black teams to play White and Black countries were not permissible, FIFA finally banned South Africa. The continued support of the FIFA President Sir Stanley Rous had kept the South African Football Association protected by official blessing, but eventually, the pressures became too great for him to ignore.

Adcock and Pollock—the former playing what will be his final Test, the latter his first series. Neither wants to lose. They score at brisk pace. 60 runs added in just 49 minutes. Pollock drives handsomely. Adcock reaches double figures for only the fourth time in Tests, goes past his career best of 17 and moves into the 20s.

At 4:30 Reid summons Motz. Yes, he can bowl bouncers to Adcock. Tit for tat and all that. The first ball flies off the pitch, high over Adcock's head. Arty Dick has to spring and stretch to collect it. The second is short again and it does not bounce that much. Adcock, taking evasive action, sees it whizz past his hip. The third ball is pitched well up, straight. Adcock is already near square leg. His stumps are all over the place. The fast bowler goes back, not very amused. As he walks he wags a finger at Motz. The New Zealander mutters something about seeing him in Christchurch.

South Africa will visit in early 1964, but Adcock will not be in the scheme of things.

Sir Stanley Rous was not an exception. Most international sporting bodies were still operated as exclusive clubs with men at the helm for whom the sun over the Empire still suggested mid-noon.

Marquis of Exeter, for example, was the President of the International Amateur Athletics Federation. In that august body, the 37 White nations had 244 votes, and 99 Black countries had 195.

The all-important position of the President of the International Olympic Committee was held by Avery Brundage, former American athlete and construction tycoon. He had fought tooth and nail against the anti-Nazi movements that had attempted to boycott the Berlin Olympics of 1936.

Dennis Brutus, the activist poet and head of the South African Sports Association, had repeatedly sent him letters about the South African situation. He never received a response.

Brutus later said that when he finally collared him in an Olympic convention, Brundage informed him that he never replied to organisations that did not have 'Olympic' in the title.

Brutus, under several banning orders and confined to Johannesburg, now formed the organisation SAN-ROC (South African Non-Racial Olympic Committee). Brundage found it too presumptuous.

Adcock bowled by Motz

An hour to go. 259 for 9. Harry Bromfield, the off-spinner, comes out to bat. Pollock decides to try and bat out time. Runs are not required any more, Bromfield scores none. But Pollock picks up a few as they doggedly refuse to give their wickets away.

Ten minutes pass. 15. 20. 35. 30. 35. The clock is ticking.

And then Frank Cameron's delivery is just short of good length. Bromfield goes half-cock, and it balloons off his bat and pad. McGregor is at silly-point to take it. Victory to the New Zealanders by 40 runs, with 21 minutes to spare. The series is 2-2.

Champagne Day summarises John Reid.

Most of the post-War stalwarts of White South African cricket, riding on whose deeds they have done so well in Test cricket in the 1950s, have now passed from the scene. It is time for rebuilding.

Early in 1962, Basil D'Oliveira was recruited by Ron Roberts to tour Rhodesia, Tanganyika, Kenya, and Malaya during the International World Tour.

30 FIRST AND SECOND CLASS

Ron Roberts would die young—only 38 when a brain tumour would call time.

But during his brief stint he was a man of boundless energy and organisational genius, who made many lives worthwhile. The International World Tour of 1962, according to *Wisden,* covered 40,000 miles and played in countries and territories as far flung as Rhodesia, New Zealand and Hong Kong. Cricketarchive lists them as Commonwealth XI.

The team was represented by 25 players including 19 Test cricketers. Richie Benaud, Colin Bland, Chandu Borde, Colin Cowdrey, Ian Craig, Tom Graveney, Norman Gifford, Subhash Gupte, Hanif Mohammad, David Larter, Ray Lindwall, Colin McDonald, Roy McLean, Roy Marshall, Ian Meckiff, Sonny Ramadhin, Harold Rhodes, Saeed Ahmed, Bobby Simpson, Harold Stephenson, Raman Subba Row, and Everton Weekes. In short, some of the brightest stars of the cricketing constellation.

It was amongst these men that Basil D'Oliveira made his first-class debut at the ripe old age of 31 at Harrison Oval, Ek Park, Kitwe, Northern Rhodesia—the current day Zambia.

One of the sides put together by Ron Roberts. Trevor Goddard seated third from right. Basil D'Oliveira standing third from right.

However, his introduction onto the world stage precedes the first-class debut and it is a match to remember.

Will he take time to adjust to the rigours of touring and find his niche as a member of such a stellar team? Questions such as these are asked often. However, D'Oliveira finds himself on the familiar territory of the Sikh Union Club Ground, where he has earlier led the South

African non-Europeans. The opponents are the known players of East Africa.

He scores just 11 in the first innings. The talking point is the magnificent 178 by Hanif Mohammad. However, he opens the bowling with Larter and picks up three wickets. Gupte's spin is too much for the local side and they are all out for 156.

It is 145 for 3 on the second day when D'Oliveira walks out to bat. As he goes out, he overhears the conversation of two spectators. Roy Marshall and Colin McDonald opened the batting, followed by Saeed Ahmed at No 3. At the crease now is the classy Tom Graveney. Hanif and Weekes are waiting to follow, not too eager for a hit because of their long outings in the first innings.

As D'Oliveira's name comes up on the scoreboard, one spectator says to another: "Never heard of him. Let's get a drink."

The comment cuts D'Oliveira to the quick. Here he is in his early 30s, as good as many of the others in that illustrious group, perhaps better than most. But circumstances have seen to it that his name has not been heard. It is the unfairness of it all that puts steel into his soul.

In England, he has learnt the art of biding his time to settle down. Here he throws such caution to the wind and starts demonstrating exactly why the world should know about him.

It is Kishore Vasani, the poor East African left-armer, who is the first to encounter the blast of the fury and then the rest of the bowlers. D'Oliveira hammers one and all, in a knock of 101 not out in 64 minutes. Eight fours and seven sixes, the second fifty coming up in 19 minutes. Later, D'Oliveira would write:

"The savagery was quite coldly planned to benefit my career. I was well aware that I was along illustrious players from all over the world and that, when illustrious players talk in this game, it is generally to important people. I wanted to make sure they mentioned me."

It certainly does work. Five years later, Everton Weekes will tell him: "You know Bas, that knock at Nairobi was one of the finest I have seen." This from someone who spent his career watching Worrell and Walcott, and later Hunte, Kanhai and Sobers.

In 1962, apartheid worked in an inward-looking way for Peter Hain and his family. Most of their extended family started alienating them. Invitations to play with cousins and family friends dwindled. Relatives withdrew.

However, Ad and Wal remained dedicated to their activism.

Mandela's trial opened at the Old Synagogue in Pretoria on 22 October. Winnie Mandela attended each day, dressed in gorgeous tribal outfits. Adelaine Hain covered the trial for the Liberal magazine *Contact*. Each day Mandela would walk into the court room and raise his fist in the traditional ANC *Amandla!* salute. And each day, he would turn to the White section of the public gallery towards Adelaine and salute her as well.

On his first-class debut, the opponent is Rhodesia. Joe Partridge is a promising pace bowler who will go on to play 11 Tests for South Africa. He dismisses McDonald and Saeed Ahmed quite early. When Weekes falls, the score is 93 for 4. This is a familiar situation for D'Oliveira.

He walks in and scores a serene 51. At the other end, once again, there is Tom Graveney. Against East Africa they had added 119, but the match was not first-class. Here they put on 95. Graveney scores an unbeaten 112.

'I want to make sure they mentioned me'.

Graveney will certainly do so.

Sympathetic officials in the Dutch and West German embassies suggested that Liberal Parties organise gatherings to overcome their difficulty of meeting non-Whites socially. These 'diplomatic parties' started taking place in the Hain household.

The tour is also memorable for several social developments and near-disasters.

On 24 February, the International XI play Rhodesia again. At Bulawayo, the main grounds are used for Currie Cup matches. Since the International XI is a multi-racial side, their game is moved to Showgrounds, with a bumpy pitch and hastily cut wicket. At a party that night, Weekes meets a well-meaning supporter. "I hope we'll see a first class hundred from you tomorrow," he says. Weekes replies: "If you give me a second-class ground to play on, then you'll get a second-class innings."

The next day, with his score on three, he hits the ball straight into the air.

The match ends in a draw on the third day. It is also the day Weekes turns 37.

"Nobody who's friends with me goes without a drink on my birthday," he declares.

D'Oliveira is a teetotaller. He is asked what he will have. "Gin and Tonic," he responds, uttering the first drink that comes to his mind. Behind the counter of the bar stands Ray Lindwall. "Right," he says. "I'm the barman, I'll fix it."

D'Oliveira has his first drink. The following morning, he has his first hangover. And it is not going to be the last.

But there are problems as well. At the Kitwe Hotel, Rohan Kanhai and Chester Watson go into the cocktail bar and are refused drinks by the barman. They are asked to go down to the lounge bar. Kanhai says in that case he will leave the country. Ron Roberts steps in and the manager apologises.

Sonny Ramadhin decides to get a haircut at the barbershop and is told to 'Go down the road'.

Tom Graveney orders three gins and tonic. The other two are for Ron Roberts and Everton Weekes. The barman looks at Weekes and refuses to serve them. An apology comes through with time, but the memories are scarred.

When D'Oliveira leaves the side after the African leg of the tour to honour his Middleton commitments, he is presented a silver tankard with the inscription: *To Basil from the Boys.* It is ostensibly for the first-class debut, but D'Oliveira is left with a sneaking suspicion that it represents his first drink.

In early 1960s, Tokyo's Yawata Iron & Steel Co. offered to purchase 5,000,000 tons of South African pig iron over a 10-year period. Without hesitation, Pretoria's Group Areas Board announced that all Japanese henceforth would be considered White, at least for purposes of residence. Johannesburg's city fathers decided that "in view of the trade agreements" they would open the municipal swimming pools to Japanese guests.

In 1962, during the visit of a Japanese water polo team, the Pretoria City Council initially refused access to the swimming pool in a city hotel, and later relented. Due to public uproar, after the team's departure the pool was drained and refilled with fresh water.

D'Oliveira scores fewer runs in 1962 but captures 72 wickets for Middleton at 15.2 runs apiece. That winter he tours with Ron Roberts again—across Greece, Rhodesia, Tanganyika, Kenya and Malaya. He plays alongside Chandu Borde, Trevor Goddard, Wes Hall, Rohan Kanhai, Willie Watson, and others.

During the overnight stay in Karachi, he is detained by the Immigration officer because of his South African passport. He insists he is a victim and not party to the regime, but that does not help.

The demand is unusual. He has to declare that he is Coloured because he has Indian parentage. D'Oliveira replies that he can conjure up any sort of parentage for the form as long as he is allowed to stay a few hours in Karachi before boarding a flight to Malay.

Next comes the demand of £200 pound bond. The teammates combine their resources to whip it up. (In *Time to Declare,* D'Oliveira says this takes place in Bombay. In *The D'Oliveira Affair,* he insists it was Karachi)

31 BLACK AND WHITE AMBULANCES

Dennis Brutus was running, weaving through the crowds. As a child, he had carried linen for wash, rushing them to a family friend through busy streets full of pedestrians, and he was adept at moving through a swarm of people.

Not so Helberg and Kleingeld, the two cops behind him. He was gaining ground, especially from the middle-aged Helberg. The streets of Johannesburg at five o'clock in the afternoon were known for maddening congestion. People were going home from work, from and to the nearby West End Station. Many of them were Africans who worked in the city, on their way to board the trains back to their respective ghettos.

Some of the folks in the streets made to grab him, mistaking him for a pickpocket or a petty thief pursued by the police. Brutus veered through, eluding their grasps.

On the Magistrates Court on the corner of the Main Street, he turned a sharp left. A bus approached, filled to the brim with Africans. Brutus sprang on. But as the bus rolled along, it did so in the direction of his pursuers. Kleingeld tried to jump on. Standing on the top of the steps, Brutus put his foot on the chest of the younger policeman and pushed. He fell off.

The relief was short-lived. The conductor was not happy with yet another passenger on an overcrowded bus, jumping on rather than waiting in the designated stops. He came from behind and shoved him off with a few angry words.

Brutus fell on a parked car, injuring his knee. He scrambled off. Kleingeld, shaken by the fall, sprinted after him. As Brutus ran, he passed Halberg coming from the other direction, puffing and blowing. The elderly policeman called out to him to stop, trying to grab him with outstretched hands. Brutus swerved past him.

It was then that he heard a loud report and felt a thump as if someone had punched him in the back. He kept running, till he saw the stain in front of his shirt. He panicked and fell.

It was from an adjacent Anglo-American office building that someone looking down on the scene phoned an ambulance. Soon sirens were heard and men in long white coats got out, pulling a stretcher behind them. Brutus lay conscious but in terrible pain as the two policemen sat beside him.

The medics took a look at Brutus, put their stretcher back in the ambulance and drove away. The face of the poet-teacher-activist registered shock. Helberg, grey haired and almost fatherly in manner, said to him, "But Brutus, you know that these men would lose their jobs if they took you in their ambulance. That is an ambulance for Whites only, and you will have to wait for a non-White ambulance."

The wait was between 30 to 45 minutes. Helberg squatted next to him and said: "Anyway, I hope you survive."

Brutus lay in a pool of blood as they waited for the non-White ambulance.

Eventually the Coloured ambulance arrived and took him to a Coloured hospital in a Coloured area called Coronationville. Brutus was operated on. His life was saved.

Ironically, the doctors who saved his life were White.

Dennis Brutus had been captured at the Mozambique border. He had escaped from South Africa while still under banning orders in order to get to a meeting of the International Olympic Committee at Nairobi. The venue was subsequently changed to Baden-Baden in Germany.

Escorted to Pretoria, he had been presented to Hendrik van den Bergh, the head of the South African secret police. From there, he had been driven to Johannesburg.

Olympics was not a mere sporting event for the South African Blacks. It was blood sport.

Dennis Brutus

In 1963 the South African government introduced the infamous 90-day Detention Law. Any police officer could detain a suspect for a politically motivated crime for 90 days without warrant. Generally, when the stipulated period was over, they were arrested again almost immediately for another 90 days.

The year started disastrously for the Hains. In January, Ad was summoned before the Chief Magistrate of Pretoria and warned to desist from engaging in activities "calculated to further the aims of communism." When asked which of her activities fell under that category, the Magistrate was unable to answer. She was advised to write to the Minister of Justice, JB Vorster, for clarification.

The reply was vague, a mesh of repeated phrases. It ended with the ominous: "Should you so wish, you are of course at liberty to ignore the warning and, if as a result thereof, it is found necessary to take further action against you, you will have only yourself to blame."

It was like McCarthyism on steroids.

Aged 13, Peter saw a newspaper cartoon which showed Vorster instructing: "Go and find Adelaine Hain, see what she's doing and tell her she mustn't."

Vorster was soon to state in Parliament that liberals were communists in disguise and tantamount to terrorists.

In the sultry heat of South African January, the swimming pool around the Durban Country Club finds members stretching out in the sun with Indian waiters hurrying across the turf, bringing them their tall drinks.

The golfers shower or sit in the air-conditioned changing rooms after their efforts in the course. The Indian chefs prepare the delightful dishes. The magnificent club building, built in Cape Dutch style, overlooks the sprawling courses.

In these settings, this year, one Indian is an exception. After years of pressure and criticism in the international press, Papwa is finally allowed to participate in the Natal Open.

They cannot ignore his two-time Dutch Open winning feats. However, there will be no tall drinks brought to him by Indian waiters, nor any delightful dishes prepared by Indian chefs. There will be no changing room with air conditioning and showers to wash off the grime after his efforts in the course.

He eats with the other caddies, lunch that is packed by his wife before he leaves in the morning. His manager Louis Nelson drives him to the course. He changes in the car. From time to time he enters the tent of the caddies to sip his tea from a thermos flask.

The first round is disappointing, but by the end of the second he is tied in the second place. The strangeness of playing alongside the 103-strong white field has perhaps worn off.

Even rains fail to deter him. He improves with each passing minute. A smart stroke with a pitching wedge, his ally from the Dutch Open, takes him to the brink. And holding his nerve, he puts in, finishing one stroke ahead of his closest rivals, Denis Hutchinson and Gary Player's brother-in-law Bobby Verwey.

Papwa has done the unthinkable. As rain pours down, it sinks in. A Coloured man, an Indian, has not only competed in the Natal Open, he has won it.

He changes in Nelson's car. The manager asks the spectators and fans who have gathered to congratulate the champion to look away. Someone calls for three cheers as Papwa pulls off his golf shoes and put on the black ones. Then an official hustles towards them and asks him to hurry. The White golfers and their wives are getting wet in the rain.

As the downpour thickens, the golfers huddle into the clubhouse. The presentation will take place there. However, there is a hitch—Papwa, the Indian man, is not allowed in the Whites-only clubhouse.

Hurriedly, the White officials shove the trophy into his hand. Some will maintain it is done through the window.

The winner out of the way, the actual celebrations continue indoors. The 1963 Natal Open Champion stays outside, trophy in hand, getting lashed by rain. But he is smiling.

Peter heard from his mother how at least one Black detainee had been subjected to electric shock torture and had gone completely out of his mind, staring vacantly into space. Assault and brutality against Black detainees were a daily course. Ad was spending hours in the courts trying to find out the names of the detainees, trying to arrange legal representation.

All through the country Liberals were getting banned. Ad and Wal warned the children that life would soon get much more difficult.

On 11 July, several senior ANC leaders were arrested in the Liliesleaf Farm in Rivonia, Johannesburg. Their most secret meeting place had been breached.

That same month, the Hain family moved to a smallholding at The Willows, to the east of Pretoria. The rented house had two large thatched rondavels on a terrace far from the road. With plenty of space, Peter quickly laid a makeshift cricket pitch.

More importantly, the move took the Secret Police by surprise. It was some weeks before they finally traced the family. Unwittingly, Adelaine Hain let herself be seen by a man who was asking the maid Eva questions about her baas. When Adelaine popped up, Eva was furious. She had been successfully carrying out her dumb kaffir routine.

On 28 August, during the March on Washington for Jobs and Freedom, Martin Luther King Jr spoke to 250,000 civil rights supporters from the steps of the Lincoln Memorial at Washington DC. *"I am happy to join with you today in what will go down in history as the greatest demonstration for freedom in the history of our nation,"* he began.

Down the line he proceeded to say: "*I have a dream that one day on the red hills of Georgia sons of former slaves and the sons of former slave-owners will be able to sit down together at the table of brotherhood.*"

In September there was a knock on the doors of the new Hain house. Two large Security Police officers loomed in the doorway, Sergeants Viktor and van Zyl, the same two who had arrested Ad and Wal in 1961. They handed Ad am envelope containing a banning order that ran for five years; it limited her to being in the company of one person at a time, restricted her movements to the Pretoria magisterial district, and prohibited her from entering places such as factories, non-White communities, school or university areas, and courts of law.

This meant that her political activities, helping detainees and challenging mistreatment were to come to an end. She could not even attend the progress meetings at her children's schools. Interpreted literally, the banning order did allow her to stand on the pavement and talk to a teacher at the primary school, but since Peter's high school was situated in a ground as a solitary building, she could not even attempt to do that.

Such was the level of ridiculousness of the bans. And such ridiculousness breeds workarounds.

She started communicating through an agent, planning clandestine rendezvous. 'Diplomatic meetings' were resumed in the Hain household, and guests came along one by one to meet Ad.

On 22 November, John F Kennedy was travelling in a presidential motorcade in Dallas, Texas, when he was shot at. One bullet passed through his back and exited through his throat. The other lodged in his head. He was pronounced dead half an hour later.

Peter later wrote that a tiny piece of hope died in a 13-year-old that day.

The Hain family could no longer afford Eva. Wal's succession of banning orders had made work opportunities limited, and it was hard to make ends meet. Eva, the Black maid, a long-term family friend, had to go.

Another major event graced the family that year. Jimmy Makoejane was a friend from PAC, associated with the party's underground POQO group. He had fled to the Rhodesian border, been captured there on the train, and been brought back to Pretoria for trial. During the trial he managed to escape during the lunch recess and now sought shelter in the Hain home. Wal drove him in a friend's car, Jimmy concealed under a rug on the back seat. From a nearby station, Jimmy boarded a train and escaped to Tanzania.

Peter was growing up in political hotbed, looking danger in the eye.

1963. The Wallabies were in South Africa. Jim Boyce remembers: "*At the end of a game three weeks into the tour, the crowd was allowed into the field. There was a Black guy … might have been a bit drunk … who approached and congratulated me. Then out of the blue a hulking Afrikaner policeman grabbed him and drove him 15 metres into the crowd … Our manager Bill McLaughlin took me aside 'Don't let situations like that develop. If Blacks come near you walk away.'*"

After the match at Ellis Park, John Vorster regaled them with stories about the fate that awaited a couple of escaped political prisoners.

And then there was the game at Port Elizabeth. Australia 2-1 up in the series. Afrikaner fans were desperate for their heroes to win and level the series.

15 minutes from full time, the referee missed a knock-on that led to a try for South Africa. The pass was thrown directly in front of the area reserved for non-Whites. A small corner stand with no cover and the worst view of the field, remembers Boyce. The Blacks wanted the Wallabies to win. They booed the referee and voiced their disapproval. According to Boyce, the Springbok fans in the open and comfortable grandstands who had been drinking heavily started throwing bottles at the Blacks and the Coloureds. The police got into action and Alsatian police dogs were turned loose on them. Later that evening, during a reception, the local police chief crowed that 'three or four' Blacks had been killed in the streets on their way home from the match.

That was not all. There was a stage-managed visit to Sharpeville. Blacks were rounded up and ordered to cheer the players as they got off the bus. The players were made to pose with local police and villagers—everyone smiling, everyone happy. The players were 'instructed' to spread their 'good impressions' in Australia and elsewhere—to 'correct misperceptions.'

Boyce recalls: "*The typical rugby administrator in those days was a deeply conservative middle-aged or elderly man from the banking, accounting or legal professions. Their parting advice to us was that South Africa was a strange country and South Africa's politics were no concern of ours. We were there to play rugby … Not a word about apartheid, or how Blacks were ineligible to play for the Springboks or the provincial teams.*"

Before the tour, Australia's first Aboriginal rugby union representative Lloyd McDermott had ruled himself out of selection by quitting the Queensland rugby union team. He was unwilling to play, even if allowed, as an honorary White. McDermott would later earn degrees in science and criminology and become Australia's first Indigenous barrister.

32 AM I GOOD ENOUGH?

Did Washbrook really say D'Oliveira was a Saturday afternoon slogger?

There is no recorded evidence. However, it is true that Lancashire did not show any interest in D'Oliveira. A pity. Naomi and Basil had come to think of Middleton as home and would have liked to carry on there.

Moreover, a doubt plagued D'Oliveira—was he good enough? Was there a reason he had not been able to break into the county circuit?

Oborne hints at equal probability of racism and stupidity. Sonny Ramadhin was recruited by the club but did not stay for long. It might have had something to do with prejudice. On the other hand, the same John Kay who had been a benefactor of D'Oliveira had suggested Frank Tyson to the club in the 1950s. Lancashire had refused, and Tyson had to bowl for Northamptonshire. So, sheer idiocy cannot be ruled out.

But it did plant the seed of doubt in the mind of D'Oliveira. He was 32 now. Time was fast running out.

"I want to make sure they mention me." That had been his thought when he went out to bat for the International XI. All the stars around him were sure to talk about him to important people if he dazzled them.

Dazzle he did. He shared two fantastic partnerships with Tom Graveney in his first two matches. Graveney was his teammate when he travelled to Pakistan with Alf Gover's Commonwealth side in 1963–64. It was a quite handy team, with Basil Butcher, Rohan Kanhai, Seymour Nurse, Charlie Griffith, and Peter Richardson in their midst. D'Oliveira had a good time, scoring 260 runs at 52.00 and capturing 13 wickets at 30.38. So did Graveney, with 500 runs at 100 per innings, blasting two hundreds in a tall-scoring encounter at Lahore.

At the Metropole Hotel, Karachi, Graveney spoke to D'Oliveira about his future. The doubts caused by the indifference of the Lancashire selection committee were slowly erased. Graveney assured him that not only was he good for county cricket, he was also good enough to play at Test level.

Graveney himself had moved to Worcestershire the previous year, after falling out with his home county Gloucestershire. Now he said, "I'd really like you to come to Worcester. You could help us win a few trophies."

There was yet another defining moment for D'Oliveira's career because of that tour. Due to his problems with the immigration in Pakistan the previous winter, Alf Gover suggested that he get British citizenship. The decision helped him not only with his international tours, it also made sure that he was eligible to play for England if he was deemed good enough.

Back in Pretoria, Peter Hain played football for the Arcadia youth team, and watched the club play at the Caledonian stadium. The Black friends of the Hain family mingled with them before and after the game, and sat separately in the non-White section during the action. The entrance, toilets, facilities were also separate.

Arcadia was an all-White team playing in an all-White league. However, Black spectators were some of their most partisan supporters—and some of their noisiest fans as well. After the government-imposed ban, the non-White friends could no longer attend the major sporting events.

Some did try to catch a glimpse of the action by climbing the trees adjoining the ground. Peter watched in horror as police dogs were used to drive them down from the vantage points, bloodied and screaming.

The eventful 1963 ended with controversies surrounding the first Test contested by *Goddard's Cinderellas* in Australia.

McGlew, McLean, Endean, Tayfield, Adcock, and Heine had all left the scene. Skipper Goddard and Waite were the only ones of the old brigade chugging along. Like Cheetham's men of 1952–53, they were not given a chance. Like Cheetham's men of 1952–53, they had Ken Viljoen as manager. Like Cheetham's men of 1952–53, they drew the series.

At Lennon's Hotel on the evening before the Test, captain Richie Benaud convenes his usual Test match dinner. Col Egar, the umpire, personal friend of Ian Meckiff, has travelled from Adelaide to Brisbane on the same train as Don Bradman. "How are ya, Chucker?" he greets the fast bowler.

"Where's your seeing-eye dog?" retorts Meckiff.

Batting five and a half hours, Brian Booth compiles 169. Australia amass 435. Peter Pollock captures 6 for 95.

Garth McKenzie starts bowling at 2.00 PM and struggles with his footing. He concedes 13 off the first over to Goddard and Barlow.

Meckiff comes in from the other end. As he sends down his second ball, Egar at square leg calls 'no ball!'

At square leg, Booth stands next to Egar. He thinks he has drifted behind square and the call is due to three fielders behind square leg.

At gully, Benaud's eyes pop out.

The next ball is a full toss that Goddard hits for four. Egar calls again.

The fifth and ninth deliveries are called as well. The rest of the 133.5 eight-ball overs of the innings are shared between McKenzie, Connolly, Veivers, Benaud, Simpson, and O'Neill.

Meckiff is not bowled even from the other end. Egar has to be given police protection at the end of the day.

The next morning Wally Grout asks him to move a bit squarer at square leg. "Col, there's a chap in the crowd pointing a gun at you. If you don't move a bit to your right, he may miss and hit me."

Jock, the team masseur, enters the Aussie dressing room with a raincoat over his shoulder, hat cocked on his head, and a newspaper over his arm. Walking up to Benaud, he demands to know why Meckiff has not been tried at umpire Rowan's end. From under the newspaper emerges a very realistic toy gun. Benaud all but falls off his chair. The prank has been arranged by Bill Lawry.

Barlow's century goes unnoticed. Meckiff never plays in a Test again—or a first-class match for that matter. There are several cries of conspiracy, but he and Egar remain firm friends all life.

33 TWO PRIME MINISTERS

January 1964.

Barlow's 109 will perhaps not stand out as his best effort, but it is an innings that has guts and bulldog tenacity written all over it, with a fair blessing of luck. Benaud has broken a thumb, Booth and O'Neill are with him in the casualty ward. Simpson captains the side, only Grout and the skipper remain from the historic Tied Test encounter three years earlier. However, Simpson is bold enough to insert South Africa on a green top. Garth McKenzie, given five slips, two leg slips and a short mid-wicket to start with, makes the ball sing.

The score of 274 looks decent in the end. But Lawry and the 23-year-old debutant Redpath add 219 for the first wicket. Lou Rowan does not see Lawry dislodge a bail while hooking Partridge. He makes good his escape, batting five and a half hours for 157. Australia score 447. Peter Pollock picks up three wickets but his hamstring snaps. Defeat by eight wickets, and the spearhead out of action—the medical opinion is three weeks.

Eddie Barlow in action

1964. Early in the year, separate trials for Whites and Blacks were arranged to nominate a team for the Olympic Games in Tokyo. The team included seven Black members among the 62-strong squad. The Government was prepared to issue passports to all the nominated members provided they didn't fly in the same plane or stay in the same quarters at the Olympic Games. It was not enough to satisfy the world. South Africa were banned from the Tokyo Olympics.

The third Test at Sydney starts just four days after the Melbourne drubbing. Somehow Pollock's hamstring recovers. He runs in to capture 5 for 83, enjoying the pace, bounce and the grass. 260 all out.

Now his brother takes over. He bats beautifully.

At the other end, the South Africans struggle. Waite and Peter van der Merwe are bowled by McKenzie in quick succession, the score is 162 for 5. Pollock and Bland take seven off his next over. For some obscure reason the fast bowler is rested after a spell of 3-2-7-2. Keith Miller calls it one of the great Test match blunders. Graeme Pollock carries on. Cover drives and hooks reverberate across the oval.

"I have never heard a sweeter note than the one young Graeme Pollock brought to Australia with his bat," writes Lindsay Hassett. "Next time you decide to play like that send me a telegram," says Bradman.

Plenty of time left in the game as South Africa take a 42-run lead. Lawry 89, O'Neill 88. The pitch is dead and Peter Pollock's bouncers lack pace and viciousness. O'Neill calls them creampuffs.

Benaud has returned, but Simpson is at the helm. Without the cares of captaincy, he hits 90, McKenzie clobbers two sixes but is otherwise sedate in hitting 76. 160 for the seventh wicket. The young Springboks are left 433 minutes to get 409 runs. They cannot afford to go down 0-2. Goddard shows the way, bats 265 minutes for 84. Bland lasts 202 minutes, Pithey 164, Graeme Pollock 101. They end at 326 for 5, high on confidence.

On 20 April, from the dock of the defendant, Nelson Mandela talked for three hours. It was a speech reviewed by his friends Anthony Sampson and Nadine Gordimer. It ended "*During my lifetime I have dedicated my life to this struggle of the African people. I have fought against White domination, and I have fought against Black domination. I have cherished the ideal of a democratic and free society in which all people will live together in harmony and with equal opportunities. It is an ideal for which I hope to live for and to see realized. But, My Lord, if it needs to be, it is an ideal for which I am prepared to die.*"

On 12 July, Mandela, Sisulu, and others were found guilty on four counts of conspiracy and sabotage by Judge Quartus de Wet. They were flown to Robben Island where the guards gleefully informed them: "This is where you'll die." Mandela was to remain there for the next 18 years, in a ten-foot by six-foot cell, with three blankets and a straw mat.

The Rivonia Accused

In Adelaide, John Waite decides just minutes before the Test that he is not fit to play. Denis Lindsay is a bit flustered at being asked to deputise at the last moment.

Australia bats. Peter Pollock breathes fire. Lawry is caught for 14. Six balls later, O'Neill fends a bouncer into Goddard's hands at gully. "How's that for a cream puff?" asks Peter Pollock as the batsman walks back.

Nevertheless, Simpson, Burge, and Booth take them to 345. Neil Hawke, with his curious ability to move the ball around with an ungainly action, dismisses Goddard and Pithey off successive balls. Graeme Pollock, beaten comprehensively off the first two, barely manages to survive. And the next ball is creamed through the covers.

What follows is four hours and 43 minutes of ruthlessness. Barlow keeps cutting Benaud's famous flipper from the stumps to the cover boundary with remarkable ease. Graeme Pollock mixes poise and grace with pure unadulterated savagery. 341 runs are added before Pollock loses his stump to Hawke. His 175 contains 18 fours and 3 sixes. Barlow pushes on to 201. But everyone, including Barlow himself, agrees Pollock's innings is classier. "I was simply the jackal picking at the corpse, after the lion has eaten his fill," Barlow observes. Lindsay flays his bat for 41. The total is a massive 595.

But the Aussies fight back. Benaud and Shepherd provide dogged resistance for the sixth wicket. The young tourists get restless.

At five o'clock on the fourth day, Barlow goes up to the skipper. "Give me a go. I have a feeling I'll do them." Goddard ignores him.

Barlow continues to badger the all-rounder. "If you don't give me the ball, you'll be in big trouble." The conviction in his voice makes Goddard relent.

In his first over, Barlow sends down a rank long hop. Shepherd pulls it and it goes skywards towards fine leg. It doesn't look like carrying to Peter Pollock stationed at the boundary. Lindsay sprints in his pads, dives full length and comes up with a miraculous catch.

Two balls later, Benaud drags one wide outside the off-stump on to his wickets.

After a few overs McKenzie hits a full-toss directly back to Barlow. 5-2-6-3. Early on the fifth morning victory is completed by a margin of 10 wickets.

Prime Minister Verwoerd continued to pursue his scheme for White South Africa as forcefully as ever, the utopia of Bantustans remaining his pipedream. In 1964, the government introduced extremely harsh influx controls that stopped housing constructions in peri-urban areas. This was the way of successfully removing 'black spots' (Black settlements in the White rural areas).

The records show that the other Prime Minister fielded an XI who registered a win against the visitors in Canberra.

But on the day, Robert Menzies is furious.

There are special rules. No one can score a duck. The match has to end in exciting fashion, in a tie if possible, but on no account can the visitors be defeated. There are two advisers to ensure this, Lindsay Hassett and Sam Loxton, the former with a casting vote.

The Prime Minister's XI makes a poor start to their chase of 267 for 7 declared. Lollypop bowling is tossed up, and recently retired Alan Davidson makes merry hitting 56. But the eighth wicket goes down at 204. More joke bowling becomes necessary. All 11 South Africans bowl.

Eventually, with nine wickets down scores are levelled. At the crease is John Gallop. An illustrious legal career has seen him become the Justice of the Australian Capital Territory, and now he also keeps wickets for second grade side of ACT. He has made most of the full tosses and long hops and is unbeaten on 28. Graeme Pollock has the ball, and he knows all Gallop has to do now is to get out. He tosses the ball up. Gallop somehow executes the best stroke of the innings. The ball crashes into the fence and the fielders are bewildered. "I was supposed to get a wicket with that ball," says Pollock.

The umpires confer but find no way to annul the boundary. In the grandstand, Menzies leaves in disgust and sacks Hassett and Loxton.

At the banquet that evening, Trevor Goddard reminds Menzies about the great setback to the Springbok confidence. John Gallop is summoned and summarily informed he will never be chosen for the Prime Minister's XI again. Hassett and Loxton are reinstated.

Robert Menzies

It was during the tour match against the Prime Minister's XI that Menzies confided to Goddard that he hoped for a South African victory in the Test series. "So as to clear away all this nonsense about your Test matches being regarded as unofficial."

There were rising voices of conscience in the Australian Board, plenty of petitions and requests they were receiving from different individuals and organisations, all appealing to end cricketing connections with South Africa. But with the unofficial Prime Ministerial backing, they felt secure enough to turn a blind eye to all the brewing dissent.

In June 1964, Charles Llewellyn, the man who somehow circumvented the colour bar, passed away in Englefield Green, Surrey. The sad news was recorded by *Wisden,* but it would be ignored by the South African Cricket Annual for five years. No South African obituary appeared.

In stark contrast, the South African Cricket Annual was quick to note the death of Lady Warner, the wife of Plum Warner, in 1955.

Back in Sydney, Goddard takes a gamble and inserts Australia. Partridge captures 7 for 91, his love affair with the ground quite famous by now. But Booth bats five hours for 102, and Australia recover from 179 for 6 to 311. Colin Bland's superb 126 and his rollicking 118-run association with Lindsay results in a lead of 100.

Booth bats five more hours, hitting 87, ending the series with 531 runs at 88.50. But with three hours to go, the hosts slump to 208 for 8, and there is more than a chance for Goddard's men to clinch the series.

But Veivers and Hawke bat an hour and a quarter to add 45 for the last wicket. The balls pop up and fall in no-man's land. When Goddard finally gets Veivers the ask is 171 in 85 minutes. Midnight, destiny hour, has found the men wanting. Hence, *Goddard's Cinderellas.* The series ends 1-1.

Instead of the usual exchange of ties, each of the Springboks are thrilled to be presented with a silver boomerang with an Australian opal in the middle. It is only the overly critical and strict management of Ken Viljoen that leaves a sour taste.

Bram Fischer was a man with impeccable Afrikaner family credentials—grandson of the Orange River Colony premier, son of Judge-President of the Free State Supreme Court. He joined the Communist Party in the 1930s and was a top-notch advocate, the defence lawyer of the accused during the trial.

In 1964, he was arrested twice. On being released on bail, he went underground. He became the most hunted man in South Africa until his ultimate capture in 1965.

When Goddard's men cross the Tasman Sea for their three-Test series against New Zealand, they are picketed in Christchurch, Wellington, and Auckland. The New Zealand Communist Party hands out leaflets titled: *Apartheid isn't cricket: Bowl out Racialism in Sport and in Life.*

The Federation of Labour opposes the tour and calls on the union movement to ban all service. Wellington newspapers, however, are critical of the demonstrators, calling them unwanted and unmannerly limelight seekers determined to spoil other people's pleasures.

Peter Pollock remembers, "In Australia we had almost forgotten our status as the skunks of apartheid as all eyes focused on cricket. Now they were back, hounding us like criminals."

The people they meet are more interested about how strong the Springbok rugby team is going to be when the All Blacks visit in 1965.

During the windy Wellington Test, they are served hot soup during drinks break. The deep trench caused by the rugby halfway line is partly grassy, and balls that pitch on one side become bouncers and on the other they shoot through. In the Dunedin Test, the players change in a glorified shed.

The tour is also marred by tragic news from back home. Peter Carlstein's wife and their three young children have died in a motor accident. Members from both the sides are shocked and accompany Carlstein to the airport as he leaves.

The departure of Carlstein, and several minor and major injuries have reduced the touring party to just 11 men by now. That, and some dogged resistance from the New Zealanders—both batsmen and umpires—in the third Test, result in a drab stalemate of a series.

This is the last time South Africa will play New Zealand till the 1992 World Cup.

During the year, the ANC set up offices in Dar es Salaam. The International Labour Organisation suspended South Africa and Universal Postal Union expelled them.

Goddard's men board the flight from Sydney and return via Adelaide and Perth. Their drawn series against Australia with an inexperienced side does not please all. Goddard's captaincy is scrutinised, and alongside the laudatory words reserved for the players, there is a suggestion that the selectors had left a lot of deserving cricketers out of the side.

Five months after their return, at the start of the 1964–65 season, this theory is even put to test. Goddard's men are pitted against the Rest of South Africa at Wanderers. The official reason given is something vague, but in reality it is nothing less than a trial. "They are trying to show us up," remarks a fuming Goddard. "I'm dead against this sort of thing. We should learn to accept the success and failure of touring teams, and not subject them to possible humility."

Most of the side are livid. Jackie McGlew leads the Rest and there is Roy McLean and a young Ali Bacher in the side.

Goddard decides not to give any quarter. He himself leads with 71. Pithey smites his way to 110. Graeme Pollock hammers 123 in less than two hours, with 23 boundaries. Colin Bland and Denis Lindsay pile up 151 and 107 respectively, adding 267 runs in just 99 minutes. Bland strikes 6 sixes, Lindsay 3. The score is 618 for 4 declared in just one day. The next morning Peter Pollock sends balls buzzing around the heads of the batsmen. McGlew resists with 49, MacLean with 52. The rest fall away. Peter Pollock captures 5. A lead of 357 and follow on is enforced. Goddard is not prepared to make allowances.

In the second innings the Rest total 242, Bacher hitting 61. The margin of victory is an innings and 129 runs. It was the better side that had toured after all.

That year Papwa Sewgolum returned to the Netherlands to win his third Dutch Open title at De Eindhovensche Golfclub, Valkenswaard.

34 BLASTING OUT CHILDHOOD

July 1964. Till now, life for Peter Hain had been a roller coaster ride on the fringes of political activism—always exciting, often tense, sometimes even scary. This month, however, it veered towards the tragic with a learning curve not suited for a 14-year-old. It was hardly suited for anyone.

John Harris was a family friend. Ad and Wal had come across John and his wife Ann a few years earlier in Johannesburg. They were both teachers, and, like the Hains, members of the Liberal Party. John had studied philosophy and Economics at the Oxford University.

He was a great sports fan as well, another shared interest with Walter Hain. Especially motor racing. Harris often joined Peter and Walter to travel to the Grand Prix in Kyalami. They would park the minibus in the Clubhouse Corner and watch from its roof.

John was Peter's great friend. He once drove Peter and his brother Tom so fast in his new car that their young hearts had been delighted and won over. He played table tennis with the kids too, hating it when he lost.

The one topic of disagreement between John and Wal was the concept of violence. Small acts of violence could result in damage in the short term, John used to say, but it would accelerate the end of the intense violence of the apartheid regime. Wal was not convinced. He had been in the war. His close friend had died from shelling right in front of his eyes. Wal believed that violence developed a life of its own.

John Harris joined the African Resistance Movement (ARM). It was formed as a militant anti-apartheid resistance movement by a group of young liberals after the Sharpeville massacre.

As Middleton started the 1964 season, Charlie Hallows came down to watch D'Oliveira in action. A Lancashire batsman immortalised by Neville Cardus in his mythical retelling of an imaginary innings on the writer's wedding day, he was now a scout for Worcestershire. Tom Graveney had kept his word.

The negotiations were brief and successful. As far as Middleton was concerned, there was no problem. They were both mature and professional enough to understand that the aspirations of a talent as outstanding as D'Oliveira's would require a canvas wider than the Towncroft Cricket Ground. But the contribution of Middleton in reshaping the history of cricket and society will be forever etched as a glorious chapter.

On 24 July 1964, a visibly nervous John Harris left a timed explosive in a briefcase 20 feet from the cubicle above Platforms 5 and 6 on the concourse of the new Johannesburg Railway Station. On the handle was tied a label bearing the words: "Back in Ten Minutes."

At precisely 4.18 PM he placed a call to a senior official at the Johannesburg Railway Police. "This is the African Resistance Movement," he said before proceeding to give the exact location of the bomb. "It is not our intention to harm anyone. This is a symbolic protest against the inhumanity and injustices of apartheid. The bomb is timed to explode at 4.33 PM. Clear the concourse by using the public address system at once. Do not try to defuse the bomb as the suitcase is triggered to explode if it is opened."

Harris also called the liberal *Rand Daily Mail* and left a briefer message. The paper, in turn, called the Security Police.

The final call placed by Harris was to the Afrikaner pro-government newspaper *Die Transvaler*.

No effort was made to clear the concourse. No warning was broadcast over the loudspeaker system at the Johannesburg Railway Station. The bomb exploded at precisely 4:33 PM. As many as 23 people were injured. The most grievous injury was to 77-year-old Ethel Rhys—who later died of horrible burns. Her granddaughter, Glynnis Burleigh, 12, also suffered serious burns.

The effects of the suitcase bomb

Most of the details that follow here have been taken from the account of the renegade Secret Police agent and journalist Gordon Winter, who published an exposé named *Inside BOSS* in 1981. The book revealed this and several other heinous deeds of the notorious South African Bureau of Secret Service (BOSS).

As the victims were taken away on stretchers, the Secret Police mounted a massive comb out of all known political activists. They were first beaten using standard interrogation techniques, before being asked to talk. With the information squeezed out, they zeroed in on the schoolteacher called John Harris.

Harris was arrested and interrogated by Captain JJ Viktor. According to Winter, the interrogation proceeded along the following lines.

Viktor sat Harris down on a chair in the middle of the room. "Look John, you are a member of the South African Liberal Party, so I know you're not the sort to go around blowing people up. So, I'm not going to waste time trying to interrogate you about the station blast."

A relieved Harris smiled as he heard this. The conversation turned informal. Viktor said they could spend their time better by discussing sport. Harris's file showed that he had been a leading figure in the SAN-ROC as well. Indeed, he had been a close associate of Dennis Brutus. Viktor asked him what his favourite sport was.

"Cricket and tennis."

"I personally am mad about rugby," said Viktor, before adding forlornly, "But I always make a hash of my drop-kick."

"I'm a keen student of rugby, but don't play the game," said Harris, relaxing. "It's too rough for me."

Viktor picked up a newspaper, crunched it into a ball and walked back to the far wall. He ran forward three or four steps and drop-kicked the paper ball towards a table in the corner.

"You are swinging your foot out as you kick," said Harris, by now completely relaxed. "This is taking the ball off-course."

"Gee, thanks," said Viktor. He picked up the crunched-up ball of paper and walked back. "Let me try again." He ran forward again, and kicked, this time at John Harris's jaw.

Harris lurched to his knees, swayed and cupped his chin, completely confused by the flurry of action and numbed by pain.

Viktor aimed another kick at his jaw. "That's how I take a penalty," he said. Kicks followed, in the stomach, on the chin. It was not long before Harris confessed.

The following day, he made a full verbal confession to the Security Police officer, Lieutenant WJ van der Merwe.

In an interview given to Gordon Winter, Hendrik van den Bergh spoke glowingly about the interrogation saying, "That will teach Harris to get involved in a scrum with one of my officers."

Van den Bergh admitted to Winter that the Railway Police had alerted him about the anonymous telephone call received at 4.18. He had in turn used his hotline to call Minister of Justice John Vorster.

They did not clear the concourse. The death of the innocents was required to whip up support among the indifferent and uncommitted White voters.

A few days after the event Ann Harris turned up at the Hain residence with her six-week-old son David. John was being held at the Pretoria Local Prison.

D'Oliveira communicated his date of birth as 4 October 1934. Apartheid had stolen some dozen years from his life, he wanted to balance the cruel hand of fate by stealing three of them back. He still looked young enough to manage it. EW Swanton even wrote that he had migrated as a teenager. The magisterial cricket commentator almost scratched through the entire stroke of bad fortune that had dogged D'Oliveira with a flourishing line of his pen.

The manipulation made him an upcoming star in his late-20s. A man in his 30s could have been considered too old by the Worcestershire selection committee. No one verified his birth certificate by asking for the original document from the Cape Town government offices.

It was after a while that Ruth Hyman, a Liberal Party friend and John's lawyer, was able to visit John Harris. He had been charged with murder, but the case had been brought up in court only after his broken jaw had mended enough to be presentable. Besides, he was still bleeding from horrendous beatings, and had damaged testicles.

Ann stayed with the Hains as John waited for his trial. The house was watched with an even greater vigilance by the Security Police. Raids became more random and frequent.

As a kid fascinated by cricket, Peter made World XIs. There was one which included the likes of Garry Sobers, Wes Hall, Richie Benaud, and Graeme Pollock … Pollock was a personal favourite, because Peter too was a left-handed batsman.

He had written down the XI as a list, with numbers next to them indicating batting order.

During one particular raid, two policemen rifled through his schoolbooks and notes. Finding the list with names and numbers, one of the cops rushed to his captain, flushed with excitement, thinking he had found a coded message. The captain merely told him not to be a damned fool.

D'Oliveira started playing club cricket for Kidderminster in the Birmingham and District Leagues.

The qualification rules prevented him from playing in the Championship in 1964. Hence, he started playing the Second XI matches. Strangely, he took a while to get going. It was not until his 13th innings for the Second XI that he registered a half-century. The first hundred took 25 innings to come. And that also arrived only after what D'Oliveira later called 'a deserved rap' from Charlie Hallows. "You can't spend this year thinking only about the next year. You haven't a divine right to a place in a county side."

When he played for the first team in the non-Championship matches, the results were different. He got a hundred against Oxford University and two fifties against Cambridge.

Besides, cannily, he worked out how to secure a permanent place in the side. He eyed the place of Jim Standen. A fine seamer, he was not that good a batsman. He topped the bowling averages with 64 wickets at 13.00 apiece during the season but had just 236 runs at 12.42 with the bat. D'Oliveira, primarily a bowler of off-cutters till now, concentrated on improving himself as a seamer. It bore excellent fruit the following season.

He played the Australians twice that year. He was bowled by McKenzie for 17 when the tourists took on Worcestershire very early in the season. The next match was at the very end of the season, the Festival game at Hastings, when he represented Arthur Gilligan's XI. Against an attack eager to fly home, and on a fantastic batting track, he hammered 119. The news was greeted with exuberant celebrations in Cape Town.

Meanwhile more Liberal Party members were being arrested and detained under the 90-day-law. In September Ad and Wal both received banning orders with a special clause—they were being given an exemption to meet each other. Personally signed by BJ Vorster.

With bans becoming the way of life, Peter was becoming more and more involved as a liaison between the Party members—communicating, passing messages, running errands.

D'Oliveira played just eight innings in first-class cricket in 1964, but the two hundreds gave him an average of 61.66, placing him in the top bracket of the English season. It was a good way to end the season, looking ahead to the following year.

The situation was completely different for the Hains and the Harrises.

On 6 November 1964, Ad waited nervously outside the courthouse, cautious not to break the clauses of the ban. A big crowd waited for the verdict outside, among them the hangman, curiously accompanied by his young son. Ann Harris sat alone inside, waiting the verdict, for neither Ad nor Wal could be with her because of banning orders.

The judge formally sentenced John Harris to death by hanging. He would have the morbid distinction of being the first White to be hanged in the anti-apartheid struggle.

The date of execution was set as 1 April 1965.

Ann stared ahead of her as she returned to the Hain house, making straight for the bedroom. Ad was visibly shaken. Peter's 10-year-old brother Tom was white with shock. He was a great fan of John. Peter had expected it. He was aghast, bewildered by it all, but kept asking himself whether something could be done.

Adelaine and Walter Hain wait anxiously as the trial of John Harris takes place

35 CRYING IN THE CHAPEL

Wally Hammond—sublime great of the game. But less than two decades after his retirement, a forgotten man, living in strained circumstances as sports administrator at the University of Natal. The world has moved on. He has somewhat reconciled and made peace with it. He is somewhat bitter, but not very. He is now more approachable than he has been most of his life.

And now, Donald Carr, manager of the visiting MCC side under MJK Smith, phones him—an idea of Ron Roberts. The phone call is perhaps the last great service Roberts will render cricket and cricketers. He will tragically die in August 1965.

Carr has known Hammond briefly during the post-War days. He asks the great man whether he would like to join the MCC players for a day's cricket and a drink or two. Hammond hesitates, he wonders whether anyone will want to see him. The team will love it, Carr assures him.

Hammond meets Carr and Smith over a drink. MJK charms him. Hammond is invited to the dressing room during the Durban Test.

The pitch is hard as a rock without a blade of grass. By the second afternoon, England are 485 for 5 when they close their innings more as an act of mercy. Ken Barrington is 148 not out.

By the end of the day South Africa are 20 for 3. On that dry pitch, the ball turns square. Fred Titmus takes six wickets, David Allen seven, Bob Barber two. The hosts lose by an innings.

Hammond, self-conscious and not completely at ease, sits in the dressing room all four days, confused and pleased at the same time. The incredulous admiration in every England player as they greet him touches his heart.

Graeme Pollock scores 5 and 0, dismissed by Titmus in both innings. The English press pounce on the small sample. Spin is supposedly Pollock's Achilles heel.

Dusty Springfield's *I just don't know what to do with myself* had reached No 3 on the UK Chart of 1964. In December, she toured South Africa, on the condition that she would perform for mixed non-segregated audiences. Two concerts in Johannesburg were extraordinary hits and mixed. At Cape Town, the government caught up with her. After performing for an integrated audience at a theatre near Cape Town, she was deported. "*Britain is a state of long-haired, third-rate entertainers with Dusty Springfield as Queen of the Mods,*" wrote an irate Cape Town resident.

The early success for England spells doom for the series. The tactics of the visitors remain uniformly negative. The placid pitches don't help either.

Dexter hits 172 at Wanderers, Barrington 121. South Africa lose their last five wickets for 46 to follow on. But Bland slams a couple of sixes during his 144 to ensure that the Titmus-Allen duo cannot bowl forever. It is a draw, quite a boring one.

At the Durban Country Club, the Natal Open had Papwa Sewgolum pitted against Gary Player this time. The Indian caddie versus the national icon.

As usual, Papwa changed and ate his wrapped lunch in his manager's car. While eating, he detected a dead myna, purposely placed under the windshield wipers.

Myna, a bird of Indian origin, brought to Durban by Indian migrants during the last few years of the 19th century. It was a fascinating addition to the biodiversity of the region. And it was not really much of a riddle why such a bird had been placed on the windshield of the car in which the Indian golfer was having his lunch.

It is a warning. Almost Corleonesque.

Papwa put the grotesque image out of his mind and rallied from being three strokes behind. Player later commented, "He chipped like a man from Mars."

Papwa won the tournament by one stroke. There was no rain this time. The prize-giving took place outdoors. Gary Player, one of the big three of that era alongside Arnold Palmer and Jack Nicklaus, was defeated by the man who could almost never tee off in a proper golf course in his own country.

Within two weeks of his win, authorities clamped down on mixed audiences watching sporting events. Papwa's non-White fans had been lucky to watch their hero at the pinnacle of his career graph.

The third Test at Newlands is equally tedious. South Africa scores 501 for 7, England 442, and the match dies an early death. But there are controversies to keep interest alive.

Barlow is all tangled feet, pads and bat as the ball from Titmus pops to gully. He thinks it has gone off his boot. The umpire is not sure. The English players cannot believe it. When Barlow crosses over with a single, Titmus mutters something about cheats. The South African retorts with colourful expletives, with the additional threat of putting the bat across the bowler's head.

Egged on by this, Barlow scores 138. The English fielders are indifferent as he crosses his landmark. Pithey hits 154 and his century sees over-enthusiastic support from every English cricketer.

During the England innings, Verwoerd watches some of the cricket. At tea, he comes to the dressing room to meet the players. Donald Carr summarises: "The Prime Minister found the players in various stages of undress, but he was very charming."

Prime Minister Verwoerd with rival captains Trevor Goddard and MJK Smith

After the break Peter Pollock pitches one outside Barrington's off-stump. It rises sharply and goes off the nick to Lindsay. Pollock doesn't even look back at the umpire as the team celebrates. But suddenly it dawns on them that Barrington hasn't moved, and neither has umpire John Warner. The fielders stand perplexed. After waiting long enough to make sure that the decision is not out, Barrington tucks his bat under his arm and walks.

The press is confused. Brian Johnston walks across to the dressing room, asking Barrington what exactly happened. The version from Carr is umpire Warner had declared not out, whereupon Barrington had walked. The pressmen debate the gesture of the batsman. If there has been no decision, some say, Barrington's walk is sporting. If the decision is not out, others argue, it is wrong to flaunt the judgement of the umpire. 'Tarnished Test' is the verdict of Charles Fortune.

It is during this Test that Fortune is joined in the commentary box by Clive van Ryneveld. The former captain has been wooed by the South African Broadcasting Corporation for half-hour views on the game. Seeing van Ryneveld come in, Fortune gruffly informs him that the deal is off since he has not confirmed his agreement. Van Ryneveld retreats in surprise. There was no confirmation clause, but there is no point in arguing.

Fortune's employers at SABC have categorically told him that he "cannot have that Progressive in the broadcasting box."

Adam Faith, one of the first major British popstars, arrived in South Africa to a Beatles welcome. However, during the first few performances, Faith found himself playing to White audiences, in spite of assurances otherwise.

As a test, the *Daily Mirror* sent an Asian journalist to buy a ticket for one of Adam's shows in Johannesburg. The box office refused, saying he wasn't allowed. At the same time, Faith was kept wondering whether the armed policemen who stood guard over him 24 hours a day were there to protect or to intimidate.

During a subsequent show, the police bundled two little Coloured girls up the aisle. To make it worse, as the girls were getting pushed out of the auditorium, the White audience applauded the vigilance of the authorities. Faith walked off the stage.

On 8 January 1965, Adam Faith flew back to London, cancelling the rest of his tour.

The *'Our English or their English'* Test match follows. Apart from the question posed by Vorster—discussed in the first chapter of this book—it is made memorable by Trevor Goddard's first ever century in Tests.

His highest so far has been 99. The best all-rounder in South Africa since Aubrey Faulkner finally crosses the three-figure mark. So excited are the scoreboard operators that 000 registers against Goddard's name. The official scorers, including the trendsetting lady Test match scorer Miss Patricia Williams, have to draw attention to the error from the other side of the ground. The correction results in yet more ovation.

In the final stages, as South Africa try to force a win, play is held up because Peter van der Merwe at silly mid-on casts a shadow on the pitch in front of the batsman. Goddard moves the fielder a few paces from the track. Immediately the sun goes behind a cloud and the shadow disappears. From the main grandstand a voice booms, "Move the bloody cloud!"

On 21 February 1965, a crowd of over 400 gathered at Manhattan's Audubon Ballroom. As people were settling down, a cry was heard: "Nigger! Get your hand outta my pocket." The security men moved in quickly to quell the disturbance, but at the same time a man rushed forward bearing a sawed-off shotgun. Almost simultaneously two other men charged towards the stage with semi-automatic weapons. It was the burst from the shot gun which caught Malcolm X in the chest. The barrage of bullets from the other weapons followed. By the time he was pronounced dead, 21 gunshot wounds were discovered on his body.

Before the final Test at Port Elizabeth, the general feeling in the England party is that Hammond should be there in the team's inner sanctum. But he lives in Durban and is not really well off.

A whip-around is organised to pay for his journey and hotel. This is one bright spot in the often-disturbed and upsetting life of the great batsman.

David Allen will later remember: "He would arrive at 10.30 every morning and hang his coat on the same peg. Then he'd shake hands with all of us as he left in the evening. In his way he was so obviously enjoying himself."

The Test is another dull draw. Graeme Pollock hits 137, scoring at will against his supposed Achilles Heel. Geoff Boycott responds to the South African score of 502 with a seven-hour somniferous yawn amounting to 117. In his frustration, Peter Pollock bowls two deliberate beamers at him. He does not even pretend that the balls have slipped or even make any attempt to apologise.

The last three strokes that took Graeme Pollock to his hundred

At lunch on Day 5, South Africa stand on 178 for 4, ahead by 245. Graeme Pollock on 77 from 77 balls. Jackie McGlew, reporting the match, is accosted by a spectator as he walks to a restaurant: "Do you think Goddard will declare? If he doesn't, I'll come back to watch Pollock. I can't bear to watch that lot (England) anymore."

Goddard does declare, and rains make sure that the spectators don't have to watch that lot for long. But Boycott spends an hour over his 7 anyway. John Murray remains unbeaten on 8 in 84 minutes. Waite catches Boycott to bring an end to his 14-year 50-Test career.

England win the pathologically boring series 1-0.

On 1 April 1965, John Harris sang 'We shall overcome' as he was hanged at dawn. A month ago, his appeal had failed. Clemency appeals were futile. Even a trip to Cape Town to meet the Minister of Justice John Vorster did not bear fruit.

Before his date of execution, Harris had managed to inform his wife Ann that he had been approached by a warder who wanted to help him escape. At great personal risk, Ad and Wal agreed to help Ann with the arrangements. But all that came to nothing, ultimately proving to have been a trap of the Security Police all along.

A sense of helplessness and fury engulfed Peter—interspersed with moments when he imagined carrying out heroic James Bond manoeuvres to rescue his friend.

On 1 April the phone rang and Ad answered. The voice at the other end asked for Ann. Recognising the voice to belong to a known Security Police officer, Ad refused. "Your friend is dead," informed the voice in a mocking tone.

Permission was sought for the body to be released for cremation. This was not a normal procedure, but the permission surprisingly came through. It was conjectured that the Security Police wanted to keep a tab on those who attended the event.

Under banning orders, Ad and Wal could not attend the cremation. Once again permission was sought and duly received. However, at the last moment, Wal's request to be allowed to read the main address was refused.

It was too late to ask anyone else. The helpless silence was interrupted by the heart-wrenching sobs of Ann. Peter felt deeply frustrated.

"Can I help?" he asked.

Ann's face lit up. Yes, Peter could indeed help.

The funeral address was two pages long. Wal had accounted for all of Ann's wishes as he had drawn it up. There was a sonnet of Shakespeare to begin with, followed by Jon Donne's:

No Man is an island, entire of itself. Every man
is a piece of the continent, a part of the man.
Any man's death diminishes me,
Because I am involved in mankind.
And therefore send not to know for whom
the bell tolls—it tolls for thee.

There followed Matthew's 'Blessed are they which are persecuted for righteousness sake' and Ecclesiastes 'To everything there is a season'. The songs were *Battle Hymn of the Republic*, and in the end *We Shall Overcome.*

Dressed in his school blazer and tie, aged all of 15 years, Peter was ushered up the raised lectern before the assembled congregation. His 12-year-old brother Tom stood squeezed between the pall-bearers. The chapel was full of non-Whites, unusually allowed to attend a White funeral. There were Liberal Party members from Pretoria and Johannesburg, people from the townships and diplomatic corps. All the names were being diligently noted by the Security Police.

Peter Hain himself wrote:

"Although the ceremony had been carefully prepared, and I had only to read out the address distributed to all who attended, I had never spoken from any platform before and had always avoided school plays and performances [...] The occasion made me even more nervous. Grown men crying and our Black maid Eva was sobbing heart-wrenchingly out loud. As I began, I trembled, my voice seeming not to want to come out. I had a stage fright moment wondering whether I could carry it off. But fortunately, that passed immediately.

"The proximity of the coffin a yard to my left, containing the body of a friend hanged only two hours earlier, made the ordeal especially unnerving."

Peter completed the address and stepped down, surrounded by a tearful Ann and his proud parents, his small brother and two sisters huddling together. Grown men came to thank him.

An hour later, he was back at school. His classmates had been told he would be late, but none of them knew the reason till they saw his picture in the papers the next day.

36 SUMMER OF TRIUMPH

It is early May. The New Road pitch is green. The air is damp with the approaching rain. Worcestershire are 58 for 3. The ball is moving around. Trevor Bailey has lost a lot of pace but has plenty of it upstairs to make things happen in such conditions. At the other end is Barry Knight, one of the most potent seam bowlers in England. The Essex attack is making the hosts sweat.

This is the situation when Basil D'Oliveira walks in for the first time in a Championship match for Worcestershire.

The ball moves, lifts, wobbles. D'Oliveira hangs in there. At the other end is Graveney. The two have developed a connection.

D'Oliveira just tries to survive. Never does he think beyond the next delivery.

An hour passes, and life becomes easier. Runs come quicker. The nasty jarring moments are over.

The innings builds. These two have already added a lot of runs in different types of cricket, in different parts of the world. Now the stand grows big.

By late afternoon the pitch has lost the zip. Knight comes back with the new ball. D'Oliveira hits him through the line, over his head, for a straight six. The bowler gives him a curious sidelong look down the wicket.

D'Oliveira's first effort at the wicket amounts to 106. Graveney 104. By the end of the second day, they are together again, having come together at 18 for 3. In the second innings D'Oliveira gets 47, Graveney 46, as the focus is on quick runs for declaration.

In between all that he bowls 20.4 overs to capture 3 for 41.

Quite a debut.

He is in a hurry to catch up.

Almost immediately after that, they go down to Brentwood to play the away match against Essex. Paddy Phelan and Robin Hobbs dismiss them for 135 on a turning wicket, clinching a first-innings lead of 167. Worcestershire is set 338 to win. D'Oliveira comes in at 51 for 3. Phelan runs through the innings with seven wickets. D'Oliveira bats virtually alone, ending with 163.

With two hundreds in two matches, both impeccable knocks in the toughest of conditions, it becomes apparent that he is knocking on the doors of Test selection.

Sir George Dowty, inventor of the first internally sprung aircraft wheel and owner of Dowty Aviation, is a patron of the Worcestershire County Cricket Club. He generally rewards impressive performances with £30. Dowty arranges a house for D'Oliveira near the city centre. D'Oliveira goes on to live there forever.

Of course, the run of centuries does not last. There are lean patches. Brian Close gets him for 1 when Worcestershire play Yorkshire. But runs and centuries continue to come.

Against Gloucestershire he scores 101 at home. When they play the county in Cheltenham, it is Graveney's grudge match. The first innings is a familiar story—38 for 3. Graveney 47, D'Oliveira 81. Partnership 102. To win they need 131 in less than three hours with the ball turning square. D'Oliveira has picked up 4 for 52 with off-spinners. David Allen and John Mortimore are almost unplayable. Graveney and D'Oliveira come together at 19 for 3.

And Graveney charges down the track, killing the spin almost halfway down. D'Oliveira stays back, plays late. The contrasting techniques yield runs from both sides. Victory by seven wickets, Graveney 59, D'Oliveira 55.

At the end of the season Graveney has 1684 Championship runs at 48.11 and D'Oliveira 1523 at 43.51. Four hundreds for Graveney, five for Dolly. Worcestershire win the Championship.

Goddard stays back as the South Africans get on the plane to London. The stalemate against New Zealand and defeat against England at home kickstarted a witch-hunt. Captaincy was the obvious target. Goddard was asked to resign on his own, with a statement that he wanted to concentrate on his game. He refused.

It means that Peter van der Merwe leads the side, yet another Springbok outfit no one wants to back—especially with the recent English success against the Kiwis.

When the visitors falter at the start and lose against Derbyshire, van der Merwe says: "I am pleased. Now we won't have an unbeaten record to worry about."

In New Zealand, the forthcoming visit of the Springbok rugby side was already creating complications. In April Maitu Rata, MP for Northern Maori, spoke out against Maori welcome for the Springboks. "Every New Zealander should re-examine his attitude towards South Africa [...] Maoris should not lower their principles just for 80 minutes of rugby."

However, opinion was divided. Maori Affairs minister Ralph Hanan supported the tour with the words, "In this country, we have some minorities with peculiar ideas. But we are living in a democracy. It is like a dog having fleas—he needs the fleas to know he is a dog."

When the Springboks arrived in Christchurch in the second week of July, one of the placards greeting them read, "Fleas Bite Again."

On 15 July 1965, ICC became the International Cricket Conference. For the first time there were associate members: Ceylon, Fiji, and the United States. A year later, they were joined by Bermuda, Denmark, East Africa, and Holland.

Nothing Bland about his movements

At Lord's, many of the South Africans get starts, but no one makes it big.

Barrington's 91 helps England get a 58-run lead, but not before Colin Bland creates a zone of terror around wherever he fields. Barrington pushes to vacant mid-on and takes off for what seems to be an easy single. Bland runs from mid-wicket to mid-on, picks up and throws down the only stump that he can see in one action.

Two hours later, Jim Parks chances Bland's arm. Realising the folly, he veers in line of the stumps, obstructing the line of the throw. Bland finds a gap between the scampering feet. The ball crashes into the stumps.

After that when he patrols the covers like a panther, no one wants to chance even safe singles. Fleet Street christens him Golden Eagle.

Bland follows it up with 70 in the second innings. England need 191 in four hours. But perhaps the inertia of the South African winter a few months ago keeps them tentative. John Edrich ducks into a Pollock delivery and is hit near his temple. The thudding noise is heard around the ground. He stands up, dazed and wobbly and then collapses. As the South African fielders gather around, someone tells Pollock, "You've lost your touch. He didn't drop immediately." Not in the best taste.

They finish at 145 for 7, effectively 8 down, Titmus and Rumsey playing out time. "We could have done it in singles," says MJK Smith.

During the Test match, the Waldorf Hotel, where the South African cricketers stayed, was besieged by anti-apartheid demonstrators. "Going to see the Whites-only South African team? It's not cricket," proclaimed one banner. It was the idiomatic expression that was at fault. It was cricket—in its purest form. Cricket has always been about privilege and discrimination. It is the gentleman's game only if we restrict the term 'gentleman' as synonymous to wealthy, influential, directly or indirectly linked to aristocracy, and, of course, White.

Back in South Africa, in 1965, the 90-day detention period was increased to 180. The station bomb planted by John Harris was used as a bargaining chip.

Trent Bridge. A Test that will forever be special in the history of South African cricket.

On a grey and grassless pitch, with the sun out, the visitors are happy to win the toss and bat. But by the time the score pushes along to 40, four men are out. Tom Cartwright makes the ball do all sorts of things. At 80 Bacher loses his stump to Snow.

Peter Pollock cannot bear to watch his brother defy the bowlers in these circumstances. Every ball is filled to the brim with tension. He locks himself up in the backroom as van der Merwe joins Graeme.

What follows is a masterclass of counterattack. Pollock, according to his brother Peter, "[takes] the English attack in his teeth and shakes it like a dog would do with a rag doll." As he starts scoring runs, his brother is locked away by his mates. He cannot be allowed to watch. Too much is at stake.

Graeme pierces the field with elan and class and finds gaps that mortals cannot see. 21 fours in his 125, the last 91 runs off 90 balls in 70 minutes during which van der Merwe scores 10—a knock that makes him a bona fide legend. When Peter is allowed to come back and watch, he sees his brother being caught in the slips.

Graeme Pollock is not happy with the dismissal. He believes he has hit the ground and the ball has deflected from one of the footmarks. He is glum as he comes back and is abrupt with the gentleman who comes up to him in the dressing room to offer his congratulations. It is only after a while that Pollock recognises Len Hutton and turns on his charm. Hutton does not often come into the visiting dressing room to acknowledge batsmen, but this is special.

The total is 269. Now Peter Pollock strikes twice before the day is over. The victims are on the wish list of every bowler. Boycott edges to slip and Tiger Lance juggles the ball for a few excruciating fractions of a second before clutching on. Barrington has his stumps uprooted. England are 16 for 2. It is also the birthday of the mother of Graeme and Peter.

The next morning, Cowdrey plays a gem. Batsmen fall around him, but he has way more time to play the ball and strokes his way to 105. Only 29 separate the sides even though Peter has five wickets.

In the second knock, Bacher, Barlow, Graeme Pollock all get half-centuries. 2 for 35, 4 for 193, 7 for 243 … the score looks alternately good and bad. The final total is 289. 319 to win.

Once again England start towards the end of the day. Peter Pollock induces an edge off Barber. Titmus is sent in to hold fort and is out soon after. Snow comes in as second night watchman. A curious ploy. That means Smith is at No 8, Parks at 9. There is a chance of running out of partners.

In any case Snow is out early the following morning, and night watchman or not the score reads 10 for 3. Barrington gloves a hook off Pollock, and it is 13 for 4. At 41 Cowdrey raises his heel a wee bit as he misses a leg-glance off McKinnon and Lindsay stumps him in a flash. At 59 Boycott succumbs to McKinnon's break.

55 runs between Smith and Parfitt and then Graeme Pollock the bowler strikes. The leg break catches the England captain plumb. But Parfitt-Parks, the last pair that can bat, put together a fighting, frustrating partnership. The score crosses 200.

Peter Pollock, for the first time in his life, summons God to help him. If he gets the three wickets, he prays, he won't touch the celebratory drink. And his prayers are answered. Parfitt and Cartwright fall at 207. At 224 Larter skies one and it is swallowed by the bucket hands of van der Merwe.

This is the proudest moment in the lives of the Pollocks—Graeme the gem in the first innings and Peter picking up 10 wickets in the match. Now the latter cannot drink. The rest sip, savour and enjoy the moment, Peter Pollock stands aloof. An hour passes, then two.

And then comes the hand of God. A policeman has been posted with the team to keep demonstrators and activists at bay. He comes enters the bathroom and looks at the fast bowler.

"Peter, why are you so glum? You guys have won a Test. Celebrate." Like a conjuring trick, this upholder of the law fishes out a beer. It is a sign from the Almighty himself. Peter Pollock drinks.

The Springboks were still in New Zealand when, on 5 September 1965, Hendrik Verwoerd spoke at the opening of the National Party's Transvaal Youth League at Loskop Dam. The Springboks had subjected themselves to the traditions and customs of New Zealand. The South African government expected the New Zealanders to do the same when they were the guests of South Africa.

It was an unequivocal reaffirmation of the government's commitment to Apartheid in sports. The Maori rugby stars were not welcome. The previous year, 10 New Zealanders had been invited to participate in the 75th anniversary celebrations of the South African Rugby Board. They had been five White players, three senior administrators and two Maori representatives. NZRFU had sent Pat Walsh and Ralph Lowe. Lowe had been chosen because he was supportive of the South African stance on Maori players. Walsh had been chosen because he was very fair skinned and could easily pass for a White.

While treated as a European through the tour, the only hitch had been when a group of players had tried to get Walsh into one of their teams. Springbok legend Danie Craven had made it clear that the time was not right for Walsh to play.

Nonetheless, the NZRFU had been encouraged to believe that there was a possibility of sending an unbiasedly representative team to South Africa in 1967. Verwoerd's speech removed every bit of confusion.

It did not matter to the Prime Minister that rugby was more than the national sport of the Afrikaner—it was life blood. It did not quite matter to him that the Springboks were there in New Zealand playing against the All Blacks. National survival—his conception of survival—

was more important than any sport.

Verwoerd: All Blacks would have to be all-white to play in South Africa

At The Oval the South Africans are in for a surprise. Starting the England attack is 35-year-old Brian Statham. Perhaps Barlow and Lindsay absentmindedly look around for the possible presence of Trueman in some corner.

South Africa, inserted on a rainy, cloudy day, finish on 152 for 5, and the following day are all-out for 208. Statham has 5 for 40. Class is permanent. Pollock responds with 5 for 43. England are out for 202.

Now Bland shows that his dazzling fielding often hides the fact that he is a terrific batsman. He scores 127, Bacher 70, Tiger Lance 53. A total of 392. England need 399 to win in less than seven hours.

This team has been excruciatingly slow in every remembered Test in recent times. People have shuddered at the thought of watching 'that lot'. Now suddenly, on the final day, they turn a side of brilliant and attractive stroke-makers. Barrington even slams sixes. Cowdrey carries on the charge.

"Don't rush through the overs," repeats van der Merwe. The South Africans don't. They wait for the promising clouds to empty their load. But they pass by.

Suddenly, it is 91 to get in 70 minutes. Pollock, already into his 33rd over, has been told that he will have to carry on right to the end. The clouds have almost cleared when, all of a sudden, a small obliging black one comes along and empties itself on The Oval. The crowd is disappointed. The Surrey members are quite bitter as the fielders walk in. The time-wasting manoeuvres have not gone undetected. But the young South Africans do not care. They have won the series.

The final innings also saw Eric Russell open for England and play a thoughtful innings of

70 on the final morning. It was perhaps the knock that tilted the balance in his way. It was Russell who went to Australia and not D'Oliveira. According to MJK Smith, it was touch and go.

Towards the end of the year, D'Oliveira had a freak accident. He had taken a winter job with the Metal Box Company. He was in a car full of employees of the company, on their way to a local hotel near Droitwich for a drink, when the car crashed. A girl was killed and D'Oliveira was knocked unconscious.

When he regained consciousness 12 hours later, he was shocked to find his right arm was badly broken. There was even a possibility that his career was over.

37 TESTING TIMES

Ron Headley—full name Ronald George Alphonso Headley. Destined to spend a career under the humongous shadow of his great father George Headley. But he was a decent enough batsman for Worcestershire. It must have been quite a curious experience for him to face the Jamaica Invitation XI at Montego Bay that spring.

For D'Oliveira, however, Worcestershire's tour of Jamaica was reassuring. Before the visit, skipper Don Kenyon had asked him how he was. D'Oliveira had replied that he could perhaps bat a bit but not bowl. Turning his arm over was painful.

After undergoing further treatment, he had travelled. In the first match against Jamaica Colts, Kenyon had made him bowl 25 overs. It felt okay.

Against the Jamaica Invitation XI, which included Garry Sobers as a guest player, he scored a second innings 101. Reassuring indeed, after that near-fatal accident. Only, he couldn't throw. He had to stand in slip all day.

The Worcestershire team knew that D'Oliveira would not be able to throw that entire season. They were okay with it. He could bat, bowl and stand in the slips. But there was a complication. After D'Oliveira scored 80 and 83 for MCC against Yorkshire at Lord's at the beginning of the season, and dismissed Boycott, Close and John Hampshire as well, the men who mattered started thing of him as an England prospect.

On 3 February 1966, Prime Minister Keith Holyoake intervened in New Zealand Rugby Football Union's approach to the South African tour.

Keith Hollyoake

Earlier the NZRFU president Tom Pearce had stated, "We have a duty to the Maoris but also to the game of Rugby." Holyoake had replied that racial equality was fundamental to the New Zealand way of life.

Now, Holyoake was clear: "Where important moral issues are involved fundamental to our national integrity, the Government has a duty to state clearly the principles which, in its view, New Zealanders should observe at home and abroad [...] In this country we are one people, as such we cannot as a nation be truly represented in any sphere by a group chosen on racial lines."

The NZRFU understood the directive. The 1967 tour was off. The small country had taken the big step.

On 4 March 1966, Beatlemania was raging through the world. John Lennon gave an interview to *London Evening Standard* voicing: "Christianity will go. It will vanish and shrink. I needn't argue with that; I'm right and I will be proved right. We're more popular than Jesus now; I don't know which will go first—rock 'n' roll or Christianity. Jesus was all right but his disciples were thick and ordinary. It's them twisting it that ruins it for me."

A few days later South Africa Broadcasting Corporation banned Beatles songs. As a result, Nancy Sinatra's *These Boots Are Made For Walkin'* and SGT Barry Sadler's *The Ballad of The Green Berets* were the greatest hits on South African radio in 1966.

Ad and Wal were trapped. The bans had all but blocked their political effectiveness. The family was struggling to survive. Wal had had to give up his job as an architect, his bans inducing the firm he worked for to fire him. He opened a private office, but having to apply for permission every time he had to inspect and survey sites outside the Pretoria magisterial district made it hard to do business. An appeal by the head of the South African Architects' Association also fell on deaf ears. In fact, word had been circulated that all private architectural firms seeking government projects were better off not employing or collaborating with Walter Hain.

Wal wrote to the architectural firm in London for whom he had worked in 1956. He got an offer immediately.

The entire family got hold of British passports, using Wal's father's Glasgow roots, Peter's birth in the British colony of Kenya and Sally's birth in England. The British Embassy helpfully registered the other two siblings, Tom and Jo-anne.

Of course, there were complications. The Security Police did not play ball. They were the Hains after all. When informed that all of them had British passports and departure permits, they withdrew the latter and issued one-way exit permits. This effectively withdrew the South African citizenship of the family. The permission to leave Pretoria was delayed till the last moment.

Ad and Wal in South Africa

It was Peter and Tom who went to say goodbye to the Liberal Party members. Because of their bans, Ad and Wal were not allowed to do so. It was a relief to escape the regime. Peter was also excited on noting the proximity of Lord's, Wembley, and Stamford Bridge to their proposed rented accommodation at Putney. He was also able to book cheap tickets for the 1966 World Cup football finals.

However, when they boarded the Union Castle Liner on 14 March 1966, there was a feeling of deep sorrow associated with helplessness. They had tried their best to change the country but apartheid raged on.

A press release was issued in Peter's name—because of the bans on the parents—which urged the Whites to change before it was too late.

On the ship Walter Hain and a Black lady co-traveller appeared together in the fancy-dress evening with their pyjamas labelled 'The Immorality Act'.

At almost the same time a ship sailed the other way, from England to South Africa. Vivian Higgs, a 19-year-old girl was on board, returning after visiting her brother Barry in London. Barry was a White ANC member in exile.

Two large suitcases had been designed by Jack Hodgson. In the false bottoms, Vivian carried subversive leaflets. When the ship docked in Cape Town, the White girl aroused little interest in the Customs. The leaflets were mailed to the addresses given to her soon after that.

The first successful operation was thus completed. A special London unit of the ANC and the South African Communist Party soon started recruiting and training young White international anti-apartheid supporters. Unknown because of their non-South African origins, and unsuspected because they were white, they would infiltrate into South Africa and carry out plenty of subversive activity that the imprisoned or under-surveillance ANC members could not. They became known as the London Recruits.

The West Indies were supposed to come in 1971. The scintillating series of 1963 had been very recent. It was all written down in *Wisden* under the heading Future Tours.

But MCC bent the Holy Writ of the cricketing bible. Double tours started taking place, with New Zealand and South Africa sharing 1965 as India and Pakistan would share 1967. It freed up 1966 for yet another visit by the great Caribbean side.

That made it an extraordinary summer of sports for England. Garry Sobers romped around the country, scoring 722 runs at 103.14, picking up 20 wickets at 27.25 and grabbing 10 catches in the five Tests (1349 at 61.31, 60 at 20.58 and 23 being the respective tour figures) It was a year in Excelsis for this magical cricketer. And at Wembley on 30 July, Geoff Hurst's hat-trick was the feature of United Kingdom's most watched television event ever. England beat the West Germans 4-2, winning their only World Cup till the time of writing—ensuring that about 90% of the football books in English would be based directly or indirectly on the 1966 theme for the next 200 years or so.

On 30 March 1966, just 16 days after the departure of the Hains, the National Party swept the polls with overwhelming support, winning 126 of the 170 seats. For the Progressive Party there was one solitary win, courtesy Helen Suzman.

Surveys showed that more than 80% of the Afrikaners disagreed with the statement that "there is no difference between the Whites and the Blacks and what exists is only a difference of opportunity." They also believed that Bantus should remain Bantus as they were different by nature and that multi-racial democracy was not practicable.

What made it even more alarming was that 66–75% of the English-speaking elites of South Africa subscribed to these beliefs.

Jackie McGlew stood for the parliament in NP colours, but he was unsuccessful.

West Indies play Worcestershire in early May. Only 8.1 overs are possible before a mean solid drizzle becomes a downpour. At half past three play is called off for the day. During the evening, Sobers speaks at a cocktail party for the visitors. "We always enjoy coming to Worcester. We always know we shall get one day off."

The next day match restarts and stops and left-arm spinner Rawle Brancker, who will never play for West Indies, proves difficult to play. D'Oliveira walks in at 152 for 3 and drives Gibbs to the extra cover fence. The following over, he plays a horrid cross batted stroke at Brancker and is caught low at slips for 7. The match sees four hours of action, 92 overs in all. The third day is washed out as well.

In February 1966, a few days after New Zealand cancelled the 1967 tour of South Africa, the England cricket team crossed the Tasman Sea for the New Zealand leg of the tour after the split Ashes of 1965–66. MJK Smith was the captain and Billy Griffith the manager. Griffith, a former wicketkeeper of England, was also the MCC Secretary. Reactions were sought and Griffith was asked how MCC would react in a similar situation.

Hypothetical question of course, but what else could Griffith say in New Zealand without ruffling diplomatic feathers than 'MCC would also cancel.'

Three drawn Tests later, as he flew home, Griffith was plagued with doubts.

The failure in that innings against West Indies did not matter.

During a game at Beaconsfield, a benefit match for Roy Booth, Ron Headley was batting with D'Oliveira when they met at the middle of the pitch. The match was held up because of an announcement over the loudspeaker. All D'Oliveira heard was "crackle, crackle, sputter, squawk."

Headley, however, did decipher the message—the names of the 12-member England team to play West Indies in the first Test at Old Trafford. "I'll tell you something," said Headley. "You're in the side." Soon afterwards, a ball from fast bowler Ray Bond rolled on to his foot and trickled between the middle and leg stumps, without dislodging a bail. D'Oliveira celebrated, scoring 104.

At the age of 34 (officially 31), D'Oliveira had overcome infinite obstacles and managed to break into the highest form of the game.

When he called Naomi to give her the news, he could make out she was crying.

D'Oliveira was chaired off the ground that day, on the shoulders of Worcestershire teammates Martin Horton and Norman Gifford. Congratulatory messages came in from everywhere—verbal, letters, phone calls, telegrams. Many were from South Africa.

But in D'Oliveira's mind there was a niggle. He still could not throw. Shouldn't he mention that to the selectors?

Don Kenyon, the Worcestershire captain, knew about his arm. He was also an England selector. We don't quite know whether he raised the issue in the selection meeting. Whatever it was, D'Oliveira was selected. There was far too much at stake for him. He was after all a slip fielder. Although, on second thoughts, Cowdrey and Titmus were in the side and they were England's specialist slip fielders. Besides, in all probability he would be a 12th man at Old Trafford. If he substituted for anyone, it would not be at slip. Substitutes were not allowed to field in specialist positions. Wasn't he better off telling the selectors about the problem?

But again, all the years—of hopelessness, of being stuck in a country where his talent had to shine unseen; and now an opportunity after 16 years of cricket. How many more seasons did he have?

"If I had to throw, I'd throw, even though my arm came out."

He remained silent about his arm.

In his position, the author at least would have done the same—or perhaps something much worse.

When D'Oliveira reaches Old Trafford, he sees some of the lads from Middleton. "We hope you play."

"Being in the twelve is enough for me," lies D'Oliveira.

The night before the game, David Allen shares his room. "I think you'll get in," he says. "There's more grass on the pitch than everybody expected."

It is a toss-up between Allen and D'Oliveira.

The next morning, the grass on the pitch is much less. Besides, Lancashire captain Brian Statham has informed Peter May that the pitch will be like the Old Trafford wicket of 1963, when Gibbs had taken 11 for 157.

Hence, MJK Smith comes up to D'Oliveira and asks, "You do twelfth, Bas?" Allen plays.

West Indies bat. D'Oliveira ventures into the field with a sweater for Titmus.

By the end of the day, Allen has failed to take a wicket. Hunte scores 135. Sometimes Sobers plays back to a yorker, sometimes he hits the ball on the up with his feet all wrong. But the end result is always the ball rebounding back onto the field from the boundary boards. At the end of the day, he is 83 not out. West Indies 343 for 5. The wicket is bound to turn later.

The next day, they stretch the score to 484. Sobers 161. The fast bowlers of West Indies have not really clicked so far. Hall has found the soft pitches slowing down his furious deliveries. Griffith has been hounded by umpires shuttling between square leg and cover point, scrutinising his elbow every delivery. With Syd Buller watching him in the Test, he becomes almost a medium pacer.

But Gibbs picks up five; one of them is Russell, caught by Sobers at short leg after going the wrong way and recovering to fly through the air. England are all out 167. They do somewhat better in the second innings, Colin Milburn somehow swivelling around with that colossal bulk to hook Hall, Griffith and Sobers. England sit pretty on 142 for 1 and the bowlers look tired when Barrington swats a long hop to Nurse at mid-on. The end is quick, with Gibbs picking up another five.

The loss of a Test at the start of a season—the English formula for a witch-hunt. Besides, the focus is on the skipper—surprise, surprise!—who has been woefully short of runs. Out goes Smith as captain, Cowdrey taking on the mantle. Out go Russell, Allen, and Brown. In come Barry Knight and Geoff Boycott, and the 39-year-old Tom Graveney is recalled into the side. And then there is D'Oliveira.

He is set to make his debut at the Mecca of Cricket.

SECTION 5
Political Intrigue

38 DOUBLY DYING SHALL GO DOWN

Peter Hain was admitted to the local state grammar school, Emmanuel, in Battersea. The career advisor, who also taught history and supervised the Combined Cadet Force, asked him what he wanted to do down the line. Peter had no idea.

"In that case, you'll be an engineer," was the verdict.

As Ad and Wal became active in the Anti-Apartheid Movement in Britain, Peter and Tom spent the summer enjoying a lot of what England had to offer. That included television, something alien to South Africa.

They watched the World Cup final at Wembley, standing next to a Spurs fan at the so-called 'Geoff Hurst end'.

They also watched West Indies play England in three Test matches, starting with the second at Lord's.

It was eerie. Peter and his family, all but forced to leave South Africa and settle in England, watching a Cape-Coloured South African who had been refused official cricket in South Africa, making his Test debut for England.

On the morning of the Test match at Lord's, D'Oliveira left the Clarendon Court Hotel in St John's Wood and walked down to the ground. The day was grey and overcast. As D'Oliveira walked towards the pavilion, he wondered how the wicket would behave.

"I went out to the pavilion balcony alone. For a few minutes I was king. I wished everybody in South Africa could see me. Until six years before, Lord's to me had been remote, almost a holy place [...] now I was not only at Lord's, but about to play for England. Very few people are allowed such a moment in their lives. After it, nothing ever matters so much again."

It had been a long arduous journey from the cobblestoned streets of Signal Hill.

Ted Swannell, the Lord's groundsman, says that the strip being used is the same as that used in the 1955 Test, when Jack Cheetham had his elbow crocked. In 1963, on a different strip, Colin Cowdrey had his arm broken by a Wes Hall lifter.

Sobers wins the toss and bats on the cloudy, windy summer day. The start leaves them tottering—42 for 2, 53 for 3. At lunch the clouds close in, and they are dark. Ken Barrington is not one to get sentimental. However, he says to D'Oliveira: "If they don't bowl another ball, they can't take this away from you. This one is yours for keeps."

They do manage to bowl a few more that day. 155 for 4, with Sobers surviving a first ball snick to slip.

35 minutes into the second day's play, Cowdrey introduces D'Oliveira. Nurse and Sobers are still there, the scoreboard looking better for the West Indians. The ball is quite new and the dew-freshened pitch is to D'Oliveira's liking. He hits a length, moves the ball either way. Nurse is bowled leg-stump from one that comes back from up the slope.

West Indies total 269. D'Oliveira 14-5-24-1.

England start their innings half an hour after lunch. Milburn is repeatedly hit on the pads and is declared out by thousands of West Indians in the crowd. Finally, the umpire agrees with them. Hall strikes.

At 8 for 1 and the packed house rises to greet Graveney. The exiled stylist. In his long-peaked cap. Graceful and grand as ever. Moving effortlessly in line. Boycott and he add 115. Gibbs induces a false stroke from the Yorkshireman. At close of play, the score is 145 for 2.

The next morning, a full house claps Barrington and Graveney to the wicket. An injured thumb prevents Graveney from carrying on his fabulous stroke-play. Barrington, out of sorts, is yorked by Sobers. Cowdrey prods around for almost an hour before being caught off the shoulder of the bat to a rising delivery from Hall. It is Parks who joins Graveney as D'Oliveira waits his turn miserably. Every passing minute is agonising. He is going insane in the age-old batsman's problem of waiting for his turn. He is never prone to such reactions, but today, the stakes are sky-high.

A Graveney hundred on comeback will be a delight. D'Oliveira would also like the familiar sight of Graveney at the wicket as he walks in for the first time in Test cricket. But the older maestro is caught committed on the front foot to one from Hall that bounces a bit too much. The attempted steer is caught by wicketkeeper Allan. Graveney out for 96. D'Oliveira passes him as he returns acknowledging the applause.

203 for 5. Hall senses a collapse. A terrifying sight as he charges in. Dom Moraes in the *Evening Standard* describes the initial plight of D'Oliveira succinctly: "*One trembled for D'Oliveira. He wore a deeply depressed look and prodded miserably at the tigerish Hall, who bowled faster every over.*"

But he survives. The new ball is weathered. D'Oliveira and Parks are still there after an hour. Hall and Griffith overpitch, D'Oliveira drives and turns them for boundaries. Sobers replaces Griffith and pitches short, and he cuts and steers him for fours.

Then Parks drives one back from Hall. D'Oliveira, standing wide of the stumps, is struck on the boot. The ball is deflected on to the stumps. He is confused. He is not out, but he does not really know what has happened. He is not sure where the ball is. Hall, with great presence of mind, swoops down on the ball and yanks out a stump. D'Oliveira is slow to react. His innings is over—a heart-breaking dismissal on debut. His score is 27.

The crowd is magnificent. The weird dismissal has garnered sympathy. Many of them have a reasonable idea—if not the full details—that it has been a miracle for him to play Test cricket. He is given a loud ovation as he returns.

England total 355 thanks to 91 by Parks. The Queen arrives and meets the players, saying a few words to D'Oliveira who will not for his life be able to remember them later. But there is a picture of D'Oliveira being introduced to the Queen by Colin Cowdrey, which will be used by *Private Eye* two years down the line.

In the second knock, West Indies is 95 for 5, only 9 ahead. Nurse has been dismissed by D'Oliveira again, caught behind trying to hit his way out of the shackles of nagging line and length.

But Cowdrey spreads the field for Sobers in order to bowl at Holford. Sobers obliges by taking easy runs. Holford is resolute. Towards the end of the day a silky cover drive gets Sobers his century, and a fan runs in to embrace him and lift him into the air. Next day Holford scores his hundred, and they are still unseparated when Sobers declares at 369 for 5.

284 to get in less than three hours. Milburn slams 3 sixes off Hall and Griffith. He brings up his hundred with two consecutive strokes towards the Tavern, one of them off the top edge. Some ill-advised English spectators emulate their West Indian counterparts and try to lift Milburn. At 110 kg, the batsman remains rooted.

It's a draw, but a fascinating one.

On 11 February 1966, District Six, the home of the vibrant Coloured community since the early 19th century, was declared a White area. About 33,000 people were affected by the decision, more than 31,000 of them Coloured. Some 1,200 were Indian. Only 1% of the residents were White.

As Ken Barrington takes a fatigue-caused break, 21-year-old Derek Underwood makes his debut at Trent Bridge. Brian Scovell scoffs: "The dearth of spin bowlers in English cricket is such that the man the selectors finally chose is not really a spinner at all. He is a slow-medium cutter and floater rather than a genuine tweaker."

The slow medium cutter and floater will go on to out-bowl Bishan Bedi and Bhagwat Chandrasekhar in India. He has come straight out of Beckenham and Penge Grammar School and has started taking wickets for Kent.

He is given only two of the 90.5 overs that West Indies bat. John Snow, Ken Higgs and D'Oliveira bowl 80.4. D'Oliveira sends down the highest number of overs for his side. 30-14-51-2. For once Sobers fails. When Parks catches him off an outside edge, 20,000 people leap out of their seats. 235 all out.

And in the last 50 minutes, Sobers turns things around. "James Bond of the 1966 series," writes Scovell. Taking the new ball instead of Griffith, he traps Boycott plumb in front. Then he catches Milburn off Hall. England end the day 33 for 3.

The following day 'Old Man' Graveney scores 109, but Cowdrey takes way too long over his 96. Typical stop-go effort, like the British economy. D'Oliveira walks into another crisis, 221 for 5, which becomes 238 for 6.

The next morning Colin Cowdrey is stopped as he tries to walk through the Trent Bridge press gate because he does not have a press card. A journalist vouches for him. "You'd better let him through, else England will be in a spot of trouble."

D'Oliveira has no nerves this time around. He drives powerfully through the covers, plays delectably late when required. Wickets tumble around him, and it is 260 for 9, and he adds 65 with debutant Underwood before Hall bowls him for 76.

Nothing can go wrong for him. Hunte is taken at slip off his very first delivery. Lashley considers him slow enough to sweep and is caught plumb. Kanhai and Butcher embark on a display of blocking that irks Denis Compton. 'Disgraceful', he summarises. Six successive maidens bowled by Underwood to Kanhai.

Kanhai reaches his 50 just before the end of the day. A West Indian girl runs in from square-leg and plants a kiss on his cheek.

After the rest day, Basil Butcher, missed five times, accelerates on the way to 209 not out. Sobers walks in at 282 for 4 and hammers 94. On the final day, England make an effort to get 393. But Milburn is out early. Boycott drives to long on and runs five. One run is deducted as the umpires decide the ball has crossed the line. The crowd boos.

But Boycott, Graveney, Parks, and Cowdrey depart one after the other. The chase is derailed. D'Oliveira bats defensively, trying to save the game. But he loses patience as he loses partners and swings at Griffith to be leg before for 54. England lose by 139 runs.

At the end of July 1966, Dennis Brutus finally managed to get an exit permit—just like the Hains—and made for England. His first stop was Wembley for the World Cup final. Peter Hain was also there, but they would eventually meet a couple of years later.

In August 1966, Verwoerd was invited to a private showing of *Othello* with the face-blackened Lawrence Olivier in the lead role. Verwoerd obviously could not dispute the excellence of the performance, but immediately after the screening, he expressed his opposition to the film being shown to South African audiences. In the racial set-up of the Republic, its showing was unthinkable. That was that. *Othello* was banished, a la Romeo.

The fourth Test is a month later. The World Cup has to be considered—neither sport would like to lose spectators or column space to the other. West Indies spend the interim period playing tour matches. D'Oliveira, like the other England cricketers, goes off to play for his county.

It rains through much of the first day of the Headingley Test. The defining statistic is read out by Bill Bowes over the press-box intercom: "Minutes played 192, minutes lost 168"

On the following day Sobers and Nurse almost match these two figures. Sobers, with 174 in a four-hour romp, forces cricket back on the sports pages, cutting through the World Cup mania. When he reaches his hundred with a sweep off D'Oliveira, a stern policeman grabs the green-skirted West Indian girl who tries to run in and kiss him. At 150, Roger Emmett, aged 12, from Ashington, shakes him by the hand after beating the defensive field set by the police corps. Nurse, 137, is more sedate but hits two towering sixes. 500 for 9 declared.

Boycott and Barber open to play out the rest of the second day. By the end of the third day, Barber is still not out … but in the second innings. On a perfectly easy batting track, England lose the first six wickets to Hall, Griffith and Sobers for just 83. When Barber slashes Griffith to lose his wicket, Len Hutton jots down for the *Observer* that the likes of Leyland or Paynter would not have played that shot even if offered a fiver.

Hall's slips are far back in the distance. He beats the bat and leaps in a curious ritual. Milburn just stands there, without playing a stroke, and receives a crack on his elbow. When Griffith lets go a bouncer at Graveney, Richie Benaud from the television commentator's box says, 'No ball.' Umpire Charlie Elliott has a word with the bowler.

D'Oliveira comes in at 42 for 3. It becomes 49 for 4, 63 for 5, 83 for 6. Just before lunch he straight drives Gibbs into the Rugby stand. After the break he short-arm pulls Holford for six more. Sobers comes on, bowling spin now, and D'Oliveira pulls him over mid-wicket for a third six.

It is back to Hall. The fast man comes charging in. D'Oliveira launches into a straight drive that lands in the rugby stand—the first time Hall has been hit for six in England with a straight bat. He claps.

One drive is not timed properly. Hunte dives forward, comes up with the ball. D'Oliveira stands his ground. Umpire Elliott asks Hunte if he has held it. The Bajan says yes. Elliott says not out. He is close to the ball and perhaps has seen it touch the ground. Hunte may have been mistaken in thinking he has caught the ball. The West Indian pressmen are shocked—Hunte is deeply religious and cannot lie.

In any case, D'Oliveira carries on in his counter-attacking ways. At 88, however, his productive slash over cover goes askew and Hall catches him off Griffith. 88 runs with 8 fours and 4 sixes. He returns to a standing ovation. This is the type of innings that had made him famous in non-White cricket of South Africa.

But England are bowled out for 240. In the second innings D'Oliveira is sent in at No 3. He survives the day but is strangely quiet the next morning. After 53 minutes he is caught at backward short leg off Sobers for 7. England fold for 205. Sobers 6 for 39. The rubber is now lost.

The same experts who had said Cowdrey should replace MJK Smith now root for Brian Close to replace Cowdrey.

In late August 1966, Hendrik Verwoerd spoke to Chief Leabua Jonathan, Prime Minister of the soon-to-be-independent Lesotho (erstwhile Batsuoland), in a historic meeting. It was the first time a South African Prime Minister had met the leader of a Black state of South Africa itself.

On 6 September, the Prime Minister was scheduled to speak in the Parliament. He was expected to make a policy speech, speak about the discussion with Chief Jonathan and also talk about South Africa's international position and the future of the Coloureds in South Africa.

Before that he and his wife spent a couple of days holidaying with members of the family at Stokkeisdraai, his farm along the Vaal river. He went on vigorous long walks—a feature of his life.

Ironically, Cowdrey is attending a dinner at The Oval when he is informed by the selectors that he is not going to lead the side there. When he rings home to tell his wife, eight-year-old Christopher asks: "What has Daddy done wrong?" 22 years later, Chris Cowdrey will be hauled out of his county ground and put in charge of a beleaguered England side against West Indies. One Test later, he will be sacked as captain and cricketer. Some patterns transcend generations.

Close wins plenty of friends by announcing that England can win the fifth Test. There are six changes to the team. Cowdrey is dropped. Even Milburn, who averages 52.66 in the series, is left out. Alec Bedser, spokesman of the selectors, says it is because his fielding is not up to Test match standard. "What are young boys watching on television to think when they see the England team fielding?"

"I was 16 stone as a kid, it's not going to be easy to lose weight just like that," says Milburn.

23-year-old Dennis Amiss makes his debut. And of course, D'Oliveira is in the side. He has made his place secure.

To break the monopoly Sobers has had with the toss, Close takes with him a Bermuda crown, given to him on his honeymoon in the West Indies. It does not work. Along with all the runs, wickets, and catches, Sobers wins all five tosses in the series.

He scores 81. It is Kanhai who gets a hundred. But apart from a belligerent Hall in the tail, no one else sticks around. The total of 268 is a bit unimpressive given the wicket.

The following day, in rising heat, Sobers bowls chinaman in a sweater. He dismisses Barber and Edrich. Hall traps debutant Amiss leg before, and then yorks D'Oliveira for 4. That is the South African's only failure in the Tests. But this is the fairy tale Test of Tom Graveney. 166 for 7, and West Indies look like making it 4-0. Cautious but glorious when opportunity presents itself, he creams 165. John Murray, the wicketkeeper in for Parks, hits 112. They add 217. And with Hall and Griffith tiring, Sobers bowling only spinners, Hunte put on to bowl, and Gibbs ineffective, Higgs and Snow have their own fun. Snow has 8 runs in the previous seven Test innings. His father, the Vicar Dr William Snow, has promised him 10s for each run he scores.

Both Snow and Higgs end up hitting fifties and adding 128. The England innings draws to an end at 527.

When West Indies come in to bat again, Snow gets both the openers. Bits of Sobers rubbing off perhaps? D'Oliveira bowls Kanhai as he tries a forcing stroke off the backfoot.

Sobers comes in on the fourth morning at 137 for 5. Snow has the ball, Close squats four yards away at a sort of silly short leg. The ball is a rank long hop. Sobers spins round to swing it to the leg side boundary. It catches the bottom of the bat and then his body and lobs gently to Close. The great man is out first ball. His average for the series shoots down to a mere 103.

West Indies are bundled for 225. Victory to England by an innings and 34 runs. West Indies take the series 3-1.

"A magnificent side to play against," says Close, before adding, "and beat."

As for D'Oliveira, Scovell writes: "I can see him playing in the England side for years to come." The tour book published in 1966 contains four chapters by John Clarke and the rest by Scovell. Clarke tragically died after the first Test.

In that 1966 book are Scovell's ominous words: "It would be a tragedy if [D'Oliveira] was left out of the next touring side to visit South Africa in 1968–69 purely for political reasons. [...] He should have been playing for South Africa years ago, not for England, but that is not his fault."

Yes, D'Oliveira made his debut in that series, when he should have had a Test career of a decade and a half behind him. He should have been groomed by Dudley Nourse and Bruce Mitchell, and perhaps Taliep Salie and Frank Roro. He should have faced Lindwall and Miller, Trueman and Statham, Laker and Lock … as well as Ramadhin and Valentine, Fazal Mahmood and Khan Mohammad, Vinoo Mankad and Ghulam Ahmed. He should have been compared to Peter May and Neil Harvey, Hanif Mohammad and Clyde Walcott. He should have batted with Jackie McGlew and perhaps Cec Abrahams; bowled second change after Neil Adcock, Peter Heine, and perhaps Eric Petersen; grabbed catches off Hugh Tayfield and perhaps sent in his returns to Lobo Abed. All these Test playing men mentioned in the paragraph had retired. All those great cricketers preceded with 'perhaps' never became Test players. D'Oliveira finally did, and was making up for lost time, trying to stretch himself through another generation, playing alongside the Amisses and Boycotts, facing the Bedis and the Gibbses.

Playing alongside all those men who had retired would have been possible in a world that Martin Luther King Jr dreamt of, not in the one D'Oliveira had lived in.

In that world, something extraordinary took place two weeks after the end of the final Test.

At about 2.15 PM on 6 September, Hendrik Verwoerd entered the House of Assembly, as the bells rang to summon MPs for the afternoon debate. As ever he looked cheerful and confident. He sat down in the Prime Minister's seat to the right of the Speaker.

The House was still filling up and members were taking their seats. A uniformed Parliamentary messenger entered, walking in great hurry. He walked in the direction of the Opposition benches, before suddenly changing his course and moving towards Verwoerd. Entering the aisle next to Verwoerd, he threw himself on the Prime Minister.

At first Verwoerd thought the messenger had stumbled upon him by accident. He smiled to indicate it did not matter. Then he saw the blood.

The messenger had stabbed him four times in the neck and the chest. Verwoerd pulled the lapels of his jacket together, perhaps to shut out the sight. But it was far too later. With a sigh, he slumped forward. The assailant was still slashing away with his knife when he was finally overpowered and taken away by the police. "Where's that bastard? I'll get that bastard," he kept shouting.

Medical doctors among the MPs tried to revive Verwoerd but it was futile. The Architect of Apartheid was dead.

The Star

PRIME MINISTER ASSASSINATED

Dr. Verwoerd stabbed to death in House by uniformed messenger

Two days before birthday

Armed bandit asked girls for a kiss

Verwoerd's attacker was Demetrio Tsafendas, a certified lunatic, illegitimate son of a Greek father and a half-breed Portuguese mother. His life was a crazy tale of drifting around, a constant battle with real or imagined tapeworms, and an incredible amount of bureaucratic hassle surrounding entry permits into South Africa. He was there illegally, and his deportation was under process. Ironically, he could not have been a messenger in Parliament if he had not been classified White. He was found mentally disordered and committed to jail as long as it pleased the State President. He had been in eight different mental institutions in four different countries.

Verwoerd had been attacked by a mentally unbalanced assailant in 1960 and assassinated by another in 1966. Curious to say the least. Mysterious too.

Private Eye commented on his death with a caption *Verwoerd—A nation mourns* accompanying the picture of several Africans in their traditional attire jumping through the air in unrestrained celebratory joy.

39 GREY AREAS

A day after the death of Verwoerd, in the festival match at Scarborough, a strong Rest of the World side took on England XI. Simpson, Grahame Thomas, and McKenzie from Australia, brothers Hanif and Mushtaq Mohammad from Pakistan, Nawab of Pataudi and Bapu Nadkarni from India, Deryck Murray from West Indies, and Colin Bland and the Pollock brothers from South Africa.

D'Oliveira dismissed Graeme Pollock for 22, catching him off his own bowling. When he batted, Peter Pollock ran in and sent down a beamer. Did it slip out of his hand? Pollock just stared at D'Oliveira with a grim look on his face and walked back to his bowling mark. No apology was rendered. D'Oliveira hit the next ball over his head for six.

Two years later, during the Datsun single-wicket competition in Australia, D'Oliveira asked all the competitors to come into his room for a drink. It was then Pollock apologised, saying he had not meant to bowl a beamer that day. D'Oliveira remained sceptical. It had, after all, taken two years for Pollock to apologise. But later, they became friends.

Oborne writes: "Pollock was a young white South African, brought up as the apartheid system reached its full savagery. White cricket in South Africa was founded on the assertion that Blacks could not play the game. D'Oliveira's mere existence of as international cricketer was a denial of everything that Pollock stood for. Pollock's beamer could appear to be an expression of pent-up rage at the Black man for his impudent defiance in faring to make his long journey from Signal Hill."

This is well reasoned, but perhaps falls under the category of speculation. We have seen that Pollock was prone to bounce tail-enders and had also sent down two deliberate beamers at Boycott without apologising. He could let his temper get the better of himself and was an aggressive fast bowler. But to say he saw D'Oliveira as a Black man who had dared to be different is unsubstantiated. The Pollocks were born into a liberal household. Peter's father, AM 'Mac' Pollock, was an editor of *Eastern Province Herald* and quite steadfastly against apartheid. He was also prone to saying, "These Nats will destroy the country." Peter Pollock had even volunteered his efforts for the anti-Nationalist movement, as a driver in Despatch. He also protested in his own way by refusing to speak Afrikaans.

This particular author would put the beamer down to competitiveness and not a to racial bias.

If one expected the death of Verwoerd to be an about-turn in the saga of apartheid, the happy thoughts came crashing down a week after the assassination. The erstwhile Minister of Justice BJ Vorster was chosen as the Prime Minister by the National Party, primarily due to his fearsome reputation. The reasoning was "one strong man should succeed another."

Vorster's first statement was, "My role is to walk further along the road set by Hendrik Verwoerd."

Grahame Thomas hit the ball harder than almost anyone else in world cricket. In the 1965–66 season, he had scored 1,171 runs with 4 hundreds at 48.55. The 229 against Victoria had come against Alan Connolly and Graeme Watson. Against Mike Smith's men, he had hammered 129, adding 156 with New South Wales captain Bobby Simpson.

But as the tour of South Africa approached, interest centred less around his batting and more on his blood. His maternal grandfather, James Evans, had come to Australia 120 years earlier from Somerset. Legend had it that Evans was a Cherokee Indian.

As Australia played England at MCG, Evans was invited to breakfast with Don Bradman at Windsor Hotel. The legend asked him how he would feel if he did not go to South Africa? Thomas said he would be extremely upset. Bradman started talking about general things to do 'when you go'.

Before the team was selected, Robert Menzies paid a visit to the South African ambassador Johan Christiaan Holm Maree. He carried a few photographs of Thomas. Patiently, Menzies explained that Thomas was understood to have some Red Indian blood, but he could hardly imagine anyone who looked less like a hawk-faced Red Indian. The ambassador informed Menzies he thought there would be no difficulty whatsoever. The objection on the part of his people being to people who presented what he called a 'negroid' appearance.

Thomas did go and managed a hundred against Griqualand West. But he did not play any of the Tests.

Vorster's first speech as Prime Minister

D'Oliveira returned to South Africa after six years, to a hero's welcome. He spent the southern summer travelling around the country, over 12,000 miles, across Cape Town, Kimberley, Johannesburg, Durban, East London, and Port Elizabeth. He was on a coaching and lecture tour arranged through the non-White cricket unions and provincial associations.

He played a few matches as well. The Transvaal Cricket Federation XI took on Basil D'Oliveira XI at the self-same Natalspruit Sports Ground, Johannesburg. The experience of playing on English grounds had not diminished his propensity for getting runs on the terrible wickets of non-White cricket. D'Oliveira batted an hour and a quarter to score 101.

At the ICC meetings, the darker-skinned representatives were starting to make their presence felt. Men like the Maharaja of Baroda were voicing their reservations about England hosting South Africa in 1970.

Gubby Allen was quite vocal in his support for the future tours. Without representative matches, South Africa's present high standards would deteriorate rather quickly in the absence of competition, with a disastrous effect on the whole of Africa.

Former Prime Minister Alec Douglas-Home maintained that 'the game should and must continue whereas politics might change'.

When the status of the Test matches played by South Africa was questioned, New Zealand's ED Blundell said that to exclude unofficial Tests involving South Africa from official records would be "burying one's head in the sand." Clichés are never recommended devices for writers, but one cannot help but pause here and observe irony dying each of its thousand deaths.

Always enjoyable. Australians at the Victoria Falls

Peter van der Merwe chooses to bat on a grassy Johannesburg strip. Garth McKenzie destroys them. 199 all out, only Denis Lindsay stands firm with 69.

Dougie Laws, the well-known radio announcer, asks the following morning, "Have you heard the latest van der Merwe joke?"

"No."

"We'll bat, Bobby."

Springbok Radio cashes in on the huge interest around the Test series.

Lawry and Simpson add 118, following which Ian Redpath and Lawry take the score to 204 for 1.

But then Goddard gets Lawry to snick. Or does he? The pencil-thin batsman cannot believe the decision. Now Barlow comes on, the usual bundle of enthusiasm, dismissing Cowper, Stackpole and Redpath—all caught Lindsay. Goddard gets Chappell, and again it is

Lindsay who holds the catch. When he snaps up Taber, Lindsay equals the world record of Wally Grout for six catches in an innings.

The lead is restricted to 126.

The next innings is almost a fairy tale. Barlow scores 50, Bacher 63. Graeme Pollock hits 90 in less than two hours, with 15 fours and 2 sixes. At 268 for 5 Lindsay comes in. Taber drops him when on 10 during the dying moments of Day 3. The next day, he smashes 182 with 25 fours and 5 sixes. When he is not hooking sixes or driving along the ground and lofting into the crowd, he rises in ballet-like pose high on his toes, left elbow well up, and the bat with handle angled forward drops viciously rising deliveries at his feet. "Champagne batsmanship at its very best," writes McGlew. His off strokes would have received full acclaim from any master of any period in terms of both artistry and effectiveness.

The total amounts to 620 in the third innings. Australia fight valiantly, but the wily old Trevor Goddard captures 6 for 53.

McKenzie skies the magnificent Goddard after a hard-hitting cameo. Mike Procter, the 20-year-old Natal all-rounder substituting for Bland, sprints and dives full length to catch him. Victory over Australia at home for the first time ever—by 233 runs with 97 minutes to spare.

But Procter is quiet as the team celebrates. What's wrong? It turns out that he had not caught it, the ball had spilled out as he fell, but was hidden by his body. And then the batsman walked, Goddard was chaired off the ground. His drop remained undiscovered.

He is told not to worry. There were 97 minutes left. They would have got that wicket anyway.

The sad bit is that Bland has run into the pickets on the boundary. He will never play Test cricket again.

In London, Peter read the *Guardian* to catch up with the sports around the world. However, he was following the politics pages with increasing interest as well.

Leading politicians being questioned on television was an entirely novel concept for a young lad from South Africa. *World in Action* and *Panorama* were stark contrasts to the state-controlled propaganda of South African radio.

Australia square the series at Newlands. Simpson and Stackpole hit hundreds while the South African dressing room resembles the casualty ward. But at 12 for 2 in response to 542 enters Graeme Pollock, with a septic toe and a strained muscle. It becomes 41 for 3, 66 for 4, 85 for 5. Pollock cannot move his leg much because of the injuries, and hence literally stands and delivers. South Africa 353, Pollock ninth out for 209. Etched with strokes of breath-taking power and perfect timing. Fieldsmen are beaten without registering a token effort at stopping the ball. This includes an 85-run ninth wicket stand with brother Peter.

Was Billy Griffith, the MCC Secretary, in the ground on that day? Oborne suggests he might have been. He may or may not have watched Graeme Pollock's masterly innings. But he was indeed in South Africa that January, with a specific task.

The question about a situation akin to New Zealand's boycotting of the South African rugby tour was no longer so hypothetical. D'Oliveira had broken into the England side and established himself. The chance of his being in the team bound for South Africa in 1968–69 was quite real. He was not only Coloured; he was a South African born in the Cape. The complications were enormous. Griffith was there to discuss the issue with the South African cricket authorities, with instructions to try and quieten things down without making them worse. Even before he left South Africa, Louis Duffus, the veteran South African cricket writer, was alluding to long and fruitful discussions with South African cricket authorities.

What Duffus claimed Griffith told him is pretty much in line with the standard 'ignoring the problem and hoping it will go away' tack often employed in delicate matters. "We discussed in principle the situation which might arise in the future but clearly there is nothing one can say about that until such time as that situation arises. I made the MCC thoughts clear to the South African cricket authorities."

However, the visit induced *Johannesburg Sunday Express* to approach PK Le Roux, the Minister of Interior. His answer was unequivocal. "Our policy is clear. We will not allow mixed teams to play against our White teams here. That is our policy. It is well known here and overseas."

Le Roux was merely parroting the lines of Verwoerd and now Vorster. However, there was a massive reaction in Britain. More than 200 MPs signed a motion calling for the tour to be cancelled almost two years in advance. The Minister of Sport, Denis Howell, had a brief meeting with the MCC All-Purposes Committee and made a statement to the Commons: "The MCC informed that the team will be chosen on merit and in this respect any preconditions that the host country lays down will be totally disregarded. The Government are confident that if, when the time comes, any player chosen for the touring side were rejected by the host country, then there would be no question but that the MCC would find such a condition wholly unacceptable and the projected tour would be abandoned."

While MCC were more than a bit uncomfortable at this comparatively direct statement that drastically reduced the area of vague shilly-shallying, Howell on his part told Prime Minister Harold Wilson that the MCC "appeared very naïve about the potential political repercussions surrounding the situation." More than naivete, it was probably the disinclination of the platonic ideal of an Old Boys' Club to open the windows of its hallowed MCC Committee Rooms and let in the winds of change that former Prime Minister Harold MacMillan had spoken about at the beginning of the decade.

At Newlands, South Africa follow on in spite of the Graeme Pollock gem. They finish on 288 for 7 at the end of the fourth day. Defeat is inevitable. Barlow and Peter Pollock, the latter unbeaten overnight, decide to drown their sorrows in drinks and disco. Early next morning Pollock and Barlow battle hangovers to get some batting practice for the former. Barlow bowls Pollock some dozen times.

When play resumes, Peter Pollock creams the first ball to the fence and proceeds to score 75 not out. This follows 41 in the first innings. "By now he can be classified as a genuine all-rounder," writes McGlew.

Four hours to get 179. Lawry, the run-digging corpse in pads, starts with a fierce hook off Pollock to the Railway Stand boundary. The chase is on. Goddard and McKinnon check the flow of runs with some naggingly accurate bowling, the latter getting sharp turn to bowl Ian Chappell. At 119 for 4, tension mounts.

But Veivers dances down the track, smites McKinnon over mid-off for six, and bludgeons Goddard over wide mid-on into the densely populated scaffold stand. At the other end, young Redpath holds firm. With victory one stroke away, however, he gives up his sheet anchor role and charges down to Goddard to loft him for the winning boundary.

"The best Test that has been played at Newlands since the War," says a sporting van der Merwe.

D'Oliveira started the summer of 1967 scoring 174 not out against Bedi, Chandrasekhar and Venkataraghavan as the Indians played their opening first-class match on tour against Worcestershire.

Just over a month later, D'Oliveira met the Indians again, this time in the first Test match at Leeds.

It was 253 for 3 when he came in to bat; Barrington, Graveney and Boycott had already batted the Indian bowling into submission. On the second morning, chairman of selectors Doug Insole visited the dressing room to berate the English cricketers for slow batting. His tirade was specifically directed at Boycott, who had batted all day for 106. Boycott accelerated on the second day, but not enough to satisfy the men in power. At least, ball-by-ball details were not available at the click of a button for objective evaluation. The selectors decided he had not been enterprising enough. Boycott was dropped for his marathon 246 not out, which did little to counter-balance his already curious attitude towards the rest of the cricketing fraternity. D'Oliveira, in contrast, played sparkling cricket, scoring 109 in three hours.

The first ball at Durban sees Barlow hitting one back to McKenzie and walking slowly back to the pavilion. Peter Pollock tries to cheer him up. "Even Bradman made ducks," he says. "Who the hell wants to emulate Bradman?" barks Barlow.

In the press box, journalists hastily turn pages of reference books to find a precedence of a first-ball dismissal till a quick eye zeroes down on McGlew. "Weren't you out first ball in a Test match?" he is asked in an unkindly loud voice. "Yes," is the embarrassed reply. "Lord's 1955."

The pressman presses on. "Didn't you get a pair?"

McGlew is red in the face. "Yes."

"But England batted first," some kindly soul interjects. "You weren't out first ball of the Test."

Cowper is suddenly introduced, perhaps to change ends, perhaps a genius ploy. He scoops out the cream of batting in the form of Goddard, Graeme Pollock, and Tiger Lance. Instead of normal off-breaks, he sends down little seamers, and at one stage has figures 10-8-5-3

94 for 6. The pairing of Lindsay and van der Merwe again. A partnership of 103. Lindsay is dropped off a miscued hook off McKenzie, but proceeds to play yet another magical innings. 137. Lifeboat Lindsay, he is dubbed. South Africa recover to 300.

The 20-year-old blonde debutant Mike Procter steams in and dismisses Simpson cheaply. Bowling with pace and hostility, he picks up three. Peter Pollock, struggling with the ball through the series, remains wicketless. Nevertheless, he strikes Lawry a fearful blow above the right eye. Ten stiches later, heavily bandaged, Lawry returns at 45 for 3, a la Sutcliffe, and scores 44 gallant runs. Barlow produces yet another uncanny spell to end with 3 for 18. Australia follow on when Procter scatters the stumps of Renneberg all over the place.

The second innings sees a spirited fight. Simpson 94, Redpath 80, the deficit removed with just one wicket down. With runs piling up, van der Merwe puts Goddard on to block one end. The man who has completed his double this very match sends down 27 overs for 23 runs.

But at lunch on Day 4, Australia are 262 for 3. Redpath and Ian Chappell are the unbeaten batsmen. It has begun to look a trifle bleak for the South Africans.

An hour and a bit after tea, Australia are 334 all out. Pollock two wickets, Procter four, the beginning of a lethal bowling pair.

It means 182 to win—not really a cakewalk. However, Bacher and Graeme Pollock make it so. A magnificent straight drive by the latter makes it 2-1.

1967. The Terrorism Act was introduced under the regime of Vorster, administered by the new Minister of Justice, Petrus Cornelius Pelser. Terrorism was vaguely defined as anything that might "endanger the maintenance of law and order." According to the Act, anyone suspected of involvement in terrorism was to be detained for a 60-day period without trial on authority of a senior police officer. This 60-day period was renewable. In practice, it was a tool for indefinite detention, 'a very handy legal lever' for the police. According to Vorster, the police were entitled to act "as if the country were in a state of war."

By 1990, a total of 73 detainees would die in custody. The death toll would include Steve Biko, the Black Consciousness leader, who would die a miserable death during security police interrogation in 1977.

It is Simpson's birthday. Perhaps that is why he is a bit whimsical. He opts to bat at Wanderers with the skies laden with clouds and a wicket that seems damp and mischievous.

After a delayed start, Australia lunch at 43 for 1. Then during a period of play between 1:57 PM to 2:08 PM, three wickets fall within 20 balls as the score is stuck on 59. Alongside Pollock, Procter, Trimborn, and Goddard, Barlow is tried as the fifth pacer. He gets Redpath, while Goddard removes Simpson and Chappell.

11 minutes later, Stackpole exposes his leg stump to a ball from Goddard that cuts back. 69 for 5.

Australia huff and puff to 143, Procter doing his usual blasting job with the tail.

The following day. "From 3:25 PM pandemonium was let loose," writes CO Medworth in *Natal Mercury.* "Everyone became a Lindsay fan, clapping his defence stroke, and roaring the offensive ones to and over the boundary edge." A lot of the South Africans spend time at the wicket, but no one gets past 50. Lindsay walks in at 120 for 4. After 110 minutes, he is 95 not out and appealing for the light. The umpires say no. Lindsay goes back to bat. Cowper bowls. The wicketkeeper batsman jumps out and deposits him into the crowd beyond mid-off.

By the end of the day, he is 111 not out, in just two hours. Scored out of 146 while he is at the wicket. Third century for Lindsay in the series.

Lindsay: Impeccable form

Algy Frames is 77, in retirement after serving the South African Cricket Association as secretary-treasurer. He has been watching Test cricket since 1905–06 when Plum Warner's men were here. He ranks Lindsay's knock alongside Frank Woolley's 154 in 1929, Stan McCabe's 189 not out in 1935–36 and Dudley Nourse's 231 in the same match, and Graeme Pollock's 137 and 77 not out against MJK Smith's men in 1965. Too bad Mr Frames did not watch any of D'Oliveira's masterpieces in the nearby Natalspruit Sports Club Ground.

Lindsay ends on 131 the following morning. Much of the third day is rained off. Australia is 13 for one, 189 behind on first innings. The fourth day sees no play—the first time a complete day's Test cricket is washed out in South Africa since the Second World War.

The final day sees Chappell batting two hours for an unbeaten 13, and Australia staring at a comprehensive innings defeat at 148 for 8 when a nasty dark cloud opens itself on the ground.

147 not out against Somerset, 156 against Essex, 106 not out against Sussex. And after a

first innings 59 at Lord's in the first innings of the first Test against Pakistan, D'Oliveira essayed his best knock of the summer in the second innings. Hanif Mohammad's colossal 187 not out had ensured that just 15 runs separated the two sides in the first innings. In the third session of Day 4, England slipped to 95 for 4. Intikhab Alam, Nasim-ul-Ghani, and Mushtaq Mohammad were a formidable trio on a spinning track. D'Oliveira played an unflustered gem, finishing on 81 not out. By the time Close declared, England were 256 ahead.

At Port Elizabeth, Peter van der Merwe elects to field. His decision is immediately vindicated through no tactical genius or dreadful conditions. The incredible pair of opening batsmen Lawry and Simpson have a misunderstanding in the middle of the pitch, and Lawry walks back, run out for a duck, without facing a ball.

Australia never quite recover. Pollock, Procter, Goddard, aided by Trimborn, are more than a handful. They manage just 173.

Peter Pollock bowls Graeme Watson

It is Graeme Pollock's turn to dazzle the spectators yet again. He completes his hundred on his 23rd birthday, a magnificent gem etched with 13 boundaries and a pulled six. Richie Benaud says without reservation that the Eastern Province left-hander is a better batsman than even Garry Sobers.

Graeme Pollock forces one to the off-side

Denis Lindsay arrives, to quote Eric Litchfield, "to the type of reception usually accorded the modern pop star [...] Schoolboys raced out to form a 50-yard human tunnel through which he had to walk." But his fairy-tale run cannot last forever. This is the innings that brings about failure.

The 103-run lead proves a telling one. Peter Pollock brings one sharply back to trap Redpath leg before for his 100th Test wicket in his 24th Test. Cowper fights hard, and the 176-run target is one of those tricky ones. But Trevor Goddard, that excellent Springbok warrior, leads the way with 59. At 5:10 on the fourth afternoon, Tiger Lance puts his foot down the wicket and hits Ian Chappell into the main grandstand. "*Six for Glory,*" writes McGlew and that goes on to become the title of the tour book.

The South Africans win their first ever series against Australia. Comprehensive 3-1. But for the rains, it would have been 4-1. Dick Whitington writes: "English-speaking South African people grow keener on cricket annually. The Afrikaans-language Press devotes more and more space to cricket. Cricket, indeed, threatens to take over from rugby as South Africa's sporting religion."

This is Whitington, and therefore has to be taken with a pinch of salt. But there seems to be a good amount of truth in the words.

The wonderful brigade of cricketers, the Pollocks, Lindsay, Procter, Goddard, Barlow et al.—will play their next Test match three years down the line. And only four more at that.

Tiger Lance ends the series with a six

Just 13 days after the conclusion of the Test series, Frank Worrell passed away from leukaemia at the age of 42.

In April 1967, Vorster spoke to the House of Assembly in Cape Town. He stated that in future, the Nationalist government was prepared to look at Black sportsmen visiting the country in a more benign light. There would be no mixed sport between White and non-Whites in South Africa itself, but they could send mixed race teams to the Olympics next year. Visiting teams of mixed race, however, had to come from countries with which South Africa had traditional sporting ties, and they were welcome only if "no political capital is made out of the situation."

It was a rather strange statement sending ambiguous signals about mixed sport.

However, Sir John Nichols, the British ambassador, cabled back to London that Vorster had "made it quite clear that Maoris might be admitted as members of an All Blacks side. And, although he did not say so specifically, it is a reasonable assumption from what he said that Mr Basil D'Oliveira may come here as a member of an MCC team."

In August 1967, the young brigade of the London Recruits struck simultaneously. Anti-Apartheid leaflets were distributed, and banners were unfurled simultaneously in Durban, Johannesburg, Port Elizabeth and Cape Town.

D'Oliveira, for his part, amassed 316 runs in the 5 Tests he played that summer of 1967, with one hundred and two fifties, averaging 63.20. In all first-class matches, his tally was 1,618 runs at 44.94 and 44 wickets at 31.09. Besides, England had won five of the six Tests played against India and Pakistan.

"You will be judged on your performance and the team's performance," had been the wise words of Tom Reddick. D'Oliveira had scored on both counts.

He was looking beyond the West Indian tour that winter. He had his mind set on playing in those magnificent arenas inside which his people were not allowed, where they had to watch the action from the segregated 'cage', where the very existence of such cricketers as himself was vehemently denied. He had set his sights on touring South Africa.

D'Oliveira coaches non-White cricketers in South Africa, 1967

40 CARIBBEAN CATASTROPHE

Writing about the banner waving days of that epochal year, historian Richard Vinen named his book *The Long 68.*

In terms of cricket and its associated politics, 1968 turned out to be a very long year as well.

You only Live Twice released in 1967 with Sean Connery in the lead, and *On Her Majesty's Secret Service* in 1969 with George Lazenby appearing for the first and only time as the most famous secret agent in the world. But the interim year in cricket saw more cloak-and-dagger drama than all the Bond movies put together.

D'Oliveira's troubles start right at the beginning of the England tour, even before the troublesome 1968 kicks off.

On the penultimate day of 1967, MCC play Barbados Colts at Bridgetown. Spurred on by the thought of imminent vacancy in the new ball department currently manned by the ageing duo of Wes Hall and Charlie Griffith, Vanburn Holder runs in with venom. He is not too quick, but moves it off the pitch deceptively. D'Oliveira is bowled, registering the first duck of the tour.

At the start of the year, a letter from the MCC dated 5 January reached the South African Cricket Association. The demand was stiff. The tour of South Africa at the end of the year could not go ahead without the guarantee of 'no preconditions about selection.' Could the SACA provide assurance on that front?

The letter was marked confidential. However, the SACA secretary Dave Bursnall forwarded it to the Board of Control for guidance. The memo asking for advice was also copied to the Sports Minister, the former Springbok rugby star Frank Waring.

As the letter sat like a ticking timebomb in the offices of the Board and the Ministry, the South African Schools took on the visiting Australian Schoolboys on 15 January at the Jan Smuts Ground in East London. Ian Tayfield, a cousin of the great Hugh Tayfield, bowled off-breaks and captured 6 for 79. He would play 43 first-class matches, mostly for Natal, and capture 132 wickets at 28.42. Of course, he would never play Test cricket. Also, batting at No 3 for the South African schools was Robert Cheetham, the son of the former captain Jack Cheetham. Very soon, we will encounter Jack Cheetham once again.

On paper the West Indian attack is fascinating. Wes Hall, Charlie Griffith, Lance Gibbs, Garry Sobers. The English think tank have loaded the side with batsmen. Cowdrey is back at the helm, with Close out of the side following infamous controversies towards the end of the 1967 season. Boycott, Edrich, Cowdrey, Barrington, Graveney, and Parks the wicketkeeper. D'Oliveira is slotted at No 7. At the Queens Park Oval, he has to sit through the first day twiddling his thumbs. Meanwhile Close sits in the press box, covering the tour as a journalist.

The vaunted bowling attack is way past its prime. Hall and Griffith lack the early sting. Boycott scores 68, Cowdrey 72. With Holford bowling, Sobers moves cannily from short leg to short gully, conning Boycott into believing that the leg-break will be more potent than the googly. The Yorkshire opener goes pack to push the short delivery that follows to find it turning back and trapping him leg-before. This is the last success for the hosts on the first day.

Barrington lofts Gibbs for six to bring up his half century. 244 for 2 at stumps.

The following day, Barrington completes his hundred. Graveney leans into his drives and plays one of his finest innings—20 boundaries in 118. By the time Parks is dismissed for 42 and D'Oliveira walks in, it is 471 for 5. He throws his bat around for 32.

He bowls a steady spell, moving the ball off the pitch. His great friend on the tour, Rohan Kanhai, tries to force him to the on side, gets a leading edge, and is caught by a tumbling Cowdrey. Nurse is missed in the slips off his bowling.

West Indies follow on, but it is already Day 5. There are very limited chances of a result. However, an inspired spell by David Brown sees them collapse to 180 for 8 at tea. During the break, English journalists file superlative descriptions of England's excellent victory.

But Hall proves that at this stage of his career he can finally bat responsibly. Sobers trusts him. With the pitch taking turn, Cowdrey errs by opting for the new ball. The 25 runs are scored to avoid innings defeat. They add a further 38 and are still unseparated when Cowdrey himself comes on to bowl. Sobers acknowledges by taking just one run off the over. It is a draw.

D'Oliveira has not done too badly, but the saga of walking in to chisel the summit of an already towering total will be the saga of the tour.

By early 1968, Peter Hain was becoming more politically involved. Family discussions revolved around the Vietnam War, with Wal and Peter both hostile to American interventions.

In Britain through the late 1950s and the early 1960s there had been massive protests against the bomb organised by the Campaign for Nuclear Disarmament. Direct Action tactics had been adopted by its militant offshoot, the Committee of 100.

Now similar protests were ongoing against the Vietnam War. Peter soon found himself drawn to these demonstrations.

Sabina Park. Yet another day is spent sitting in the dressing room. England 222 for 2 at the end of Day One. Edrich caught off a Sobers chinaman for 96.

The following day, Cowdrey hits 101, Barrington 63. D'Oliveira finally comes out with the score on 318 for 5. The sudden dismissals of Barrington and Parks make Sobers crowd him with close in men as Holford bowls. A big leg break beats him as he stretches forward. Murray whips off the bails and asks the question. Out is the decision, although there has not been any perceptible movement of the back foot. A duck. His first in Test cricket.

John Snow is in a belligerent mood the following day. Kanhai and Sobers are dismissed off successive deliveries—it does not get better than that. The roar that greeted the arrival of Sobers is matched by the hush as he walks back. Only the third time he has been out first ball in a Test match, and twice it has been Snow. In the press box, Close does not forget to write that the last time it had been he who had caught him at short leg.

Snow gets deliveries to kick up viciously, and first Butcher and then Holford edge. Griffith slashes and D'Oliveira at fourth slip takes a one-handed blinder. Hall bowled second ball. Snow takes 7 for 49. West Indies 143 all out. They follow on.

D'Oliveira gets Camacho with one that keeps low. And then the controversial dismissal. Parks catches Butcher off a leg glance. The crowd does not like the decision. Or is it that they don't like the score?

204 for 5, only Sobers among the recognised batsmen still around. Bottles are being thrown, tear gas is being used, the crowd stampeding on to the playing area, one man even managing to ride his bicycle across.

In all, 75 minutes are lost and England ask for an hour and quarter's play on the sixth morning to compensate for it. If required.

But in the interim, something happens that blots D'Oliveira's tour. Sobers snicks Brown through second slip for four. Graveney gets a finger on it, splitting it. He goes off for reparations. D'Oliveira is asked to move from the outfield into the vacated position.

The following ball is edged again. It flies towards D'Oliveira at knee height. He seems to have his hands ideally positioned. The ball goes in and out.

The final 75 minutes are not only required, they almost get West Indies a miraculous win. Sobers and Holford add 110, Sobers and the rest of the tail another 77. Sobers unbeaten 113, and he declares at 391 for 9.

80 minutes left in the day, 155 in the match. Sobers takes the new ball. Boycott is bowled shouldering arms to one that jags back in. Cowdrey is leg before to the last ball of the over. By the end of the day England 19 for 4, requiring to survive the 75 minutes they had asked for.

The following morning, Parks is leg-before to Gibbs. Controversial decision, but he has to walk back. D'Oliveira is in at 38 for 5, with 41 minutes to survive. He is dropped at slip off Gibbs before he has scored. Graveney sweeps Gibbs for what seems to be a certain boundary. It bounces off the left hip of Camacho at short leg and Griffith catches him at square leg. Titmus falls to Gibbs. D'Oliveira is dropped by Holford again. Brown hangs on for 12 minutes before Sobers bowls him. Time has run out. England survive on 68 for 8—D'Oliveira is unbeaten with 13. Unlucky in the first innings, terribly lucky in the second.

But his lack of runs and the dropped catch make people wonder. And make the typewriters rattle. Is he too social on the tour? Is he going for too many parties? Is he spending too many nights out? Why is he hardly seen during breakfast?

D'Oliveira offers a rather weak excuse in his memoirs that he generally never breakfasted, preferring to stay in his room. However, the truth is that he was enjoying himself. West Indies was full of people eager to entertain this Coloured man who had defied all the injustices of life and managed to make it to the top level of cricket. He was invited to parties, to dances, to inaugurate shops and stores. He struck up a friendship with Rohan Kanhai, who, according to Oborne, was a fantastic batsman and an unreliable companion. And the introduction to alcohol that had come hand-in-hand with international cricket had not really helped matters. If we see his pictures through his career, the boyish young man ages quite quickly from 1967–68 onwards. It does not seem unrelated. Even the testimonies of his teammates during the West Indies visit confirm this. He was away much too often. The manager, Les Ames, was even required to have a word with him.

By now MCC was getting worried about the non-response of SACA. The letter sent to them had been clear. The answer had not come in as yet.

MCC Secretary Billy Griffith was soft-spoken, gentle, and decidedly not racist. A former England wicketkeeper, in 1948–49 he had been as shocked as John Arlott on seeing the inhuman conditions in which the Blacks had to live. His son Mike Griffith, who would later become MCC President, was at present playing for Sussex. Mike was not short for Michael—he had been named after Mike Jackson, the schoolboy cricketer, hero of the early PG Wodehouse school stories and one cricket-based novel. Wodehouse was, in fact, his godfather.

What Billy Griffith needed to resolve this D'Oliveira situation was a Jeeves. But unfortunately, in the inner sanctum of the committee rooms of Lord's, Jeeves and his mates from Junior Ganymede were reduced to performing the role of stewards. He could be used in his capacity to check that the visitors were wearing the correct ties, and at best clear his throat like a sheep coughing in the distant Alps and remind an errant visitor that cameras were not allowed in the Long Room.

"May I suggest, Sir, that you sheathe your photographic apparatus till I make my way out to the Grace Gates to receive Lord Cobham," one can almost hear him saying to a camera wielding visitor. "A quick draw of the equipment compounded with an admirable shutter speed may suit your purpose to satisfaction, Sir. I may add that the other stewards were all born before the Crimean War and hence their eye sights unfortunately, or fortunately in this little matter, are not quite what they used to be."

In the inner sanctum of the club, however, one was more likely to come across Lord Emsworths and Lord Ickenhams.

Griffith and the likes of Gubby Allen zeroed in on Sir Alec Douglas-Home, the Prime Minister between Macmillan and Wilson, and recent President of MCC, who had accompanied Chamberlain to diffuse the Czechoslovakian situation with Hitler. He was the only Prime Minister of Britain to have played first-class cricket. Sir Alec was travelling to Southern Africa in relation with the Rhodesian crisis. He was supposed to meet Vorster in the course of the visit. Could he discuss the D'Oliveira issue as well?

Sir Alec said he would be happy to. According to Jim Swanton's biography of Gubby Allen, Sir Alec 'tested the ground with other sections of society including the cricketers.' His advice on return was not to press an answer for a hypothetical question. He told the MCC Committee that in his view, if D'Oliveira were to be chosen, the odds were 5/4 on his being allowed in. Looking back, he should have charged thousands for adding no value whatsoever, so closely he did he manage to resemble the modern-day corporate consultants in this errand. Galahad Threepwood would have perhaps delivered better results.

Sir Alec Douglas-Home

Bridgetown. The score reads another healthy 319 for 5 when D'Oliveira comes in to bat on the fourth afternoon.

Rain has delayed the start of the first day, and the West Indies innings dragged well into the third day to end at 349. D'Oliveira has bowled 19 overs for 36 runs, economic but not successful.

Edrich 146, Boycott 90. The first wicket partnership yields 172. Graveney 55. The England batting makes merry in front of 'King Dyall', England's biggest supporter in the Caribbean. He is the island's most colourful figure, turning up each day in a different coloured suit.

When Edrich nicks a leg side delivery from Griffith to Murray, D'Oliveira is left with the tail—one of the perils of batting low down the order. But he remains calm, hogging much of the strike. He starts slow but is in command down the line, not afraid to lift the ball over the infield. Hall bowls him with the fastest ball of the day, reminiscent of the bowler he was five years ago. Someone dubs it 'flashback in the pan'. It is D'Oliveira's 51, his first substantial knock of the series, that gets England a commanding lead.

Strangely, Cowdrey allows the innings to run its course on the final morning without major urgency. That means four hours and 20 minutes to try and bowl West Indies out.

D'Oliveira drops Camacho early on at leg-slip—another bad miss. Despite his fifty, questions continue as the match ends in a draw.

On 1 March, the second day of the Bridgetown Test, Dave Bursnall, the SACA secretary, wrote back to the MCC Secretary Billy Griffith: "I have to advise that the South African Cricket Association has always given MCC its loyal support [...] The SACA would never presume to interfere with the manner in which you choose your side to tour South Africa, nor has it during the 80 years of tours between our respective countries. Regarding the treatment of your team whilst in South Africa the SACA has no reason why the hospitality and courtesy normally extended to all visiting teams should in any way be changed."

Diplomatic answer. Sidestepping all the critical questions with the dexterity of a Nijinsky.

It was Jack Cheetham who carried the letter to Billy Griffith and the MCC Treasurer Gubby Allen. However, basing their strategy on Sir Alec Douglas-Home's advice, the MCC were no longer looking for a reply to 'hypothetical questions'. According to Oborne, "When Jack Cheetham cheerily produced his laboriously produced document, Gubby Allen waved it away."

Lord Cobham

Meanwhile, in South Africa, the 10th Lord Cobham was having dinner with SACA official Arthur Coy. Yet another ex-President of MCC, the 10th Viscount Cobham was also an ex-Worcestershire captain and hailed from the famous Lyttleton family.

Yet another cricketing grandee and a former Governor-General of New Zealand, he had a South African mother and business interests in South Africa.

After the dinner, Coy sent a letter to Cheetham in England, informing him that Cobham had assured him he would do everything necessary to ensure that the tour went forward.

Cobham had agreed with Coy that it would be disastrous for D'Oliveira to tour because 'the obvious problems would be' exploited by the press and the cricket would be subject to possible West Indian behaviour.

Here the hint was towards the bottle-throwing and tear-gassing incident at Kingston a few days earlier. What follows in Coy's letter to Cheetham is even more intriguing. Cobham promised that he would talk to D'Oliveira "with ideas that would suit us." In other words, Cobham would have a quiet word with D'Oliveira to tactfully make himself unavailable—the same quiet word Laker had hinted at in relation to Raman Subba Row.

After his dinner with Coy, Cobham was summoned to visit Vorster. It was not a formal meeting, and Vorster was way more forthcoming than he had been to Sir Alec. In concise terms, he let Cobham know that the tour would be cancelled if D'Oliveira was chosen. It was left unsaid but was clear to everyone that Vorster wanted the message to be passed on to MCC.

Cobham passed on the message, albeit in an unconventional manner. Here is Swanton again, "[...] in the form of a letter not to any officer of the Club but to a senior member of the Committee." Marked private and confidential, the letter was nevertheless passed on to Billy Griffith, who in turn passed the letter or the information to the treasurer Gubby Allen and the President Arthur Gilligan.

Oborne argues that Cobham chose this unusual way of delivering the message since he wanted to keep it private, instead of addressing it to the MCC Committee and thereby making it known to the world.

Allen, Gilligan and Griffith recognised that the message from the horse's mouth was at odds, so to say, with the odds suggested by Sir Alec. However, they decided to remain silent.

At the other end, the silence was uncomfortable to the South Africans as well. With SACA, and thereby South Africa, not given a clear assurance about the non-selection of D'Oliveira, Vorster was starting to pay MCC a sort of compliment that would shake the foundations of that august body if made public. He was starting to consider MCC a dangerously left-wing body of subversives.

Queens Park Oval again. Yet another pitch with nothing in it. West Indies bat well into the third day, declaring at 526. Knott plays in place of Parks and Lock is back in the team. Camacho skies one and Lock remains standing, looking like England's ancient monument, as Knott makes his way 20 yards to get under the ball.

Kanhai and Nurse hit big hundreds. So dominant are the batsmen that when a splutter of rain comes as relief, fieldsmen go galloping for shelter. The umpires don't leave, the covers never make it to the middle, and the batsmen look annoyed as time is eaten up while the fielders get back. Kanhai makes his feelings known by hitting Lock for a huge six.

D'Oliveira toils for 15 overs. Brian Close writes that he bowled intelligently, but the analysis is nought for 62.

And then he waits his turn, which has become a habit. The match is proceeding to a dull, drab draw for the fourth successive time. Cowdrey is on 62, England 204 for 2 at the end of Day 3.

The next morning, when Graveney falls to leg-spinner Rodriguez, it is 260 for 4. With Parks out of the side, D'Oliveira walks in at No 6. The first ball is a googly that he does not read. He is bowled for a first-ball duck—his second duck in real quick succession.

Cowdrey's 148 notwithstanding, West Indies lead by 122 on first innings. The last day seems to be a waste of time, with players going through tiresome motions. But as JS Barker writes, "Half-way through the funeral rites on the final day of the fourth Test, Sobers took the corpse out of its coffin, dusted it off and set it back on its feet."

Perhaps he is bored as well. It is 92 for 2, Carew and Kanhai are the not out batsmen, Lloyd, Sobers, Butcher yet to bat. Ahead by 214, with 165 minutes to play, he calls his men in. Later, he is to say that he had been sure he could not lose the match and might possibly win. One wonders why. English cricketers face such targets regularly in County Championships of the 1960s and are used to chasing these scores. The decision is even more surprising with Hall not playing this Test and Griffith unable to bowl in the second innings. He doesn't even ask his men to accelerate before closing the innings.

Sobers starts the attack with his medium-fast pace at one end and Gibbs at the other. Boycott and Edrich don't get bogged down by the off-spinner as they have often done in the series. At tea, England are 72 for 1, with 144 to get in 90 minutes.

Cowdrey plays a superlative innings, fast-paced without the indication of hurry. He gets to his half-century in just 35 minutes. An hour to go 85 to score. 65 to get in 45. In the last half hour they need 40.

Cowdrey falls for 71 made in 75 minutes with 10 fours. Gibbs removes Graveney almost immediately thereafter. D'Oliveira comes in with 33 needed in 27 minutes, promoted ahead of Barrington. Boycott and he get the remaining runs, with a number of smartly judged singles. Boycott is unbeaten 80, D'Oliveira 12. Jones and Brown lead the others in a celebration sing-song around bottles of champagne at the Queen's Park Hotel. The Test has been gifted on a plate.

Things were far from ideal for D'Oliveira. He was failing—not getting runs, not getting wickets, and dropping catches. He was being bombarded with letters and phone calls. It piqued him to note that many of his people thought he had sold himself to the White man, deliberately underperforming in order to avoid selection for South Africa.

No such proposition had been made through any channel yet, but in South Africa, Vorster and Coy were discussing along the same lines. Was it possible to offer a very generous coaching contract to buy him off? A 'well-wisher' had suggested the same to Coy. The contact with D'Oliveira could be made in United Kingdom. "We are not neglecting the other 'string to our bow' in this respect," Coy wrote to Vorster.

It was also around this time that a security file was opened on D'Oliveira.

Guyana hosts the final Test. The declaration of Sobers has been volatile enough for the teams to be escorted by a policeman on an American-built motorcycle with sirens screaming. Riots have taken place in the aftermath of the defeat and heated arguments are still going on.

It is blisteringly hot near the equator and the pitch looks a beauty. D'Oliveira bowls just eight wicketless overs as West Indies pile up the runs. Kanhai 150, Sobers 152. At 322 for 3, the press-box sweepstake put their money on a 650-plus score. But Kanhai pulls Pocock into the hands of Edrich and the innings falls away for 414.

It looks like the repeat of tall-scoring matches, a dead Test that only a crazy declaration can bring to life. Even considering the six-day duration. Boycott scores 116, Cowdrey 59, and then there are rains interruptions for most of Day Three. But then England collapse. Proceeding to 27 without much trouble, D'Oliveira swings a long hop straight down the throat of Nurse at mid-wicket. The tour cannot get worse. Or so it seems.

Lock hits an exhilarating 89, his highest score in Test cricket. And England finish on 371.

This time the West Indies innings loses its way after an excellent start. Snow creates havoc, dismissing the openers after 78 is put on by Nurse and Camacho. It is Sobers again, a one-man exhibition of clear thinking and powerplay. The innings proves he is the king of the cricketing world. He remains 95 not out. West Indies 264.

308 to win in five and a half hours. They are up in the series and it is not worth taking the

risk and losing all.

But within a span of 25 minutes they lose five wickets, and things get tricky. From 33 for no loss to 41 for 5. The last one is D'Oliveira—the final bit of misery on the tour—trying to hit himself out of trouble and managing to send it straight back to Gibbs.

A nightmare of a series for him. 137 runs at 22.83. Just three wickets at 97.66. Terrible figures. And all those dropped catches.

Alan Knott, in only his fourth Test match, joins the skipper. Gibbs and Sobers the spinner, they keep sending down over after over. Fielders crowd the bat. Cowdrey pushes his pad forward, again and again. Plus, there are adjustments of the gloves, discussions between batsmen. Cowdrey even refuses to take strike unless the uproar dies down. "Timesmanship," writes Barker.

The crowd jeers. At tea, it is 153 for 5. Cowdrey 75, Knott 31. The England captain is unpopular. Not one man in the crowd claps as he returns.

After the break the new ball is due. Hall comes back, and so does King. Knott is up to it; he plays them without worry. And finally, Cowdrey pushes his pad at Gibbs once too often. The crowd is ecstatic. Knott is left to shepherd the tail to safety.

Snow stays with him for 45 minutes, scoring just one run. The Vicar must be glowing with pride back home. And then Sobers dismisses Snow and Lock. Gibbs picks up Pocock, while he appears to have hit the ground. Still seven minutes to go.

Ten men crouch within two yards of the bat. Gibbs in operation. Jeff Jones the Welshman will end his career with a first-class average of less than 4. But here he lunges forward, makes contact and keeps it out.

Knott faces the next over. Sobers with his spinners, mixing them up. The Kent youngster is confident, a scrapper. He plays them out without any problem. And Gibbs comes in again. Final over. Fielders breathe down on the neck of Jones. The match can still be won, and the series squared.

It is a poor over. Gibbs tries too hard. Twice the batsmen meet for a talk. Only once does Jones have to play it with the bat. He does it, with composure that belies his batting record.

The match is drawn with England on 206 for 9. Knott is the hero with an unbeaten 73. The series for England. The most lengthily reported series in West Indies till date—around two million words dispatched by Cable and Wireless staff from the Test grounds.

"Now for Australia in England, South Africa next winter," writes Brian Close. "To prove England are worthy to take over leadership of the cricketing world once more." South Africa in the winter …

It can perhaps go without a hitch because D'Oliveira is in the midst of the worst phase of his career.

Far away Waring, Coy and the others heaved sighs of relief and sent their reassurances to Vorster. It would be difficult for D'Oliveira to be picked against Australia during the summer's Ashes.

In South Africa, the Liberal Party was formally banned in June 1968. The following year, the infamous Bureau of Secret Service (BOSS) was formally launched, headed by the notorious Hendrik van den Bergh. It was independent of the South African Police and accountable only to the Prime Minister.

However, for all practical purposes, most of the members of the Liberal Party had been banned much earlier. And according to Gordon Winter, the BOSS had come into being in 1963, as an alliance between Vorster and van den Bergh.

While interned for pro-Nazi activities during the Second World War, van den Bergh had come across Vorster and had saved the latter's life. A pact had been formed.

SECTION 6
A Diplomatic Drop

41 DROPPED

Six princes, one marquis, two counts, three barons, five generals, one rajah, two sheiks, a sprinkling of millionaires, and a comrade or two. They had met in a casino spa overlooked by turreted castles. That was the scenario for the meeting of the International Olympic Committee as they had gathered in Baden Baden to discuss the fate of South Africa in 1963.

It is of little surprise then that, although pressured into axing them from the 1964 Tokyo Olympics, the South African affair went simmering on for another five years. When John Vorster provided the concession that the contingent would be multi-racial, they were prepared to turn a practised blind eye to the process of selection and segregated trials and readmit their comrade-in-arms. The three-member committee that visited South Africa to investigate conditions in the sporting facilities had not been convinced. However, Avery Brundage was adamant. "No matter what countries withdraw, the Games will go on"

On 4 April, Martin Luther King Jr was shot dead at the Lorraine Motel Memphis, Tennessee. Perhaps the sad event played a role in the debate. Even the IOC voting system weighted towards the West did not manage to pull it off, King's death was heavy on everyone's mind. Readmitting a nation built on racism and repression was simply not justifiable, even by IOC. Several of the top Black athletes of America threatened boycott. The African nations and the Soviets were all aligned in the protest, 50 nations threatened to boycott the Olympics if South Africa were readmitted.

Congolese representative Jean-Claude Ganga did not mince words when he told the IOC: "We do not wish that the Blacks in Africa appear like costumed apes presented at a fair and then, when the fair is over, sent back to their cages." The zoo-like Congo Village exhibit of the 1958 Expo World Fair in Brussels was still recent enough.

The IOC executive board met on 21 April 1968 to seek a diplomatic formula under which to exclude South Africa, finally agreeing that "due to the international climate, the executive committee was of the opinion it would be most unwise for South Africa to participate."

It was a tumultuous month.

On the day prior to the IOC executive board meeting, on 20 April, at a meeting of the Conservative Political Centre in Birmingham, British MP Enoch Powell delivered his infamous Rivers of Blood Speech. "In this country in fifteen or twenty years' time the Black man will have the whip hand over the White man," he shared his fears. "Like the Roman I see the River Tiber foaming with much blood," he continued.

In Birmingham, Powell's speech, filled with unresearched and unsubstantiated anecdotes, received enthusiastic applause. That night, he received a call from the Conservative Party leader Edward Heath informing him that he had been sacked from the Shadow Cabinet.

Early in the following month, it poured in Worcester as the Australians under Bill Lawry arrived for their opening match of the tour. It was still raining when the umpires went for their first inspection the following morning. It became the first Australian tour match to be completely washed out. Thus far, strangely, washouts had affected only Test matches.

"How did Sir Donald Bradman get 1000 runs in May?" asked one of the younger members of the team. "I don't look like getting one innings."

Rain would play a defining role all through the story of this singularly important tour. It was probably compensating for Paris, which was burning all over with the student rebellion.

Enoch Powell

Would Basil D'Oliveira manage a place in the side after his rather ordinary performances back in West Indies? He was helped by the rain. There were few opportunities for the challengers to his spot to showcase their skills because of the weather. He himself, not in sparkling form yet, nevertheless got fifties against Oxford University, Gloucestershire, and Glamorgan.

When MCC played the Australians at Lord's, he was out hooking the big Victorian Alan Connolly for 10. But he had probably done enough to show he had recovered his touch. Besides, there was the old adage about not changing a winning combination.

So, there it was. D'Oliveira retained his place in the playing eleven at Manchester.

It is ironic that in a season of rainfall, Manchester remains dry. Australia slip to 29 for 2, with John Snow making the dents. However, as Lawry and Doug Walters steady the ship, Cowdrey has to bring in D'Oliveira as first change.

D'Oliveira bowls well, but England is impatient. This is a series they are supposed to win. They have just beaten West Indies in their backyard. This Australia is one of the weakest to have come to the shores. Simpson is there only as a journalist. The batting, bar Lawry, is raw. The bowling is spearheaded by the ageing McKenzie. So, why not go with an attacking third pace bowler rather than a defensive trundler? Especially with David Brown shifting restlessly in the dressing room.

The lack of depth in the bowling makes the Australians confident. When Pocock comes in to bowl the first over after lunch, Lawry throws his right foot down the track and slogs him twice. One reaches the fence on the first bounce, the other on the full. A crashing drive through the covers and a hoisted six over midwicket follow. Lawry and Walters both hit 81, and both fall to the part-time leg-breaks of Bob Barber. But Ian Chappell and Paul Sheahan stitch together another big partnership. 319 for 4 at the end of the day.

The next morning, they lose their last six wickets for 31—a sordid collapse. D'Oliveira 25-11-38-1. His job is to hold one end up and pick up the occasional wicket, and he has performed it to perfection.

It grows dark as England start their innings. They go off, come back in, an appeal for the light is turned down, Boycott grumbles. Another appeal, and it is upheld. 60 without loss. It is a short day, but a good one for England. However, the wicket seems to be deteriorating.

Back in South Africa, Frank Waring turned morose. He had not expected England to persist with D'Oliveira after the West Indian tour. But there he was, playing the first Test.

Frank Waring

It rains on the following morning. Lawry paces restlessly in his hotel room. The windshield wipers are used at double pace on the way to the ground. But Bert Flack and his staff do a superb job. Play starts just 20 minutes after schedule.

The outfield is rendered less than lightning quick. Boycott's square cut is pulled back by a scampering Walters and Edrich is caught short of ground as he comes back for the third run. According to Simpson, Walters has kept the throwing arm hidden from the Englishmen till now—deception that works only once in a Test career.

The dismissal triggers a collapse—from 86 for none to 97 for 5 when D'Oliveira walks in. He cracks a fantastic straight drive off the naggingly accurate Cowper. But when on nine, a ball from Connolly ducks in late from the off and hits middle. Yet another failure with the bat.

England fold away for 165.

When Australia bat again, they are painstakingly slow in the beginning. D'Oliveira sends down five overs for seven runs and dismisses Lawry. The following day the pitch turns, the Australians are adventurous and Pocock does most of the bowling. Walters plays another fine knock as the off-spinner picks up six wickets. 413 to win in 9 hours and 15 minutes.

The limpet-like English top order decide defence is not going to get them anywhere. Boycott goes for a 10-ball 11—a man who had been dropped for his slow 246 a season earlier. Cowdrey looks in excellent nick but is undone by a brute of a delivery. It is back to the wall stuff after that.

Edrich and Amiss both depart at 91, Simpson writes that he has never seen a sadder sight than the 11 minutes Amiss spends for his duck. At 105, Graveney is out to Gleeson's mystery spin. The score is 105 for 5 and D'Oliveira is in again in the face of crisis.

By the end of the day, he is 21 not out. Off the last over from Chappell he hits three blistering boundaries. The following morning, he carries on where he left off. Simpson writes that he looks the best batsman in the England side. He even grits his teeth and sees off a dangerous McKenzie bowling at his body from round the wicket.

At 185, Barber flashes at Hawke and is caught at gully. D'Oliveira moves on to his 50, with 10 fours studded in the innings. He follows it up, striking Cowper beautifully over the sightscreen for a six.

Knott gets two lives but cannot capitalise. Snow comes and goes. So does Higgs. 219 for 9.

With Pocock at the other end, D'Oliveira knows the end is in sight. He slams three more boundaries, making runs in a tearing hurry. But Gleeson's googly foxes the last man. 253 all out. Defeat by 159 runs. D'Oliveira unbeaten on 87.

He returns to Worcester satisfied with himself and quietly confident. Now that he has established himself in the side again, his sights are once again set on South Africa.

On 19 June, D'Oliveira travelled to Lord's on the eve of the second Test. In South Africa, Frank Waring was in a sombre mood as he sent his missive to Vorster. "His last performance in the First Test against Australia merited his selection for their next game. They have persevered with him, when in fact his record on paper in West Indies hardly justified this."

It was also the 200th Test match between England and Australia. Advance bookings had swelled as the event had been billed with extraordinary fervour: "The takings [are] close to £73,000, or £14,000 more than the previous best for any cricket match," notes *Wisden.*

From Clarendon Court Hotel, just as he had done two years earlier on the day of his Test debut, D'Oliveira walked to the Grace Gates for the pre-match dinner at Lord's. The evening was filled with glitterati of the cricket world and the cricket patrons. A number of these patrons were South African grandees. Lord's swarmed with them for most of the days of the Test match that followed. The MCC archives are full of invitations sent to the South African guests for this celebratory occasion. Wilf Isaacs was one of them. And some were interested not merely in watching the cricket or partaking in festivities. Arthur Coy was being entertained in Lord Cobham's private box. Coy was there on a mission—to look for a solution to the D'Oliveira problem.

A hand touched D'Oliveira's shoulder in a friendly way. It was Billy Griffith, the MCC Secretary. The confused cricketer was drawn away to a secluded corner of the room.

The question asked by Griffith was a curious one. Would D'Oliveira consider declaring himself unavailable for England, but likely to play for South Africa if permitted?

The unexpectedness of the entire premise of the question stunned D'Oliveira. For a few moments he remained silent, trying to unravel the strangeness of the proposal. Then he angrily retorted: "Either you respect me as an England player or you don't."

The following morning, D'Oliveira was practicing in the nets. After a while he sensed the figure of Colin Cowdrey hovering nearby.

As Billy Griffith had done, Cowdrey took him aside. The Kent legend was never very comfortable bearing bad news. A man who excelled at exuding charm, he could fumble and fret when the situation was not ideal.

Barry Knight was the man they had decided to go for. A former Essex all-rounder who now played for Leicestershire, he was not remotely as accomplished a batsman as D'Oliveira but was a decidedly better seam bowler. England needed penetrating bowlers. In short, D'Oliveira was out of the side.

"I know you did very well at Old Trafford and you're disappointed," Cowdrey said. "But before the season is out, you'll be back."

D'Oliveira kept his head down as he put on his blazer and started running the errands of a 12th man. Part of his job took him out of the pavilion to the Lord's premises between the library and the Grace Gates. The early spectators did not yet know he was not playing. They warmly wished him luck.

It is tempting to link the omission with the suggestion of Billy Griffith the previous evening, surmising that something sinister was going on. However, they appear to be quite independent and there is nothing to suggest that the change in the team had any external influence. Indeed, as we will see in the fifth Test, it was not so through the whole series.

Bobby Simpson did voice his surprise. England had left out D'Oliveira and Pocock, the two men who could be classified as success at Manchester. However, when Barber and D'Oliveira had started their partnership in the second innings of the first Test, Simpson himself had written of their effort: "Australia had two ends open and the all-rounders of the team, Barber and D'Oliveira, were at the wicket without the benefit of a recognised batsman at the other end."

This underlines the problem D'Oliveira was facing. He was one of the great batsmen of his era without having the opportunity to prove it. Now, after all these years, when he had finally made his way into the England side, his role was fuzzy. He was categorised as an all-rounder, a batting all-rounder but an all-rounder all the same. To use a much-maligned modern term, 'a-bits-and-pieces player'—a precursor of the Mark Ealhams and Ronnie Iranis and Derek Pringles that England would be using down the years. He was often slotted to bat after the wicketkeeper Jim Parks, when he was, in reality, a frontline batsman.

The categorisation was at fault. As a batsman who could send down an over or more, he had done a fabulous job at Manchester. But if he was considered as a pure all-rounder, it made sense for England to look for a more penetrative bowler. And Knight thoroughly justified his inclusion.

Incidentally, they also removed Pocock and Barber, and Underwood was the one filling in the role of the spinner. It would prove an excellent move down the summer and the years. The other open slot was filled up by Colin Milburn. 1-0 down in the series, the onus was on a more balanced side with genuine bowlers and stroke-players.

As Colin Cowdrey spins a new gold sovereign, presented to him by the former Australian Prime Minister Sir Robert Menzies, Bill Lawry calls wrongly. England bat. Edrich is dismissed early, fending to second slip, after which Milburn and Boycott are involved in a firm stand.

D'Oliveira sits in the pavilion, bordering on despair. However, the strange sequence of events dogging him continues to take place.

Jim Swanton, correspondent of *Daily Telegraph,* came sauntering up to D'Oliveira. Swanton, a most respected cricket writer, was as much a face of the old-world establishment as Gubby Allen. In fact, it makes perfect sense that it was Swanton who wrote the definitive biography of Allen. Enormously influential, Swanton's columns in the *Daily Telegraph,* to quote Oborne, smacked of "gentlemen's clubs, the golf course, and public schools."

Swanton repeated the same suggestion as made by Griffith. He received the same response.

Was Arthur Coy, at that moment being entertained by Lord Cobham in his box, the man behind the proposal suggested by both Griffith and Swanton? One wonders.

Arthur Coy (standing third from right) in an SACA meeting

McKenzie pummels Milburn. The batsman receives two sickening blows to his groin. Numerous balls thud into his colossal bulk. The score is 53 for 1 at lunch. One ball is bowled after lunch, in an already threatening drizzle. It becomes stronger and play is halted. It builds up into a hailstorm, of immense velocity. The ground is white with hail. The Lord's ridge stands out like the bank of a river. That is the end of cricket for the day.

Doug Insole, chairman of selectors, now brought Wilf Isaacs into the English dressing room. A leading sponsor of South African cricket, Isaacs was close to the MCC establishment. He greeted D'Oliveira warmly, expressing how much he looked forward to seeing him in South Africa during the forthcoming tour. D'Oliveira was by now wary of all that was happening around him. Cautiously, he replied that he would be glad to accept his hospitality if he went on the tour.

Two years earlier, D'Oliveira had returned after his first day of Test cricket at Lord's and slept with the England cap under his pillow. This evening, the head that hit the pillow was ready to capsize with worry.

The following morning, Milburn tears into the Australian attack. The first over from McKenzie costs 13. When the faster bowlers bounce, they disappear in front of square. When Cowper pitches short he is pulled into the scoreboard under Father Time. Milburn is on trial, for this Test and the rest of his career. But he has no worries. He plays the only way he knows.

He is the first one to depart, for 83, with 12 fours and 2 sixes. One pull goes askew, the top edge carrying it up rather than far. Boycott follows five runs later, for 49.

Barrington and Cowdrey add 97. At the end of the day England are 314 for 5, Barrington retiring hurt with an injured finger. They have slowed down in the final session.

As people flocked to London for Saturday's cricket at Lord's, D'Oliveira, his duties as 12th man completed, departed for Glastonbury where Worcestershire were playing Somerset. There was no solace for him in the cricket, as rains continued to dog the season and no play was possible on the first day.

The bulletins came in from Lord's. The weather was only slightly better in London; 27 minutes of play was possible before lunch. Two and a half hours later, the game resumed, and Knott was run out by a throw delivered with a flick of his wrist by Redpath. The Victoria batsman had spent the previous match trout fishing, and he claimed that his practice of flicking the fly had aided his aim.

In the little play that was possible, Barrington resumed his innings to compile 75 and Knight was unbeaten on 27 as England finished on 351 for 7. A frustrating day for the spectators, but the torment of D'Oliveira at Glastonbury was far more excruciating.

Neither at Lord's nor at the Morlands Athletic Ground was there any possibility of a result. But as D'Oliveira continued his frustrating journey with a low score of 6 on Monday, on the television he snatched glimpses of David Brown and Barry Knight tearing through the Australian batting line-up, dismissing them for 78, their lowest in a Test in England since 1912. Cowdrey caught Redpath to level with Wally Hammond's record of 110 Test catches and went ahead by pouching Gleeson and Hawke. Knight's 3 for 16 from 10.4 overs fully justified his inclusion, coming on the back of his unbeaten 27. It could not have been happy tidings for D'Oliveira.

On the final day of the Test, D'Oliveira took a breather in Worcester before taking on Nottinghamshire the following morning. A persistent, pouring rain allowed only a little more than a couple of hour's play at Lord's. The match ended in a draw with rain emerging as the star performer, but not before Underwood had walked away with incredible figures of 18-15-8-2.

42 CALLS AND CALLED BACK

Knight retains his place, but Milburn has to sit out. His aggressive collaring of the Australian bowling turned things around at Lord's. All that has come at the price of a badly bruised wrist.

Strangely, Ray Illingworth is the man who comes in for the batsman. Like for like is no longer the chosen course.

But they have to wait as umpires abandon the first day at Edgbaston after taking a look at the wicket at 10.30 AM. Weather is the winner around the country.

The following morning, Cowdrey wins the toss in his 100th Test match. He has 6,940 runs and 112 catches—a rather impressive record.

England bat. Eric Freeman, replacing Hawke, opens with McKenzie. Boycott flicks McKenzie off his toes to bring up his 1000 runs for the season. But the start is slow, only 22 runs in 13 overs, 50 in 28.2. At lunch it is 65 in 35. The wicket is easy. Hard to imagine that England is trailing in the series, such is their crawl.

It does not improve after lunch. The score inches to 75 in 42. The first wicket falls for 80, Boycott 36 from 148 balls. Good old days of Test cricket.

Cowdrey comes in to a glorious round of applause and plays delightfully. He drives and cuts boundaries. The 100 is up in 56 overs.

By the end of the day, England accelerate to 258 for 3. Cowdrey, much of his innings with Boycott as runner, is unbeaten on 95.

On South African Freedom Day, 26 June 1968, the London Recruits distributed leaflets in Port Elizabeth, Durban, Cape Town, and Johannesburg. Banners were unfurled from high places. A loudspeaker was used to broadcast information from a car as well.

The leaflets disclosed the otherwise suppressed news of the Wankie Military Campaign, the operation launched by the Rhodesian Security Forces in response to the group of Zimbabwe People's Revolutionary Army and Umkhonto we Sizwe fighters crossing the Zambesi River.

D'Oliveira's sequence of scores since his departure from Lord's till the time of the third Test at Edgbaston was 6, 2, 4, 10, 6, 16, 9, 0. One can perhaps gauge his state of mind during this period.

He gave up thinking about England. There hardly seemed any hope now of getting back into the team. He virtually lost all interest in cricket for a while. He didn't socialise back in Worcester and moped around. It hurt him to be dropped after doing so well at Old Trafford, and it hurt and confused him to have been offered that unthinkable option by Griffith and Swanton.

To make things even worse, two weeks after meeting him at Lord's, Wilf Isaacs made a statement to the South African press that D'Oliveira would not be selected for the South African tour. He did provide the disclaimer that he had not spoken about the selection matters with the MCC officials.

Cowdrey is stuck on 99 for 17 minutes. McKenzie continues to bowl a bit short of a length. Cowdrey continues to defend his wicket and his ribs. At the other end Freeman keeps Graveney stationary. The crowd waits for the occasion—century in the 100th Test. It comes at long last, with a single to the backward of point. Boycott is still doing the running. Cowdrey departs at 104.

Graveney, driving with gorgeous ease moves to 96. Connolly comes round the wicket and angles it from the leg stump. There is a man at deepish cover, point and mid-off, to cut off his favourite areas. The maestro tries to drive him through the on-side and loses his middle stump.

The English approach remains slow. It is the final pair of Snow and Underwood who show some urgency, adding 33 in 27 minutes. 409 in 172.5 overs. It is already the third day. The possibility of a result is remote.

Snow starts for England. Lawry hooks the first ball for four and the second for two. The fifth ball of the over rises sharply and cracks him on the little finger. He calls for plaster, throwing off his glove in pain. He plays just one more ball and leaves the ground. X-rays show it to be a fissure fracture. Redpath does not last long, but Cowper and Chappell rescue the visitors from an impending collapse. Graveney leads the side in absence of Cowdrey, while Chappell and Cowper take Australia to 109 for 1. Cowper even takes the unhittable-for-right-handers Underwood for runs.

On 12 July 1968, the second day of the third Test, the International Olympic Committee passed a rule to balance the question of altitude related performance in Mexico City (7,347 feet) and the difficulties of the 'amateur' athletes in acclimatising to the conditions through focused and sponsored training in high altitude locations. "To achieve fairness as far as possible between competitors, no athlete other than those who usually live and train in such heights, shall specially do so at high altitudes for more than four weeks in the last three months before the opening of the Games."

The American track team soon set up camp in Echo Summit, at 7,400 feet, and trained on a specifically constructed tartan track for more than a month. They named it 'The South Lake Tahoe United States Olympic Medical and Testing Programme'. The Russians had stayed at Alma Ata for months. The West Germans were at Flagstaff, Arizona, at 7,000 feet.

Cricket was not the only sport struggling to come out of the ridiculous amateur-professional divide. All organised sports and competitions that evolved from the elite minds of privileged grandees wrestled with problems that had no logical solution.

Strangely, it is the Australians who play aggressive cricket on the fourth morning. Chappell sweeps and cuts Illingworth with elan. But when Knight beats his attempted on-drive to bowl him for 71, the visitors stumble. Underwood and Illingworth run through the lower order. 222 all out—a lead of 187. Two spinners are in form and the wicket is bound to deteriorate, perhaps that is why Cowdrey does not enforce follow-on. Quick runs are required.

But Boycott and Edrich inch to 41 in the 16 overs till tea. It is when Graveney, comes in that the rate is improved. Edrich drives Connolly back over his head and almost decapitates umpire Yarnold. Knight comes in at No 4, Knott at 5. The instructions are to get on with it. England declare at 142 for 3.

The target is 329 in 373 minutes. But the following day, just as Underwood and Illingworth are getting their vice-like grips around the game, the rain comes in. It lashes Birmingham relentlessly. Shortly after 3 PM the umpires call off play. As if on cue, a torrential downpour submerges the whole city under a sheet of water.

There was an illusion of form as D'Oliveira scored 22 and an unbeaten 29 at Eastbourne against Sussex. The 51 he made at Bramall Lane was undoubtedly a superb innings. Yorkshire won by four wickets and the scores were Worcestershire 99 and 105, Yorkshire 79 and 126 for 6. His was the only half-century of the match and achieved against an attack of Ray Illingworth, Don Wilson, and Brian Close.

But the runs dried up again as the season progressed—13, 4, 0, 0, 16.

It was a period of misery. The wetness of the summer did nothing to help.

Neither did it really help D'Oliveira's case that Ted Dexter had announced his intentions of making a comeback, and appeared in his first County Championship match in two years. On 20 July, Sussex lost three wickets for 17, four for 27, five for 85. Dexter held one end firm before cutting the Kent attack—including Derek Underwood—to ribbons, hitting a magnificent 203. Arthur Milton, David Green, Phil Sharpe, and Roger Prideaux—all scored hundreds.

As the England side reach Headingley they are a crumbling lot. Boycott has injured his back. Cowdrey has not recovered from his injury. England management decides to bolster the batting. Hence, Ted Dexter is recalled, debutants Keith Fletcher and Roger Prideaux are in, the latter as opening batsman. Barry Knight is 12th man.

Injuries galore, but there is still no place for D'Oliveira with all the fresh talent streaming in. To be fair, the run of scores has not been really encouraging to say the least.

There are more scares in store. Tom Graveney is to lead in the absence of Cowdrey. He himself is nursing an injured ankle. And to compound it, he cuts himself in a household injury. Normally such an injury would require stitches. But Graveney is informed that if stiches are made, it would take two weeks for him to play again. Graveney decides to risk it.

Illingworth also has an inflamed throat and David Brown is carrying a slightly strained leg.

Phil Sharpe is called up as backup.

As for Australians, Bill Lawry has not recovered from his finger injury. Barry Jarman will marshal the troops from behind the stumps. Keenest gambler in the side. He has a flutter on the toss and wins it. Australia bat.

It was around this time that D'Oliveira received the call.

Tienie Oosthuizen, marketing director of Carreras, the tobacco company, wanted to meet him for a most important interview. When could he travel to London?

Carreras was part of the great South African tobacco manufacturer Rothmans. The company, founded in London, was acquired in 1954 by the legendary Afrikaner businessman Anton Rupert, one of the stellar members of the Broederbond. Rupert's ventures had gone a long way in addressing the imbalance between the Afrikaner and the English businesses in South Africa leading up to 1948.

Rothmans was, and continued to be for many more years, a major sponsor of cricket. D'Oliveira himself had played in many of the Sunday 'Rothman's Cavalier' matches. He was not uninterested, especially at a time when his cricketing fortunes seemed to be stagnating.

Yes, he was willing to meet Mr Oosthuizen, the man with the very Afrikaner name.

Inverarity, the replacement of Bill Lawry, trips on the large shoes that he has to fill. Snow yorks him for 8. Thereafter Cowper plays the limpet for two and a half hours before another of Snow's yorkers crashes against his stumps. Redpath creams some classic drives, looks in control, but misses his century. Frustrated by Illingworth's nagging line, he sweeps him, misses and is bowled for 92. Walters looks good in patches, but Underwood gets him to snick on 42. Sheahan resists against Underwood, but Snow with the second new ball induces a drive and thereby an edge. 258 for 5 at the end of a keenly contested day.

The next morning, they lose the remaining wickets for 57. Underwood accounts for three of them.

The England reply starts on a positive note. Prideaux drives Freeman and hooks McKenzie to demonstrate that he is at home in Test cricket. Edrich 62, Prideaux 64. The openers put on

123. But once they are gone, the dream comeback does not materialise. Dexter inside edges McKenzie into his stumps. 163 for 3 at the end of Day Two with Graveney and Barrington at the crease.

Oosthuizen's offices were at No 8, Baker Street. D'Oliveira's family waited in the car as he went to the first floor for the mysterious interview. The office was large, plush and impressive.

"My friends call me Tienie, you can do so as well," Oosthuizen seemed friendly and approachable.

He explained to D'Oliveira that a cricket coach and sports organiser was required by an organisation known as the South African Sports Foundation. D'Oliveira nodded. He knew of the organisation. He knew that Trevor Goddard was in charge of cricket there, at least for the White South Africans.

They needed a man to look after the sporting facilities for the Coloured Africans, Oosthuizen continued. He had discussed the job with Ted Dexter, who had suggested Kenny Suttle, his Sussex teammate. The foundation wanted someone who had reached the end of his career and would take the post permanently.

Up to that moment, D'Oliveira had never thought about his life beyond cricket. In his thoughts, he would be playing for Worcestershire for years to come.

Oosthuizen now produced a copy of the recently published *D'Oliveira: An Autobiography.* "Somewhere you said that you'd like to go back coaching among your own people." It was while reading the book, Oosthuizen said, that it had hit him that D'Oliveira was indeed the man for the job.

D'Oliveira was in two minds. His career was far from over. He had been playing for England a couple of weeks ago. But he wanted to keep his options open.

Besides, there was the benefit season to think about. That was due. Oosthuizen made it clear that financial matters would not be a problem.

"I want you to know that there is nothing about politics in this at all. I'm not interested in politics," he suddenly added out of the blue.

Would he take the job? Oosthuizen pressed for an answer.

D'Oliveira said he would at least wait till the tour party to South Africa was named.

It was then that the amount was mentioned.

"It will be at least £4000 a year, with all expenses thrown in—a car, a house and that type of thing."

D'Oliveira was taken aback. That was a seriously huge amount of money in cricket. What was the catch? He did not ask it in precise terms, but the catch was revealed at this juncture.

"I have to let the Foundation know by 14 August. Could you make up your mind by then and let me know?"

The selection of the team was due on 28 August. What was the rush? "I can't jeopardise my chances of going to South Africa with MCC."

Oosthuizen looked at D'Oliveira. "If you knew for a fact that you were not going out there would you then take the offer?"

D'Oliveira was not sure how he was to ascertain the decision of the selection committee. However, he replied that it would definitely weigh in strongly.

"If you knew you would not be accepted in South Africa as a member of the tour, would you then take the job with the Foundation?"

It was a loaded hypothetical question.

"No one can possibly know this," he offered.

"Well, I can," said Oosthuizen conclusively.

D'Oliveira was speechless. After rearranging all the bits in his mind, he promised to give

Oosthuizen an answer if he did indeed get him the information.

As he left the office, Oosthuizen let D'Oliveira know that the contract could be for five years or ten.

This was indeed the second string in the bow of JB Vorster and Arthur Coy. There is enough evidence now to substantiate that Oosthuizen was acting on behalf of the South African cricket establishment and the Prime Minister in offering this job, which can be safely called a 'bribe'.

It is a topsy-turvy third morning. Graveney and Barrington, years and years of experience between them, take England to 209 for three. Then Graveney edges a drive off Connolly. Fletcher, having dropped three catches at slip, now touches one from the same bowler down the leg side and Jarman moves smartly to the left to hold it. A duck to go with his fielding lapses on debut.

After lunch McKenzie and Connolly maintain the pressure. Barrington is rapped on the pads by Connolly several times by ones that cut in. He loses his stumps to one that goes away. Two snicked runs later, Knott plays back to one from Freeman that cuts in from the off and the umpire gives him out. Illingworth tries to heave Connolly out of the attack and is taken magnificently at mid-on by Gleeson. Suddenly it is 241 for 9.

And then comes the counter-twist. With fieldsmen crowding him, Underwood swings lustily. Two boundaries to the leg side, a cover driven couple, a hooked boundary. A thumping high drive off a no ball, and the 10th wicket partnership is over 50. A sweep off medium paced Connolly takes the total past 300. Cowper bowls Brown to end the fun, but Underwood's 46-ball unbeaten 45 has taken the score to 302. England trail by just 13.

At the end of Day 3, Australia is 92 for 2, 105 ahead.

The week that followed saw D'Oliveira hounded by Oosthuizen. Calls were made to his house, at the ground. Could he confirm his acceptance of the offer?

On Sunday, Oosthuizen called to set up another meeting. D'Oliveira was playing at New Road that day. Hence, they decided to meet halfway, at a roundabout on the way into Oxford from Worcester.

Oosthuizen was late and D'Oliveira sat in the café waiting for him. On arriving, the South African apologised for being late and ordered himself a full English breakfast. D'Oliveira sipped his coffee.

"The only information I can get about your situation is that, while I can't definitely say that you won't be allowed in, I have it from the highest possible source that, if you are included in the MCC side, you'll be an embarrassment to the Government and Mr Vorster," Oosthuizen paused, before going on. "Surely you can read between the lines what that means? If you are an embarrassment, well, quite obviously you can't go."

The information was nothing new. D'Oliveira pointed out that he had not told him anything that he did not already know. On this information it was not possible for him to give up his chance of being picked for the tour.

Oosthuizen warned D'Oliveira not to get involved in politics.

"It's not politics," answered D'Oliveira. "It's my people. They're not fools. They know what's going on. They know nothing at this stage can persuade me to withdraw. I just can't do it."

They parted with D'Oliveira saying he would think further but was not sure that he would change his mind.

Some of his close friends did advise him to take the money and plough it back into non-White cricket. Damoo Bansda was one of them. Naomi told him to decide for himself.

But despite his form, D'Oliveira could not let go of the slim hope that he could still make it to the team.

It is weather that plays the spoilsport again, aided by the Australian reluctance to try and force the issue. A delayed start, appeals against light, and rather tardy batting see 191 runs in the day. Chappell plays an excellent innings, as does Walters, but there is no urgency. This is surprising given that their stand-in captain is a punter.

The 326 required by England on the final day is beyond them, especially with the pitch becoming tricky. Dexter attempts to cut loose, but it is too difficult. But at least the crowd get to see this flamboyant batsman for 100 minutes before he is bowled by Connolly's quicker ball. Barrington and Fletcher play out time. Series is 1-0 in favour of Australia as The Oval gears up for the final Test.

Early in the morning on Sunday, 18 August, Oosthuizen rang D'Oliveira at his home. Worcestershire were playing Middlesex and D'Oliveira was busy preparing. He was not really prepared for a call.

Oosthuizen said that he had been due to fly to Malaya but had changed his mind. He was now going back to South Africa, leaving on a plane at 3.30 PM. He needed D'Oliveira's answer before he left.

D'Oliveira was still not decided. The thought of letting his people and his ambitions down weighed heavy on one side, but he would be able to give the wife and kids a lot more with the money being offered.

On the spur of the moment he decided to lie and play for time.

"Look, I'm very sorry but I've been asked to make myself available for the tour," he said.

"Who by?"

"That's not important. I've been offered a lot of money to say I'm available."

"How much?"

D'Oliveira made up a sum. "Between £2000 and £3000."

There was a pause. "Look Basil, I'll tell you what I'll do. I'll offer you anything they offer. I'll do even better if you'll take this job now. This new offer has nothing to do with the job, it's my personal guarantee."

D'Oliveira could make out how vehemently Oosthuizen wanted him to say yes. He was cornered once again. He mumbled something about having to rush to the ground.

"Basil, I've got to catch my flight. Be sure you ring me before I leave."

D'Oliveira rushed to the ground. As he waited in the dressing room, there was a call to the ground. Oosthuizen was at the airport and wanted to speak to him before boarding his flight. D'Oliveira brushed him off, saying he had to go to bat.

That day he made a quick 40 against an attack that included John Price and Fred Titmus. Around tea, the team to play in the fifth Test was announced. He was not included. With his run of scores, he had not expected to be either. Later that day, he sent a note to his agent Reg Hayter, setting up an appointment in London for Tuesday.

On Tuesday morning there was a call. The operator asked him whether he was willing to take a call from South Africa? D'Oliveira informed that he was leaving for London. The operator insisted that Mr Oosthuizen wanted to speak on an urgent matter, and could he go to the Baker Street office at 11 to take the call?

Hayter, earlier a Press Association reporter, had set up an agency of his own. His client list today reads almost like a cricketing Who's Who, including Denis Compton and Ian Botham.

On hearing D'Oliveira's story Hayter doubly confirmed if the amount was really £4,000. £400 would be more in line with a winter contract in South Africa. Many cricketers did go on coaching assignments, like Clive Radley and Dickie Bird.

The second thing Hayter did was to make arrangements to record the telephone call. The taped conversation was reproduced in *The D'Oliveira Affair* and also in Oborne's book on D'Oliveira.

In short, D'Oliveira informed Oosthuizen that he could not take the offer. Once again there were assurances by Oosthuizen about the money. Once again there was insistence on the part of D'Oliveira that they wait till the selection of the team for South Africa. Oosthuizen also mentioned that unless D'Oliveira accepted the offer he would get "caught in a vice that would 'squeeze you helluva lot.'"

Once the call was over, with Oosthuizen promising to call again, Hayter set about enquiring from his sources whether D'Oliveira had a chance of making the touring squad. From his 'source', which Oborne surmises most likely to be Colin Cowdrey, he got to know that D'Oliveira had a 'bloody good chance'. He would certainly be among those who were being considered.

With this news, D'Oliveira started on a rather slow drive home.

It was evening when D'Oliveira reached Worcester. On the way home, he stopped at a pub. As he was going in, he bumped into Fred Trueman.

The following morning, Worcestershire were supposed to play Yorkshire at New Road. D'Oliveira engaged in a bit of banter.

"I'll give you some stick tomorrow, Fred."

"What do yer mean?"

"You've slowed down mate, and I'll give you a bit of stick."

Trueman looked at him quizzically.

"You won't be here, cock."

"Where do you think I'll be?"

Trueman realised that D'Oliveira was in the dark.

"You're in Thursday's Test, Basil. They've put you in. Although I can't bloody well understand why."

The news had been released about two hours after D'Oliveira had left London.

A week before the perplexing sequence of phone calls with Oosthuizen, Colin Cowdrey had played at The Oval. Kent had been playing Surrey, and Cowdrey had got a hundred.

Alan Dixon of Kent and Stewart Storey of Surrey were medium pacers. In the match Dixon picked up four wickets, Storey one. But Cowdrey perhaps found Storey difficult to negotiate during his long innings. He also saw the effectiveness of Dixon.

It dawned upon him that a medium-pacer would be handy. The selectors seem to have outvoted him, opting for Snow, Brown, and Higgs, three fast bowlers. Cowdrey, however, asked whether he could call up another player before the Test if conditions remained unchanged.

Tom Cartwright of Warwickshire was his first choice. Barry Knight the second. And since both of them had fitness issues, there was a third option as a backup. Basil D'Oliveira.

Three days before the Test, Cowdrey was warned that Cartwright was not fit. Knight was the next choice. It turned out Knight also had fitness issues.

Cowdrey asked for D'Oliveira to be included in the Test squad. The probable 12th man.

This was the news that D'Oliveira and Trueman discussed in the pub, and no doubt celebrated.

There was a further twist.

At lunchtime on Wednesday, 21 August, Roger Prideaux pulled out. He had a virus infection—or so he said. Later he admitted that he did not want a failure at The Oval that could mean foregoing his chances of selection for the South African tour.

But Cowdrey had a ready solution. Milburn would be pushed up the order to open, and D'Oliveira would be in the middle order, as a batsman who could bowl.

Perhaps it was Cowdrey the great theoriser about cricket at work. Perhaps it was Cowdrey the charming gentleman, niggled by the thought that he had to keep the promise made to D'Oliveira, that he would be back before the end of the season. We will never know.

Fate works in mischievous ways.

At 8.30 AM the following day, the International Exchange Operator rang D'Oliveira at his Worcester home. "The call booked to you from South Africa for 8.30 AM has been cancelled. The caller is not able to talk to you."

That was the end of the Oosthuizen affair.

43 OVAL RENAISSANCE

22 August 1968.

The troops had rolled into Czechoslovakia the previous day. Alexander Dubcek had been arrested by the Soviets. On this day, 1,192 of the 1,543 of the Communist Party delegates assembled at the CKD factory in Vysočany, a suburb of Prague, to select a new party central committee and a new presidium. The leaders unanimously re-elected Dubcek as the KSČ First Secretary.

At The Oval, the sun was out for the first time in the season in all its blazing glory. England went in with another majorly changed team, which took the number of players used over the five Tests of the series to 20. Only John Edrich, Tom Graveney, Alan Knot, and John Snow appeared in all five. Dennis Amiss, Bob Barber, Keith Fletcher, Pat Pocock, and Roger Prideaux played just one. Basil D'Oliveira managed to squeeze in at the beginning and the end.

But it was just minor relief.

The previous evening there had been the usual pre-Test dinner. Doug Insole had announced that all those who had been asked if they were available for the South African tour should provide answers before the end of the match. D'Oliveira heard the announcement, realising that he was perhaps the only England player in the room who had not been asked. The onus was on him to prove himself.

As he prepared for the Test that morning, he was contacted by Reg Hayter. A 'highly placed MCC official' was apparently peddling a rumour that he had received several thousand pounds to keep himself available for the tour. It is likely that whatever D'Oliveira had told Oosthuizen to buy time had reached the MCC through Arthur Coy or some other channel in a snowballed Chinese Whisper.

D'Oliveira had to seek out captain Colin Cowdrey and assure him that the rumours were not true. "The skipper had always shown extreme courtesy towards me." Cowdrey believed him, or at least did not care about the rumours. In any case, he had won the toss and that made him happy. The Oval wicket looked a beauty for batting, which was significant because the ground had been under water after a storm in the weekend. Lawry, having recovered from the finger injury, led the Australians into the field.

The Test match starts with a hiccup for tradition. Climbing into the Surrey Members' Pavilion early on the first day, Gubby Allen is absolutely appalled. His 66-year-old eyes zero in on something that they have never witnessed before.

Straight ahead, at the Vauxhall end, there is a board that rests around the boundary, announcing 'XS Insurance'—the first advertising board ever seen in a Test match in England.

Turning to the members around him, Allen points his finger and asks with an audible shudder: "What on earth is that?"

Seated beside him is Bernie Coleman. A South London publican, he has recently joined the Surrey Committee. And according to Stephen Chalke's excellent *Summer's Crown*, Coleman's reply is simple and to the point: "That, Mr Allen, is £500, and we're broke."

Times are indeed *a-changin'*.

By the time the Test match will draw to its dramatic end, there will be plenty of other hiccups of much greater magnitude for both Allen and the rest of the stodgy keepers of the archaic flame.

Milburn flashes a square drive for four and the impact can be heard in the nearby Vauxhall Station. And then his bulk leads to a comical interlude. Edrich drives McKenzie through the covers, with Sheahan in hot pursuit. By the time Milburn turns his massive frame to see Edrich charging down for the second run, the quicksilver Sheahan has already stooped down for the ball. "No," bellows Milburn, but Edrich is too far down the wicket. Luckily, Sheahan hastily throws on the turn and it runs away for overthrows.

Connolly, canny, and calculating, cleverly swings a bunch of deliveries away from Milburn and then ducks one back in to sneak through the guard of the large man and bowl him. Early wicket, but the pitch is a featherbed. Cowdrey is slotted as the No 3, but it is Dexter who makes his way out. The bowlers will have to work extra hard. Australia have fielded two spinners in Gleeson and debutant Ashley Mallett. Walters is in the role of a third seamer. He has not bowled much on the tour and it shows. The first delivery is a wide.

Gleeson comes on soon. England are 48 for one after the first hour. The sun ensures that drinks are brought out for the first time in the series.

22 August. The 1968 Democratic National Convention opened in Chicago. This would continue until 30 August. During the event, riots would break out, with severe clashes between the police and the anti-war protesters. It was a year of world-wide protests, especially by the students.

Dexter decides that Gleeson's mystery can be unravelled by attack. He tries to dominate but cannot get him away. Frustrated, he tries to drive Connolly at the other end, whose round-the-wicket angle takes it away from the batsman. The snick travels hard and wide of Ian Chappell at first slip. The catch does not stick as Chappell sprawls. But the following over, Dexter goes forward and tries to drive Gleeson. It is a wrong 'un that he hasn't read. The ball sneaks through the open gate and bowls him for 21. 84 for 2 at lunch.

Cowdrey takes 22 minutes to get off the mark. The malaise is catching. Edrich joins him in a synchronised saga of maidens.

Suddenly the sleeping giant in Cowdrey reawakens. Three quick and classy boundaries follow. Then debutant Mallet comes on—quiet, unobtrusive, hence nicknamed 'Rowdy' by teammates. His fifth ball in Test cricket is a quicker one and it grips and turns as Cowdrey plays back; the result is leg-before wicket.

Graveney struggles with his timing at first, but then there are the familiar drives through the covers. Edrich is untroubled as he moves into his 90s. At tea England sit pretty on 175 for 3.

22 August. The same day Ringo Starr briefly quit The Beatles after frustrations with the recording session of the song *Back in the U.S.S.R.* On vacation with his wife and children he would write *Octopus's Garden.*

Edrich places Gleeson round the corner to get his 100. It will be like Morris's 196 at The Oval 20 years ago. People will ask him whether he indeed played that match. Some milestones are like that.

200 for 3 in 85 overs. After three more overs, Bill Lawry opts for the new ball. McKenzie runs in and Graveney unleashes a magnificent drive down the ground. Fifty for him.

At 238, McKenzie comes round the wicket. Graveney leans into the drive. The angle induces an edge. At gully Redpath swoops low and grabs it. Arthur Fagg looks questioningly at his colleague Charlie Elliott. A nod confirms it. Graveney walks back for 63.

There are 45 minutes left in the day when D'Oliveira walks in to bat. He is keen to get into the middle and is jogging in even as Graveney leaves the ground. For someone who has spent the last two months going through the leanest of patches and the meanest of crisis, caught in political intrigue worthy of a spy novel, he is without apparent nerves. He is serene and peaceful as he faces the bowling.

McKenzie bounces and is resoundingly hooked for four. Mallett floats it up, and down the wicket comes Dolly, creaming him through the covers and lofting him over mid-on.

At stumps Edrich is 130, D'Oliveira 24. England 272 for 4. Perhaps the best day's cricket in the rather tepid series so far.

That evening was perhaps the worst for D'Oliveira in the entire Test. He had a room to himself in the hotel, hence all he was left with were his thoughts. What lay in store for him on the following morning? D'Oliveira did not drink that evening. He went to bed after a light supper.

The following morning, he got up feeling refreshed and confident. He phoned Naomi. "I'm all nerves," she said. "I couldn't sleep."

23 August 1968. Czechoslovakia's Prime Minister Dubcek was brought to Moscow from the prison, where Soviet First Secretary Leonid Brezhnev, Premier Alexei Kosygin and President Nikolai V. Podgorny discussed the invasion with him.

The sun remains smiling as the players take field the following day. "Wonder of wonders," says Simpson. Best conditions for batting.

As D'Oliveira gets to the bowler's end, umpire Charlie Elliott approaches him. "Get your head down," he advises.

Edrich and D'Oliveira propel the score along, at almost a run a minute. Lawry starts with Gleeson and Connolly, the two most impressive bowlers so far. Edrich is aggressive, perhaps for the first time in the series. He moves to 149.

Lawry makes the first change. Ian Chappell is asked to bowl his leg-spinners. He hits the spot right away. D'Oliveira on 31, goes back. The ball turns, takes the edge of his bat, and—Jarman spills the catch.

Later Jim Swanton will write of this lapse as "the most fateful drop in cricket history."

Edrich comes down and has a word with D'Oliveira. He has been a bit too confident. "Snap out of it, Bas. Get your head down. The wicket is better than yesterday. You can have a hundred here."

Chappell has an average of over 100 with the ball. He hardly bowls five overs a Test. But today he keeps excellent control, and the wicket suits him. D'Oliveira tries to drive him, several times, but does not get hold of his strokes. But when he errs by pitching short, Dolly goes back and late-cuts him with finesse to the fine boundary. The first hour has brought fifty for England. A sweep off Mallett takes D'Oliveira to 50 as well.

As D'Oliveira raises his bat, umpire Elliott mutters: "Well played—my God, you're going to cause some problems."

By now he is in full command. The score moves quicker. The partnership reaches 100.

It is Chappell who gets the breakthrough. Edrich moves down the wicket to drive. The ball dips a little, gets through the bat and pad and hits middle. Seven hours and 40 minutes for his 164. Few will remember the innings, so pathbreaking is the event unfolding at the other end. D'Oliveira is on 77.

Before lunch, D'Oliveira decides to break the stranglehold of Chappell and lofts him high over mid-on for four. He is 85 at lunch, Knott on 4.

23 August 1968. Colonel Benjamin Adekunle led Nigeria's final assault on the short-lived secessionist republic of Biafra. His instruction to the Third Nigerian Army Division was to "shoot anything that moves." In the month that followed, thousands of civilians would be killed as half of a yellow sun would set on an ephemeral nation.

D'Oliveira establishes his upper hand immediately on resumption. Lawry continues with Chappell, and he drives the part-time leg-spinner straight down the ground for four. A few defensive strokes and he sends him to the boundary through the covers. When he pitches short, D'Oliveira back-cuts him for two.

Perhaps Lawry has left the irregular bowler on for too long. Mallett takes over. D'Oliveira is on 96 and fretting for his hundred by now. He tries to drive the off-spinner, a bit too early. The ball is in the air, but falls short of mid-off. A scare.

The 400 comes up, five wickets down. D'Oliveira 98. Knott is keeping the scorers busy with square cuts and glides. He is dropped by Chappell at 400.

Mallett is worrying D'Oliveira. The Cape-Coloured South African knows the value of the hundred. To his people. To the non-white cricketers. To Naomi. To Damoo Bansda. And then to Johannes Balthazar Vorster. To Tienie Oosthuizen. To the suggestions of making himself unavailable for England. To the England selection committee, who have not yet asked him whether he is available to go to South Africa.

And the enormity of it all makes him nervous. Mallett raps him on the pads several times. A push for a single. He is 99.

Gleeson comes in from the other end. Three good balls. Two of them take the edge as he tries to turn them to the on. The edges are thankfully along the ground.

And then, a ball comes straighter. A nurdle to fine leg. And he runs. Century. He raises his bat. The Oval stands up. The value of a three-figure knock cannot be undermined. From 99 to 100 is the transition that makes the innings impossible to ignore. 87 not out in the first Test could be set aside without attracting critique. It is impossible to do so when there is a three-figure mark fresh in cricketing, public and journalistic memory.

The reactions are varied. "Oh Christ, you've put the cat among the pigeons now," says Elliott. Gleeson shakes his hand and mutters: "Well done, Bas, it'll be interesting to see what happens." Everyone knows the stakes.

No one more than the people in the office of BJ Vorster.

The telephone rings in the office of Geoffrey Howard, the secretary of the Surrey County Cricket Club. The caller is from the Prime Minister's Office in Pretoria. "A fellow called Tienie Oosthuizen, a director of Rothmans," Howard will recall later. Oosthuizen is trying to get hold of Billy Griffith.

"I can't get hold of the MCC secretary, so will you take a message to the selectors?"

Howard says he will pass it on.

"Tell them that if today's centurion is picked, the tour will be off."

Short, concise. No beating about the bush or walking on eggshells.

Howard passes the message on to Doug Insole.

Hundred in 195 minutes with 13 boundaries. D'Oliveira is now the frontrunner for the £250 prize for the fastest century in the series. However, that is not what he is playing for.

A break in concentration? As so often happens when one crosses a landmark? D'Oliveira tries to drive Gleeson to mid-on, and it pops back off the leading edge. "'Dolly' of a catch," writes Simpson. Gleeson can hardly believe his luck. He snatches at it and it falls out of his grasp. The earlier drop, according to Swanton, is the most fateful in cricket history. This one, Simpson says, is the easiest ever.

D'Oliveira capitalises. He back-cuts Mallett through the vacant slip area for four. He drives wildly a couple of times, lofting the ball into vacant regions of the outfield, and then lifts Mallett over mid-off and finds the fence first bounce.

That same over, he swings at one, and Connolly, perhaps unsighted, grasses the knee-height opportunity at long-on. After two months of terrible run of luck, today he seems predestined to make a huge score.

The new ball is taken at 447. D'Oliveira is on 137, making runs at will. Wickets fall at the other end, but the Worcestershire ace brings up his 150 with a single down to gully. Tea is taken at 457 for 8.

23 August 1968. Judge Edwin M Stanley ordered Caswell County, North Carolina, to integrate its schools. It was the last remaining racially segregated school system in the United States. After years of getting deferments for submitting a desegregation plan, the Supreme Court ruled: "The time for procrastination is over."

Luck sides with D'Oliveira even after the tea break. A hook off McKenzie goes skywards and Gleeson drops yet another sitter. But finally, he has to go. Debutant Mallet gets his wicket as he sweeps hard and low to Inverarity at backward-square leg. 158 in a little more than five hours, with 21 fours. The crowd stands up as one as he returns to the pavilion.

Two months of endless suspense, tension, drama and disappointment, and finally everything culminating in a great, great innings. No innings in cricket has changed the fate of man as much as this.

The show goes on. Sheahan dives forward at cover to catch Brown off Gleeson to end the England innings at 494.

Before the day is over, John Snow sends Inverarity packing. The hurried jab nicks the ball on to his pads and lobs to short leg where Milburn dives to his left and takes the catch. It is quite a sight to see the enormous bulk diving through the air and holding the offering in an acrobatic fashion. However, Milburn's reflexes make him a far better fielder than he is given credit for. Lawry and Redpath are together as stumps are drawn at 43 for one.

Late that afternoon, Colin Cowdrey was called away to take a telephone call. It went on for a while. When he returned to the dressing room, the rest of the team had left. Only D'Oliveira was there, absorbed in thoughts.

By now, the consensus in the dressing room was that he was a strong candidate for the tour. Cowdrey who had not been in South Africa since the 1956–57 visit, was keen to have a word.

"You must know the problem better than most people."

D'Oliveira knew of course.

"Can we get away with it without getting too involved in politics?" Cowdrey asked.

According to Cowdrey's memoirs *MCC*: "D'Oliveira was under no illusion at all about how the microscope would be on him every day, every hour, every moment [...] 'Everyone will be looking for the slightest flaw in my behaviour, both on the field and off it. There will be plenty of them just longing for me to get involved in an incident.' He had worked it out, even down to the kind of social functions he would attend and those he would not [...] I was very impressed by his outlook."

At some stage Cowdrey turned eloquent. "What'll it be like? What will happen if it's a Saturday afternoon at Newlands. You are batting. Pollock's bowling and we are on a high, just getting in command of the game. Pollock bowls, the whole South African side goes up for the catch, and you just stand your ground and refuse to walk."

At the end of the conversation, the skipper said: "I want you in South Africa. If anyone at the tour selection meeting asks me if I am prepared to accept responsibility for anything that might happen on the tour should you be selected, I shall say I am prepared to do so."

This dialogue took place after play on Friday according to D'Oliveira's conversations with Oborne, and on Saturday according to both D'Oliveira's and Cowdrey's written accounts. Whatever be the day, D'Oliveira came away convinced that he would be chosen.

However, it was not always prudent to take the charming Cowdrey's promises verbatim.

It is Bill Lawry who holds Australia together. On Saturday, he adds 129 with Redpath, but just before tea the visitors lose their way. Chappell, Walters, Sheahan and Jarman fall away, mainly through a lack of discretion.

At lunch, Doug Insole comes up to D'Oliveira. Is he available for South Africa? D'Oliveira says he is. "I thought as much," says Insole. Everything is falling in place.

Lawry continues his vigil, and with wickets falling so rapidly Cowdrey persists with the old ball. It is 103 overs before he opts for the new ball and Brown clips McKenzie's off stump. 49 invaluable runs are added. Lawry is still there as the third day ends, unbeaten on 135, as Australia struggle on 264 for 7.

Sunday, 25 August. Day of rest at The Oval. And of peace for D'Oliveira. The knock of 158, and the talk with his captain have laid his worries to rest. At least for the time being.

In Moscow's Red Square, a motley group of physicists, writers, poets, and linguists joined together in a congregation and unfurled the Czechoslovakian flag. Eight people were arrested. Seven of them would receive sentences ranging from three to five years of exile in Siberia.

Lawry falls for his overnight score, but Gleeson plays the aggressor and Mallett demonstrates immense maturity on debut. The follow-on is averted and the score creeps past 300. When Gleeson falls, Connolly frustrates the Englishmen alongside Mallett. The Australians survive through to lunch and Cowdrey is at his wits end.

It is only eight minutes after the break that Connolly edges Underwood on to his stumps. A total of 324. England's lead amount to 170. Less than what England had hoped for, but Cowdrey is determined to press home the advantage.

The hosts go for the runs early. Lawry responds with just one slip for his opening bowlers. Hopes are pinned on big-hitting Milburn. He hooks Connolly for a mighty six, but the cordon of fielders in a ring cut off most of his strokes. A frustrated Milburn tries to repeat his stroke and is caught at mid-on.

Most of the English batsmen get starts, try to accelerate and depart. Edrich 17, Dexter 28, Cowdrey 35, Graveney 12. D'Oliveira cannot recapture the magic of his first innings. Trying to hit Connolly back over his head, he skies a catch to Gleeson.

There is some hasty running, resulting in two run outs. But they keep scoring at a run a minute. Perhaps Cowdrey would have been happier to close the innings on his own terms, but it runs its course for 181 in 179 minutes. 395 minutes to score 352 runs for the Australians. Simpson feels Cowdrey has been a bit too cautious.

And then things start to happen. Lawry strikes Brown sweetly through the covers, and gets a fine edge off the next ball. Once again, the gigantic frame of Milburn crashes into the ground. Once again, he comes up triumphantly holding the catch.

It takes just seven overs for Cowdrey to introduce spin. Five close men surround Redpath. The batsman tries to push the fielders back with a crashing drive through the covers. In the last over of the day he pads up to Underwood and realises to his horror that it is the arm ball. 13 for 2. The Australians are in desperate strife.

The British Lions were busy touring South Africa during the same period as the Test series. The incident-free games at home lulled the Springboks into a false sense of security. 1969–70 would be very, very different.

The Lions won 15 of their 16 non-international matches, losing only in the Afrikaner stronghold of Transvaal. However, they were decimated in the internationals, losing 3 of the 4, managing one draw.

Tuesday, 27 August.

The final day of the Test match is the first without bright sunshine. A pleasant enough morning, but not as cheery as the previous ones.

Underwood is let loose upon the Australians right from the start. A quicker one in the third over, Chappell shuffles across and is rapped on the pads. The lethal finger goes up. 19 for 3.

Walters has been stroke-less for almost half an hour. And then one turns and pops up shoulder-high. It feathers the bat and Knott holds a reflex catch. 29 for 4.

Cowdrey stations eight men in catching positions for Underwood. The battery of close in fielders, helped by the batsmen looking to push and prod. The Australians are almost anchored to the crease.

Sheahan tries to break free. With fielders all around the bat, he gets four every time he wields his willow aggressively. After admirable resistance for more than an hour, he plays a dreadful stroke. Illingworth pitches short and Sheahan, shaping for the pull, does not go through with the stroke. Snow moves to his left from square leg to hold it.

65 for 5. 257 minutes to go. Deep, deep trouble. Barry Jarman, the next man, is in dreadful form with the bat. But unlike the previous batsmen, he does not thrust forward; rather, he allows the ball to come to him. It works—he strikes two boundaries. Inverarity is holding his end up with solid defence.

81 for 5 after 57 overs. Jarman strikes yet another boundary. And suddenly dark clouds appear. Another single and it starts to rain. The batsmen appeal and the umpires agree.

The players just about reach the dressing room when a cloudburst breaks. "The storm came in from nowhere," Bill Gordon, later the head groundsman at The Oval, will narrate to the author. "And it was a storm. The field was flooded, there was water-logging everywhere. The outfield in those days had not yet been re-laid, it meant water would find its way to the top."

The rain continues through the lunch break. It does not yield until just after time for resumption. By now, the ground looks more like a lake. "Colin Cowdrey came out and asked the head groundsman [Ted Warn] what he reckoned," Gordon says. "He said if we got cracking for a couple of hours there could be play. And we did it."

The reflection of the stands stares ominously back at Cowdrey from the huge pond like water-body stretching across the outfield. The England team have just started to pack their bags when the captain makes his way to the middle, trousers pulled high over his boots. He starts by urging the Oval ground-staff to do something about it. And he quickly realises that just those hands would not do.

The captain turns to the spectators for help, appealing on the loudspeaker. And the crowd swarm in, with personal blankets, handkerchiefs and parts of their clothing. At 2.15 PM, they start their mopping operations under the astute guidance of the groundsman Warn. Hessian bags are used in large numbers. Gradually water drains away. Patches of green become larger and larger and linked up. By 4.45 PM, the miracle is achieved. The large hand of the Vauxhall Lane stand clock shows fifteen to five when John Snow runs in. Just 75 minutes of play remain.

"It was a different game back then. Nowadays the match referee wouldn't allow all those people on the turf," Gordon remembers.

Cowdrey hopes that the pace of Snow will get some bite. His first ball has as much pace as a plum pudding. Underwood runs in from the other end. All 10 men breathe down the neck of the batsman.

At Snow's end, Cowdrey tries D'Oliveira, then Illingworth, then Brown, then Illingworth again. No success. For 11 overs Jarman and Inverarity keep their wickets secure. The latter steps inside Underwood's line and pulls him twice to the boundary to bring up his 50.

And then he is dropped. Dexter at silly mid-off fails to hold on to a bat-pad offering. Illingworth groans in despair. 110 for 5. Time is running out.

Once again Cowdrey summons D'Oliveira—the magic man for this Test match. He pitches just outside the off. Jarman tries to pad it away. It cuts back, flicks the inside of the pad and removes the off bail.

5.24 PM. The defiant stand broken.

Illingworth bowls the next over, and Cowdrey takes D'Oliveira off and brings back Underwood. The first ball to Mallett kicks up. The debutant manages to fend it off the middle. At silly mid-on lurks the six-foot-four-inch frame of David Brown. He scoops up the catch almost from Mallett's boot laces. McKenzie survives four balls. The last ball of the over is played forward, head in the air. It touches bat and pad and is on the verge of dying down into the ground when in lunges the huge frame of Brown, diving forward, coming up with the catch, wet and muddy like a soccer goalie.

Three wickets are lost at the same score of 110. In just six minutes.

Cowdrey does not have to place the field anymore. They just circle the batsman like vultures. For the last two balls of Illingworth's over, however, they drop back on to the ring. Preventing the single.

Gleeson sweeps a boundary and then hits Brown with a sweep and gets a single. Inverarity snicks one between Knott and Cowdrey for four.

Underwood bowls over the wicket now. Gleeson inexplicably offers no stroke to a straight ball and is bowled.

Connolly walks in. The last man.

Six minutes remain on the clock when Inverarity faces Underwood. He tries to push his foot forward to pad up, but his boot is caught in the mud. Anchored on the crease, he has padded an arm ball. Fatal. The question is almost rhetorical. England have squared the series. Underwood 7 for 50.

A victory that will be savoured, with the final moment captured as one of the most famous photographs of cricket.

"You'll be judged by only two standards—your own success and your team's success," Tom Reddick's words echo in D'Oliveira's mind.

He cannot be left out now, can he?

D'Oliveira returned to Worcester late that night, caught in the celebrations.

Colin Cowdrey got into his Jaguar, with the number plate MCC 307, and drove northwards. Across the Thames, past Hyde Park, along Edgeware Road, all the way to Lord's.

The selectors' meeting commenced at 8.00 PM in the Lord's committee dining room. It went on till 2.00 AM the following morning.

44 RESELECTED FOR A CANCELLED TOUR

The minutes of the meeting are lost forever. We will never quite know exactly what took place during those six long hours.

However, we do know certain details. For example, we do know that the meeting need not have taken place. The message from Vorster, communicated by Lord Cobham in his unconventional manner, was clear enough. The telephone call from Oosthuizen to Billy Griffith, received by Geoffrey Howard, could not have been clearer either.

MCC had already refused to agree to preconditions. Hence, there was no need to select a team. The Prime Minister of South Africa had played his hand, dictating the selection, threatening cancellation if a certain player was selected. The tour should have been called off then and there.

The problem was that the four selectors were not informed of the message. Peter May, Alec Bedser, Don Kenyon, and Doug Insole were asked to choose an England side. As chairman of the selection committee, knowing fully well about the complications surrounding D'Oliveira, Insole did play his role in urging the decisions to be made as if they were choosing a team for Australia—in short, ignore the complications and choose the best team.

Billy Griffith, Gubby Allen, and Arthur Gilligan were the only ones who remained aware of Vorster's clause. They chose to remain silent.

Swanton tries to defend his friend Allen for not disclosing the message to the MCC Committee by saying: "There was a practical difficulty from which there was no escape. Two of the four selectors, Insole and May, were on the MCC Committee. Their job was to pick the sides against Australia without any other consideration. The knowledge of Cobham's talk with Vorster would be an unfair burden to out upon them, if it could be avoided."

This defence is understandable, Swanton being the pro-establishment champion of Allen. However, it falls apart on two accounts.

One, as pointed out, trying to force MCC's hand in selection matters should have automatically cancelled the tour without bringing the selection committee into the picture.

Two, by the time the team for South Africa was being chosen, the Australia series had already been done and dusted. So, Allen, Gilligan, and Griffith could have used the window between the end of the Oval Test match and the beginning of the selection meeting to disclose the message and spare them the ordeal of a long night.

Instead, Griffith and Swanton had both approached D'Oliveira with suggestions to withdraw his availability. It cannot be concluded to have been anything other than trying to ensure the long-lasting cricketing connections between the two friendly nations carried on smoothly, and hoping that through minor manoeuvring the problem of D'Oliveira could be resolved independently.

The D'Oliveira issue was discussed in the Cabinet that day in South Africa. In the Cabinet minute book for 27 August, a handwritten note records: "MCC kriekettoer 1968/9. Als D'Oliveira gekies word is die toer af." (Should D'Oliveira be chosen, the tour is off). A three-page press release was prepared for the contingency in case this happened and Vorster was obliged to intervene and cancel the tour.

There is not really any empirical evidence to suggest that the selectors were swayed by the controversy surrounding D'Oliveira. However, it is impossible to deny that the South African complications were at the back of every mind.

Eventually, the team that was formed did not include D'Oliveira. From the several detailed analyses we have of the meeting, Peter May did not speak for D'Oliveira. Neither did Alec Bedser. Don Kenyon, D'Oliveira's captain in Worcestershire, was not a strong enough voice for him. And Insole, the chairman, did not weigh in on any issue; he gathered the opinions and evaluated them.

Finally, Cowdrey, who had promised D'Oliveira that he would stand up for him, and in all probability believed it himself when he said so, did not plump for him. In *MCC,* he writes: "D'Oliveira himself, I feel sure, believed he had done enough to justify his selection for the tour. On purely cricketing grounds, I was not so sure." It is in stark contrast to his earlier promise to D'Oliveira, which again is something he writes in *MCC.* The analysis that D'Oliveira had not done enough was perhaps a retrofitted logical chain concocted by Cowdrey himself—to explain his own decision to himself after the incident.

Cowdrey, before driving to the selection committee meeting at Lord's, had said to Jack Bailey, the MCC assistant secretary: "They can't leave Basil out of the team. Not now." Perhaps he really wanted him in the team. Perhaps somewhere along the line, some other charming consideration took precedence.

He was a man of charm and perfect manners. The 'spirit of cricket lecture' of MCC is named after him. Often, the burden of maintaining such a squeaky-clean straight-walking image makes one prone to stumbling on ridges and fissures where the lines of demarcation between right and wrong are not that straight.

Cowdrey sometimes walked when he was out. Sometimes he did not. Some say he chose his moments, walking only when the situation was not critical. It could have been so, or individual cases could have been in line with other parameters that he was balancing in a mind burdened all along by his image. It just confused the hell out of the umpires.

Here, it confused D'Oliveira. A cricketer to the hilt, someone who was too steeped in his game to think much of the complications of complex minds, D'Oliveira kept trusting Cowdrey. Even after the shock of his omission was made known to him the following day.

Private Eye's take on D'Oliveira's Omission

In cricketing terms, D'Oliveira was not considered as an all-rounder. As Insole explained in detail, the selectors were not confident of his bowling in the South African conditions. Tom Cartwright was the man chosen for that role. As for batsmen, they went with Cowdrey, Boycott, Barrington, Edrich, Graveney, Fletcher, and Prideaux.

Both Fletcher and Prideaux had played just one Test apiece. However, they had scored plenty of runs in the English season.

Prideaux had 1,993 runs at 41.52, Fletcher 1,890 at 41.08. In contrast, D'Oliveira, even after the 158 at The Oval, ended the season with 1223 runs at 33.05. The two younger batsmen were included because of their potential.

Hence, one can argue that there was cricketing merit in the omission, and there indeed was. But D'Oliveira had proved himself at the Test level, and his last two Tests had seen him score 263 runs at 87.66. From that point of view, it was a bit strange to omit him when considering him as a pure batsman.

Worcestershire was playing Sussex. D'Oliveira heard the news on the transistor radio of opening bowler Brian Brain. The BBC commentator Brian Johnston started reading out the team list. When he was done, D'Oliveira put his head in his hands and wept.

Tom Graveney, chosen vice-captain of the side, arranged for the grieving player to be taken into the private room of Bill Powell, the Worcestershire physiotherapist. Alone in the room, he broke down completely.

In Potchefstroom, Louwrens Muller, Vorster's newly appointed Minister of Police, was addressing a Nationalist rally. He interrupted his speech with the news that D'Oliveira had not been chosen. The announcement was greeted by loud and jingoistic cheering.

Prime Minister Vorster was a relieved man. He rang up Coy and thanked him for his contribution in the matter. Coy wrote a letter to Vorster appreciating the Prime Minister's gesture of telephoning him. This letter demonstrates how much hand-in-glove SACA was with the South African government and its policies. "We (SACA) do indeed appreciate your help and guidance in a matter which was important to our Country in many respects."

While Insole explained the omission of D'Oliveira in cricketing terms, Billy Griffith took pains to reiterate that there had been no preconditions to the selection based on South African influence. He followed up this statement of tenacious technical correctness with a not-so-correct follow-up: "Never at any time was pressure put on the selectors by anyone in South Africa." It was not even a half-truth. Doug Insole had received the message from Prime Minister Vorster's office on that very day of selection, a few minutes after D'Oliveira had completed his century.

The reactions were varied, and mostly scathing. Sir Learie Constantine, great West Indian cricketer and influential Trinidad politician, termed the omission of D'Oliveira as suspicious. *"To say he is not in the best 16 cricketers of England is nonsense. I am convinced that if Dolly was White he would be packing his bags."*

Closer to home, the Worcestershire secretary Joe Lister was fuming. *"We have been told all along that the best side would be chosen and internal politics not brought into it. It is hard to believe the real reason for not choosing him is his form."*

In the *Mirror,* Peter Wilson wrote: "*In the bad old days the colour of your tie was of paramount importance. Now the colour of the skin seems to transcend all logical and sporting concerns.*"

Weighty voices in the press sided with D'Oliveira. Jim Swanton, the very man who had whispered the proposition to make himself unavailable, now said that "*the idea that a man who learned his game under the shadow of the Table Mountain is not suited for South African conditions was ludicrous.*"

Michael Parkinson in the *Sunday Times* was as scathing: "*Last Wednesday a group of Englishmen picked a cricket team and ended up doing this country a disservice of such magnitude that one can only feel a burning anger at their madness and a cold shame for their folly."*

It was as usual John Arlott, the man with perhaps the greatest influence on D'Oliveira's career, who summed the matter up in lucid prose: *"MCC have never made a sadder, or potentially more damaging selection than in omitting D'Oliveira from their team to tour South Africa [...] There is no case for leaving D'Oliveira out on cricketing grounds [...] No one of open mind will believe that he was left out for valid cricket reasons; there are figures and performances less than a week old [...] It could have such repercussions on British relations with the Coloured races of the world that the cancellation of a cricket tour would seem a trifling matter compared with an apparent British acceptance of apartheid."*

Reactions were strong in the political world as well. Labour MP Ivor Richard wrote to Mark Bonham-Carter, chairman of the Race Relations Board, to open an investigation into the failure to select D'Oliveira. Several Labour MPs demanded a government enquiry. While sports minister Denis Howell dismissed these suggestions, his remark was loaded: "On team selection, as a Minister, I am expected to be officially speechless, and I certainly am at the moment."

From the cricketing world as well, there were voices that joined the chorus. Ted Dexter insisted that he would always pick D'Oliveira as his No 6. Trevor Bailey observed that the Worcestershire pro was unlucky not to be chosen and his style of bowling could have been handy in South Africa.

Indeed, if we look at the statistical tables, in the 1960s bowlers like Eddie Barlow and Tiger Lance, similar to D'Oliveira in their styles, had been successful in the Test matches. During the 1964–65 series, even Geoff Boycott's slow medium pace had got him reasonable success, five wickets at 31.40. One would imagine D'Oliveira, a bowler of far greater ability, would do better. Dismissal of his bowling abilities just because of the West Indies tour, where wickets were decidedly the flattest of decks, was somewhat myopic.

Yet, there were voices which supported the selectors as well. According to many, Colin Milburn's exclusion was a bigger case of disappointment.

Jim Gallaghan in the London *Evening News* wondered what would have been the case if Jarman had latched on to the offering at 31: "*Would they have been describing the MCC decision as 'shameful', 'damaging' [...] if Dolly had been White?"*

John Woodcock wrote that next to the other batsmen he failed to make the grade. If he had gone, the tour would have been as much a political whistle-stop as a cricketing exercise.

Michael Melford, John Thicknesse, Brian Scovell and, most tellingly, EM Wellings, came out in support of the decision. Wellings, in fact, had written a lengthy article on the eve of the selection underlining why the selectors should not choose D'Oliveira. He had dwelled on the failures in West Indies: "He had opportunities galore because he was nominally the only all-rounder. The more chances he had, the more obviously he became a liability to the team."

In South Africa, Louis Duffus observed that there would be "a national sigh of relief."

Amongst the non-White community of South Africa, there was dejection. They had hoped for years for the moment when Basil D'Oliveira would walk out in the very grounds he was not allowed to be in other than in the 'cage' and show the White man what a Coloured cricketer was capable of. Now, as their dreams were shattered along with D'Oliveira's, letters kept streaming into the Worcester residence of the cricketer. The phone was ringing off the hook. Tom Graveney's wife took Naomi aside and advised her to pack her bags and take the family away from all the furore.

And somehow, D'Oliveira continued to play. While his omission was being announced, he hit 128 against Sussex and captured 3 for 36 in an innings win. Against Surrey, he hit a classy unbeaten 92 and bowled with plenty of guile.

However, at the same time, he could not get away from the South African issue.

Through the agencies of Hayter, D'Oliveira was contracted by *News of the World* to travel to South Africa to report the tour.

Vorster reacted to this new development, slamming down on "guests who have ulterior motives or have been sponsored by people with ulterior motives." The Afrikaans newspaper *Dagbreek en Landstem* wrote that the British Sunday newspaper was "[a]pparently paying a tremendous sum to embarrass South Africa." Additionally, under the Group Areas Act, D'Oliveira's visit would have been disastrous. He would have had to report sitting in the non-White stands, have his meals separately, and could not have interviewed any player.

It was a time when intrigue and rumours flew about without restraint. And in *The Times,* Charles Barr, a 28-year-old lecturer and associate member of MCC, published a classified advertisement in which he called on "fellow members, unhappy with the club's handling of tour selections and cricket relations with South Africa" to get in touch with him. He received about 70 calls and a meeting was arranged in his flat at Essex Road. Among the attendees was the long-time anti-apartheid voice, Reverend David Sheppard. It was decided to press for a special meeting of the MCC to call off the winter tour.

EM Wellings, an intemperate critic of D'Oliveira, attacked Sheppard saying that the step was "strangely intolerant for a Christian." After 20 years of apartheid, protests against the regime still cut several of the old-world proponents to the quick. Wellings of course cloaked his pro-South African arguments with the rather curious view that continued sporting contact was the way to confront apartheid. Obfuscating journalistic prose has never quite required rational deductive reasoning.

Rand Daily Mail cartoonist Bob Connolly summed up the situation

On 4 September, a week after the team was announced, D'Oliveira went down to Lord's for Worcestershire's final match of the season, against Middlesex.

There were three men who came to meet him. Billy Griffith entered the visiting team's dressing room, expressing how sorry he was that D'Oliveira had been so bitterly disappointed. He added that he was grateful that the cricketer had accepted it as an honest decision. The same message was reiterated by Donald Carr, the assistant secretary.

The third person who visited was from a very different world and a very different direction. It was Dennis Brutus, the poet-activist and founder of SAN-ROC.

A decade ago, it was Brutus and his SASF who had derailed the proposed tour of West Indian Black cricketers to South Africa. In a way, his negative effect on D'Oliveira's cricketing ambitions had prompted the cricketer to seek opportunities in England. After that, the two men had met once or twice in South Africa and in England. Brutus had been quite insistent that D'Oliveira, as a Test cricketer, voice his support for the organisation. D'Oliveira on his part did not want to focus on anything other than cricket and had refused.

Now, during the Middlesex game, Brutus invited D'Oliveira to join him for a drink. They had a couple of beers in the Tavern. The conversation remained centred around personal matters. There was no broaching the subject of protests.

However, later that week D'Oliveira received an invitation from Brutus's wife to open a church bazaar in North London. D'Oliveira refused, being committed to a match that day. In any case he would have refused.

But Brutus was becoming more and more active in his relentless struggle against apartheid sports.

No doubt Tom Cartwright was in prime form in 1968, with 68 Championship wickets at 15.17 apiece. Six fifers, two ten-fors. But then, Championship figures need to be analysed further to get a proper perspective. Against Hampshire, for example, Basil D'Oliveira captured 11 for 68 in late July. Against Gloucestershire 10 for 80 in middle of August. He himself had 58 wickets at 15.74, and he was not considered a bowler.

What is significant is that Cartwright played just 16 of Warwickshire's 28 matches that season. He had missed nine of the last 10 matches of the county. He had trouble both with his shoulder and his knee.

The selection of Cartwright as the all-rounder in the side was a bit surprising given his fitness problems. Over the last few years, his batting had also deteriorated.

Cartwright himself was not having an easy time with the developments. "[A woman calling from BBC] asked me very aggressively how I felt. 'Aren't you sorry?' I remember saying, 'I'm sorry for a lot of people. I'm sorry for Alan Jones of Glamorgan. He's had such a brilliant season, and he's very unlucky not to be picked'."

He had read in the paper that the MPs in the South African parliament all cheered when they heard D'Oliveira had not been picked. It did make him uneasy.

He was receiving cortisone injections on his shoulder in order to be fit for the Gillette Cup final on 7 September. His 3 for 26 had been instrumental in beating Middlesex at Lord's in the semi-final three weeks earlier.

He spent the night in Clarendon Court Hotel on the night before the final against Sussex, and hardly slept a wink. The following morning, he reached the dressing room, turned his arm over and found it impossible. He did not even go to the nets.

Donald Carr approached him. "You're our property now." He wanted Cartwright to see Bill Tucker, an orthopaedic surgeon with consulting rooms in Park Street, off Park Lane. He had taken care of Denis Compton's knee.

Tucker's report to Carr did not look promising. There was a chance of his never being able to bowl again if he did go to South Africa.

On 16 September, Cartwright received a call from Colin Cowdrey. Could he confirm his availability? If something went wrong during the tour, Don Wilson or someone else coaching in South Africa could be brought in, assured the England captain. Till then, there was no suggestion of any D'Oliveira factor.

Cartwright said no. Cowdrey accepted the decision.

Cartwright's biographer Stephen Chalke says: "Tom withdrew for three reasons: his injury, the effect on his family of being away all winter and his unease at the reaction of the South African parliament when Basil D'Oliveira was not selected. The three factors did combine in his mind to make him think, 'I just don't want to go.'"

All of a sudden, a position had opened up.

Like-for-like replacement would have been Barry Knight. However, he had fallen afoul of MCC. In a newspaper feature, he had disclosed secrets about his marriage break-up, bankruptcy, and contemplating suicide. He also had his problems with Essex, and had earned the wrath of MCC because an article had been published under his name without their knowing it.

The selection committee was stumped. The previous couple of weeks had been harrowing for them, and they were still being roasted in various sections of media, public and cricketing fraternity.

According to Cowdrey's *MCC*, it took them just 10 minutes to reconvene and come up with the name of the replacement.

Basil D'Oliveira was having dinner with Naomi and several cricket friends on 16 September in the Astral Hotel, Plymouth, when the news came in. His reactions were mixed.

"It was the greatest moment I can remember. I think I knew then in my heart, however, that the tour would probably not take place."

In London, the selectors were trying hard to pull the inequality sign into something resembling comparability.

"There is no direct replacement for a bowler of Cartwright's specialist abilities. Therefore, the balance of the touring side has to be altered."

Billy Griffith was again going through the painful process of justification. The selectors had apparently "rethought the entire issue and decided that Dolly could pick up a few wickets. The selectors have been desperately honest all along the line."

Prime Minister Vorster was about to make the opening speech in the Orange Free State Nationalist Party Congress in Bloemfontein—the veritable heartland of the Afrikaner. He erupted. "The MCC team as constituted now is not the team of MCC but the team of the Anti-Apartheid Movement, the team of the South African Non-Racial Olympic Committee and the team of Bishop Reeves."

This Bishop Reeves was the Anglican Bishop of Johannesburg who had been deported several years ago for his outspoken criticism of apartheid. One wonders why Vorster, who had already typecast MCC as a leftist organisation under direct control of the Labour Prime Minister Harold Wilson, chose this surprising combination as the constitution of the team. Perhaps the news, after what he had considered the end of the matter two weeks ago, came as too unpleasant a surprise to frame a reasoned response. In any case, he received a frenzied and enthusiastic ovation.

"We did not want to play selection committee for them. The ultimate decision was theirs and theirs only and they made their choice on merit. There was an immediate outcry because a certain Gentleman of Colour was omitted on merit, as they themselves said. From then on D'Oliveira was no longer a sportsman but a political cricket ball."

On the following day, British ambassador John Nichols cabled London with the ominous words: *"MCC's decision to include D'Oliveira after all is likely to run us into serious trouble."*

It was D'Oliveira's inclusion in the team as a replacement, that too of a bowler, that lent weight to Vorster's argument that it had been a political ploy.

In the heated exchanges that followed, Billy Griffith came out of the Yellow and Red MCC shell. "Basil D'Oliveira had been left out of the original team by a bee's whisker and has now been picked as a replacement. It is as simple as that. We picked our best side and assumed this would be acceptable. If it is not, then the tour will be off."

As a desperate measure to save the tour, Arthur Coy and Jack Cheetham flew to London under assumed names. But it did not help. Ben Schoeman, the important political ally of Vorster and a pillar of the National Party, pointed out: "Cartwright was a specialist bowler and D'Oliveira is a batsman. Yet, the MCC had the impudence to say that D'Oliveira had been selected entirely on merit and that no political considerations had been involved. It will be a waste of time to send a peacemaker."

The 1968–69 tour to South Africa was cancelled.

In 1968, almost simultaneously, The Separate Representation of Voters Amendment Act abolished the remaining parliamentary representation for Coloured people. The Coloured Persons Representative Council Amendment Act replaced it with an elected Representative Council with limited powers.

To end this chapter on the selection fiascos and the reactions, it would be appropriate to quote parts of an article by Louis Duffus, the most respected South African cricket writer, that was published in *The Star.* The idea is to lay bare the warped thinking of White South Africa and the Old Boys' Club of cricket prevalent in those days.

"D'Oliveira was for so long a dagger directed at the heart of South African cricket that surprise and shock at the cancellation of the MCC tour seems synthetic [...] the law of the land says drive on the left, D'Oliveira was told to come out and drive on the right.

"England knew the law when a much greater cricketer, KS Duleepsinhji, could have been chosen to tour this country. He was not selected and nothing was ever said about it.

"MCC [...] which exists solely to further the interests of cricket [...] made the most crippling decision in the history of the game through blatant ignorance or deliberate ignoring of South African conditions.

"Because of one cricketer, the great players produced in this country and the game itself have both been victimised.

"Posterity will surely marvel how a player, helped to go overseas by the charitable gesture of White contemporaries, could be the cause of sending the cricket of his benefactors crashing into ruins."

Louis Duffus

Duffus might have been terribly wrong about posterity, but the reactions to the article were exhilarating.

"The headmaster of an Afrikaans school, of whom I had not heard since we were contemporaries at King Edwards nearly 50 years previously, said extravagantly, "Your article should be hung in every cricket pavilion of the country."

"For the remainder of the afternoon [on the day it was published] and night there was a succession of calls from people, some unknown, anxious to offer their praise.

"There were telegrams and letters and for some weeks, people I met had something to say about it."

It restores faith in humanity a little when we read Duffus admitting that not all the messages had been complimentary.

On 3 December 1967, 53-year-old Louis Washkansky received the first ever human heart transplant in the world, at Groote Schuur Hospital in Cape Town. It was performed by Surgeon Christian Bernard of the Cape Town University.

The country would have to wait much longer for a change of its own heart.

Eastern Province

HERALD

JACK'S

VORSTER: We will not have a team thrust upon us by people wishing to make political capital.

GRIFFITH: The team has been chosen all along with no shadow of doubt only on cricketing ability.

TOUR BY M.C.C. OFF

Dolly's inclusion not acceptable–Vorster

Public servants and teachers get rise

'Team of Sanroc'

Policy

Correctly

No notice taken of pressures says M.C.C.

LETTER

TRAGEDY

Tribute to Portuguese Premier

Helicopters search for killer

POLICEMAN SLAIN BY FUGITIVE GUNMAN

Graaff deplores tour decision by Premier

On merit

SEATS AT BARNARD LECTURE ALL GOOD

Warning

Performing whales for City hope of museum director

Maternity wear in fashion pages

How much will it cost you to replace all your possessions tomorrow?

R1,000?
R2,000?
R5,000?
R10,000?

How LITTLE will it cost you

The sensational front page of the Eastern Province Herald

SECTION 7
Stop The Seventy Tour

45 PLAN OF ACTION

February 1969. Steel had been forged into the quagmire of charm that constituted the psyche of Colin Cowdrey.

If the proposed, and eventually cancelled, South Africa tour had been designed to test the moral makeup of the English team, the hastily arranged Test series in Pakistan was no longer just an ethical dilemma. It was as close a cricket team would come to actual warfare before the Sri Lankan team bus would be shot at by terrorists 40 years down the line in the same country.

It had been the exclusiveness of the founding members of the Imperial Cricket Conference that had almost seen the England side tour apartheid South Africa. Now, it was the more practical alliances struck up to swim abreast the frigid undercurrents of the Cold War that landed the team in a dangerously explosive Pakistan.

Ayub Khan was at the helm of the disturbed dictatorship. A former President of the Pakistan Cricket Board, he was struggling against the irritating growth of the Pakistan People's Party of Zulfiqar Ali Bhutto and the Awami League of Sheikh Mujibur Rahman.

In fact, East Pakistan was on the verge of a bloody battle for independence which would form the country of Bangladesh two years down the line.

But in this explosive environment, Ayub struck up an alliance with the United States and Britain, mainly due to the strategic location of West Pakistan near the countries of Soviet Union and Afghanistan. And while the MCC looked for a proper winter assignment for the contracted players after the annulment of the South African odyssey, the British Foreign Office encouraged them to send the players off to Pakistan. The itinerary included a Test in the combustible East Pakistan capital of Dacca.

Horror stories, including tangible death toll, reached the players daily as they went about apprehensively from tour game to tour game. Karachi was under curfew from dusk to dawn even as they reached the country.

When the MCC side was forced to get up at 5.30 AM and fly in to Lyallpur to play the Central Zone immediately after their match against BCCP XI at Bahawalpur had ended the previous evening, it was too much for Cowdrey.

Cricket, to him, was still a game of old-world charm and antiquated values. Cowdrey was the confused link between the supposed pristine past and the troubled present. Most often, this resulted in indecisive floundering, as had been the case in the D'Oliveira affair. However, today, he took a stand. Things had gotten a bit too out of hand.

Or it may be that he was just not a morning person.

"No English side has ever started a game of cricket without having a cup of tea," he announced. As Saeed Ahmed waited for toss, and the crowd grew impatient, Cowdrey refused to go in until they had been served tea and had partaken of it in leisure.

There was a two-hour delay before John Snow bowled the first ball to Hanif Mohammad. On the second day of the match, Basil D'Oliveira stroked his way to an unbeaten 102.

The special meeting of the MCC proposed by the rebellious group (mentioned in the previous chapter) was actually held on 5 December 1968. David Sheppard had assumed leadership.

Three motions were proposed at the meeting.

First was that the members of the MCC would publicly regret their committee's handling of the matter leading up to the selection of the team for the 1968–69 South Africa tour.

Second, no further tours to and from South Africa were to be undertaken until evidence was obtained of actual progress by South Africa towards non-racial cricket.

Third, a special committee needed to be set up to examine such proposals as were submitted by the SACA towards non-racial cricket.

The 26-year-old Mike Brearley took the incredibly bold step of seconding these proposals.

Sheppard and his rebel group were invited to a supposedly informal meeting at Church House in Westminster to discuss the points. When they arrived, they were confronted with the full MCC-committee, including ex-Prime Minister Sir Alec Douglas-Home, all thirsting for battle. Sir Alec had flown down from Scotland to attend the meeting.

In the meeting, there was deliberate deceit. There can be no other way to describe the conduct of MCC. Sir Alec reiterated that 'hypothetical questions' to the South African board had not made sense, sidestepping the fact that Lord Cobham had actually brought an answer that took away every bit of the hypothetical quotient of the questions. Secondly, Gubby Allen addressed Sheppard saying, "You may as well know that we did write, and we never got a reply." There had been two replies. A letter brought by Cheetham, and an answer passed on by Lord Cobham. After much acrimony, the motion was put to vote. The rebels lost by 382 votes to 341. When the postal votes were counted, the margin was in the order of 4,000 to 1,500. According to Peter Hain, "[t]hese [votes] were from typical cricket backwoodsmen opposed to any moves aimed at ending compromises with racialism in sport."

[The results of the voting:
Proposal 1: For 1,570 Against 4,357
Proposal 2: For 1,214 Against 4,644
Proposal 3: For 1,352 Against 4,508]

In October 1968, Peter Hain attended the big anti-Vietnam War demonstration in Grosvenor Square, witnessing violent clashes between the police and protesters determined to storm the US Embassy. As the march proceeded from Victoria Embankment to Mayfair, the city was eerily boarded up. "London Paris and Berlin, we shall fight and we shall win!" he joined in with the voices. Or the questions asked to US President Lyndon Johnson—"Hey hey LBJ, how many kids you killed today?"

In Putney, there was no youth branch of the Liberals—Peter had to form one himself. There were two other youthful members, Miranda and Mike. The office posts were divided among themselves. Peter was the chairman.

It was also the time he read up left-wing books and pamphlets. Those were the years of student protests—anti-Vietnam, anti-Soviet, Paris uprisings, Chicago, Mexico. There was a new iconoclastic left, with the slogan 'Neither Washington nor Moscow.' Peter was caught up in the libertarian socialism wave. Passionate debates, conferences, demonstrations, sit-ins.

That same year, the Young Liberals formed a 'South African Commission' (SAC). As the only ex-South African among those involved, Peter found himself becoming more and more prominent, in touch with leaders of the wider Anti-Apartheid Movement. In October he was elected to the National Executive Committee of SAC. As part of his activities, he visited the London office of the African National Congress. Among those who participated in the discussions was Thabo Mbeki, a student at the University of Sussex, who would become the President of South Africa in 1999.

It was also in 1968 that Peter was introduced to the men in exile running the SAN-ROC. He had a special attachment to this organisation even before he had joined. John Harris, the family friend and Peter's hero who had been hanged in the station bomb case in 1965, had been involved in the movement.

Peter carried from 10 Downing Street after a Young Liberal Protest 1969

The cancellation of the 1968–69 tour seemed to have been just a minor hiccup in the long saga of England-South Africa cricketing relationships. On 22 January 1969, MCC unabashedly announced that the South African team would visit in the summer of 1970.

After a long debate, the Council unanimously approved the tour. The *Cricketer* reported: "By [approving the tour] it said in effect to the South African Cricket Association: *'Although we were obliged to call off our tour to you last autumn because your government would not admit the team we chose—and, incidentally, despite a good deal of gratuitous abuse directed at MCC by your Prime Minister—we as a cricket body hope you will fulfil the visit to England in 1970.'*"

Even *Cricketer* acknowledged: *"By publishing their approval without any accompanying statement they disappointed the liberal opinion, which sees the governing body ... as prepared to maintain the old link with South African cricket irrespective of the situation of the Non-European cricket community there."*

Later Hain would write, tongue in cheek, "Perhaps the MCC ought to be commended. Perhaps they were playing a much cleverer game against racialism in cricket than we have given them credit for."

That very same issue of *Cricketer 1970 Spring Annual* contained an article by Louis Duffus which 'clarified some misconceptions' about non-White cricket in South Africa. "*The indigenous African does not readily take to cricket [...] Only a small percentage of non-Whites in South Africa are interested in cricket. To some extent their opportunities to play the game are limited but there is nothing in this country to compare with the national enthusiasm for cricket which is evident from childhood in the West Indies.*"

It may be that if Duffus had really tried to clear the actual misconceptions about non-White cricket, he could have embarked on a trip to Robben Island. But the White South African media did its bit in extending the Saramago-esque white blindness.

Whether fortified by the tea or not we will not really know, but in the first Test at Lahore Colin Cowdrey struck a pleasing hundred. But it is what took place two days before the Test match that remains hilarious.

Aftab Gul, the man who would go on to represent Salman Butt as his lawyer in the spot-fixing scandal of 2010, was at that time a promising cricketer for Lahore and Punjab University. More importantly he was an important student organiser, and the right-hand man of Bhutto.

With student protests for democracy a very tangible threat, Ayub Khan personally ordered the Tests to be cut short from five days to four. Two days before the Test, D'Oliveira asked Gul whether the Pakistan team had been selected. Gul replied, "No, but I know I'm playing. If I don't play, there's no Test match."

The Test took place without protests mainly because Gul played and opened the innings.

March 1969. As a brainchild of Vorster, the South African Games were held at Bloemfontein—as a consolation to the White South African sportsmen against the expulsion from the 1968 Olympics. Invitations were sent out to White athletes only from mostly-White countries. Even then, three of the countries ordered their athletes not to participate because of overwhelming anti-apartheid pressure. A team from West Germany withdrew after African countries threatened to boycott the 1972 Munich Olympics. New Zealand declared that the Kiwi athletes were there as individuals and not representing the nation. The U.S. Amateur Athletic Union denied permission to compete to four invitees, as did the U.S. State Department to two employees stationed in South Africa.

Competitors complained of shabby, dirty, and overcrowded accommodations. Even the Johannesburg *Sunday Express* reported that the Games had failed to become a spectacle comparable to the Olympics.

South African National Olympic Committee held the racially-segregated games under the Olympic insignia. The Olympics rings were used without the approval of the IOC. Along with multiple counts of sporting segregation, this particular violation of the Olympic Charter led IOC to expel South African National Olympic Committee in 1970.

In 1970, a separate Black Games was held in SOWETO.

GUS, WEDNESDAY, MARCH 26, 1969

MARGARET AUTON (right) the British swimmer who set a South African all-comers record in the 110yd. butterfly at Newlands bath last night, is pictured talking after the race with (from left) Springboks Nancy Harris and Katinka Germishuis and team-mate Alex Jackson.

A Cape Argus press cutting about the South African Games

The second Test at Dacca was held while the East Pakistan city was sieged by rioters and the police and military had pulled out of the city. The English players wanted to leave but were informed that their coach would not make it to the airport if they did.

The cocktail party with the British Deputy High Commissioner Ray Fox on the eve of the Test match had to be cut short. Another group of representatives from the British and European community had rushed in to meet Fox. The agenda was to discuss plans for evacuation.

Perhaps the circumstances and the terribly underprepared wicket of hardened mud made D'Oliveira reminiscence of the days back in Cape Town. It was almost the cobblestone streets of Green Point once again. With the ball stopping, squirting, turning sideways, he stood alone among the ruins, compiling an unbeaten 114, taking England from 130 for 7 to 274. He acknowledged it as the greatest innings of his life.

Sport governed the life of White South Africa. Peter knew this better than most. He was a sports fan himself, by his own admission a mediocre left-handed batsman. He had grown up watching the fanaticism that surrounded rugby among the Afrikaners. Sport was a gateway to international acceptance and legitimacy.

The other big influence in Peter's life was the concept of direct action. That had been more to do with his post-South African period, the last few years in London, witnessing all the political protests that took place around him in those heydays of the 1960s.

And then there was the contact with SAN-ROC members. The idea of anti-apartheid activism in the field of sport was taking form in his young mind. He was not the first one to try it, but he brought into it something unique.

In the third Test match at Karachi, Aftab Gul is back in the side as the series is back in West Pakistan. The match is extended to five days because the series is still undecided. England bat for over two days and are 502 for 7 on the third morning. Milburn and Graveney hit hundreds, Knott is unbeaten on 96. But even Gul's presence cannot prevent the crowd from invading the ground.

Cowdrey's men have had enough. The Test is abandoned, and they take the flight home that night.

However, the England they returned to would soon witness several protest-linked ground invasions throughout the next calendar year.

46 STST IS FORMED

HART—Halt All Racial Tours—was an organisation started by Trevor Richards, Tom Newnham, and others in New Zealand to protest against tours to and from South Africa. One of the leaders of the organisation was Dave Wickham, who lived for sports.

Activism to stop sporting tours rarely went down well with sports fans. During one of his talks, Wickham was heckled by someone in the back row alleging the organisation to be anti-sport. Wickham turned on the accuser.

"Who said that?"

The offender identified himself.

"Okay, so we're anti-sport are we? Let's take the 1960s All Blacks. You name the backs and I'll name the forwards—or would you like to do it the other way around?"

He got a walkover. Apparently, the accuser was not really a good sport.

Peter Hain, by now a first year Engineering student at London's Imperial College, was also a sports fan, as he would remain all his life. Even as a Cabinet Minister, it was to the sports pages he turned first when he got the papers.

We remember him as a young boy in South Africa, making cricket world elevens including Garry Sobers, Wes Hall, and Graeme Pollock.

Yet, it was his idea to disrupt sporting events in an effort to stop the proposed South African cricket tour of 1970.

Is this a contradiction?

The oft-voiced question was "Why bring politics into sport?" Keeping sports and politics separate was often the argument offered by the defenders of sporting ties with South Africans.

Having come this far in the book, I don't think we need to respond to apologists any further.

However, a couple of points perhaps need to be made, because we will come up against such arguments again and again during the course of the narrative.

As we can see from the tour of Pakistan amidst riots, sports and politics are seldom separate. Sports, especially the ones tailor-made for bilateral relationship like cricket, will always be used as tools for political propaganda and alliances. It is quite naïve to expect the two to be carried out in separate worlds.

That is precisely why Sir Alec Douglas-Home headed MCC, William Milton captained South Africa and Ayub Khan became President of the Pakistan cricket board.

Besides, the issue with South Africa was not political, it was human and moral.

If we give the politics tag to the apartheid policies, it perhaps makes sense to look at what Peter Hain himself wrote:

"Politics are part and parcel of South African sport, as they are in no other country in the world. Politics decide, on a racial basis, what sport any South African may play, where he may play it and with whom he may play it. Politics regulate non-Whites to inferior facilities and opportunities. Politics bar non-White South Africans from representing South Africa—although White immigrants and White Rhodesians may do so."

Hence, argued Peter, if British sport bodies invited racially chosen sides to play, as MCC had done, they were obviously responsible for introducing politics in British sport.

Many English cricketers, who enjoyed some of the best times of their lives in South Africa, often argued that they were against racial bias, but hampering sporting relationship with another country was not going to change anything. And why pick on South African cricketers?

They were not the ones responsible for the situation in South Africa.

The argument against that is that if sportsmen from other countries insisted on engaging with racially picked sides on the sporting fields, they were condoning and also encouraging the discrimination. "Inhumanity is every man's concern," as Hain said.

As far as the White South African cricketers were concerned, they could indeed be pitied; they were extremely talented men caught in the wrong place at the wrong time. But so had been the Frank Roros, Taliep Salies, Ben Malambas, Cec Abrahams, the Abed brothers, and hundreds of Black cricketers for too many years. While we can of course wonder what sort of records a Barry Richards or a Graeme Pollock could have set had they continued to play Test matches, we have to think of the multitude of Coloured cricketers, the Basil D'Oliveiras who were not aided by the same sort of fortunes. What sort of Test records would they have had?

According to Peter at that time, "White South African sportsmen have enjoyed the best of both worlds far too long: internationally, the acceptance which non-racial societies accord to all; at home, the privileged status which is the denial of that same acceptance to non-Whites ensures for them."

Besides, sports boycott, as the likes of Trevor Huddleston and David Sheppard had divined long earlier, would hit White Apartheid South Africa where it hurt the most.

When MCC nonchalantly announced that the South African tour of 1970 would go ahead as usual, Peter Hain was getting ready.

Sports had been targeted by anti-apartheid demonstrators, but mostly with banners and placards around the stadium. What Peter had in mind was something bigger.

In May 1969, during a public meeting of SAN-ROC in London, the young man raised the question of direct action to stop the tour. Dennis Brutus thought it was a good idea. Former champion South African weightlifter, Chris de Broglio, was a major anti-apartheid activist and SAN-ROC co-founder. He also felt the idea was a sound one.

Hain drafted a motion for the Young Liberals that pledged to take 'direct action to prevent scheduled matches from taking place unless the 1970 tour is cancelled'. It was approved by the South African Commission. The pledge stated: "The moral opposition to the scheduled tour cannot be underestimated. Should this tour take place, Young Liberals will take every measure to ensure that the matches are not allowed to go unhindered."

The motion got a small mention in *The Times*. It was also sent to the MCC Secretary Billy Griffith during the 12 June Cricket Council meeting at Lord's.

In March 1969 South African government rejected the visa application of reigning US Open champion Arthur Ashe. That was in spite of South African Lawn Tennis approving his request to play in the South African Open tournament.

Jim Swanton had meanwhile kept writing about the advisability of South Africa sending mixed-race teams. Even if for unofficial tours to England. However now, as one of the characters we have briefly come across earlier became prominent again, it was yet again a White side that came over.

In the summer of 1968, Wilf Isaacs had entered the England dressing room at Lord's and charmed D'Oliveira with promises to entertain him during the proposed 1968–69 tour of England. Subsequently, he had told the press that D'Oliveira would not be selected. A known benefactor of South African cricket, he now assembled a team of South African cricketers on a tour of matches in England during the summer of 1969.

This was not the first time he was bringing a side over. In 1966, another Wilf Isaacs team had toured England; among the members had been the old hands Roy McLean and Ken

Funston, as well as the young guns Lee Irvine and Barry Richards.

The side that Isaacs brought over in 1969 was led by former South African wicketkeeper batsman John Waite. It included off spinner Ian Tayfield, the cousin of the great Hugh Tayfield, and the towering young swing bowler Vincent van der Bijl. And of course, there was Graeme Pollock.

The international cricket of the summer was lukewarm. It is true that Garry Sobers brought his West Indians over once again, but by now it was a poor shadow of the fantastic unit that it had been half a decade earlier. The bowling department was plain weak.

With Colin Cowdrey snapping his Achilles tendon on the very day that he had been appointed captain for the summer, it was Ray Illingworth who led the side.

At Old Trafford Illingworth won the toss with a newly-minted 50p piece given to him by his friendly neighbourhood Midland Bank manager in Pudsey. They had a plan for Sobers, that included a half-volley about two feet wide, and a slip catcher standing wide. The bowler was required to pitch it in the right spot. In the first Test Sobers was caught Edrich off Brown for 10 and then caught Sharpe bowled Knight for 48. A 10-wicket win for England.

In July 1969, Arthur Ashe started splendidly in the Wimbledon semi-final against Rod Laver, taking the first set 6-2. However, the great Australian struck form, winning the next three sets 6-2, 9-7 and a whopping 6-0. The same day, when delegates from over 40 nations met in Wimbledon, a Polish-Hungarian proposal to expel South Africa from the Davis Cup was stopped from coming to a vote due to a procedural manoeuvre.

The tour opener of Wilf Isaacs' XI is against Essex at the Carrera's Ground, Basildon, on 5 July.

Eight Young Liberals gather at Waterloo Station, London, early in the morning. The group, mostly in their late teens and early 20s, make the journey with growing excitement. For some it is their first demonstration.

They are joined at the ground by two others from the Basildon district. The walk to the ground is jaunty. They make their way past the ticket-box to the field. However, the announcements of probable disruption have been taken seriously. The young men and women notice police constables, squad cars, motorbikes, even a mobile radio headquarter.

The visiting team is batting. After watching a bit, the youngsters make their move. Immediately plainclothes detectives pounce on them. Peter struggles with them as the others break free and run, unfurling banners. Making their brisk way into the ground, they sit down on the pitch.

The man who holds Peter down asks him for his name and address When Peter asks him to show his police-ID, he seems quite hurt, but the card he pulls out is authentic.

Meanwhile, the other demonstrators are on the pitch. The bowler is Keith Boyce, the West Indian quick. From behind the stumps, wicket-keeper and captain Brian Taylor, playing his 20th year for Essex, asks him to bowl directly at the protesters. Boyce refuses.

It may be just the irritation at having games interrupted by teenaged activists, the archetypal troublemakers. There may not be any significance other than the fact that Taylor enjoys the game and lives for it. He also plays football.

However, urging Keith Boyce, a Black man, to charge in and hurl down his fast stuff at anti-apartheid demonstrators is somewhat stupid. Boyce is embarrassed and refuses. Taylor comes around the wicket and kicks a demonstrator on the back.

The police are rather undecided for a while. And then they come in and drag the protesters off the field. They have to be carried. The match is held up for 10 minutes. The movement is afoot.

West Indies went into the final Test at Headingley having lost one and drawn the other. The pitch was green in early stages and got progressively easier. England 223, West Indies 161. Knight pitching the ball perfectly as a wide half volley and Sharpe holding a stinging catch off Sobers. The same ploy, the same result.

In the second innings, Sobers came at them with the new ball under overcast conditions. 5 for 42 from 40 overs by the superman. England 240 all out.

With 35 minutes to go for stumps on the fourth day, West Indies were on 219 for 3, requiring 84 to win, Butcher and Lloyd at the crease, Sobers still to bat. Later, Reg Hayter asked D'Oliveira if at that time he felt they had lost the match. "No. If they had got 30 or 40 more, I would have said it had gone. At this stage I felt Illy was still on top of his job and we were still dictating the course of the game."

Butcher reached forward to Underwood and the snick was held by Knott. And then Knight ran in to Sobers with the score reading 224 for 4, 79 runs to win. The wide half volley was perfectly pitched. Sobers, trying to beat the trap, got right across to make sure he did not get an outside edge. He went through with the drive, his illustrious head in the air. This time the ball came in off the inside edge on to his stumps. Sobers averaged just 30 in the three Tests and crossed 50 only once.

Illingworth, who replaced Underwood himself as soon as the left-armer had snared Butcher, sent back Lloyd. By the end of the day they were 240 for 7. The next morning, they lost by 30 runs. Ray Robinson remarked that it was one of the finest bits of captaincy he had ever seen.

Peter Hain was not the only young man making waves in the political world in 1969. In South Africa, 23-year-old Steve Biko gave up studying medicine in the University of Natal to devote himself to the cause of his fellow-countrymen. That year, he founded the Black Consciousness movement.

The Wilf Isaacs' XI is a testing ground for the following season. However, it is in the match against Oxford University that the side comes up against the most disruptive demonstration.

Three days before the start of the match, demonstrators dug up the pitch. However, groundsmen got it repaired in time.

On the first day, Pollock is dropped at slip before scoring. At 26, he is once again put down. Thereafter he feasts on the insipid bowling, hammering a majestic 231 not out. The second highest score is 22, and the total is 351. After that van der Bijl runs through the University men, capturing 6 for 35, skittling them out for 128.

On the second afternoon, following on, Oxford University are 33 for 4, when there is a shrill whistle. Over 70 protesters run into the ground, including members of the Oxford Anti-Apartheid, student protesters, trade unionists, and others. It is much more than a Young Liberal demonstration. Play is halted and abandoned for the day.

A similar demonstration follows when the side faces Surrey at The Oval.

Towards the end of the tour, policemen swarm around the venues.

In the final match of the tour, against MCC Schools, every spectator is asked to state his business by a policeman before being allowed entry into the Roehampton Bank of England ground. The mother of one of the schoolboys participating in the match, who is pushing a pram, is turned away from the ground because her answer is not convincing enough.

All this security does not really amount to much. A group of Young Liberals bluff their way into the ground and disrupt the match for several minutes.

Illingworth's side followed up the victory over West Indies with a similar 2-0 win against New Zealand when Graham Dowling's men toured in the second half of the summer.

Basil D'Oliveira, however, did not really set the grounds on fire, hitting only one half-century in his nine Test innings.

By the time Wilf Isaacs returned to South Africa in August, he was sick and tired of it all. In an interview to the *Eastern Province Herald,* he said, "Some of them are definitely paid. Their tactics were usually to insult the biggest player in the team in the hope that we would retaliate. Their behaviour was disgusting. I was spat on. They were crude and their language was filthy. Some of them were drug takers."

It was news to the demonstrators that they were being paid. By whom? While the other charges dwelling around the filthy language and spitting could not be proved or disproved, one wondered how Isaacs could make out that some of them took drugs.

Isaacs, as we have seen earlier, could be quite cavalier with the truth while talking to the press. And those were the days of the 1960s, when long-haired hippies were common, and so were protesters, as were sex and drugs and rock and roll. To members of a generation who prided themselves on the more conservative virtues, long hair was often the connecting link between the different groups and the boundaries blurred when their inexperienced and uninformed analysis tried to categorise the other side. Student protesters with long hairs were easily confused with hippies with long hair and thereby with marijuana-smoking-long-haired zombies. Anyway, the activists who disrupted play were quick enough to get through the security barricades, which does not tally with drug abuse.

On 11 July, SAN-ROC and the Young Liberals delivered a letter similar to the one they had sent to MCC. Only, this time it was handed to the Lawn Tennis Association. The language was quite the same, and the event targeted the Davis Cup Zonal final between Britain and South Africa held at Bristol from 17 to 19 July.

It is another journey fraught with excitement as Peter drives down to Bristol with two other members of the Putney Young Liberals—Helen Tovey and Maree Pocklington. They have a vague intention of interrupting the game by sitting on the court, without any concrete ideas. They are inexperienced, green, and apprehensive.

At Bristol they are joined by another Young Liberal, Mike Williams. The written warning has borne fruit and the police security is tight. But they manage to buy tickets and take their seats as ordinary spectators, pretending not to really know each other.

It is a closely contested match. Mark Cox was the Quarter Finalist in the Australian Open two years ago. The previous year, he reached the fourth round at Wimbledon. Bob Maud, the South African, on the other hand, is more recognised as a top-ranking doubles player. But they produce a close fight.

It is Maud who takes the first set 6-3, while Cox draws level winning the second by the same margin. In between sets, the demonstrators take up their places in different points in the stands.

And as the players change over, in a synchronised move, they jump into the court, unfurling their posters and displaying them to the crowd. Maree Pocklington even tries to give leaflets to the officials and the players, who are not really interested.

After a few confused minutes, a leading official comes up and asks the group to leave. Peter says that they are sorry, but they cannot leave. The police make their move now, and promptly all the demonstrators sit down on the court. They have to be carried off. As he leaves, hauled by two constables, a reporter keeps pace with Peter, asking questions. And Peter speaks to him over the arm of the constable who is clutching on to his armpits.

They are held for three hours at the Redlands Police Station, Bristol. While they wait nervously, they neatly scratch the date: 'Young Liberals 17/7/69.'

Cox wins the match 3-6, 6-3, 6-4, 3-6, 6-4.

The following day, South African doubles specialist Bob Hewitt beats Graham Stilwell in another marathon five setter 7-9, 6-3, 3-6, 6-2, 6-3 to restore parity.

While Cox and Peter Curtis battle out the doubles match against Hewitt and Frew McMillan, two more demonstrators run into the court and disrupt play. Outside, the Bristol Anti-Apartheid group, supported by other organisations, organise a march. As demonstrators pass by, a flour bomb is thrown over the walls of the tennis club, disrupting play for another 20 minutes.

The British players won the doubles after another five-set tussle. The hosts won the tie 3-2. But the memories of the exciting tie would be forever intertwined with the disruptions.

The Wilf Isaacs matches and the Davis Cup Tie provided extensive press coverage to the demonstrators—one of the obvious benefits of targeting sporting events.

The initial success paved the way for more focused manoeuvres. Peter was starting to contemplate a broad-based direct-action co-ordinating committee, beyond the ranks of Young Liberals. His idea was to draw in all who were prepared to take action against apartheid sport.

The crucial feature was that the events were taking place around the country, and action could be initiated locally. A network was soon developed.

On 29 July, Arthur Ashe put the South African government on the dock. With the South African Lawn Tennis Union hedging for time, claiming to support Ashe and remaining noncommittal about the government giving him a visa, the tennis star announced that he would reapply for a South African visa. "This time I won't be silent. I'll go right to the South African embassy in New York. If they want to turn me down, they'll have to do it right there, in front of [the press]."

On 22 August, a letter from Peter was published in the *Guardian.*

"At its coming council meeting, the MCC will have the opportunity of calling off next year's tour by a [W]hite South African cricket team to Britain.

"The consequences of another refusal by MCC to cancel the tour should not be underestimated. The token disruptions during the recent tour of Wilf Isaacs XI to Britain and the Davis Cup match at Bristol demonstrated the seriousness of threats to massively disrupt the 1970 tour: *Next summer could see a season consisting of an endless series of protests and disruptions.* The MCC ought to have the courage to call a halt to collaboration with racialism in sport. White South Africa should be made to realise that there will be no further compromise with apartheid either inside or outside sport. There is a need for a clear moral lead from British sportsmen on this issue and MCC has the chance to provide this."

[The bit in italics was in the original letter but edited out when published in the paper]

In September 1969, with encouragement of Dennis Brutus and Chris de Broglio, Peter teamed up with Hugh Geach, a Reading University Student, to launch the Stop The Seventy Tour Committee (STST). Geach became the secretary and Peter the spokesman.

A press conference was called on 10 September at the Fleet Street pub 'The White Swan'. The aim was to announce the formation of the committee. Representatives of all the groups that had pledged support for the Committee were invited. These included the Anti-Apartheid

Movement, CHURCH, International Socialists, the Movement for Colonial Freedom, the National Union of Students, the Reading Joint Anti-Apartheid Committee, SAN-ROC, United Nations Youth, United Nations Student Association, Young Communist League, and Young Liberal Movement.

The goal was simple—to stop the 1970 summer tour. The D'Oliveira incident was playing on the psyche of all the pro- and anti-sports apartheid groups. However, the upcoming Springbok rugby tour later that winter was also coming into focus.

Peter announced: "We will be organising mass demonstrations and disruptions throughout the tour [...] next summer's cricket season could collapse into chaos should the tour take place. We are fighting British collaboration and racialism in sport. And this is a fight we are confident of winning. We are today issuing a clear warning to the British sport authorities: that their complicity in apartheid sports will no longer be tolerated—all future tours, including the Rugby tour starting in November, will be severely disrupted."

The Young Liberals Chairman Louis Eaks added:

"I believe that many people are prepared to risk arrest and even imprisonment on this crucial issue of principle. We have asked the MCC on numerous occasions to take a reasoned stand against apartheid in sport. It is they who will be responsible if Lord's becomes the Ulster of the sporting world next summer."

The following day, the newspapers mistakenly reported Peter Hain as the chairman of STST rather than spokesman. And that is what he became, elected by the press.

There was mention of the group in the newspapers, but apart from *Guardian* and *Morning Star*, none of the others made any effort to analyse their motives and potential.

Peter Hain, the young activist in 1970

47 TRIPPING IN TWICKENHAM

4 October 1969. Johannesburg. Five Springbok selectors sat down in a hotel room to select the team for the 1969–70 rugby union tour to Britain and Ireland. The Currie Cup final between Northern Transvaal and the Western Province was just over.

Some of the members to be selected required no discussion. Avril Malan was assistant manager and coach. A former captain, he was also a member of the Broederbond and younger brother of Magnus Malan, later chief of the South African Defence Force and minister of defence.

And of course, the captain was Dawie de Villiers, another Broederbond member, who would go on to be a National MP and Cabinet minister.

At the same time, preparations were proceeding in a frenzy for the STST. All the colleges and universities had received letters and even telephone calls. Hugh Geach used the Reading University base to team up with the Reading Joint Anti-Apartheid committee. A 'Fireworks Day Committee' had been formed in Oxford to organise a demonstration at the first Springbok match scheduled on 5 November.

That the movement had already made some impact was revealed in a curious way. In early October, Peter Hain received a registered letter from the South African Minister of the Interior informing him that his right as a British citizen to enter South Africa without an 'alien temporary permit' or a visa had been revoked. Having neither intention nor means to visit his former home country, Peter took it as quite an achievement for a 19-year-old.

On 23 October, it was announced that weed-killer had been sprayed on Oxford University's Iffley Road Ground. At the same time, the words OXFORD REJECTS APARTHEID appeared in huge letters five feet tall on the pitch where the game was scheduled to be played.

The following day, the University Rugby Club officials called off the match. Apparently, they had been advised to do so by the Thames Valley Police. The reason cited was 'risk of violence and danger to genuine spectators and club facilities'. Of course, the decision was also influenced by the massive protests in the town and the university.

This early win served as an enormous fillip to the young protesters. As Peter put it, "Public interest was immediately focused on our plans."

From then on started an espionage thriller, with the Rugby Football Union trying to find a new venue for the Oxford match and at the same time trying to keep the information under wraps, and the demonstrators trying to deduce the venue by piecing together different bits of clues.

On 26 October, Bill Lawry's men completed their sojourn in Ceylon. They would now cross the Palk Strait and embark on one of the most challenging twin tours undertaken by an Australian side.

A year ago, a series of political ripples around the world had merged to convolute the cricket calendar. While the D'Oliveira affair had scratched the MCC tour of South Africa off tour schedule, the military government of Yahya Khan had implemented strict exchange controls for Pakistan. While MCC toured the volatile land that winter, the Pakistan leg of the

Australian tour to the subcontinent had to be amputated because the financial terms could not be agreed upon.

Famished of international cricket, the SACA had promptly offered to host Australia instead. Hence, the 1969–70 season for Lawry's men included five Tests in India and four in South Africa. It was about to turn into the most difficult season for most of the cricketers on the voyage.

The South African rugby contingent left by VC10 on 29 October and arrived at the Heathrow on the morning of Thursday, 30 October. The Reading group had volunteered to attend to the arrival. About 30 of them staged a protest. The slogans were innovative.

"No to 'Boks" were all over the place, while a particularly interesting one declared "Don't Scrum with a Racist Bum."

JBG Thomas, whose book *Springbok Invasion* is dedicated to "the British Police without whose help the tour would not have been possible," writes that there was a one-off scuffle between the demonstrators and the airport staff. Peter Hain says that the exchange of blows actually took place between an airport official and a small group of South Africans who had come to welcome the side.

But apart from this minor incident, it was the word of warning by Geach, voiced to the press after the demonstration, that made it memorable: "We are going to hound them everywhere they go."

Tommy Bedford had been overlooked for captaincy because the Broederbond suspected him of liberal opinions. The suspicions were justified, but the overlooking was not. He said later that on landing in Heathrow, "[i]nstead of proudly stepping out wearing our Springbok blazers, we were smuggled out in a coach to a golfing hotel."

The midday press conference was held at the Park Lane Hotel in London. The manager Corrie Bornman steered clear of all the potentially explosive political questions with the standard line of "We have come to play rugby and not engage in politics. We want to mix socially and create a favourable impression among the British people."

When asked whether the team would mix with Coloured people in Britain, he replied, "Certainly, provided they are rugby players."

Unknown to them, there was an STST representative in the room, but because of very limited number of questions allowed and only a few journalists being permitted to ask questions, he was unable to put forward queries that were considered vital by the protesting organisation.

However, the movement did make breakthroughs in spite of utmost security. As the following morning dawned, painted slogans were discovered on the stands and on the pitch of Twickenham.

The following day the Springboks trained at the Richmond Athletic Ground. It was near the Hain household, and on hearing the news of the upcoming practice session, a small group of local STST volunteers were assembled.

Hence, running in for their training, the Springboks were greeted by banners and slogans. JBG Thomas is quite eloquent about David John, the 61-year-old club secretary, former rugby forward, referee, and Metropolitan policeman, who broke up the demonstration by breaking some banners over his knee, executing a diving tackle and barking, "Clear off, this is private property." The practice session was not really interrupted. But the very presence of the demonstrators received massive press and television coverage.

That evening the Springboks arrived in their coach to the South Africa House at Trafalgar Square for a reception given to the team, rugby VIPs and members of the British Rugby Press by the South African Ambassador. About 40 demonstrators of the Anti-Apartheid Movement greeted them, jeering and picketing. The police made an avenue for the players to walk through into the reception. There was another demonstration, on a smaller scale, when the Springboks left the reception. By now all the protests were receiving wide coverage by the press and television.

All the while, speculation about the venue of the Oxford match continued. Twickenham seemed the logical option; however, during the reception at the South Africa House a rumour was started that the match had been transferred to the United Service Ground, Portsmouth. Nothing was confirmed, but *Daily Telegraph* was confident enough to announce it the next morning. The RFU Secretary, Robin Prescott told the *Guardian* that if the match was played, it would definitely not be at Twickenham.

The Springboks, meanwhile, watched Harlequins play Bristol at Twickenham and moved into the Dormy Hotel in Ferndale, on the outskirts of Bournemouth. There they stayed, with five plainclothes policemen and dogs stationed along the perimeter of the tree-studded property. It gave credence to the Portsmouth venue rumour.

A contingent of demonstrators arrived from the local technical college. Three of them were allowed to walk along with the police and hand over their petition to manager Bornman. The manager was not there, engaged in clandestine meetings in London with the rugby boards of both the countries about the venues and security. While the delegation of students went up to the English liaison officer, who received the petition on behalf of the Springboks, the detectives dashed about trying to get hold of a camera to photograph the three 'troublemakers' for future reference. By the time they got hold of a camera, they realised it was too dark.

"For God's sake, somebody, get a flash-bulb!"

By that time, the demonstrators were busy walking back to the bus to join their friends. But the placards and banners remained unfurled as a group of policemen and a rather unfriendly looking Alsatian kept them from parading.

On 4 November, the morning before the match, the *Guardian* carried an exclusive report that the Ministry of Defence had banned all Service rugby grounds for the match. The decision had been taken by the Minister of Defence for Administration, Roy Hattersly, and endorsed by the Prime Minister. So, Portsmouth was out. Rumours were buzzing around. Someone even suggested that the match was going to be played on the Channel Island of Jersey, a ploy that would definitely have allowed it to proceed free of demonstrations.

The night before the match, while the reporters and the demonstrators waited for the tip off about the venue, Bornman addressed the press. "The demonstrators are just a bunch of kids," he proclaimed. "There have been a few demonstrations so far—so called shows of strength. If these are a show of strength, they have no strength at all."

It was 9.30 PM on 4 November when the phone rang. Peter heard a familiar voice informing him, "Twickenham, 3 PM, good luck."

The organising activities went on deep into the night.

"Tomorrow marks the beginning of our fight against the racialist Springboks," Peter was quoted in the papers.

"What a way to start a tour," remarked some of the seasoned rugby journalists as they made their way to the shuffled venue early in the morning.

The Springboks left in their coach, shepherded by police escorts. As they got to the outskirts of Camberley, on the Surrey border, they left the highway and drove into a heavily wooded copse. As they sat eating their very well prepared picnic lunch packed by the Dormy Hotel—cold chicken, ham, hard boiled eggs, rolls and cheese, coca cola, milk, and fruit—there also took place the official handover of police responsibility from the Hampshire-and-Dorset detectives to the Surrey Constabulary.

As they resumed their journey, one police car drove in front of the coach, one behind, and one by the side. Hundreds of policemen were lined up outside the ground when the team arrived. No bars, no tearooms, no sweet stalls, no tobacco kiosks—none of the amenities Twickenham was famous for. A journalist who had run out of cigarettes was told that there was a place half a mile along the road, before being cautioned that if he went out there was no guarantee that he would get back in.

There was yet another development. On the morning of the match, the frizzy-haired, fuzzy-bearded London Welsh loose forward John Taylor announced that he had decided not to play against the Springboks for reasons of conscience and politics. It led to another *Guardian* exclusive written by Christopher Ford, a reporter who had already refused to cover any Springbok match.

The stand was brave indeed, coming from a 24-year-old. And for the demonstrators it added enormous credibility to all the protests they were carrying out. However, in the eyes of traditional rugby reporters, it did not make sense.

JBG Thomas wrote scathingly about how Taylor "had decided not to play against the men whose hospitality he had experienced 15 months previously." Wallace Reyburn was a bit more balanced, calling it, perhaps satirically, "a great gesture" adding that he "respected his struggle with his conscience." At the same time, he could not help wondering what 'Basil Brush' achieved. "All he achieved was doing himself out of a much-coveted cap against one of the great rugby touring countries. Sure, he got his name in the papers and TV interviews and all. Then, Press and TV, with their usual callous search for fresh news, went on to other things, which can place a man in that sad position of thinking he is being ignored, when he is merely forgotten."

Twickenham resembles a concentration camp. Accommodation for spectators has been restricted to the West Stand, and the standing enclosure in front of it. The rest of the ground is sealed off with stout wire netting, patrolled by police. The rest of the stands are empty, apart from the press box in the middle of the East Stand with all the phones and typing equipment. To get to the press box, the journalists have to pass through cordons of policemen and a wire netting barricade. The 10,000 spectators, who have managed to change their plans and turn up at the new venue, do not get the usual printed programmes. There is instead a mimeographed list of the two teams produced on pale puce duplicating paper. Just beyond the playing area, outside the touchline, there is a row of policemen standing shoulder-to-shoulder.

Peter Wilson writes: "Sport comes to a pretty pass when a tour opens like this." *Morning Star* will later reflect: "It was proved that it is possible for White-to-White rugby contact to be maintained if the stadium is turned into a police State."

Just before they trot out to the field, the Springboks are told: "Make sure you have your overcoats handy, to cover up your Springbok gear if things get out of hand and you need to make a quick getaway."

Seldom has a more troubled team run into an arena.

A thousand or so demonstrators pour in among the spectators. The chants start soon enough, almost immediately after Piet Visagie, mine paymaster from Kimberley, kicks off. "Sieg Heil!" "Fascist pigs!" cries are interspersed with "Go home Springboks go home" sung to the tune of *We're here because we're here.* There are slow claps, and the blowing of referee's whistles all over the West Stand.

An over eager Oxford forward is caught off-side. And Visagie kicks a penalty on the 25, ten yards from touch. Springboks lead 3-0. But three minutes later, a Springbok is caught doing the same over-eager run. Mike Heal, the Oxford full-back, will play 22 first-class matches in his cricket career, score an unbeaten 124 against Warwickshire in 1972, and play for the Gloucestershire Second XI. Here he scores from a kick from a similar position. 3-3.

With half-time approaching a couple of Springboks enter a ruck from the wrong side. Heal scores his second penalty. Oxford 6 Springboks 3.

Peter Hain falls into the arms of the waiting policemen as he climbs over the five-foot concrete and metal fence into the perimeter. However, two demonstrators manage to get into the playing area.

Peter made a rather nasty habit of getting 'carried away': Here by policemen during the Twickenham game

One youth tries to climb a goal post before being escorted off. The other is even stranger. As the teams line up for the second half, an elderly gentleman in a rugby pullover emerges from the dressing rooms and sets off for the centre of the field even as Oxford captain Chris Laidlaw and referee Mike Titcomb confer. All around the ground, even by the press and the players, the man is assumed to be a reserve touch judge or a slightly elderly ball boy or trainer. However, things become a bit confusing when he proceeds to kick the ball away from the half line and take off his pullover with a flourish to reveal a white jersey with AA (Anti-Apartheid) in red. He is escorted out of the field.

The demonstrations do not manage to stop the match for more than a few minutes, but the curfew environment and the constant presence of the demonstrators take their toll.

Just on the call of full time, Visagie makes a gallant effort to score, but his long-range drop at the goal goes wide. The Springboks lose 3-6. Even the presence of the redoubtable Wilf Wooller in the stands, professing absolute support for the game and disgust for the protesters, does not really help matters. One of the big rugby upsets of the decade.

Even then some of the press reports claim that the protests have been a damp squib. The *Daily Mail* headline runs "Twickenham Victory for Oxford and the Police."

Writing about David Griffiths, an Australian, replacing Peter Dixon during the second half, JBG Thomas noted, *"[Griffiths is from] a country [...] that allows no Coloured immigrants, but whose players in all sports are never demonstrated against."*

In fact, even Reyburn dwelt on the Australian question before the tour: "*In Australia, the aboriginees (sic) are not permitted to vote, they are forced to live on reserves and are in all ways second-class citizens. In addition the Government forbids entry of Blacks except for those 'with special skills needed in Australia.' Why don't demonstrators hound visiting Australian cricket teams?*"

He turned to New Zealand as well: "*In New Zealand, proud of the fact that Maoris have full voting franchise, racial discrimination is exercised against immigrants. If you hold a British passport and are White you may enter freely. If you hold a British passport and are Black you must apply for an individual entry permit and such applications can be and have been refused. Other would be immigrants who are Coloured have been barred because their entry would 'disrupt the cultural pattern of the country'.*"

While perhaps arguing for the wrong cause, both these writers underlined the racial problems prevalent in the world in the late 1960s. In fact, the horrid 1965 South African experience of the Wallaby star Jim Boyce had actually made him aware of the casual racism in behaviour and even use of idioms that he himself indulged in as an Australian.

Yes, there was racism in places other than South Africa, but that would not change by letting the world go on as usual, indulging in White blindness.

The effectiveness of the STST during the Oxford match was reflected in the scoreline—the first time an actual English club side had beaten the Springboks.

It was hardly a damp squib.

But it was just the start.

48 SWANSEA AND ALL THAT

In his zeal to revive the temporarily extinguished fire of Springbok enthusiasm, coach Avril Malan dislocated a finger during training and had to receive hospital treatment. The party moved to Leicester, where they stayed at the Abbey Moor Hotel, seven storeys up on the roof of a multi-storey car-park.

As they moved rather freely around Leicester, the consensus was that the demonstrators had run out of steam. They enjoyed pleasant and rather expensive lunches at the hotel.

Nevertheless, all police leave in the city was cancelled for the Leicester game against Midlands East, a trend that was to follow all through the tour. The STST organisation was still not robust enough in terms of network and coordination. Nonetheless, 3,000 protesters had managed to march to the ground. Tickets were heavily restricted but about 100 of the demonstrators managed to get into the ground. Peter himself got four tickets by showing his Rugby Club card.

Some 30 mounted officers charged from one street to the next to halt the marching demonstrations. Slogans were displayed and shouted, and leaflets were distributed. Swearing matches were aplenty between the protesters and the fans.

There are 1,017 policemen employed on special rugby duty. But with the score on 3-3, the first demonstrators run in, foxing the cordon around the ground formed by police and stewards. The stoppage is brief as they are escorted off. After that the intrusions are sporadic and always brief. But the Springboks are visibly annoyed.

The interruptions continue, in fits and starts. But the Springboks manage to win 11-9. They leave to a standing ovation, not for their performance, but from the fans who feel for the visitors who are putting up with the 'demo bores'.

Nine people are arrested, and 12, including three policemen, are taken to the hospital for medical treatment.

The match is interrupted only briefly, but the movement is on. The atmosphere is almost one of siege. The Afrikaans pro-Government newspaper *Die Beeld* reports: "*We have become accustomed to Britain becoming a haven for all sorts of undesirables from other countries. Nevertheless, it is degrading to see how a nation can allow itself to be distracted by this bunch of left-wing, workshy, refugee, long hairs who in a society of any other country would be rejects.*"

Long hair—once again the perennial peeve of the conservatives.

In the meantime, the tour moved on to Wales. The next match was at Newport.

Arriving quietly in Cardiff, the Springboks spent the evening in the hotel's television room. It was still a device not allowed in the southern land. And on at that moment was a heated debate on the Malcolm Muggeridge show, dealing with apartheid and its side effects on sport. Two ex-internationals, Rev. Robin Roe and Wilf Wooller, fought spiritedly for the Springboks.

By now the training venues were not being publicised for fear of demonstrations. Instead of the expected University College Ground, the Springboks trained at the Glamorgan Wanderers Ground.

In cooperation with the police, the Newport Club made elaborate arrangements. Cops from several parts of Monmouthshire were drafted in.

The night before the match, there was a 200-strong torchlight procession through the town.

On the day of the Newport match, 700 demonstrators protest outside the ground, making the heavy precaution of the police somewhat superfluous.

Once again, the police and stewards cordon off the ground. However, one lone demonstrator manages to run onto the pitch during the game. He is marched out of the ground, and ironically turns out to be a South African White, a former member of the South African Liberal Party. He is detained for several hours by the police. According to Peter Hain, "[h]is faith in the British police was shaken when some pills mysteriously appeared in his clothes while he was being searched in detention, and the Newport police attempted to charge him with illegally possessing drugs."

Newport turns out to be a sort of a brief lull, with the on-field demonstrations limited to a single incident. But the Springboks are quite shaken by now. In the 19th minute, Newport captain Raybould makes the opening, making a half break with Dave Cornwall up beside him. Cornwall takes the clever slip pass and lobs a long one out to Ian Taylor, a fellow centre. With Grobler coming in to cover Taylor, he is not at hand to stop left winger Alan Skirving from going over. Newport thus go 3-0 up and by the first few minutes of the second-half have extended it to an eight-point lead. The final score is Newport 11, Springboks 6. South Africa's second defeat in three matches.

John Anthony, the Newport captain, is chaired on the shoulders of his teammates after the final whistle. "The happiest moment of my life," he says.

The tour moved to Swansea.

The team was put up in the Dragon Hotel, in the centre of Swansea. All through the day, the demo pickets were present, along with placard waving students, sometimes in thinning groups of dozen, sometimes in larger turnouts of fiftyish. The chants were constant "Go home fascist pigs! Sieg Heil!"

Uniformed police stood guard outside the main entrance.

Peter and the STST demonstrators were not the only young people involved in the massive protests against apartheid South Africa.

On 14 November 1969, an extremely innovative subversive technique was used across South Africa by the London Recruits. In Cape Town, Port Elizabeth, Johannesburg, East London and Durban, bucket-type leaflet bombs were set off. A simple device, equipped with toy snakes or spiders to keep curious people away, the bombs were uncomplicated and designed not to hurt anyone. However, once exploded, they flung hundreds of ANC leaflets into the air.

Prototypes had been tested in Bristol, in the Somerset countryside, on Hampstead Heath, and in Richmond Park. They were extremely successful.

15 November. At Wanderers, Transvaal plays Eastern Province in the Currie Cup. Replying to 351, the visitors lose two early wickets. Graeme Pollock walks in at 4 for 2. He cuts Aldworth straight into the hands of gully and is put down. Thereafter he launches a blitzkrieg. After two hours, he is third out with the total on 151. His score 123, with 20 fours, 1 five and 1 six.

15 November is also the day of the Swansea match. The Springboks leave early, but the coach parked on the side of the hotel is a decoy. Local rugby men have 10 cars parked in the

hotel's parking lot, and they slip out in them.

Over 2,000 demonstrators arrive in coaches, assembling in front of the Guild Hall, before walking to St Helen's. Everything seems well organised and peaceful.

According to Peter Hain, "At matches prior to Swansea the police had tried to maintain some degree of impartiality. At Swansea, all pretence was forgotten. The police were in open collusion with rugby supporters and self-styled vigilantes, who openly attacked the demonstrators. The South Wales Constabulary seemed determined to use apartheid methods to protect an apartheid team."

As the march nears the ground, the police and the demonstrators clash for the first time, starting a near riot. It kick-starts a series of events that will go down as the worst incident of mob violence in Britain since the 1930s.

It is the same ground that has seen Garry Sobers slam Malcolm Nash for 6 sixes in an over just about a year ago. The police have blocked off the traffic on the adjoining Mumbles Road, to allow the parade of protesters.

The chanting protesters march up the road, shouting 'Shame Shame Shame' at the ticket-holders. And they march back along the road again.

It is in front of the players' entrance that the police and the demonstrators clash. It is a chaotic scene. Opinions about who is at fault will vary. But soon, hundreds are wedged between the shoulder-to-shoulder police barricade and the six-foot retaining wall along the high ground.

And now Reyburn produces almost as an ode to police heroism. "*Three policemen grabbed a struggling demonstrator and yanking at him to get him free from where he was stuck in among the crowd they eventually got firm hold of him by the arms and legs and as he swung away his body went head first against a concrete stanchion of the grandstand. He hit the ground like a dropping from a high cow. The policemen turned to a batch of rugger fans and said: "There you are, boys, he's all yours." And the fans were quick to show their obvious pleasure at coming to watch rugby and having a demonstrator to boot.*"

Reyburn actually sees this happen. He also writes about what he does not see, but hears of: *"I cannot confirm, through not having actually witnessed it, that later the police were pulling demonstrators out of the melee and saying to rugby supporters: 'Who wants this one.'"*

In retrospect, it does not make very proud reading for the British Police to whom JBG Thomas dedicated his book.

The atmosphere inside the ground is inflammable. The rugby fans are already seething at all the fights, and some are hankering for more. The anti-apartheid slogans of the demonstrators inside do not really placate things.

The Springboks, however, put on a good show on the field. When van Rensburg is carried off with a neck injury, the massive Mof Myburgh comes into the ground. Someone calls out: "We asked for one replacement not two." They lead 12-0 at half-time.

And then it gets ugly. Uglier than ever.

A few minutes after the start of the second half, a clutch of demonstrators break through the police cordon in a well-planned execution. They have taken advantage of a diversion caused by some incident in one of the terraces. After Swansea, the police will have learnt their lesson. Terrace trouble will henceforth be dealt with by mobile task forces while the cordon will stand their ground.

However, here there are some 50 demonstrators running in, with two young girls in the lead. This is cue for an onslaught from the other end of the ground, running full tilt across the cricket pitch, coming at the police with such momentum that they cannot help but break through. The match is stopped, as the whole field is full of people running around, screaming, fighting, chasing. From the grandstand, bloodthirsty, vicious advice is doled out to the policemen and the stewards.

Play is held up for five minutes while the police and the 'stewards' turn brutal. The protesters are assaulted even as they sit on the ground, and even the girls not spared. After being dragged by the hair, kicked and punched off the field by the police and the helpful stewards, some of them are thrown into the rowdy sections of the crowd to be beaten up. Even some of the rugby fans end up booing the violence.

Mobile television crews get hold of some of the most gruesome shots of the tour. One of them show a demonstrator who got on the field being bundled back over the fence of the metal railing on to the terrace, momentarily impaled on the small of his back.

Some of the Welsh rugby fans are skinheads with heavy boots, and they bring them to use against the 'long hairs'.

The official line of the police is: "We were met with force and had to retaliate." Chief Constable Melbourne Thomas of the South Wales Constabulary says: "Five constables were taken to hospital. One sergeant was severely injured in the chest and abdomen from blows with a sharp instrument."

Littered among the debris are broken posters, poles, piles of torn placards and banners, and burnt out smoke bombs—the ugliest scenes in a rugby match.

The score does not change after the first half. Springboks win 12-0.

Dawie de Villiers in action

Sections of the STST were thoroughly demoralised after the Swansea fracas, especially the Reading group. One of the members had a broken jaw and was in danger of losing an eye. A girl had been admitted to the hospital in a state of shock. Geach had been dragged off the ground by his genitals and repeatedly beaten in the crowd where the police had thrown him back.

A letter was immediately despatched to the Home Secretary, calling for an immediate enquiry. Peter contacted the MP of his constituency, Hugh Jenkins, and another Labour MP from Reading, John Lee. They added their voice to the public call for an investigation. About 200 statements were collected from demonstrators and they were quite gruesome to say the least.

On the day after the match, Peter released an STST statement: "We are demanding a full public enquiry into the Swansea demonstration and particularly into the role played by the rugby vigilantes. This private army of rugby thugs was responsible for some of the most systematic and brutal mob violence ever seen on peaceful demonstrations in Britain. The introduction of the vigilantes into the protest area must now call into question the whole future of the tour. Unless something is done now, someone may get killed."

The next match against Gwent was in three days at Ebbw Vale. Peter ended with the words: "Ebbw Vale could make Swansea look like a tea-party."

In reality, the Ebbw Vale match proceeds peacefully. The demonstrators, led by the Gwent Socialist Charter, march into the ground and hand leaflets over to spectators.

In relatively quieter circumstances, the Springboks lead 8-6 at halftime. However, in the end, they surrender 8-14 to the local side, mainly due to the ineptitude of their backs. Their third loss in five matches.

The letter to the Home Secretary did not bring about the public enquiry. However, the Home Secretary, James Callaghan, did summon all the chief of constables from the remaining venues of the tour for a conference. The agenda was "to discuss the best way in which police responsibilities can be carried out." It did result in an internal police enquiry as well. Subsequently, calls were raised in the House of Commons to cancel the rest of the tour.

The following match was once again scheduled in Twickenham, against the London Counties. Since it was in the headquarters of STST, meticulous planning took place before the scheduled game. Briefing meetings were held to prepare for the match.

The Springboks left Wales on the morning of Thursday, 20 November, and travelled to London on an express train. Arriving in the city they checked into the Park Lane Hotel. The Thursday afternoon and evening were spent seeing the sights at West End and being entertained by the Rugby Writers' Club at the RAF Club in Piccadilly.

Thomas writes this about gathering in his book on the tour: *"The chairman of the Rugby Writers' Club, Pat Marshall of the* Daily Express, *emphasised the fact that many brave South Africans had used the RAF Club during World War II while helping to win the Battle of Britain. A good point this, for without our victory in the Battle there would have been no freedom for the demonstrators to demonstrate. I have many South African ex-servicemen as friends, especially one who flew as a rear gunner in a bomber without a parachute because there was no room for both in the 'Tail-end Charlie' cockpit! One does not forget these things easily, and it was one of the reasons why the 'militant' demonstrators left me cold during the tour."*

What were you fighting for, Mr Thomas? Preserving your White social club, and thereby condoning the pathetic policies of the country of your White buddies? A lot of the policy-makers in the country of your comrades-in-arms, the same country of the brave men who flew without parachutes, were actually pro-Nazi during the War. A major example was the Prime Minister BJ Vorster.

Such defence of apartheid sport does read lame and contrived in retrospect. But no doubt, a shared War gave some sense of entitlement to above-the-law grandeur and postponement of the palpable sunset on the Empire.

On Friday, the Springboks toured London by coach. At the same time, John Jones, who played for the Swansea Rugby Club in 1939, spoke to the *Guardian* about "dissociating himself from the Rugby Union in disgust after seeing suede-jacketed toffs acting like thugs and bullying demonstrators." At Swansea, he had seen a former player he knew acting as a steward, pulling a girl 30 yards by the hair and then he and the fellow stewards "openly boasting about it while they caroused with the Springboks."

This was flashed in the *Guardian* on the morning of the Twickenham match, on Saturday, 22 November. Another steward was quoted in *London Evening News* as saying: "If any of the demonstrators interfere with the game, we'll sort them out."

There had been some criticism of the STST. They were supposedly victimising individual members of the team who might well have been against apartheid in sport. So, it was decided to give the players the opportunity to make their positions clear. On the morning of the Twickenham match, members of SAN-ROC delivered a personal letter to each player of the Springbok party. Each player was asked for an individual declaration that he was opposed to the exclusion of sportsmen from national and international sport because of their colour.

It was too complicated. None of the Springboks could realistically answer the letter. There was no response forthcoming.

The conditions are perfect for the match—bright sunshine on a warm spring-like day. London Counties are star-studded, and at the headquarters of rugby this is expected to be a thriller.

It turns out to be an absolute disappointment for the spectators. First, this match witnesses one of the biggest demonstrations of the tour. Secondly, the home team puts up one of the weakest shows against the tourists.

Chanting and whistling start immediately after the kick-off. Hiller places a penalty from the halfway marks between the North Stand posts to put London counties ahead. However, the chanting and booing don't stop. Visagie, visibly disturbed by the demonstrations, fails to convert a couple of penalties.

Just 11 minutes into the match, the demonstrators run in. Having taken position in several corners of the ground, they now sprint in from all angles. The players and referee Meirion Joseph are surprised into transfixed stillness. The police hurry after the 'miscreants' and a few stewards lend them enthusiastic help.

One of the demonstrators grab a corner flag and run to plant it in the middle of the field. The rest perform well-rehearsed 'sit in'. There are more than a hundred of them on the ground. The match is stopped completely for six minutes before the field is cleared of the squatters.

As the game restarts, the protesters are herded into a room under the stadium. Most of them are ejected, but 15 are taken to the Twickenham Police Station. Six policemen and three civilians are taken to the hospital.

But the game is interrupted again and again on occasions. None of the interruptions are major, but they add to the irritation factor. In the terraces, there are the usual scuffles between the fans and the demonstrators.

However, according to the London Counties coach Gerwyn Williams, the interruptions help the Springboks. The plan was to tire out the heavyweight Springbok forwards by switching play back and forth across-field. The interruptions helped the big boys recuperate.

Indeed, the Springboks recover. By halftime it is 6-6. On resumption, Visagie converts two tries, Bedford scores by snapping up a loose ball and Carelse delivers a monster kick which goes through high up between the posts. 22-6 in favour of the visitors.

The report in the *Guardian* is headlined: "Protesters claim their finest hour."

By Monday, 25 November, there were further developments. The Home Office was persuaded to agree to meet an STST delegation to discuss the role of the police and specifically the Swansea demonstration. Also, the Home Secretary announced that stewards were to be barred from clearing demonstrators from the pitch and interfering with the protesters.

There were contradicting voices as well. Lord Ferrier, President of Edinburgh Academicals, one of Scotland's eldest clubs, stated in public that he thought the leaders of the demonstrations were contravening the section of Race Relations Act dealing with 'inciting people to violence.' He continued, "I am against apartheid, but I think people are getting tired of these demonstrations. We run the risk of a backlash."

The next match at Manchester saw about 7,000 demonstrators march to the ground. It was coordinated from the Manchester University Students Union. At the same time the scheduled match at Ulster was cancelled because of the threat it posed "to the preservation of peace and the maintenance of order." Ulster being a potential timebomb of a city about to erupt over civil rights, it was quite prudent to avoid mass demonstrations. However, it was an indirect win for the campaign anyway.

The Manchester match was not interrupted, mainly because there was a problem in obtaining tickets. A number of protesters tried to get in with forged tickets but that did not work. Outside, clashes between the demonstrators and the police continued, and 150 of the people in the march were detained. Of these 77 were arrested, which included some who had managed to get in and were about to run into the field.

But with every demonstration, the STST was learning. The techniques were developing and becoming more streamlined. And they were also learning to pick their moments. With the Ulster match called off, the focus shifted to Scotland where the Springboks were to play two matches, at Aberdeen and Murrayfield, Edinburgh.

Aberdeen became vitally important to the impetus of the campaign.

49 BUS HIJACKED

Two days before the match against The North at Aberdeen, David Sheppard, now Bishop of Woolwich, expressed his admiration and full support for the majority of peaceful demonstrators while questioning the violence perpetrated by some of the militant members among the protesters.

In Wales, former Olympic long jump gold medallist Lynn Davies spoke out against the Springbok tour. At the same time, the Bishop of Monmouth, the Very Reverent Errol Thomas, refused to welcome the tourists, and instead joined communist leaders and others in Cardiff at a special anti-apartheid rally.

"The way of Christ was to help all men and not discriminate in any way, and it was sad to see men of the church take this action," wrote JBG Thomas.

Well …

About 1,000 demonstrators march to the stadium—the biggest the city has ever seen. A mass meeting is held outside.

Immediately after the start, about 100 demonstrators invade the pitch. Two even mount on the goalposts, flashing out the Nazi salute from atop. The police dance about underneath, asking them to come down. Some of the policemen have donned shirtsleeves and football boots for easy tackling. It takes more than 10 minutes to remove the protesters.

The match continues after that, bar two small interruptions. It is one-sided, the first real easy game the Springboks have had. The final score is 37-3.

The Scottish authorities had made clear that invading the pitch would be a breach of peace in accordance with the Scottish law. The invaders were charged and 98 were arrested, including 29 girls. The fines amounted to a whopping £1,500, quite shattering for the students.

One of the protesters who had been arrested had spent some time working for New Musical Express. His bright idea was to phone the NME office, get hold of the New York number of John Lennon, and leave a message. Would Lennon consider doing a concert to raise the £1,500?

Within the week, a letter arrived from Lennon. No, he did not see the need to do a concert, but he could shell out the money. Enclosed was a cheque for £1,500.

According to a press statement released by Billy Griffith, a sub-committee, responsible to TCCB, was being set up to consider the practical side of staging the cricket tour. It also stated that TCCB was "unanimous in their resolve to uphold the rights of individuals in this country to take part in lawful pursuits, particularly when these pursuits have the support of the majority." It was quite evident that the authorities were deflecting the issue of racism in sport into their 'concern' for law and order—a tack that is always handy for the pro-establishment voice.

Murrayfield, 6 December. The first international of the tour.

A scrum just outside the Springboks' 25. Duncan Paterson goes right, and John Frame works a dummy scissors with Chris Rea. Through the gap in the hedge, Frame speeds ahead and sends a long and beautiful pass to full back Ian Smith. The Scottish Army captain takes the ball on the burst. Bedford and Nomis challenge the full-back. But the long striding Smith eludes them and dives over, one of the most beautiful international tries for many a year. The Scottish win 6-3. The Springboks have lost their first international.

The match goes through without interruptions, but the security arrangements mean 30,000 spectators attend instead of the anticipated 55,000. There are 2,000 protesters marching outside the stadium. Inside hundreds clash with the police as they try to break into the field. The action in the middle takes place in a state of continual unrest.

By the time the tour reached Cardiff, all pretence of an ordinary rugby match was abandoned. A massive barbed wire fence was put up around the field. A 2,000-strong demonstration went on around the game, but it was not interrupted.

It also raised a question of financial figures in very tangible terms. During the TCCB meeting on 10 and 11 December, the questions of costs was raised. The rugby tour had proved so far that police would have to be employed in huge numbers for the cricket series to take place. The cost was estimated at some £6,000 per day for the proposed 28-match tour. The cricket authorities were hoping to come to an agreement with the Home Office on reducing police hire charges. There was also speculation that Cheetham and Coy, once again in England representing SACA, had offered to bear part of the cost [according to some, the offered figure approached £250,000]. However, this was denied by Lord's.

BREITLING
R98.50
John N. Miles

Eastern Province
HERALD

WHOLESALE!
J. MARKUS

Unanimous vote delights cricket lovers

M.C.C. DECIDES 1970 TOUR WILL GO ON

Anonymous committee to probe all aspects

VINDICATION OF CRICKET SAYS CHEETHAM

Report back

No offer

Convinced

GIRLS FIGHT FOR LIFE IN FLOOD

Survey ship calls for help

CITY POLE SIT MAN BATTLES FOR CASH

State Department supports Ashe

HUNT OFF CITY FOR TWO SHIPS ADRIFT

'Bull' talk wins in heated City Council debate

Elizabeth Arden has a gift for making Christmas happy

Eastern Province Herald reports that the tour is on

Some of the county club secretaries were finding the concept of hosting tour matches under siege increasingly disturbing. However, the members representing the counties in the TCCB meetings were most often the chairmen, quite detached from the logistics of the ground realities. According to a comment to *The Observer* on 14 December, one club secretary mentioned: "This was their [the chairman and his ilk] opportunity to apply all their dislike and loathing of permissiveness, demonstrators and long hair. Staging matches is their chance to make a stand against these things."

It was thus clear that a 'generation gap' was playing a role as well.

The focus of the rugby protests was now on the Twickenham match against England, the second international, on 20 December. It was a testing time for the STST. The matches were becoming ticketed-only, the security was beefing up, Christmas holidays were closing in. Momentum needed to be sustained.

The Hain phone was tapped, a familiar but disconcerting experience for the family. They had enough experience to get around the problem.

The protesters bought tickets by the bulk at agencies. At one stage, Peter had 400 tickets for the Twickenham game hidden in his bedroom. Plans were being finalised with rigour.

The three matches in between the internationals had taken place in comparative peaceful conditions, and there was a lull that was taken as proof of the fervour dying out. However, the authorities were not easing up on security measures.

On 16 December, Jack Cheetham, President of SACA, came up with the now-famous statement: The South African team would now be chosen purely on ability and irrespective of colour considerations.

The Cricket Council hailed this as a great step forward and "complete vindication of our policy of maintaining contact with South Africa."

However, multi-racial cricket in the land remained an impossibility, with the laws of the land strictly forbidding any such event. Besides, the government would hardly be amenable to allowing a mixed-race team to leave the country. Hassan Howa, the President designate of the SACBOC, dismissed Cheetham's statement as "mere window dressing for the British public." If anything, it smacked of a public relations exercise to reduce the opposition to the summer's tour.

Meanwhile, the STST received plenty of recognition from important voices against the tour.

John Arlott wrote in the *Guardian* on 19 December: "The demonstrators, by their action against the rugby tour, have in a few months achieved more than the cricket authorities have done by 15 years of acquiescence."

The endeavours were getting more innovative.

Two of the members of the STST were booked into the Park Lane Hotel where the Springboks were staying. One of them was the vivacious Rosemary Chester, later to become Lady Kirkwood, wife of former Liberal MP Lord Archy Kirkwood.

At the same time, Mike Findley and Peter Twyman, two members of the Putney Young Liberals, went through a hilarious training session. Gathering in the garden behind the Hain house, they spent the evening running up from the edge of the patch and handcuffing themselves to a pole planted in the middle.

The night before the match, the two STST members in the hotel set out pouring metal into the locks or the Springbok rooms, so that the players would be locked inside. Early in the morning, a locksmith had to be engaged to free these locked players, and to let in those who were locked out of the room.

The team managed to prepare in time and get into their coach. The bus waited in the kerb beside the hotel. The passengers included Danie Craven, now the President of South African Rugby Board. At this moment, Michael Deeney, a member of STST, emerged from the hotel, impeccably dressed, and made his way to the coach. The driver looked up questioningly, and Deeney informed him that there had been a change of plans and he was wanted inside the

Hotel.

The driver left the bus, making his way towards the hotel. Deeney promptly sat down in the vacated seat of the chauffeur and chained himself to the steering wheel.

This far it was according to the plan as hatched by the STST. The modification that came about now was a product of the circumstances and certainly not very laudatory. The driver, in his confusion, had left the engine running. Deeney eyed it, felt the vibrating throbs of the vehicle, and could not restrain himself. He drove the coach away.

His driving skills, what with it being a big coach and his hands being chained, was less than ideal. The coach made its faltering way into the rear end of a Post Office van about 100 yards up the road.

By now the Springboks were alarmed, and justifiably so. For his troubles, Deeney was punched in the face by a Springbok player and had his jaw broken.

The policemen arrived on the scene quickly enough but had a difficult time freeing Deeney. The chain was hardened steel, and he had to be cut free with cutters from a nearby roadworks gang. Deeney was fined £40 and barred from driving for six months.

"What do you have to do to get locked up in this country?" the Springboks asked, exasperated.

That was not the only hiccup on the way to the ground. As the coach actually departed for the match, it was further delayed by demonstrators sitting on the road.

There was a 5,000-strong rally going on around the ground, with a gathering of MPs and other public figures, including Rev David Sheppard. Folk singer Julie Felix even entertained the demonstrators afterwards.

But here is what JBG Thomas had to say about the demonstrations of the day, *"Such demonstrations aroused me not, and I wondered what they would have done in 1939–45. I had been to South Africa several times and to many parts of Black Africa where the atmosphere was far more Nazi-like than in South Africa[...] The militant demonstrators were all so naïve, so ready to absorb, in parrot-like fashion, any critical propaganda of South Africa, while the majority wanted to see a good game of rugby."*

Before the match, Danie Craven gave an interview to 'Atticus' of the *Sunday Times*. "The Blacks, the Coloureds, and the Whites are separate nations. Like Scotland, Wales, and England. They are different stock, so they won't ever play in the same side. But maybe, perhaps, like your Lions, one day, we would have such a team, combining the nations. What happens ultimately, that we must leave to the future. See what history has to say."

Did he see Scotsmen and Welshmen travelling to England with passbooks, herded into ghettos, and forbidden to meet together in gatherings, forbidden to inter-marry, play against each other or have sexual relations? I wonder who were the naïve ones—the anti-apartheid demonstrators or the likes of Craven and JBG Thomas.

The start is delayed because of the problems faced by the Springboks in reaching the ground. The royal family has announced that they will not be paying their customary visit to the International.

The barricades are difficult to penetrate, with an extra fence erected behind the already existing one, and policemen standing shoulder to shoulder in between.

However, immediately after the start, Findley and Twyman leave their ring side seats and sprint to the nearest goalpost. The policemen are hard at their heels. Twyman is tackled by an agile bobby ten yards short of the post, but Findley wins the photo-finish. Even as he is grabbed by a diving constable, he arrives at the post and snaps his handcuffs home. Play has to be interrupted till he is cut free.

Orange smoke pellets thrown amongst the players disrupt play as well, resulting in dramatic pictures on television and the papers.

Purely as a game, the International is a cracking one. South Africa take the lead through a Visagie penalty from 28-yards. A Greyling try makes it 8-0 in favour of the tourists. A sequence of slick inter-passing in confined quarters leads to Larter diving over to make it 8-3 at half-time. In the 20th minute of the second half, Hiller goals a 35-yard penalty to make it 8-6. Finally, a bit of indecision in the Springbok line allows Pullin to beat Dawie de Villiers to the touchdown, followed by Hiller's conversion, which makes it 11-8 in favour of England.

The Springboks lose their second International as well.

The experiences of the day were trying. Corrie Bornman said that he might have to take his team home if their safety could not be guaranteed. This was supported by Danie Craven.

However, after further discussions, Bornman said on Monday, 22 December: "I see no reason why the tour should be called off for one isolated incident, but if this trend of violence continues, there may be cause for consideration."

That was the day Craven flew back to Johannesburg. On landing in Jan Smuts airport, he told the army of press reporters: "The Springboks will try to see out their tour of Britain for the sake of the Springbok cricket tour next year. There is real possibility that the rugby tour could be called off unless there is an improvement in the security arrangements for the players, as these had left much to be desired."

On the following day, Peter issued a counter statement for STST:

"With increasing security on the game itself, the Springboks can expect direct action protests to follow their every movement. Demonstrations will no longer be confined to the matches. We welcome the suggestions that the tour should be stopped and suggest to Dr Craven that he make every endeavour to have his boys home safe and sound by Christmas."

The Springboks spent Christmas quietly in their London Hotel before travelling to Exeter for their next match.

At the Rougemont Hotel, a special group of the STST infiltrated their way inside, past the battalion of police and plain-clothes detectives. The slogan 'White Rugby equals Racialism' was daubed on the room doors of some players. One demonstrator, painting 'Go Home Springboks' on the walls of the toilets, was surprised by the detectives and locked himself in the lavatory. He was charged with malicious damage, and there was a worried phone call from his wife in London who asked the Exeter police whether her husband had been arrested.

There was even more trouble in Bristol. The demonstrators paraded up and down outside the Unicorn Hotel, while young detectives waited eagerly to nab them if they trespassed into the forbidden boundaries of the establishment.

When a long-haired youth pushed open the glass doors and made his way in, the plainclothesmen pounced on him, pushing him down to the floor, pinning his arm behind his back. The head porter ran forward, "Stop, he's one of ours. He works here."

Long hair.

At 2.30 AM on the morning of the match, the hotel's fire alarms went off. It was an ear-shattering sound, and the Springboks and the other guests huddled together in the lobby in visible panic. The scrumhalf Dirk de Vos, however, slept right through the commotion, although his room was the closest to the scene of trouble.

Two of the demonstrators had gotten into the building and one of them had rigged up two crowscarers and a marine flare. The idea had been to set off the fire-alarms. But a hotel attendant had discovered them before the five-minute fuse had burnt itself.

Thus thwarted, the STST member had broken the glass of the fire alarm switch on the wall.

During the half-time break in the game against the Western Counties, a demonstrator ran in with pockets full of ¾ inch tacks. In order to maintain the cordon, the police had divided their responsibilities into two categories. The cordon would remain there to stop invaders. If someone managed to breach it, a special force, wearing rugby boots, would run in and drag the miscreant away.

At Bristol, the second team was slow off the mark. The demonstrator managed to sprinkle enough tacks before the front runner of the task force brought him down with a flying throat tackle. This delighted the fans in the crowd, but play had to be held up as the players and officials cleared the ground of tacks. They did not really do a thorough job. After the match, a magnet dragged across the turf drew up more than 200 tacks that had not been detected.

The other serious matter that the tack-sprinkling event unearthed was that the Springboks had by now reached the end of their tether. The official policy was to do nothing in retaliation but take everything the demonstrators aimed at them. But while the invader had been busy with the tacks, the 18-stone prop Hannes Marais had tried to go after him; with Piet Visagie in hot pursuit and Tommy Bedford, captain for the day, waving his arms frantically. Luckily, the police tackled the demonstrator before Marais.

The police also confiscated 28 pounds of sugar that the demonstrators had brought with them with the intention of putting it into the petrol tank of their coach.

In the New Year's Eve speech to South Africa, Vorster issued a tough statement reaffirming his unequivocal commitment to apartheid in sport. South Africa would not deviate from its sports policy in spite of recent statements by some sportsmen to the contrary.

The STST statement released in response read: "If the MCC ever needed a final prod in the back, then Mr Vorster's predictable pronouncement that apartheid would remain firmly within sport must surely have done so. The MCC cannot honestly go ahead with the tour if it really has the interests of all cricketers—Black and White—at heart."

Vorster: As unrelenting as ever

50 HOME RULE FOR ESKIMOS

At 11.25 AM on 2 January 1970, the BOAC VC-10 touched down at Jan Smuts Airport, Johannesburg. In the plane were Bill Lawry's harried and hassled men—most of them underweight, undernourished, and sick. The 3-1 series victory in India had come at high cost, including pathetic hotels, inedible food, riots, heat, and dust.

Alan McGilvray, the ABC ace, was shocked to see the contingent as they stepped out. "They looked haggard. Their eyes seemed to be standing out of their heads and some of them looked positively yellow."

That was not the only cause of concern.

As South African journalist Eric Litchfield watched the plane touch down on the tarmac, he heard a senior SACA official voice his concern: "I wonder if we are not welcoming the last cricket touring team to South Africa for a long, long time."

The fear was genuine. The newspapers were full of reports of the STST and their incredible demonstrations were hounding the Springbok rugby players wherever they went.

In fact, the news on that very day from Newcastle-on-Tyne was as follows: "An extreme left-wing group of 'revolutionary' students will be in charge of the anti-apartheid demonstrations when the Springboks play North-Eastern Counties at Gosforth, Newcastle." Several Newcastle councillors and at least one MP were supposed to participate.

The report ended with the burning question: "How much longer can the players be subject to the mental agonies and emotional strains imposed by the new wave of violence by militant anti-South African demonstrators? There is little doubt that at the moment several of the players just want to get this tour completed as fast as possible."

Ali Bacher and Bill Lawry

On the same day as Lawry's men arrived in Johannesburg, Dr Glyn Simon, Archbishop of Wales and a member of the Glamorgan County Cricket Club, called upon all the fellow members of the club to resign if the tour went ahead. This brought forth a stinging retort from Glamorgan CCC Secretary and former rugby international Wilfred Wooller, denouncing the Archbishop as "in a sporting sense, a completely useless member."

On 5 January 1970, Australian cricket board secretary Alan Barnes was visited at Cricket House by representatives of 13 religious orders. They were all involved in the new Australian group called CARIS (Campaign Against Racialism in Sport). The 13 representatives submitted "a petition to the board against its continuance of cricket relationships with South Africa and called upon it to cancel the current Australian visit there." Barnes undertook to submit the petition during the next Board meeting. In reality it was an empty gesture on the part of Barnes. The next meeting was three and a half weeks away and by then, Australia would have already played their first Test.

The reactions of the Springbok players had by now ceased to be passive. At Coventry, as several demonstrators ran in, the fiery three-quarter Mannetjies Roux lost his temper and threw a ball at one of the protesters. JBG Thomas speculates that 'poor' Roux must have "received a friendly warning from the management."

The Coventry protest was a particularly successful one, with the Bishop of Coventry joining in the march outside and scores of white balloons tied with black crepe paper released from outside the ground flying over the playing arena. Spectators were asked to look under their seats because of a bomb warning.

There was more disturbing news for the South Africans. The MCC's tour of East Africa and the Far East had to be changed into a tour of Ceylon and the Far East after Uganda refused to play the MCC in Kampala as a protest against the Test and County Cricket Board's decision confirming the South African tour of England in 1970.

Litchfield was horrified. *"What monstrous impertinence by the East African cricket officials. They are 'nobodys' in world cricket. They ought to have been extremely grateful that the MCC agreed to send a team to their area."*

After this, Kenya also declared that MCC would not be welcome because of continued sporting ties between them and South Africa.

Meanwhile, on 7 January, demonstrators applied weed-killer to the outfield of the Worcester ground "as a warning of things to come."

As the Springbok rugby team flew to Ireland, their flight from the Birmingham Airport was delayed by the report of a possible bomb in their luggage. There was no such thing, but every bit of their luggage had to be meticulously searched. As they stepped into the Dublin International Airport, eggs were thrown at them and stones at their coach.

Pickets besieged them as soon as they took up accommodation in the Royal Starlight Hotel.

Reyburn writes colourfully about the protesters in his *There Was Also Some Rugby:* "The genuine anti-apartheid demonstrators were surrounded by as fine a rabble as you would wish to see, representing every breed of political and religious trouble-maker, trade union agitators, Sinn Fein, Young Socialists, communists, Britain-haters, Maoists, anarchists. In fact, the only group not represented seemed to be the anti-vivisectionists."

But loud as the pro-tour voices screamed, by now it was impossible to ignore the coordination and the extraordinary success of the demonstrations.

The march in Dublin is the largest in public since the S-Plan days of the late 1930s. Over 10,000 people march on to the Lansdowne Road Ground, led by Bernadette Devlin, MP. In red sweater and jeans, she tells reporters that she has come down "[b]ecause the #### demonstrators aren't being tough enough with the #### Springboks."

There are other prominent public figures in the march as well.

The International takes place with 30,000 spectators and 2,300 policemen, the latter figure a record. No official programme is on sale. The preparations have focused on security, the pitch encircled by barbed wire and hundreds of policemen standing guard behind it.

The match is a close one, the South Africans leading 8-5 towards the end before Tom Kieran's simple penalty kick ensures a draw. The 8-8 result ensures that the Springboks have the worst record in the Internationals in Britain of any touring team barring the 1957–58 Wallabies.

The demonstration continued with increased vigour as the Springboks left the ground. The reception for the teams was at the Hibernian. On their way, bottles and stones were thrown at the bus, the players pelted with eggs. Bernadette Devlin walked into the hotel and put her case to Dawie de Villiers.

A watch had to be kept while the teams had dinner.

The *Evening Press* headline read "What a demo! Dublin's massive protest." In *Sunday Independent* the show was called "The siege of Lansdowne Road."

When the Springboks left Ireland and reached Edinburgh, Tommy Bedford allegedly "jumped up and down a couple of times, to feel the good, sane soil of Scotland under my feet."

Ireland had been a nightmare.

Meanwhile, as the Australians proceeded through the first-class encounters in South Africa, they received all the hospitality that had made the land the favourite touring destination of the white cricketing world. As usual, the Oppenheimer family of diamond merchants from Kimberley entertained them lavishly at their farm Mauritzfontein. Apart from Lawry, Chappell, Redpath, and the other Australian cricketers, the night was attended by Arthur Coy, Roy McLean, Jack Plimsoll, and Eric Rowan.

The tour was generating extreme interest among the South African spectators starved of international action. Advance bookings for the Tests had already been supremely encouraging.

During the final day of the tour match against Griqualand West, SACA official and former captain Jack Cheetham approached Australian manager Fred Bennett proposing a fifth Test match. Bennett forwarded the request to the Australian Board.

While the Springbok rugby team went through a quiet interlude in Scotland, other actions were being planned. Arriving in Wales, they heard of a coordinated daubing raid on the county cricket grounds on 19 January. Anti-apartheid and anti-tour slogans were written across the premises of 14 of the 17 county clubs in a coordinated protest—specifically Surrey, Middlesex, Gloucestershire, Somerset, Essex, Lancashire, Hampshire, Leicestershire, Kent, Yorkshire, Sussex, Glamorgan and Warwickshire.

In addition, in Cardiff, a hole was dug on the Sophia Gardens Ground square. The car of the Glamorgan County Club secretary was besmirched with paint.

The reactions were fast and furious—with calls for the demonstrators' blood. However, there was some confusion about who had carried out this particular synchronised action. While

Peter adamantly denied the involvement of the STST, Louis Eake, chairman of the Young Liberals, did mention he was associated with the raids and that 'some of the Young Liberals had been involved.' Apart from getting the cricket establishment frothing at the mouth, the statement also sparked off a row within the Liberal Party.

Who was actually responsible for the daubing? Such a brilliantly clandestine coordinated movement?

It remains a mystery. Fifty years down the line, the author asks Peter Hain about the incident. Sitting in his office at Millbank House, House of Lords, London, Lord Hain of Neath laughs and says that no one knows. "I know," he adds mischievously, and it is quite apparent that it will remain a secret secured by the pact of the movement.

The other result of the 19 January action was that security and guard dogs were introduced around most county grounds.

On the same day, 19 January, the third day of the tour match between Australia and Eastern Province, Graeme Pollock, batting on 78, faced an over from the off-spinner Ashley Mallett. The first ball was a dot. The next five took him to 102. The sequence was 4,4,4,6,6—all of them executed with the straightest of bats.

It was just a taste of what the Australians were in for during the series. Unfortunately, it was also a taste of what the international cricketing world would be missing for most of that great batsman's career.

On the following day, the Springboks took on Llanelli at the Stradey Park. Carwyn James, the coach of the local side, publicly refused to attend the match. After a special session with the team, he left the ground and returned home. Another major strike for the movement.

JBG Thomas, a friend of James, lamented that the former international should have divorced politics from sport. That and his abhorrence of long hair pretty much summed up the pro-tour mentality.

22 January. The start of the Newlands Test match. Making his debut is a cautious but enormously talented blonde youngster called Barry Richards. He is slow, watchful. He gets off the mark after 24 minutes. But when he cuts a short of length delivery from Connolly crisply for four, the class is palpable. Ian Chappell drops him at slip off Mallett, but he cannot really capitalise. A ball from Connolly cuts back to bowl him for 29. New captain Ali Bacher, the peerless Graeme Pollock and vice-captain Eddie Barlow score sedately. Australia bowl 109 overs, but the South Africans score just 254 for 4.

Bill Lawry has reason to be satisfied by the disciplined Australian attack which has not allowed the South Africans to get away. However, just after five in the afternoon on the second day, some cynic among the spectators manages to get to the flagpole between the scoreboard and the Kelvin Grove end sightscreen and lowers the Australian flag to half-mast.

There is reason for this. Barlow, playing in front of his home crowd, has earlier in the day stretched his score to an unusually restrained 127. By 5PM, he has caught Stackpole, Redpath and Sheahan at first slip. Peter Pollock and Mike Procter look like the most threatening new ball pair in the world. Grahame Chevalier, playing what will be his only Test, has taken a wicket in his first over. The Australian score stands at 58 for 5. At the start of the tour, Bill Lawry has said somewhat controversially that Ian Chappell is equal to any batsman in the world on all wickets. The South Africans are not happy with the assessment. Peter Pollock bounces him out for a duck off the fourth ball he faces.

By the end of the day it is 108 for 6 and only a dogged fifty by Walters gives them some respectability.

The following day the innings finishes at 164. Bacher declines to enforce follow on. The South Africans bat dourly again, not very convincingly, but by the end of the day they are in an impregnable position. But the Australians are disgruntled. According to them, they are at the wrong end of as many as six umpiring decisions. Lawry even snatches the ball from umpire Billy Wade, the former Springbok wicketkeeper.

The South Africans end the day at 179 for six, 397 ahead. Former skipper Peter van der Merwe sums it up: "If the batsmen could do only this well on the third day, how can one expect them to do any better on the fifth?"

The last International at Cardiff is once again played in a near-fortified stadium. Over 3,000 demonstrators march to the stadium. The match remains uninterrupted, on a wet day with the ground muddy.

South Africa take the lead through a HO de Villiers kick, but soon a blunder by HO allows Wales to draw level. It is brilliant play by Ellis in the second half that results in a try and the Springboks go 6-3 up. The muddy conditions see players sliding about. The visitors dominate till late in the game.

But in the injury time, there is confusion among the South African backs. Gareth Edwards gets the ball from a ruck and goes flat out through a gap in the right flank before diving over by the corner flag. 6-6.

The Springboks finish the Internationals losing two and drawing two, without a single win.

The press back home was by now divided between lambasting the demonstrators for spoiling the sport and criticising the team for their poor performance.

On the cricket front, the sporting press of South Africa have plenty to cheer about.

Set 451 to win in 10 hours and 35 minutes, the Australians coast at 130 for 1 after tea on the fourth day. But as it so often happens in such cases, one wicket alters the course of play. A ball from Procter does not rise as expected and a revealingly aggressive Lawry is leg before for 83. Chappell, after spending an hour and quarter for 13, turns a benign ball into a yorker. Walters slashes away from the body. 136 for 4, three wickets falling in a decisive 17-minute period.

181 for 5 at stumps on the fourth day. Eric Freeman breakfasts the following morning asking with forlorn hope about chances of rain. There is a spirited show by the tail. But in the end the hosts win by 170 runs.

The Springbok rugby match with the Southern Counties had been shifted from Bournemouth to Gloucester. The Kings Park in Bournemouth had been determined to be extremely vulnerable to demonstrations. The ploy did work, there was no definite stoppage of play despite attempts to run into the field. There were the usual protests outside the ground, but the match proceeded without interruptions.

The focus was now on the final match of the tour, the showdown against the Barbarians, once again scheduled to be played at Twickenham on 31 January. It was all-ticket, and the STST purchased hundreds of them beforehand of which 80 were bought by a white South African visitor to Britain, her accent removing all suspicion.

Two days before the match, the South African government refused Arthur Ashe a visa to play the South African Open. Frank Waring explained that the government's decision was a simple matter of law and racial preservation. "He is aware of the accepted practice in South Africa," Waring said referring to Ashe.

JBG Thomas mentioned that Ashe was apparently thought to favour 'Black Power' and Prime Minister Vorster could not lean towards this in any way so near a general election in the country. He idly speculated that had the election already taken place, Ashe would have been allowed. Thomas even wrote he was sure of this. All around him, protests had flared because a Coloured cricketer had not been admitted a year ago, and yet he was sure of Ashe being admitted if the elections were through.

Reyburn had another take: "In America Arthur Ashe rants about not being allowed entry into South Africa to play in a tennis tournament. It would be interesting to see how far a South African Black would get if he sought entry into the average American tennis club. Or golf club. How many Coloured players are in America's famous golfing circus who tour the world? Should they not be boycotted until they are picked on a Black-and-White basis?"

As a humour writer, Wallace Reyburn had convinced a wide range of readers into believing that flush toilet was invented by Thomas Crapper. One can see why.

For the younger generation, for whom the broad mind and narrow waist had not exchanged dimensions, the refusal of Ashe was yet another cause to charge full steam ahead of the final match.

On the same day, 29 January, the Australian Cricket Board met to decide that the fifth Test proposed by the South African Cricket Association could take place if the 15 tourists accepted an offer of $200 on top of their $2800 tour fee.

To provide the STST a further shot in the arm, it was announced in the BBC television programme *Sports night with Coleman* that the White South African cricket officials had declared that the International Cavaliers side was unacceptable because it contained 'non-White personnel'.

That season, the 'non-White personnel' in the International Cavaliers side comprised of Garry Sobers, Mushtaq Mohammad, and Younis Ahmed, the Pakistan cricketer who participated in non-White cricket in South Africa.

With time frozen still in its premises since the days of the Empire, the Long Room at Lord's distanced itself from the International Cavaliers, stating that it was a private club.

Over 3,000 demonstrators march to Twickenham for the usual out of ground protests, while 500 enter the stands. While the demonstrators march outside, Wilf Wooller makes a close inspection, trying to single out the militant ones.

There is no second fence as there was for the international at the venue a month and a half earlier, but 1500 policemen are present, and it is difficult to breach through.

The novelty in this demonstration is the presence of white powdered dye, in polythene packets. When damp, the dye turns mauve-black. The idea is to throw the dye on the field where the players will fall in. It is notoriously difficult to remove. The aim is to send back a 'multi-racial' South African side back home.

Soon after the start, the demonstrators start throwing the dye into the field. Immediately, fighting breaks out on the terraces between plainclothes detectives and the dye throwers. For good measure, orange and grey smoke bombs are also tossed. The chanting of 'Springboks go back', 'Sharpeville', and other slogans make rounds throughout the match.

However, finally, after disappointing through much of the tour and in the Internationals, the Springboks play a superb game. Perhaps the thought of leaving the country two days later spurs them up. They trail 0-6 at first, 8-9 at half time. But in the second half, they dominate. Dawie de Villiers scores 9 points in the game, and his team wins 21-12.

The after-tour dinner took place at Savoy. The protesters shouted and chanted at the reception. There was an attractive STST girl as well, whom Peter refers to as STST's Mata Hari. At Bristol, she had struck up a friendship with a Springbok and had made him agree to accompany her with some of his colleagues to a party. Of course, the party was being hosted by the STST and the idea was talk to the Springbok team members. But when this 'Mata Hari' arrived at the Park Lane Hotel, she found her date completely drunk and interested only in groping her.

By now, the MCC delegates were busy talking to Home Office over arrangements for the summer's tour. The forthcoming Commonwealth Games stood a good chance of being boycotted by the African, Asian, and West Indian countries. West Indian cricket officials were starting to voice their dissent about MCC's position regarding the South African question.

On 1 February, the Australian cricketers were summoned to a meeting in the lounge of the Casa Mia Hotel of Johannesburg. The proposal was that the final two first-class matches against Western Province and Orange Free State would be scrapped and there would be an additional Test at Wanderers. The tour would be extended by two days.

Vice-captain Ian Chappell was aghast. "$200? That's bullshit. The board can get fucked. If they want us to play, we should get at least $500."

Bennett responded that he did not see the Board agreeing to that.

Bill Lawry pointed out that it was all in or all out. If one of the touring party disagreed, the Test could not go ahead.

A lot of the players were actually on Chappell's side.

On 2 February, in a television programme, the Conservative Party leader Edward Heath said that the cricket tour should go ahead. It was becoming increasingly clear that the Conservatives were determined to use the tour as a 'law and order' campaign against the Labour Government.

The Springbok team departed for Heathrow on 2 February. A large group of demonstrators tried to follow in an old Bentley, with a loudspeaker attached to the top. The idea was to talk to them on the way to the airport. However, several police cars boxed them in as the coach left with the players. After 10 minutes, the demonstrators were allowed to go, after the usual queries about identification and license. As they followed, the coach reached the airport by a back entrance and the team slipped away.

Corrie Bornman was not really diplomatic with his last words about the tour: "The last three months have been an ordeal to which I will never again subject young sportsmen [...] the violence we have seen leaves me in no doubt that any future South African team in Britain will be in danger."

Reyburn was rather sarcastic in his appraisal at the end of the tour. "I felt a moment of sadness for the demonstrators now that the departure of the Springboks had denied them a focal point for their demos. What was there for them to turn to next? Home rule for Eskimos?"

Casual racism shines through the writings of those times. Reyburn need not have worried—the STST at least had other issues to focus on.

The unprecedented ordeal was over for the rugby players. For the STST, it was a hugely successful trial run and an opportunity to focus totally on the forthcoming cricket tour.

51 LAST DAYS IN THE SUN

The Australians flew from Johannesburg to Durban on the 7 AM flight on 3 February. This was quite lousy scheduling, since a mid-morning flight would have been quite adequately timed for their scheduled late-afternoon nets. On arrival at the Eden Roc Hotel, quite a few of them went back to sleep.

Most were not around to hear Fred Bennett announce that due to three of the players holding out against the Australian Board's proposed payment amounts, the suggested fifth Test was shelved. It broke the hearts of the South African cricket authorities. The craze over the tour had continued unabated. The tour match against Transvaal between the first and second Tests had seen a profit of R30,475.

On 3 February, Frank Cousins, Chairman of the Community Relations Commission of Britain, sent a letter to the Home Secretary. It stated that if the South African cricket tour did take place, it would do untold damage to community relations.

The following day, 4 February, the Lord's authorities announced the arrival of 300 reels of barbed wire.

5 February, Kingsmead, Durban. There is controversy when Frank Lange, the head groundsman and a Durban City councillor, marshals his ground-staff to cut the wicket after the toss. "I was instructed quite early in the morning by the umpires to make the last cut at ten o'clock—half an hour before the scheduled start," he says in his defence.

However, all that is drowned in an avalanche of flowing runs. Early in the morning Barry Richards, playing in his home ground, hooks and back cuts Eric Freeman for two boundaries and then hooks Connolly for another four. By the time he reaches 19, the hundred seems to be a mere formality, but nonetheless a dazzling one.

Another hook off Freeman and a cover drive for his seventh boundary and he reaches his first fifty in Tests. And when Gleeson comes along, he advances down the wicket to launch him into the grassy bank beyond the long-on pickets.

When the veteran Trevor Goddard hits a Gleeson full-toss straight to Lawry at silly mid-off, he departs for 17. The score has rattled along to 88 in 83 minutes.

Richards continues in the same vein, sweeping Gleeson and then advancing down the wicket to drive him through the covers with apparent hours to spare. With every passing minute there looms the possibility of this young man joining Trumper, Macartney, and Bradman as the only men to have scored a century before lunch on the first day of a Test match. He is on 94 when the Memorial Tower clock shows 12.30 PM. It is the scheduled time for lunch, but umpires Gordon Draper and Carl Coetzee walk to their positions for the start of the next over. Lawry asks Coetzee about the time. The umpire's watch is not in sync with the ground clock. Connolly bowls.

Ali Bacher is on strike. He tries to nudge the second ball behind square leg, to allow Richards a chance to get to his landmark. But he fails to make contact and the ball clips the leg stump. The second wicket falls for 126, and lunch is taken. Richards has to wait.

The arrival of the barbed wire at Lord's, alongside the constant security around the grounds all over the country, indicated that the money spent on preventive measures was already considerable. STST issued a statement challenging the MCC to state publicly whether it was getting money from South Africa to subsidize the tour. The query went unanswered.

Barry Richards

Seven minutes after resumption, Richards completes his hundred. Several of the Australians shake him by the hand. There is a minor break in concentration as he charges down the wicket and drives Gleeson. The outside edge jars with the excellence of the innings, but travels safely towards point.

By now, the mayhem is being carried out with a two barrelled gun. Paul Sheahan recalls that: "[w]hen [Graeme] Pollock came to the wicket, it felt like he said: 'Well, you've seen the apprentice, now have a look at the master.' Richards did bat beautifully, but Pollock smashed us all over the shop [...] At one stage Garth McKenzie was bowling with four in the covers, but Pollock was still beating them. The only good thing was you didn't have to run far, because the ball would career back from the fence."

50 in 58 minutes for Pollock. McKenzie is bowling with a 7-2 field and he is threading through the off-side with brutal finesse.

Meanwhile, Richards is scoring runs with absolute majesty. There is nothing that Lawry or any captain can do. This is a symphony of two extraordinary virtuosos.

A cover drive from Richards and the stand is worth 103. The following ball is a slower one which bowls him for 140. With 20 fours and a six. The 103-run partnership has been registered in 61 minutes.

"Every so often a grandiose diamond is found in South Africa—a jewel that glows with richness," Lichfield cannot quite control his emotions. "Now there is a new sporting diamond. To the list of such gems, which includes the names of Bobby Locke, Gary Player, Karen Muir and, of course, Graeme Pollock, add Barry Richards." No place for Dolly or Papwa.

Barlow does not last long. "After the Lord Mayor's show, there was no room for me out there," Barlow will recall later. "I was embarrassed. Those two have made a mockery of batting."

Pollock carries on to his seventh Test hundred. At 117, the Murphy scoreboard can no longer keep up and is stuck. It remains static as Pollock hammers three successive fours, a two, and then an overthrow for five off Walters—19 off an over.

He is 160 not out at the end of the day. The total 386 for 5.

On the second day, 15,656 spectators flock to watch the action. And Pollock does not disappoint. There are men placed on the fence at cover point and extra cover. He still strokes boundaries through them. "Unique day for the South African reporter," writes Lichfield. "Never before have we spent an entire day with the record book remaining open alongside the typewriter."

At 196, he is temporarily subdued. Connolly bowls a frugal spell, round the wicket with two short legs and a man at mid-wicket. After a spate of maiden overs, he overpitches. Connolly will recall later: "Soon as I realised it, I said 'Oh Shit'. And he smashed it back past me at 2,500 kilometres an hour, and a split-second later it hit the sightscreen."

A superb on-drive off Stackpole takes him from 254 to 258, past Jackie McGlew's 255, which has stood as the highest score by a South African for 17 years. The spectators are already aware, as thunderous applause greets the boundary. However, for some reason, the milestone is announced on the loud-speaker which holds up play for a minute.

His final score is 274, with 43 fours and a five. Anything after that is anticlimactic, even the terrific run of play that sees Australia lose four wickets for four runs to slump to 48 for 4.

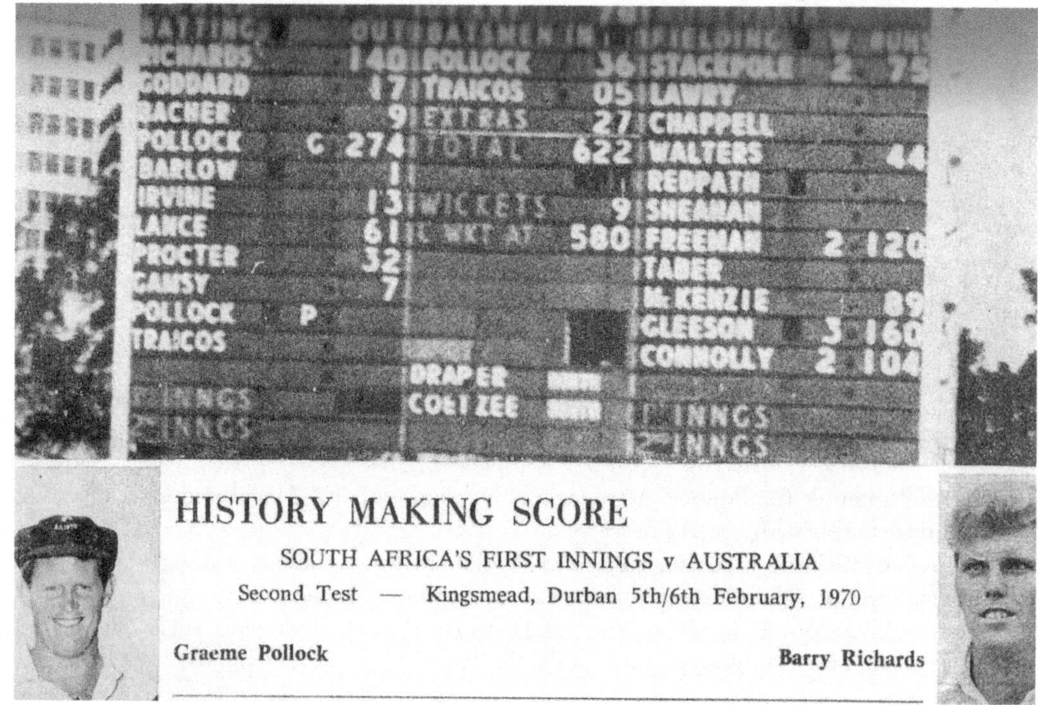

'That' scoreboard celebrated in the South African Cricket Annual

Barlow gets Lawry with his first ball, Chappell with his fourth, and Walters with his ninth. When bad light ends play, his figures read 1.4-1-4-3. The following morning, a fan parades the ground with the banner "Barlow for President."

622 for 9 declared. In reply Australia manage 157 and 336. The second innings dismissal of Lawry is controversial. Phil Tresidder writes in *Sydney Telegraph:* "Inquiries revealed that Lawry missed the ball by a foot when he was given out by umpire Draper to a solitary half-hearted appeal." Lawry leaves the ground in stunned disbelief and retires to the seclusion of his hotel room immediately after the day's play. At the end of the match, it is Bennett who addresses the press. However, there is no doubting the superiority of the South Africans.

The SAN-ROC had been busy all the while. On behalf of non-White cricketers, letters had been sent to all first-class county cricketers not to play against the South Africans. The Trinidadian cricketer Bryan Davis, who played for Glamorgan, had already announced that he would not play against the tourists.

As far as STST was concerned, the trade union group organiser of the group, Brian Thomas, had written to all the trade unions asking for their support against the tour. Over 20 unions had already replied, with the 285,000-strong National Union of Public Employees announcing its opposition to the tour on 9 February.

At the Jan Smuts Ground, East London, Australians took on Border. Lawry, along with Sheahan and McKenzie, stayed behind on the Rand.

LEW Glass, the Mayor of East London, welcomed the tourists at a civic reception by saying: "The first Australian team to play in East London was led by Vic Richardson, the grandfather of Ian Chappell who is leading the team in this particular fixture."

On the same day, as the Cricket Council meeting took place, the Anti-Apartheid Movement handed in a 13,000-name petition against the tour. In addition, STST sent in a letter asking the Council 'to have courage to take a positive stand against racialism in sport' and cancel the tour.

That same day, a STST banner made its first public appearance outside the Grace Gates. In the freezing snow and cold, the banner was held aloft by STST Committee members Rosemary Chester and Mike Craft.

That evening, an announcement was due from Lord's about the tour. Mike Craft and Peter sneaked into Lord's along with the pressmen and were directed to the Long Room by the stewards. Peter later recalled that the famed Long Room of which he had read so much turned out to be bare and dull.

What can one say? It definitely lacked the feminine touch to brighten things up. Women would not be allowed there till the late 1990s, although the Queen remained a patron. The history of marginalisation in cricket establishments transcended colour and bore down heavily on gender.

Peter was recognised by some of the journalists, who gathered around the STST duo and started a conference within a conference. This must have shaken the foundations of the old pavilion. The security at the ground, where the leader of the protest movement could walk in posing as a journalist, did invite some comment.

Eventually some rather embarrassed-looking MCC officials made their way to the young men and asked them to leave. Peter did manage to cast a glance at the hallowed turf through the window of the Long Room. It looked eerie with the dark barbed wire surrounding the pitch.

The press conference that followed was sensational. Billy Griffith announced that the original tour, consisting of 28 matches in 22 different grounds, had been cut down to 12 matches in eight grounds. Additionally, to ensure that play could go on in spite of unwanted nocturnal visitors to the ground, artificial all-weather pitches were to be installed.

This not only revealed the degree of intimidation inflicted by the STST and their coordinated efforts, the detail about the artificial pitches underlined the embarrassingly excessive lengths the establishment was prepared to go in order to preserve the sporting ties between the two countries.

Meanwhile, Peter had walked out of the Lord's pavilion and was waiting in the Tavern. The reporters rushed there to jot down his reactions to the announcements. "It is a major victory to have the tour cut by more than half before we have even started. It is the case of the first round to us. The tour is assuming the proportions of a military operation and we regard the Cricket Council's decision as an open declaration of war on the campaigners."

Mayor Glass was in the ground the following day as Australia played Border. Ashley Mallett, ignored in the previous Test in favour of Gleeson, turned in an impressive performance. Buster Farrer had played in the singles, doubles and mixed doubles of the 1956 Wimbledon, after which tennis trips proved too costly for him. A veteran of six Tests against

New Zealand and by now known in Border as 'the forgotten man of South African cricket', in this match he hit an aggressive 154. Unfortunately, with the team for the third Test already selected, no national selector was there to watch the innings.

Border put up 299 in their first innings.

In England, the Conservative Party entered the fray by aiming the 'Law and Order' arrow. Sir Peter Rawlinson, the Shadow Attorney General, called for injunctions to be taken out against Peter and Louis Eaks, alleging that the public statements by the two had constituted a "direct threat to illegal action." According to Rawlinson, the Home Secretary, James Callaghan, had remained 'neutral' and thus had "acknowledged the license to riot."

At East London, Ashley Mallett followed up his eight wickets in the match with a stubborn unbeaten 23-run partnership with Connolly to clinch a close 2-wicket win against Border.

That night, Alan Connolly's wife gave birth to a son back in Australia. The order for champagne at the Deal Hotel, East London, reached a staggering 17 bottles. After the tour, the Australian cricketers would rate Deal, alongside Eden Roc, Durban, as the best hotel of the tour.

The day after the match, 17 February, was an eventful one across the two countries of South Africa and England. A group of White South Africans, headed by Nicky du Preez, communicated their intention of coming over to guard the South African cricket team. In a statement given to the *Daily Telegraph,* du Perez said, "If it comes to a punch-up with the sort of long-haired hippies who tried to disrupt the Springbok rugby tour, we will take care of that."

The party who found themselves in the most awkward of positions as a result of this 'assurance' was undoubtedly the MCC. In a cautiously worded statement, they responded that attempts at disruption would be 'adequately dealt with' and that outside help was not needed.

That same day, there was support from another sparklingly important quarter. George Best, the Manchester United megastar, professed his support: "I think that it is an absolute disgrace that we are allowing the South African cricketers to tour this summer [...] We have been playing them for years but they have done nothing about their scandalous apartheid policies ... Put them in isolation until they see sense." Best also reiterated that he would have joined the rugby sit-down demonstrations had they not coincided with his football season.

On his part, Peter described the White South African band of self-appointed guards 'the importation of apartheid thuggery' into Britain. The STST, in fact, welcomed such development and similar moves that came out of South Africa, because "the arrogance of this typical white South African approach would further antagonise the people in Britain."

Peter was by now giving interviews to journalists in between classes, appearing on television in his jeans and anorak. Polo shirts and polo necked jerseys were his personal badge. He did not possess a suit. At a political meeting at the Durham University, a 'Jeeves-like valet' 'showing him to his room freshen up' was distinctly aghast when he came back to find that he was in the same polo shirt and anorak.

With two brilliant leg side stumpings in the match, off Connolly no less, Ray Jordon fancies his chances of making it to the Test team. After all, Brian Taber has been struggling with asthma and his keeping has been ordinary. Thus, when he is not named in the team for the third Test, he is rather pissed. He asks Fred Bennett whether he can be excused from the team meeting, since he thinks he may say something he will regret. He watches *Battle of Britain* by himself.

The Australians are not happy. In spite of their complaints, Carl Coetzee has been appointed umpire for the third Test match. However, on the first day at Johannesburg, they enjoy their best day of the series.

Bacher has to borrow a 20-cent piece from English cricket writer Henry Blofeld in order to save time for the toss. He wins the flip of the coin.

As Trevor Goddard plays an ultra-cautious hand, Barry Richards strikes the ball with the youthful conviction that nothing untoward can happen to him. A considerable proportion of his boundaries come off parts of the bat distinct from the middle, and one eludes the bat altogether and races to the boundary off his gloves. But these are interspersed with strokes of such dominance that once again there is speculation about a hundred before lunch. He falls well short, edging a drive at 65, with 12 fours and a six off just 74 balls.

However, Goddard manages 6 in an hour and Bacher 30 in well over two. Even Pollock, dropped twice, battles over two hours and 37 minutes for an unclean 52. An interruption due to thunderstorms does not help the batsmen. South Africa end the day at 191 for 5.

The cricket craze continues in Johannesburg. Bob Connolly's cartoon in *Rand Daily Mail* is captioned: "If manpower shortage becomes more serious, we'll have to recall staff from Wanderers."

In the middle, Lee Irvine's heroics manage to take South Africa along to 279. With Traicos, the last man, at the crease, Irvine runs even when the ball has been gathered by fielders, once even when the said fielder is at gully. He lifts Gleeson into the crowd beyond long on, and then into the scoreboard. The last wicket partnership produces 33 of which Traicos contributes a solitary run.

And then Peter Pollock and Mike Procter harry the Australians. Stackpole, Lawry, Redpath go back with the score just 12. Chappell spends 191 minutes over 34, choked for runs by Goddard and eventually snared into slashing to point. Towards the end of the day, Walters falls for a well-compiled 64. Australia 122 for 5.

1970. In April, the National Party romped through the elections once again—winning 118 of the 166 seats. The This was the first time in South African history that the House elected was responsible entirely to White people. The seats of the four MPs elected separately by 'qualified' Cape Coloured had expired. During the next decade, population in the Bantustans would increase by 69 per cent.

That same year Papwa Sewgolum was banned from the Natal Open. His passport had already been revoked. In the ensuing years he would be denied the right to play golf altogether.

He would die a pauper in 1978.

Mike Procter gets another wicket.

A total of 28,258 have paid admission in advance for Day 3. Joe Pamensky, the Transvaal Cricket Union treasurer, reports that another 301 enthusiasts have been permitted to purchase tickets. These, plus the non-Whites who take up spare accommodation, bring the day's paid attendance to 28,863.

Yes, non-Whites still sit separately in the stands. And Jack Cheetham would like the world to believe that the South African teams will be selected on merit without any consideration of Colour.

On 22 February, during the rest day of the Johannesburg Test, British Prime Minister Harold Wilson voiced his reservations about the tour quite openly for the first time in a radio interview.

The same day, the London Labour Party announced that they would be organising peaceful mass demonstrations at The Oval and at Lord's.

Pollock 5 for 39, his lean patch far behind him. Procter 3 for 48. Australia 202. Lead of 77. Eddie Barlow opens with Richards because Goddard is not feeling fit. The South African side teems with all-round excellence. Barlow fits in snugly at the top of the order and gets his sixth Test hundred. Graeme Pollock plays yet another dazzling innings of 87. They add 139 in quick time.

Irvine comes in and flogs the tiring bowling for 73. Tiger Lance heaves a six, Procter slams two. It becomes obvious that magnificent pace bowler that he is with his unusual delivery stride, Procter is a raw talent with the bat as well.

And then he runs in to dismiss Stackpole. There is a brief phase of counterattack by Lawry which looks more like desperation. Peter Pollock is hooked for six. Barlow is in with the ball now. Sleeves pulled up, run up measured out. The first over sees three balls go past Lawry's broad blade. The second ball of the second over gets the edge to first slip. The very next delivery is a yorker that sneaks under Ian Chappell's bat and hits middle and off.

"There is probably not a better allrounder in the world than Barlow," writes Eric Lichfield. Well, Garry Sobers is still around and will go strong for four more years, but West Indies is not really part of the cricketing world that White South Africa deals with.

But there is the sombre tale of another great all-rounder that follows.

Goddard picks up the final three wickets. 24.5-16-27-3. Those are most Goddard-like figures. He has career economy rate of 1.64. No one with more than 30 Test wickets has been so miserly, before or since. Goddard ends with 123 wickets at 26.22. And then there are 2,516 runs at 34.46 and 48 catches. 74 of his 78 innings have been as an opening batsman. He is perhaps the most unsung of all-round greats of cricket.

And suddenly, he discovers that his career is over. A Test too soon.

As he showers and dresses, Goddard is approached by the selectors, Arthur Coy among them. Pat Trimborn is to be tried out in the final Test. Since Goddard has made himself unavailable after the series, it is time to look ahead.

Just like that, a 15-year career comes to an end. Goddard is numb and keeps his head down. He blinks back tears and thinks: "That's nice, after 15 years of loyal service that's the way they drop you."

After a while, he is philosophical. "I wouldn't be human if I did not say I was disappointed, but that's life."

Even Bacher, who has just won his first series as captain, says with considerable emotion: "This was one of the saddest [days] since I first played Test cricket for South Africa." Several Springbok players have tears in their eyes.

Coy admits that the decision to leave Goddard out of the final Test may seem inhuman, but mouths the inane cliché of the game being bigger than the individual and "with the series won, we have got to think about the composition of our touring party for England."

Coy, of all people, should have known that the summer tour of England was a long, long stretch, and the final Test would prove to be Trimborn's last as well. In fact, it would be the final Test for all the South African cricketers except for the young Rhodesian off-break bowler John Traicos who would go on to play a few for Zimbabwe at the age of 45.

Goddard receives a warm round of applause as he emerges to bat for Natal at No 3. He strokes the ball fluently and gets 70 against McKenzie, Connolly, Gleeson, and Mallett. He is cheered all the way back to the pavilion. On the second day, Redpath and Chappell hit hundreds.

Stackpole and Sheahan meet Keith Miller, on tour as journalist, as the latter comes into the Eden Roc Hotel.

"So, how'd you get on today?" Miller asks.

"We did pretty well," says Sheahan. "Didn't you go?"

"No, I went to the races."

"But didn't you write a story?"

"'Course I did," says Miller. When he finds the two cricketers looking at him with eyes falling out of the sockets, he explains "You boys don't bother paying any attention to that stuff, do you?"

The Wanderers Club offers to make up the difference between the $500 demanded by the players and the $200 offered by the Australian Board for the additional Test.

"No way," says Chappell. He wants to use the issue to stand up for their pay. "If we don't, we deserve to be pushed around for the rest of our lives."

Laurie Mayne says that there are enough players to make an XI even if the others do not want to play. Chappell is furious. He pulls out his chequebook. "If $200 means so much to you, I'll give it to you now. We've got a chance to stand up to the bastards, we should do it."

Lawry insists that it is all-in or all-out. McKenzie and Gleeson confirm their opposition. The Test plans are cancelled.

South Africa remain starved of Test cricket, only these four morsels coming their way in the last three years.

Bacher is armed with a brand-new Kruger rand for the toss at Port Elizabeth. Lawry calls heads and loses for the fourth time in succession—rotten luck in a rotten series.

The misery piles up as Richards and Barlow add 157 for the first wicket. Dropping Richards twice does not help matters. The wicket is not easy, with a green patch at the Park Drive end. It is simply through high-class batsmanship that the openers put on that many runs. Mayne resorts to sending down bouncers in succession, and Barlow hooks him nonchalantly for six. Richards goes for a hook and skies the ball. He starts walking even before Taber gets under the ball, and then has to retrace his steps back to the wicket as the wicketkeeper drops the sitter.

South Africa lose Barlow, Richards and Graeme Pollock within the space of two runs. And by the end of the first day, their position is not as solid.

Connolly's hard work pays off as he bags a career-best 6 for 47. The South African first innings ends at 311.

By now, every move that Bacher makes is bearing fruit. Eric Rowan thinks he is a hell of a good captain.

Barlow and Lance are put on to bowl once the combination of Procter and Pollock have spent their venom after earning one wicket—the two part-timers in action before Trimborn. Lawry glances Lance and Lindsay dives to hold a stunning catch. When Trimborn bowls, he gets Chappell and Walters off successive balls spread across two overs.

And just when Redpath and Sheahan start making merry, Procter comes back and Trimborn holds a stinging catch at gully. Before the second day is over, Procter strikes Mayne on the shoulder and on the ribs.

The following day, Mayne is flogged with the bat. Cushioned on a 99-run lead, Richards hooks Mayne for two boundaries in one over and does not look back. Gleeson, when he comes on, is twice pulled for four and swept for six in between —all in the same over. Walters is cut for four and pulled into the lower rows of the grandstand. McKenzie is crashed through cover and mid-off and then swung into the grandstand.

In the final 50 minutes before tea, 63 runs are added, of which Richards scores 51.

He finally departs for 126, with 16 fours and 3 sixes. With Bacher he adds 126 in two hours. Keith Miller acknowledges that he has no equal in the world as an exciting opening batsman. To which he adds that Richards is the most technically correct opening batsman in the world—which is perhaps the deadliest of combinations.

Sadly, this will be his final innings in Test cricket.

All smiles after his second hundred. Barry Richards in his final Test innings

On 7 March, STST held a national conference at Hampstead Town Hall, attended by over 300 group delegates. The speakers during the morning session included Mike Brearley.

Brearley—while he was not really in favour of direct-action tactics—was dead against the South African tour. It was indeed rather courageous of the young cricketer to come out in support of the movement while still in the early days of his career.

Besides, the afternoon session included group discussions about organisational problems. It underlined the growing maturity of the group as a potent body.

However, the most hilarious interlude was when an MCC member usurped the speaker's role with the statement that "he was occupying the pitch." Having made some stinging remarks about STST, he departed.

Ruth Craft, one of the STST members, also recognised a plainclothes detective who had made his way in with a suitcase, in spite of all the precautions taken by the group in admitting members.

The conference was instrumental in setting up a powerful STST Trade Union group with contacts throughout the country.

The morning after the rest day dawns with a south-west breeze across the ground. To those familiar with Port Elizabeth, this means rain. With the skies getting darker, Bacher and Irvine go for quick runs.

The captain looks set for a hundred when his back-foot slips after a stroke and dislodges the leg bail. Lindsay comes in to slam a 54-minute 43-ball 60 with 10 fours and a six, the over-boundary a magnificent straight drive off McKenzie. It is ominously like the same Lindsay who had scored those mountains of runs against Simpson's men three years earlier.

He hits Gleeson for 5 fours off successive deliveries. When Lawry keeps the spinner on, Irvine lofts him for four and six. Gleeson goes for 35 runs in two overs.

At 92 Irvine hooks a six off Connolly. Off the following ball, he repeats the stroke and is dropped on the ropes by Redpath. In the next over he reaches his century. Procter comes in to smash Connolly for a six over extra cover.

At 470, Bacher declares. Australians are left to get 570 in just a bit less than nine hours.

In his second over Peter Pollock pulls his hamstring yet again and hobbles off. But it no longer matters. Procter and Barlow knock down the first four wickets. The following morning, even as reports of rain in the early hour increase the anxiety of some fans hungry for a whitewash, Procter and Trimborn finish off the rest.

Victory by 323 runs. Procter 6 for 73.

During the final stages, Ian Chappell and Doug Walters disappears from the dressing room to play golf.

Chappell, touted ahead of the tour by his captain as equal to any batsman in the world on any wicket, finishes the series with 92 runs at 11.50.

Bill Lawry refuses to say a few words at the end of the series. Umpire Coetzee enters the Australian dressing room with an exotic gift—a souvenir plaque made of lion hide. Lawry refuses. "I am not a hypocrite," he says. The Australian camp is not a happy one.

On the other hand, Bacher is chaired off the ground. Modestly, he suggests that the 1970 side is so great that a captain is redundant.

This is true to a great extent. Graeme Pollock 517 runs at 73.85; Barry Richards 508 at 72.57; Eddie Barlow 360 runs at 51.42 and 11 wickets at 23.36; Lee Irvine 353 runs at 50.42; Mike Procter 26 wickets at 13.57 and 209 runs at 34.83; Peter Pollock 15 wickets at 17.20.

It is indeed a supreme side. Player for player it is the best in the world. And it will never be seen in Test cricket again.

Goddard knows it, Trimborn and Chevalier do not. But they continue to share the distinction of taking wickets with their respective last deliveries in Test cricket.

Only John Traicos, far from a finished product during this series, will somehow reappear two decades later.

In March, South Africa was expelled from the tennis competition by the Davis Cup Committee of Nations.

The Victorious Captain

52 PRESSURE

A few months after returning to Australia, Fred Bennett recalled to Bob Parish, "I have a great affinity for the South African people [...] bearing in mind that on tours of this nature you don't see the 'seamy' side of the whole question of the Black situation."

In Durban, Bennett had been asked by one official about the domestic scene in Australia—what they had to do on a daily basis and so on. Bennett had answered, "Well, you know, I cut the lawns, wash the car." The official had replied, "That would never happen in South Africa [...] we've got the Black people who do those sorts of things."

The voices in the White cricketing world were still conservative about mixing 'politics' with sport.

On the other side of the world, in Britain, March was slightly slow in terms of sporting and demonstration action. However, the STST remained active.

The Nottingham STST group was formed with Bob Gregory as Secretary. Along with the Leeds STST Secretary Maureen Baker, he was to become the key campaign organiser outside London.

Towards the end of the month there was a major development.

On 23 March, *The Observer* chapel of the National Union of Journalists proposed a motion at the next meeting of the Central London NUJ branch. The call was for a complete newspaper, radio, and television ban on coverage of the sports aspect of the tour.

It was quite an unusual suggestion. The Branch covered all the national daily and Sunday papers, which sparked off a serious debate about the meaning of news reporting.

At the same time, Wilfred Brutus, brother of Dennis, and Chris de Broglio travelled to Cairo for the General Assembly of the Supreme Council for Sports in Africa. Several actions were discussed to isolate South Africa from the sporting world. Eventually, this would lead to the coordinated threat of boycott of the Commonwealth Games, and play a major role in the STST campaign.

As the month ended with the Easter Weekend, there was fresh opposition to the tour. One of the most unexpected quarters from where call for cancellation was voiced was the Association of Child Care Officers.

By this time the West Indians working on London Transport were discussing the feasibility of the one-day token strike coinciding with the first match at Lord's.

On 5 April, the Bishop of Woolwich, David Sheppard, launched his own organisation to stop the tour. The final aim was the same—stopping the proposed tour. However, the methods were to be peaceful. There would be no direct action in the STST style. Sheppard had always disagreed with such tactics. The intention of a massive and peaceful protest march of conscience was announced, to be held on 20 June, the route going past Lord's. It was to coincide with the Saturday of the Lord's Test.

Some parts of the press saw this new organisation as a sign of a split in the campaign to stop the tour. However, they were two independent groups linked by a common cause, and they did have constructive intersections. As Peter said: "I welcomed the formation of a new group as adding to the strength of the campaign by bringing in a large portion of hitherto untapped support—support which included people who had never demonstrated in any way before."

Two days later, on 7 April, there was an announcement that the 14,000-strong Association of Cinematograph, Television, and Allied Technicians were urging members not to cover the tour and was guaranteeing full Union support to any member who refused to do so. The threat of radio and television blackout was by now very real.

Various trade unions representing diverse categories of workers were by now lending their voices against the tour. The election planned in June was also playing an important role. If there were serious disturbances over the tour during the general election campaign, they were bound to react unfavourably on Labour's chances.

With the tour just six weeks away, on 15 April, the Pakistan Board of Control for Cricket stepped into the fray, advising the Pakistani players in the counties not to play against South Africa in the tour matches.

However, the biggest boost came on the evening of 16 April. Interviewed on Thames Television, Prime Minister Harold Wilson came out strongly in opposition of the tour. According to him, MCC had "made a big mistake" in inviting the South African team—"a very ill-judged decision." He added that with the proviso that any protests must not be violent, "Everyone should be free to demonstrate against apartheid—I hope people will feel free to do so."

The opinion was polarised about the Prime Minister's statement. While the demonstrators were elated, the faction supporting the tour were vehement in their criticism. And while non-White South Africa celebrated, the White South Africans were fast feeling the heat of resentment that was building against the tour.

On 11 April, at a political rally in Uitenhage, BJ Schoeman, the Transport Minister and number two in the South African Cabinet, said that if he had his way he would not send a side to tour England. "Why should we allow our boys to be insulted by those long-haired louts?"

Long hair. A recurrent theme.

The next important voice was that of cricket itself. John Arlott, who had broadcasted every tour since 1946, now announced that he had decided not to do so for any South African match that summer. "Commentary on cricket demands, in my professional belief, the ingredient of pleasure; it can only be satisfactorily broadcast in terms of shared enjoyment. This series cannot, to my mind, be enjoyable."

By now the summer season of 1970 was about to get underway. Newspapers soon made a habit of publishing pictures of county cricketers emerging on the grounds to practice with the barbed wire in the background producing a concentration camp sort of atmosphere.

It became a new campaign objective for STST to prove that the elaborate security could be breached. The new mini-project was to get into Lord's and carry out a multi-racial cricket match at the home of cricket.

For two days, the young activists watched the ground, hatching a complicated plot. Next, 12 demonstrators were packed in the back of a van in their cricketing gear. They were accompanied by a few press reporters and photographers. The van was driven to the Grace Gates. The driver flashed an MCC member's card and requested the steward to let him in while the one on the passenger seat got busy pulling out a squash racket from his bag. The story was that as MCC members they wanted to use the squash courts.

The man at the gate, however, was not accommodating. He had been instructed, along with the other gatekeepers, not to let in any van that week. The driver insisted, asking him to phone through to the Lord's office.

The phone call did not go through. The driver was insistent. He was an MCC member after all.

The gatekeeper looked like relenting.

"I just have to take a look in the back of the van."

There was no other alternative. The driver got out and opened the back door. And there they were, the demonstrators in their cricketing whites and the pressmen with their cameras.

"I certainly can't let *them* in, Sir," the steward rushed to his phone, closing the gates firmly.

So out came the protesters. On to the St John's Wood Road. Clad in their whites. Stumps were set up on the thoroughfare. Two batsmen took guard, the field was set, and a game of street cricket kicked off.

As if on cue, a television crew that had been tipped off appeared on the scene. The filming started. A Rolls Royce pulled up and the owner poked his head out asking: "Will I really be on telly tonight?"

Traffic on one side of the road was completely blocked. From the Lord's Tavern, customers spilled out to watch this weird game of cricket. A cover drive was cheered while the ball disappeared under a No 159 bus. A bus passenger, flustered at being held up by this impromptu demonstration, barked at a van at the other side to drive 'over the wicket'. This was stopped by something the players were really good at—a sit-down was staged on the road in front of the van.

It was a short enough game, but an exciting one. The Lord's turf remained protected, but the game was covered extensively by the media.

On 21 April, the British Council of Churches called for peaceful demonstrations against the tour. On the following day, Trades Union Congress called for a complete boycott in a statement by its General Secretary.

Finally, it all came down to money. The cost of protecting the grounds for play was proving to be enormous, and it would go up exponentially if the tour did take place and the protesters carried on in the same vein as they had done during the rugby tour.

On 23 April, the MCC launched 'The 1970 Cricket Fund', with a minimum target of £200,000. It was approved by the Cricket Council. The fund was launched at Lord's under the chairmanship of Lt Col Charles Newman, VC, and with a distinguished list of patrons including the Duke of Norfolk, Viscount Portal, Lord Wakefield, Judge Sir Carl Aarvold, Sir Peter Studd, MJC Allom, Alec Bedser, Brian Close, and Colin Cowdrey.

To steer clear of any controversy, the Chairman made it clear that no donation would be accepted from South Africa.

On the same day, two other distinct developments took place.

It was reported that the Queen would not make her traditional visit to the Lord's Test Match and neither would there be the normal invitation to the South African side to Buckingham Palace. The MCC 'explained' that it was a precautionary measure in case there was a display of 'bad manners' inside or outside the ground. However, it remains a fact that the Buckingham Palace had indicated as early as February that the Queen would not be attending.

In another significant development, 13 African countries threatened to withdraw from the Commonwealth Games in Edinburgh scheduled for July. The statement was made by

Abraham Ordia, the President of the Supreme Council for Sport in Africa. The timing of the pressure—no doubt a well-thought-out action—could not have been more potent. It soon blew up into a major issue.

By now, the STST were no longer making things happen—the juggernaut had been set off and the movement was snowballing on its own.

On 25 April, Granada Television announced that they would not be screening any of the play during the tour.

Two days later, BBC Television invited a debate on the issue during an episode of the programme *Panorama.* On one side were the MCC officials. On the other, there were David Sheppard, John Arlott, Dennis Brutus, and Peter Hain. There was also heavy-duty political presence in the form of Sir Peter Rawlinson of the Conservative Party and Brian Waldon for Labour.

On 28 April, STST sent a three-point letter to the Home Secretary. The demands were public and unequivocal assurance that Coloured demonstrators would not be singled out by the police, a ban on the police photographing of demonstrators not arrested, and general protection of the demonstrators' civil liberties.

The letter continued: "Unless we resolve these issues and unless the authorities are seen to be positively acting in an impartial manner, then the 'riots' that certain public spokesmen with rather dubious motives have been predicting have a much greater chance of occurring."

By the end of April, Rowland Bowen, the brilliant and eccentric editor of the *Cricket Quarterly,* came out with a stinging point by point counter of the Cricket Council's 'remarkable apologia' on why the cricket tour '70 should go on.

The statement of the Cricket Council started with "During the last 18 months much has been said and written about the policies of the South African government and about the position of South African cricket in relation to these policies." Bowen attacked the essay right from the first line: "*At once we get the perspective wrong: much has been written for over half a century on the policies of the South African government and for the last ten years on its attitude to sport.*"

The entire statement was thereafter torn to shreds by the unapologetic typewriter of Bowen. Some examples of his scathing comments are as follows:

"There is no 'Coloured Board of Control' [as mentioned by Cricket Council] The draftsmen at Lord's do not even understand South African terminology. There is a South African Cricket Board of Control, a non-racial body, to which the 'White' body should affiliate.

"The Cricket Council reveal their innate attitude. We, they say, 'are not going to be intimidated even into doing what is right. We are the rulers, and we intend to persist with that we have decided.' It is the attitude which, in terms of politics, lost the American colonies, San Domingo, the Afrikaners in 1832, and much later, Southern Ireland, India, Burma, Ghana, Kenya. 'We will not bow down to mob rule.' Does anyone seriously imagine that it was anything but a minority in each country named which achieved their independence? These people are froth blowers and live in a romantic past which never existed.

"The whole point is that the document is the most miserable piece of hypocrisy and special pleading ever to have been issued from Lord's. (and as usual by no means free from error or ignorance)."

Bowen did not mince his words.

On 30 April, a letter sent by Peter to the *Guardian* and *The Times* was published in both papers. Starting with a request to pause for a moment and ask what the tour was all about, he wrote:

"Lord's is in the dock now. Is cricket prepared to bear responsibility for poisoning race relationships in this country? [...]

"This is a time for courage, not for retreat. In cancelling the racialist cricket tour, even at this late stage, the Cricket Council will have shown a dignity worthy of the game itself."

By the end of the month, Alex Ross, the Chairman of the British Commonwealth Games Federation, had flown to Nigeria to talk to Abraham Ordia. It did not help. He was informed that the boycott would go ahead.

The television technicians were by now demanding BBC cancel its contracts worth over £50000 with the MCC for tour coverage. There were various important organisations voicing genuine concern about what the tour would do to race relations.

At Leeds, the Lord Mayor announced that there would be no reception for the South African team.

By the time Basil D'Oliveira walked out on the last day of April 1970 and top-scored with 40 in an unofficial one-day match against Northamptonshire, the tour had become a major political issue and the MCC were squirming in discomfort.

53 CANCELLATION

May 1970 kickstarted with more support from the Prime Minister. Harold Wilson appeared on BBC's *Sportsnight with Coleman* and said that he hoped the Cricket Council would think again and call off the tour. The Conservative leader, Edward Heath, however, sided with the MCC, merely asserting that the players should be treated with respect.

For the Cricket Council, Assistant Secretary Jack Bailey said that the pressure of the African and Asian countries amounted to nothing less than political blackmail. "If for political or other reasons the Government decides that the tour should not take place, then let them come out into the open and say so."

Bailey was merely voicing the opinion of the majority of the MCC members who wanted the tour to go forward.

At New Road, Worcester, it was a rather ageing bowling attack of the International Cavaliers that showed up on May 2. Jack Flavell, Fred Trueman, and Trevor Bailey bowled decently enough, but even the youthful pace of Bernard Julien teaming up with them could not stop D'Oliveira from stroking his way to an unbeaten 83 and taking his side to an eight-wicket win.

The same day, the Bishop of Woolwich formally launched his own group for stopping the tour. David Sheppard himself assumed the role of the chairman of the Fair Cricket Campaign. Sir Edward Boyle, the former Conservative spokesman on education, was appointed a vice-chairman. A week later, Reginald Prentice, another Conservative MP, would become the second vice-chairman.

Meanwhile TCCB took the precaution of writing to players to say that the English cricketers appearing in the five Tests and for the Southern and Northern County sides would have their lives insured for £15,000. This was a result of alleged threats of violence received by the two overseas professionals of Lancashire, Clive Lloyd and Farokh Engineer, if they appeared against the touring South Africans.

Peter Lever, the Lancashire fast bowler, announced that he would not be playing against the Springboks.

With political pressure building on the MCC due to the Commonwealth Boycotts and also the support of the Conservative MPs for FCC, the STST now decided to keep a low profile for a few days. Background organisation carried on, but action and provocative statements were reined in. This was a deliberate ploy to jettison any possibility of establishment lobbying.

The first three matches were to be held at Lord's, Trent Bridge, and Headingley. All these centres were being readied for action. During the first two weeks of May, 7000 posters were sent out to the campaign action groups.

The other concentrated point of action was the Heathrow airport, where the scheduled arrival day was 1 June. However, there were rumours of last-minute switch of arrangements whereby the team would get in a day earlier without being accosted by protesters. Hence, STST were busy forming contingency plans as well.

Tickets for the first Test at Lord's were also being fast arranged for. Since ticket application forms could only be obtained from club officials, several measures were being found to circumvent this problem. One of the supporters of the STST, a middle-aged Australian woman associated with the Campaign Against Racialism in Sport (CARIS) presented herself at Lord's and persuaded the office to give her 25 application forms for her friends—equivalent of 100 tickets.

A focus group of STST even analysed the surrounding geography of Lord's and found the existence of an underground tunnel running right under the venue, with an opening nearby. The possibility of a dramatic entry into the ground was very much in the plans.

The local expats were also getting involved. Leaflets publicised the proposed Explanation Day on 30 May, when young West Indians, Pakistanis, Africans, and Indians were supposed to march from Hyde Park Corner to Lord's to ask: "Why are the MCC insulting us in this way?"

A flat overlooking Lord's was rented by a TV news team in order to install sophisticated television equipment which could "pick up individual blades of grass on the ground."

Speculations were aplenty. From the possible changes in the date of arrival, to reactions of players and people of different races, to the practical questions of chasing a ball in the outfield and running into the barbed wire—everything was being discussed.

Pressure was being piled on from every quarter now. On 5 May, India announced the intention to join the boycott of the Commonwealth Games. The following day, Guyana followed suit.

The statement released by STST in reaction to the withdrawals was succinct: "The White tour of the South will be complemented by a White tour of the North, making a sorry picture of racial sport in Britain. The multi-racialism of the Games is in direct conflict with the racialist cricket tour. Unless British sport as a whole is prepared to stand up and be counted against racialist sport, the Games could be sacrificed—so making a grand slam for apartheid."

At this juncture, in spite of the immense controversy surrounding the boorishness of the stewards in manhandling protesters during the rugby tour, the MCC nonchalantly announced that they had written to all club members inviting them to become 'honorary stewards' to help the police in the event of trouble.

The subsequent announcement of MCC did little to assuage matters. With typical unflinching steadfastness against the flow of events, the august body announced that the new MCC President would be Sir Cyril Hawker, Chairman of the Standard Bank—a major affiliate of the Standard Bank of South Africa.

By now, disturbing reports were coming in from schools in London where racial divide was rearing its ugly head in the playground. Most of the teachers in predominantly multi-racial schools argued against the South Africans being allowed to play at The Oval. The ground was, after all, in the middle of the boroughs of Lambeth and Southwark, with large immigrant populations.

On the day of the AGM of the MCC, three members—Rev David Sheppard, Sir Edward Boyle and Mark Bonham-Carter, Chairman of the Race Relations Board—were vocal against the tour. The Fair Cricket Campaign group lobbied heavily among the members. Frank Cousins, chairman of the Community Relations Commission, also delivered a letter to the MCC President Maurice Allom in which he stressed the adverse effect of the tour on race relations across Britain.

The tour, however, remained scheduled. MCC and its Cricket Council refused to budge from their stand.

On the same day as the AGM, sodium chlorate was sprinkled on the wicket at the Gloucestershire County Cricket Club. The west county ground had no scheduled tour match, but this was probably in reaction to Mike Procter being one of the overseas cricketers recruited by the club.

Innovative protests reached a new level with the ingenious David Wilton-Godberford—a 20-year-old London biology student, who had decided to unleash a plague of locusts on the grounds to stop the tour.

By the time he talked to *The Times*, Wilton-Godberford had already bred 50,000 locusts, mostly desert and African migratory, at his Colwyn Bay residence. The insects, up to 1.5 inches long, were kept in glass-fronted cages, and were kept warm by electric bulbs. He also had many eggs in his possession. The eventual target was 100,000 locusts.

The 11 May edition of *The Times* quoted him saying: "Anything up to 100,000 locusts will be let loose at a particular ground and I think the plan is fool-proof. They will ravage every blade of grass and green foliage. The greatest care will be taken to ensure they are in the correct physiological stage. So that their appetites will not be impaired they will not be fed for 24 hours before the moment of truth [...] It takes 70,000 hoppers [locusts] 12 minutes to consume one cwt. [about 51 kg] of grass. The crack of a solid army of locusts feeding on the grass will sound like flames. The South Africans are going to dread this trip; they will see more locusts than they have ever done back home"

Wilton-Godberford had thought out the entire thing. At the time of the 'onslaught', the insects would not have grown wings, and the weather would kill them within a month, before their wings would develop.

As Abhishek Mukherjee later wrote: "Cricket has seen its share of insect invasions. Swarms of bees have stopped even Test matches; flying ants, grasshoppers, and leatherjackets ... have caused hold-ups; and flies often disrupt batsmen's concentration in Australia (Kevin Pietersen even swallowed one at Melbourne)." So, this incredible direct-action method was not extremely farfetched.

At the same time, more conventional methods of protest were also proceeding in full blast. As Basil D'Oliveira and the rest of the Worcestershire side completed a frustratingly wet and interrupted match against Middlesex at Lord's, West Indian, Pakistani and Indian High Commission representatives had talks with the top brass of MCC in the exclusive rooms of the old pavilion. Alex Ross of the British Commonwealth Games Federation announced that he would be meeting Billy Griffith on the following day.

Speculations had by now reached a crescendo. Only repeated denials by the Cricket Council managed to ward off rumours that the tour had already been cancelled. Billy Griffith also reiterated the same establishment lines after his meeting with Ross.

On 12 May, two significant announcements were made by Pakistan. The government had called off the under-25 cricket tour to England, scheduled to take place at the same time as the visit of the South Africans. Pakistan had also pulled out of the Commonwealth Games.

The proposed 1971 tours of India and Pakistan seemed to be tottering on a knife's edge.

What took place next was termed "a rare event in British life" by Irving Rosenwater in

Wisden. It was a House of Commons emergency debate on a sporting topic.

Arranged at the insistence of Philip Noel-Baker on 14 May, the tour issue was threshed out for three passionate hours. According to the Minister of Sport, Dennis Howell, never in his experience had he had to deal with a question where the issues were as deep, as emotional, and as involved as this one.

Pointing out the effect of the proposed tour on law and order, implication on the Commonwealth Games, the long-term interests of sports and, most importantly, racial harmony, Howell announced the latest resolution of the Sports Council for Great Britain (of which he was the chairman). The Council strongly urged the Cricket Council to withdraw the 1970 tour invitation because of its belief that it would have harmful impact on sport, especially multi-racial sport, extending far beyond cricket itself.

Reginald Maudling, Deputy Leader of the Opposition, argued that it would be a positive gain to encourage people to come to England to play games so that they could learn from the system of freedom and tolerance. "I believe our basic principle must be that any man is entitled to do what is lawful and to expect that the State will protect him from unlawful interference. Once a man is denied the right to do what is lawful because other people at home or overseas may disagree with his views it would be striking at the roots of freedom under the law. Once we admit the right of people to enforce their views by violent means with impunity democracy is at risk."

Sir Edward Boyle explained to the House why he had agreed to become a vice-chairman of the Fair Cricket Campaign: "I did so because, as someone who utterly deplores and opposes violence and disorder, I had come reluctantly to the view that the South African cricket tour was likely to be bad for community relations in this country, bad for the future of cricket, bad for the future of sport generally, bad for Commonwealth, and bad for law and order in Britain."

The Home Secretary James Callaghan summed it up: "When I hear the list of organisations who oppose the tour, when I consider the possible damage that can be done, I repeat to the Cricket Council that it is for it to consider whether its judgement to proceed with the tour is right [...] What I fear is that there will be damage done to racial relations and other matters ... There seems a lurking belief, that I detected in the Cricket Council when they came to see me, that they are a lonely band of heroes standing against the darkening tide of lawlessness. I can relieve them of that burden. What we are discussing here is the judgment of the Council in inviting a team here in the face of an unparalleled crescendo of opposition [...]. It is not unfair to the Cricket Council to throw responsibility upon them. They invited the South Africans, and they can uninvite them if they choose to do so."

This was one of the toughest appeals by a Government Minister for the cancellation of the tour so far.

One day later, White South Africa was dealt another crippling blow in the *Voortrekkers'* land. In Amsterdam, during the 69th International Olympic Committee's congress the IOC withdrew recognition of the South African National Olympic Committee, thereby severing all ties with the country. This meant that until the decision was reversed, and the body was re-recognised, South Africa would not receive invitation for any Olympic Games.

This marked the first time any nation has been expelled from the Olympic movement since the inception of Modern Olympics in 1896.

The reason for expelling was violation of Rule One of the Olympic charter, which stated that "no discrimination is allowed against any country or person on grounds of race, religion, or political affiliation." The charges were brought up by Abraham Ordia of Nigeria and Jean-Claude Ganga of Congo. After the vote, IOC issued a statement: "The act of an organization which has so little respect for the rules and constitution does not warrant comment."

The Olympics thus joined the list of individual sports like boxing, fencing, gymnastics, basketball, soccer, table tennis, and weightlifting, whose international bodies had already banned the country.

The ban pleased Dennis Brutus no end. While predicting that it would lead the other international sports relations still enjoyed by the country to fall like dominoes, he added: "This has definitely helped in the drive to stop the cricket tour."

It was reported that the IOC had the Arthur Ashe and Basil D'Oliveira incidents on the top of their minds as the resolution was put to vote.

A spokesman at Lord's merely responded: "It will be noted."

By now, several important members of the cricket establishment who had originally supported the tour were turning against it.

Swanton was one of them. Ted Dexter was another.

The Royal Commonwealth Society, known for its impeccable record of good sense and responsibility, expressed great concern at the harm that would be done by the tour to multi-racial sport and good relations within the Commonwealth.

The Fair Cricket Campaign had by now started sending over 20,000 invitations to organisations and individuals to stop the tour. The Archbishop of Canterbury and the Chief Rabbi added their voices to the opposition.

An unofficial source stated that even the Queen, in her personal capacity, was opposed to the tour.

To complicate matters further, on 18 May the Prime Minister announced that the election date had been set for 18 June, the first day of the Lord's Test. It was proving quite difficult for any party to gain any political leverage in the explosive atmosphere surrounding the tour. Visions of race riots on the polling day could not have been a welcome thought for any political party.

At the same time, the West Indian Board of Control sent in its formal opposition to the tour from Barbados, adding that "irreparable harm" would come from it. The Board also stated that forthcoming tour of the West Indian Young Cricketers, scheduled in July–August 1970, would be cancelled if the South African tour went forward.

As the Cricket Council met for a secret session on 18 May, a meeting that went on long into the night, the council of the 14,000-strong Inner London Teachers' Association deplored the prospect of the tour and the "inevitable repercussions" in schools. Several hundred people living near Lord's also presented a last-minute petition to Lord's to halt the tour.

While the developments did give rise to plenty of optimistic speculation that the tour was about to be cancelled—even to the extent of congratulatory calls to the STST headquarters—Peter was not sure. "I felt quite firmly that the cricket authorities were incapable of responding predictably or logically."

In the end, he was proved right.

At 7 PM on 19 May, while the protest groups paraded outside the Grace Gates with their banners and placards, the pressmen gathered in the Long Room. The statement was read out by Billy Griffith:

"The Cricket Council have decided by a substantial majority that this tour should proceed as arranged. It has always been believed that cricket in South Africa should be given the longest possible time to bring about conditions in which all cricketers in their own country, regardless of their origin, are able to play and be selected on equal terms. The SACA have taken the first step by announcing that all future touring teams will be selected on merit. The Council have confirmed the present tour in the hope and the belief that this intention will be capable of fulfilment in the future.

"The Council have informed the SACA that no further Test tours between South Africa and this country will take place until South African cricket is played and teams are selected on a multi-racial basis [...]

"In reviewing their original decision to confirm the invitation to the SACA, the Council had to consider whether the desirability—so often repeated—of maintaining contact with South Africa had in any way changed. It was agreed that in the long term this policy was in the best interests of cricket, and cricketers of all races in South Africa.

"The Council discussed the Commonwealth Games in Scotland and deeply regretted the attitude of those countries who had threatened to withdraw if the cricket tour took place [...] They hope, in view of their statement as to the future, that these countries will reconsider their attitude.

"Two other issues should perhaps be further elaborated:

"First the question of community relations. The Council recognise that there has been a growing concern in the United Kingdom with the unacceptable apartheid policies of the present South African Government. The Council share this concern, but wish to re-emphasise that cricket has made an outstanding and widely acknowledged contribution to the maintenance of good relations between all people among whom the game has been played.

"Secondly, the question of freedom under the law in this country. The Council do not consider it the duty or the responsibility of cricket to campaign for freedom under the law at the expense of the game itself. But the Council and its constituent members are aware of the dangers of a minority group being allowed to take the law into their own hands by direct action. However distasteful to this minority group, the South African tour this summer is not only a lawful event, but as shown by the outcome of the recent opinion polls, it is clearly the wish of the majority that the tour should take place."

The wording of the statement, with verbose padding over critical issues, and rather unscientific opinion polls to tide over the opposition, pleased no one in particular. Even the supporters of the tour were ballistic at being informed that the future tours would be stopped.

In the summer issue of the *Cricket Quarterly*, Rowland Bowen sliced through the arguments yet again.

"Bear baiting is illegal, cock-fighting is illegal: boxing other than under the Queensberry Rules is illegal: coursing would have been illegal but for the late election. Each of these sports or games was brought to an end by a 'vocal minority'.

"The question of whether one has a right to do something abhorrent to others is a highly debatable one, and majorities or minorities do not enter into it. If in undivided India a Hindu majority threatened to do something repugnant to a Muslim minority (playing music outside a mosque), it was the majority that was always forbidden to perform its repugnant act, an act which was not of itself, of course, illegal, but became undesirable in the particular circumstances.

"And the question of whether there was, in recent months, any majority in favour of the tour is much more than doubtful: a scientifically conducted postal research survey found most emphatically there was not, and the so-called opinion polls to the contrary (though they indeed show a movement) were either for samples which were far too small for any kind of validity, or were based on simple yes/no questions, which are the most unreliable method of sampling opinion."

However, the tour was on, and so were the activities to stop it.

At the same time, in South Africa, Sports Minister Frank Waring was fuming over the decision of the IOC. "Politics have triumphed over sport," was his usual clichéd response.

In the Republic, plenty of realistic fans by now thought that the tour was an impossibility. Even the *Rand Daily Mail,* a strong supporter of the tour, was of the opinion that the team could make the journey but would not be able to play much cricket. "Only a clear, unambiguous statement by our cricket authorities on the principle of non-racialism in sport can help the tour," reported the paper.

The statement by captain Ali Bacher was guarded. A medical doctor working in a hospital for non-Europeans near Johannesburg, he said that he would welcome multi-racial cricket as soon as it was considered practical by the Government. He discussed with Dawie de Villiers about what to expect in England. While stating that he would love to speak to a demonstrator provided the latter was polite, Bacher insisted that they should not be allowed to break up a tour.

For a man who would later perform quite incredible things to keep cricket alive and fair in South Africa during and after the isolation years, his statement included that perennial cliché: "We are not politicians, we are going to England to play cricket." However, he did publicly defend the right of protesters to stage peaceful demonstrations.

The tour manager Jack Plimsoll stated that he was not against mixed-race cricket in South Africa. "There are a lot of non-White cricketers who, in better company, would improve with increased competition, and could force their way into the Springbok side."

But there was opposition to the tour as well.

While many papers depicted the wives of the South African cricketers hoping and praying for the return of their husbands, Kevin Craig of *Johannesburg Sunday Times* warned SACA that unless they called off the tour they would "expose our cricketers to physical danger and maybe death."

In view of the adamant stand of the Cricket Council to go forward with the tour, STST called an emergency press conference. Peter Hain attacked the decision and said that they would be pressing ahead with renewed attempts "to stop this racist spectacle." "The tour is not on until those cricketers arrive at the Heathrow airport. We had held our fire the last few weeks in the hope of a courageous advance from the Cricket Council. We now intend to regain the initiative and press ahead with more militant protests. In the coming months we shall see the greatest show of opposition to the tyranny of apartheid ever in Britain."

On 20 May, the Home Secretary stepped in. James Callaghan invited the Cricket Council to meet him at the Home Office on the morrow: "I want to hear from them their reasons for going on with the tour, after deciding that future tours should be cancelled. We shall have a very full discussion into the possible consequences if the tour goes on. There have been many requests to me from trade unionists, teachers, church leaders, and others to intervene and I would be failing in my responsibilities if I did not meet them."

The Chairman MJC Allom and the secretary Billy Griffith attended a three-hour meeting. The letter drafted during the session on behalf of Callaghan stated:

"When you and Mr Griffith came to see me this morning, we discussed the statement issued on behalf of the Cricket Council on 19 May. You explained that the Council have come to the conclusion that the tour should go on after reassessing their own responsibilities, which were limited to the impact of the decision on cricket and cricketers, both in the United Kingdom and throughout the world, and on other sports and sportsmen. You emphasised, however, that although the Council were naturally concerned with various other matters of a public and political nature [...] these matters fell outside their own responsibilities and that it was beyond their competence to judge what significance to attach to them. This, they felt, was the responsibility of the Government who were equipped to judge and act upon them.

"I accept the distinction.

"The Government have therefore been very carefully considering the implications of the tour, if it were to take place, in the light of the many representations that have been received from a wide variety of interests and persons. We have had particularly in mind the possible impact on relations with other Commonwealth countries, race relations in this country and the divisive effect on the community. Another matter for concern is the effect on the Commonwealth Games. I have taken into account too the position of the police; there is no doubt as to their ability to cope with any situation which might arise, but a tour of this nature would mean diverting police resources on a large scale from their essential ordinary duties.

"The Government have come to the conclusion, after reviewing all these considerations, that on grounds of broad public policy they must request the Cricket Council to withdraw their invitation to the South African Cricket Association, and I should be grateful if you would put this request before the Council."

It was as good as a Government directive. The Cricket Council did not even pause to take a vote.

On 22 May came the final communication from the Cricket Council:

"At a meeting held this afternoon at Lord's, the Cricket Council considered the formal request from Her Majesty's Government to withdraw the invitation to South African touring team this summer.

"With deep regret the Council were of the opinion that they had no alternative but to accede to this request and they are informing the South African Cricket Association accordingly.

"The Council are grateful for the overwhelming support of cricketers, cricket lovers, and many others, and share their disappointment at the cancellation of the tour. At the same time they regret the discourtesy to the South African Cricket Association and the inconvenience caused to so many people.

"The Council see no reason to repeat the arguments, to which they still adhere which led them to sustain the invitation to the South African cricketers issued four years ago. They do, however, deplore the activities of those who by the intimidation of individual cricketers and threats of violent disruption have inflamed the whole issue."

And just like that, the tour was cancelled.

Peter Hain was in a BBC television studio when the news came through. Hearing the entire statement must have given him quite a feeling of satisfaction; even in their condemnation of the direct-action measures, the Cricket Council could not really ignore the enormous contribution of the young men and women had in triggering this decision. The final lines were a true testimony to their efforts.

Peter, the 20-year-old engineering student who had made this campaign his life's work at that point, received the news with calm dignity. There was a quick gathering at The White Swan, the pub where it had all started. Dennis Brutus, Mike Craft, Rosemary Chester, Jeff Crawford, and all other major players of the STST were there. They were also joined by Walter

Hain.

Under the glaring arc lamps of the TV cameras, with reporters swarming in the room, Peter gave his reaction. It was quite charitable.

"I don't believe the Cricket Council has backed down—in fact it has moved forward towards a position where racialism is rejected in cricket and international sport. It was an extremely courageous step by the Government in getting us out of a depressingly entrenched position where there seemed no fluidity about the situation at all … The decision is a great boost to the fight against racialism and to those working for better race relations in Britain."

That evening, Peter received calls and visits from friends, many of them Black South Africans. A cable arrived from the Cape Reserve in his hometown of Pretoria, a simple message from some non-White friends—Poen Ah Dong, Alban Thumbran, and Aubrey Apples—who had waved them goodbye in 1966: "And so say all of us." Brevity was not just the soul of the wit here; it was also the brain and instinct behind survival. A slightly more elaborate message would have been flagged by the secret police.

That was what South Africa was all about. In terms of human rights, playing cricket with them and watching the action from a window in the Long Room came a distant second.

Eastern Province
HERALD

UPTONS

TOUR OFF
DECISION MADE RELUCTANTLY

Racial blow-up fears 'inflamed issue'

Delight at cancelled visit

Express demand

Accede

World XI not for us say Springboks

Grim 'farewell' to Pollocks

Faithful three show emotion

WARING UPSET BY WILSON'S ATTITUDE

Statement

Cancellation disappoints 'Dolly'

No reason

Answer to ore port question imminent

Features today

The tour is off: Eastern Province Herald documents the disappointment

Conservative reaction was, of course, scathing. The Conservative Home affairs spokesman Quintin Hogg called it "a classical illustration of the inability of this government to preserve freedom in this country or to maintain law and order." Enoch Powell, the man behind the 'Rivers of Blood' speech, compared it to the loss of the 'Prince of Wales' and the 'Repulse … beneath the waters of the Gulf of Siam.' There was something very liquid about the man.

Jack Bailey of the MCC believed that "the rule of threatened mob violence had won the day."

And on his part, Hoofleier Vorster was ballistic. "It is not cricket or sport that loses, but the forces of law and order."

While Bailey lamented the isolation of South African cricketers as representatives of their country, Vorster's stinging remarks put into perspective why sportsmen of the maligned nation could not be considered independently from their government.

"This particular cricket relationship between South Africa and Great Britain was a relationship of the MCC with White South Africans. Even in the previous years, when there was nothing against it whatsoever, Britain did not include Coloured players when sending a team to South Africa, because they recognised the particular sporting relationship which existed between the countries."

Obviously, to the curiously convoluted mind cultivated in the White bubble, that sounded like justification. It is really difficult to unravel exactly where in that statement the Prime Minister of White South Africa found a platform to complain.

A sum of £75,054 was paid to the SACA in compensation.

Half a century later, sitting in the current times and having shed [to a great extent] the blinkers of the 'good old days' of the 'Gentleman's Game', we do realise the long-term implications of the movement by the 'long-haired bunch of delinquents'.

Peter Hain reflects: "First of all that victory came at a time when the internal resistance had been crushed, the leadership had for many years been in Robben Island, ANC had been suppressed, external campaign and internal resistance were very limited. It was a big, important victory for the anti-apartheid campaign. It was also very important for Nelson Mandela and the others to learn about it through the news blackout in Robben Island.

"Beyond that, White South Africans knew that the apartheid system was reviled across the world. At the same time they enjoyed collaboration, military support, economic and trade support and crucially they were welcome and feted at the international sports stadia of the world—whether it was Twickenham or Lord's or Australia or New Zealand, they were given lavish hospitality and a big warm welcome. International sports participation was very important for them psychologically or practically as a way of reconciling international opposition to apartheid with being welcomed abroad.

"Everybody will tell us in South Africa that for Whites it was a big body blow and for some it awakened the start of a reconsideration of their own attitude and future. For Black South Africans what it did was it connected into the struggle in a very profound way."

54 BANISHED

Lord's, 17 June 1970. It is an experimental batting line-up for England. Cowdrey and Boycott are not in form and have asked the selectors not to consider them. Edrich has an injured hand. Brian Luckhurst and Alan Jones open the England innings.

Captain Garry Sobers comes on first change. Held back by an ageing and rebuilding side for the last few years, now he is at the helm of some of the best cricketers of the world. He bowls fast and swings it. Luckhurst edges to Barry Richards in his third over. In his sixth, D'Oliveira snicks to Engineer. In his eighth Phil Sharpe is caught in the slips by Barlow. In his ninth, Knott is snapped up by Kanhai. 4 for 9 off 8.1 overs.

He ends with 20-11-21-6.

And then he hammers 183, with one six and 30 fours.

MCC had shown remarkable enterprise in arranging a replacement tour by the Rest of the World.

Ironically, the team had four South Africans—Barlow, Richards, Graeme Pollock, and Mike Procter. There were Sobers, Kanhai, Lloyd and Gibbs from West Indies, Intikhab Alam from Pakistan, Garth McKenzie from Australia, and Farokh Engineer from India.

Unequivocally mixed-race side, including four White South Africans, led by the greatest cricketer of the world—a Black man.

Wisden recorded the matches as Tests. The players were told that they would be considered Test matches. Alan Jones assumed that he was making his Test debut. Commenting about Eddie Barlow's 119, *Wisden* says it was his seventh Test century.

However, all that would be struck off the records. The rather pedestrian match at Sydney in October 2005 would surprisingly be bestowed Test status.

Intikhab's leg breaks and googlies ensure an innings win for the Rest. Illingworth gets 94, but Sobers dismisses him, bowling spin this time.

Over 35,000 turn up to see the contest. The Rest Day is taken on 18 June, and in the polls the Conservatives pull off a surprise win. Edward Heath takes over as Prime Minister.

"Maybe we didn't want to read the signs," wondered Peter Pollock in retrospect.

There was some optimism in the South African camp that the tour of England would take place till the tiding came through on 22 May. However, to none of the players was it a complete surprise.

Peter Pollock called on his fellow sportsmen to demand multiracial sport and requested the government to assist. Eddie Barlow clearly said that the country's cricket authorities would have to overcome racial problems and choose their Test cricketers on individual merit or face international isolation.

Peter Pollock was perhaps unlucky not to make the cut as a member of the Rest of the World side. However, too many South African players in the side could have instigated more political reactions.

The *Morning Group Newspapers* sent him over as a journalist and Pollock accepted.

At Nottingham, the ball moves around under cloudy skies for the first three days. Clive Lloyd compiles a memorable 114, but the Rest of the World manage just 276. D'Oliveira uses the conditions to perfection and captures four wickets. His partner in crime is Tony Greig, the enormously tall Sussex all-rounder. He picks four wickets as well. One a Coloured South African and the other a White South African, both will end up as stalwart Test cricketers for England. Curiously, the other two wickets are taken by Brown. Quite a colourful story.

The first half of the match sees all-rounders shine with their lesser-known skills. Barlow picks up five wickets, and Illingworth hits 97. A wafer-thin three-run lead for England.

Less than two weeks before the first Rest of the World vs England 'Test' at Lord's, a very low-profile South African wandering side did make it into England. The Penguins had a few useful first-class cricketers from the Eastern Cape. Alan Hector, who started his career for Eastern Province and then played for Transvaal, was an impressive medium pacer who would end up with 117 first-class wickets. James Young was an Eastern Province all-rounder of yesteryears, who, at the age of 57, bowled well enough to capture 14 wickets. Arthur Rudman was yet another first-class cricketer from Eastern Province. Jeff Levey, a slow-left arm bowler from St Andrew's College Grahamstown and University of Cape Town, would later play a solitary and successful first-class match for Eastern Province. He joined the team late but topped the bowling averages taking 44 wickets.

Manager SHW Levey, who had emigrated to South Africa in 1935, called the tour a great success. "We arrived at Heathrow in some trepidation, not daring to wear our club blazers for fear of demonstrators. We were very worried about the reception we would receive from both the public and cricketers. And we found nothing—exactly nothing. There were no matches disrupted—there was nothing but kindness, sympathy and understanding from people in every walk of life."

He went on to say that they played cricket with (he preferred to say 'with' rather than 'against') many West Indians, Pakistanis, and Indians "who in our country are termed non-Europeans. From the start, there was absolutely no tension; to each other we were just cricketers [...] If only political boys would leave sport alone."

It remains quite probable that the tour was so low key that Peter Hain and other demonstrators did not even come to know of it. Or perhaps they did not think it was worth making a fuss about now that the actual tour had been cancelled. The 'trepidation' hinted at makes it quite clear that the team had no intention of publicising their visit. Besides, they played against rather obscure sides in rather obscure locations.

They opened the tour against Aldershot Services at the Officers Club Services Ground, Aldershot, played at Sutton, Esher, Lyminton Road (Hampstead), Church Road, Wimbledon, and so on—the highest profile ground being The Saffron's Eastbourne where they faced the Sussex Second XI.

However, it remains an indication that there continued to be plenty of encouragement for White South Africans to undertake such cricketing tours.

When the Rest bat again, Barlow hits his second century of the series, underlining that he is indeed one of the best all-rounders of the world. D'Oliveira and Greig scalp three more wickets each. The target is 284, steep considering the scores so far. However, after the third day the sun smiles and the conditions are perfect for batting. Luckhurst carries his bat to the end, with 113 not out. Cowdrey hits 64, and *Wisden* records that he has passed Wally Hammond to become the highest run-getter in Test cricket. It will all have to be rolled back, though. He would eventually get there at Brisbane in December.

England win easily by eight wickets. The series is getting interesting, but only 16,000 turn up to watch the cricket.

"I shed no tears when the 1970 Springbok tour to the UK was called off by the Government [...]," recalled D'Oliveira. "I disagreed with plans to disrupt the matches, but I agreed that the anti-apartheid campaigners were right to try to get the tour halted. I thought some sporting isolation would do South Africa some good. It would make their politicians realise things were wrong in the eyes of most of the free world."

D'Oliveira had never been too keen on campaigning himself. He had not refused to play when he knew that the South Africans were coming. To some of his people, it was an unthinking and insensitive stance.

But he maintained: "I was stepping away from the limelight of race-relations. I was happy to leave the campaigning to articulate, able, and sincere men like Brutus and Hain. I told Brutus, 'Use what I'm doing on the cricket field for your campaign but don't pull me this way and that for public statements'."

The Edgbaston 'Test' is played under some unfortunate limelight. It is made known that during the course of the match a decision is going to be made about whether Illingworth or Cowdrey is going to lead England to Australia.

Before the start, Barlow has lobbied heavily to replace out of form McKenzie with the best fast bowler of the world who is sitting in the press box. Peter Pollock does not say no. Hence South Africans Barlow and Richards open the batting and South Africans Pollock and Procter share the new ball.

After the English openers put on 56 for the first wicket, Sobers sends back Luckhurst, Cowdrey, and Fletcher without conceding a run. D'Oliveira walks in at this juncture and his second scoring stroke is a six. His aggression compels Gibbs to bowl with a long off and a long on. With Greig he adds 110. After his century, he hits one straight back to Clive Lloyd.

After England score 294 in the first innings, the crowd is delighted by the two West Indian left-handers. Lloyd and Sobers get together on the second afternoon and bat into the third morning, adding 175 in two hours, and ensuring a crowd of 12,500 on Saturday. Procter, who has captured five wickets in the first innings, hammers 12 fours in a majestic half-century.

Trailing by 269, England fight back. D'Oliveira punishes pace and spin with equal felicity, hammering 41 in his first hour at the wicket. When Sobers gets him caught at slip, he has 81 against his name. Cowdrey resists for 71, Knott an unbeaten 50, Illingworth 43. Brown and Snow help Knott add 92 for the last three wickets. The target is 141 in three and a quarter hours. At 107 for 5, Underwood and Illingworth getting the ball to turn, Graeme Pollock injured, hopes of an unlikely win peep through for England. But Procter comes in to hit some lusty blows and Intikhab plays quite an eloquent second fiddle. Victory by 5 wickets.

"Distasteful though it was for the Cricket Council to submit to minority threats and extraneous pressures (including not least the oblique invitation to demonstration, on a scale likely to degenerate into violence, by the Prime Minister himself) I hoped they would themselves cancel for the sake of cricket," wrote Swanton. However, he added: "It's hard really to know which of the extremes is the more pathetic, the violent young demonstrators of the left or the elderly skinheads of the right."

Yes, we cannot deny that for all his noble qualities, Swanton was still at home with the stiff-upper-lipped Gubby Allens with their excellently tailored suits and, most importantly, the right colour of tie.

On a slow, drying Headingley pitch, Sobers puts England in. There are three Yorkshiremen on their home ground—Boycott, Don Wilson, and a 21-year-old Chris Old. Peter Pollock is back in the press box and Mushtaq Mohammad plays for Rest of the World.

England totter to 91 for 4, recover to 209, and then lose the last six wickets for 13. With the new ball, Barlow dismisses Fletcher for 89. Then, in three successive deliveries, he castles Knott and Old, and gets Wilson off bat and pad caught by the substitute. Interestingly, it is Mike Denness, the 12th man for England, who fields for the Rest as they struggle with the damaged back of Richards and the bruised hand of Kanhai.

Hattrick for Barlow, four wickets off five balls. *Wisden* gushes about the first Test hattrick since Gibbs and his emulation of the four wickets in five balls captured by MJC Allom against New Zealand in 1929–30. Yes, the same Allom who is the ex-Secretary of the Cricket Council, and the ex-President of MCC.

Deryck Murray, having replaced Engineer behind the stumps since the previous Test, now opens with Barlow in place of injured Richards. He gets 95. Sobers hits 114, and then declares at 376 for 9, to keep the injured Richards from batting.

England come back strongly in the second innings. Boycott and Luckhurst add 104, Fletcher gets 63. Illingworth's 54 and a sound 37 by Old set a reasonably decent target of 223.

That fourth afternoon sees sensational drama. Snow, charging in at fiery pace, removes Barlow and Murray. Mushtaq and Lloyd steady the ship before falling to injudicious sweep shots off Illingworth. Snow comes back to bowl Pollock. 62 for 5. In spite of sending in a night-watchman in the form of Intikhab, Sobers has to walk out to bat. They end the day at 75 for 5. Kanhai and Richards are injured.

With the light much clearer on the final morning, Sobers and Intikhab chip away at the runs. Greig drops the latter and the match starts to swing the way of the Rest.

At 177, Snow gets Sobers to edge to Cowdrey at slip. Intikhab hits the last ball before lunch to D'Oliveira. After the break, the injured duo of Richards and Kanhai come out. And soon Kanhai falls trying to cut Illingworth. 183 for 8, still 40 to get. Gibbs at No 11. Procter joins Richards.

The two ice-cool young Springboks overcome nerves and the new ball to take Rest to the series clinching victory.

Dennis Gamsy

Three days after the official announcement of the cancellation of the tour, Dennis Gamsy, the White South African wicketkeeper, wrote an editorial in the *Rand Daily Mail* calling for a national sports conference. His view was supported by Alf Chambers of the White tennis body.

On the first day of the fifth 'Test' at The Oval, the London Recruits carried out leaflet bombings and loudspeaker broadcasting in five cities: Durban, Cape Town, Port Elizabeth, Johannesburg and East London. In *Port Elizabeth Evening News*, Douglas Alexander reported: "Two bombs exploded today scattering hundreds of leaflets attacking South Africa's government [...] The pamphlets were headlined: The African National Congress says to Vorster and his gang: 'Your days are coming to an end [...] we will take back our country.' A police expert said charges found in some unexploded bombs averaged about one and a half ounces, enough to inflict burns or damage to the eyesight of anyone close to a blast."

The apartheid regime had their hands full with youthful movements.

The fifth 'Test' at The Oval is a magnificent game of cricket. In response to England's fairly decent 294, Rest score 355 aided by a 165-run association of left-handed heaven between Graeme Pollock and Garry Sobers. Pollock, off form for most of the series, is dropped at 18 and makes it count. Sobers continues the exhibition of his genius. The two add 135 in the last two hours on Friday, making sure that the stands will be full on Saturday. Pollock's 114 contains 16 fours and a six, and comes in just two and a half hours. Sobers is castled at 79. It is the young Lancashire fast bowler Peter Lever who bowls both Pollock and Sobers, picking up 7 for 83. Yes, the same Peter Lever who refused to play the South Africans.

In England's second innings Geoff Boycott bats half of the third day and most of the fourth, piling up 157. With the wicket taking increasing turn, England look to be sitting pretty at 289 for 3. But then they lose their way, and the unlikely bowling hero turns out to be Lloyd. Boycott leaves after six and a quarter hours, Illingworth is snapped up at the same score. Sobers and the back-in-side McKenzie account for the rest.

284 is by no means an easy target on a crumbling wicket. Barlow is cleaned up by Snow early in the innings. Richards and Pollock both try to counter the turning ball by stepping miles down the pitch and are bowled. But Lloyd and Kanhai, a trifle more selective in their strokes than the South Africans, add 123. Lloyd falls for 68 when Snow charges back. Kanhai just manages to complete his ton before he is also sent back by the Sussex poet-speedster. He accounts for Mushtaq as well. However, Sobers is once again a thorn in the English flesh. He slashes Lever to the thirdman boundary to bring up the winning runs.

The Rest take the series 4-1.

"It would be a mercy for humanity if this unpleasant little creep were to be dropped into a sewerage tank. Up to his ankles. Head first." This was the opinion about Peter Hain as published by Sir John Junor, editor-in-chief of *Sunday Express.*

However, what Peter Hain's direct action achieved went a long way towards shaping the destiny of the South African Whites and non-Whites. Sporting isolation was about to take a vice-like grip.

Besides, as Peter put it, "For the first time since Sharpeville, Black South Africans and Whites involved in the resistance had something to cheer about. For them it was a clarion call in the wilderness, a flash of light in the dark."

EPILOGUE

2 April 1971. The eve of the Van Riebeeck festival match at Newlands. Practically a trial match for the proposed Test tour of Australia in 1971–72. It was a celebration of 10 years of being a Republic, and also the anniversary of the 1652 arrival of Jan van Riebeeck to the Cape.

It is Rest vs Transvaal. Ali Bacher is absent, his medical practice keeping him busy. Eddie Barlow is away on business in New Zealand. But there is no shortage of stars.

Barry Richards is guesting for Transvaal, back from Australia after scoring 1,538 runs at 109.85 for South Australia with a best of 356. Mike Procter has just hammered a world record sequence of 119, 129, 107, 174, 106, and 254 in the Currie Cup. Graeme Pollock, leading the Rest, is sporting new glasses. There are Peter Pollock, Pat Trimborn, Grahame Chevalier, and the towering young Vintcent van der Bijl. It is a star-studded encounter.

In September 1970, an official invitation to tour Australia was issued to the SACA. On 27 January 1971, the conscience vote proposed by Clem Jones was defeated 12-1 and the Australian Cricket Board decided to go ahead with the proposed South African tour.

Less than a month later Jack Cheetham visited Don Bradman. The legend told him that "the Australian Board by a majority decision, made purely in light of their cricket requirements, wish the tour to proceed." However, the Don was wary of the dangerous demonstrations that had marred the Springbok rugby tour of Britain in 1969–70 and had eventually got the cricket tour cancelled. It would be better if the side sent to Australia was not all-White, he suggested.

At a dinner on that evening of 2 April 1971, Peter Pollock drew brother Graeme and senior cricketers Mike Procter and Denis Lindsay aside. The time had come to take a stand. The premier fast bowler of South Africa discussed his plans.

Cheetham persuaded the SACA to make an official request to include two non-White players in the South African squad to tour Australia. It was not that the Government had not known of this. Cheetham had been in discussion with Vorster in private. Dik Abed and Owen Williams had been approached by Cheetham, on his own initiative, and had been requested to join the side.

However, Hassan Howa, the SACBOC President, saw this gesture as empty. "SACBOC wants to have nothing to do with two token non-Whites in the team, like dummies in a shop window," he said.

On 26 March, Vorster forwarded his Government's response to the proposal of the SACA directly to Cheetham. Four days later, at a Press Conference, Vorster reiterated that it was the sole responsibility of the various non-White bodies to contact overseas countries and establish their own international links.

The communication with SACA was done in private and was supposed to be made public on the final day of the van Riebeeck festival match. But Cheetham was to fly to London on that day. The announcement had to be moved forward to 2 April. By the time the players had the pre-match dinner, the news of Cheetham's disappointment was well known. A perennial isolation looks starker than ever.

The initial plan hatched by Peter Pollock was to boycott the match. However, the four cricketers saw Charles Fortune sitting nearby. Respected veteran commentator, friend of the cricketers and a 'sage'—or at the very least sagacious. The Pollocks, Lindsay and Procter invited him into the discussion. Barry Richards was also drawn in.

Fortune was shocked. It sounded quite preposterous at the beginning. However, then he mellowed and advised the cricketers to adopt a different form of protest. The match was sold out and leaving the holiday crowd high and dry would not be the canniest of methods when it came to protesting.

They decided on a symbolic gesture. A draft statement was prepared by the core group and finalised by Fortune and Peter Pollock. The elder Pollock, being a journalist, was well-suited for the task.

Some other things had to fall in line. The Rest had to field first, so that the four organisers of the protest could lead the players off the ground in their symbolic walk-off. Therefore, Don Mackay-Coghill, the acting captain of Transvaal, was brought into the group.

Not all the Transvaal cricketers were convinced. But eventually no one refused to participate. Transvaal opening batsman and ex-Oxford University captain, Fred Goldstein, made his position clear: "If this is just an attempt to save the Springbok tour to Australia, I'm not interested. But if it is a genuine effort to promote equality on the sporting field, count me in all the way."

The explanation of the Pollocks and the others thoroughly convinced Goldstein. He committed himself all the way.

The players were smart enough to keep the plans away from the ears of the Transvaal manager. He was none other than John Waite, who had written in 1961 that there was no non-White sportsman who could displace a White sportsman in any Springbok side.

On 3 April, Barry Richards takes guard as Peter Pollock marks out his long run. The ball is straightish and is pushed to mid-on for a single. Thereafter the batsmen lay down their bats, and together with the 11 fieldsmen walk towards the players' entrance. There, they are joined by the other nine members of the Transvaal side.

The spectators, including four Cabinet Ministers in their midst, sit in surprised silence as the players make their way to the dressing room. Ron Delport, manager of the Rest, is handed a statement which he relays to the press.

Thereafter, the players make their way back to the ground and the game is restarted.

The statement reads: "We cricketers feel that the time has come for an expression of our views. We fully support the South African Cricket Association's application to invite non-whites to tour Australia, if they are good enough, and further subscribe to merit being the only criterion on the cricket field."

Minister of Sport Frank Waring describes the gesture as "a political demonstration designed for overseas consumption." According to Geoffrey Chettle, in the *South African Cricket Almanack 1971*, "[Waring was] clutching at floating straws [...] In the manner of a petulant schoolboy, he immediately dissociated himself with the prize-giving ceremony at the end of the match." Waring also cancels the traditional *braaivleis* (barbecue) after the match where he is supposed to host the players.

The wording of the statement is hardly revolutionary. But for the South African government, it is positively shocking. However, according to Patrick Ferriday, "this was not a group of Black demonstrators who could be restrained with batons, tear gas, and bullets, this was an elite group of privileged White males interrogating the very foundations of their sport, and through that their society. As a sporting elite they were role models and national heroes."

Of course, the event had repercussions. Eric Rowan, one of the selectors, sought out Mackay-Coghill, perhaps due to the erroneous conclusion that he was the ringleader, or perhaps because he was the only lightweight among the identified group of organisers. Rowan was quite short with Mackay-Coghill as the acting Transvaal captain was informed, "You've done your dash." He was not selected for the Australian series, which in any case remained a phantom tour.

Don McKay-Coghill

The match turns out to be a drab, dull encounter, with Barry Richards and Graeme Pollock getting hundreds and Grahame Chevalier picking up 10 wickets. At the end of the match, Vintcent van der Bijl is greeted by the relieving news that he has been chosen for the tour. However, two days later he gets a letter from his father Pieter, the man who scored 125 and 97 and had two haircuts in the Timeless Test at Durban, 1939. The letter advises him, "not to harbour any hopes of the tour taking place."

For a while the Australian tour remained on the cards, with the new Australian Prime Minister William McMahon parroting the 'sport should be divorced from politics' cliché.

However, things changed with the Springbok rugby team landing in the country on 26 June.

Fortified by the incredible STST success, CARIS, AAM, and the Aboriginal activists produced a heady sequel to the 1969–70 Springbok tour to England. It was a mayhem that deserves a full book for itself. Peter Hain was invited to support the campaign, and after successfully completing his first-year university exams he left for Sydney on a 31-hour flight.

Every match was disrupted with increasing frequency. To make matters worse, Ansett and Trans Australian Airlines refused to ferry the players and they had to travel around 1,700 miles in cramped Royal Australian Air Force flights.

At the Sydney Cricket Ground, the Springboks met the Wallabies and Don Bradman was in the stands to watch the match.

"There was no food and drink provided, the unions rebelled against it. They put barbed wire all around SCG and dug holes all around the outfield," Bradman remembered later.

"What on earth are all these holes for?" he asked one of the organisers he was with.

"You'll soon find out when the match gets underway," he was told.

He did find out. They were to extinguish smoke bombs thrown by demonstrators. The activists also made attempts to saw down goalposts. There were 2,000 policemen at the SCG that day, but they had grave difficulty containing the demonstrators who were armed with bolt cutters. The noise was impossible.

Bradman was convinced. "It became clear as crystal it was a sheer, physical, utter impossibility to stage a cricket match under those circumstances. It literally could not be done."

On 8 September 1971, the Australian Cricket Board unanimously agreed to the Clem Jones motion of cancelling the tour. In a drafted statement, Bradman hoped that the South African government would "in near future relax its laws."

The Australian tour was also formally cancelled. Garry Sobers led yet another World XI side to play five 'Tests' against the Australians. The team included Graeme Pollock, Peter Pollock, and Hylton Ackerman from South Africa.

Peter Hain reflects, "My two weeks in support of the campaign was of assistance, but the main campaign was generated from inside Australia. I think my role was more symbolic. We had had the victory and I came saying that you can secure a victory too—which they did. The organisation, the momentum, the activism, the courage was all from Australia. But that campaign, repeating our success of 1970 a year later, was critically important. South African cricket and rugby teams never toured either Australia or Britain again till after isolation."

The next time South Africa played international cricket was in 1991. A year after the release of Nelson Mandela.

Their first opponent was India. They visited the country to play three One Day Internationals.

Their first Test match was against West Indies.

The complete cricket isolation was not for the lack of trying on the part of the passionate supporters of South Africa in the traditional cricketing establishments. Even in 1983, there was a requisition raised to the MCC Committee by fifty of its members, stating that a private club team (MCC posing as the private club in this case) should be sent to South Africa in 1983–84. Firmly in favour of the MCC tour was Denis Compton.

Wiser counsels prevailed—mainly with an eye on the global repercussions. Though the South Africa Cricket Union (SACU) had been established in 1976 to administer the game on a multi-racial, meritocratic basis, the effectiveness of their actions was still being debated in 1983. Joe Pamensky, president of SACU, was still trading blows around the issue with Sam Ramasamy, Chairman of SAN-ROC.

The only way the South Africans could get an ersatz taste of international cricket was by arranging 'Rebel' tours of mercenary cricketers from various Test playing nations.

The Rebel Tours can perhaps be recognised in retrospect as a sign of progress. Along with two England teams and two Australian teams, there were two West Indian and one Sri Lankan side who visited the shores on defiant tours. In order to survive isolation, mixed race cricket did find its way into the grounds of South Africa.

Other sporting contacts were reduced to bare minimum.

1969–70 was the last time the Springboks toured the British Isles before the end of apartheid. Similarly, 1971 was the last time the South African rugby side toured Australia.

Touring other countries on official sporting contests became difficult. The 56-days of the 1981 Springbok tour to New Zealand saw over 200 demonstrations in 28 centres, with 150,000 people taking part—the largest civil disturbance since the 1951 waterfront dispute in the country. Even the Springbok-All Blacks series were suspended after that till the abolition of apartheid.

Official tours to South Africa were comparatively easier, with the protests easier to control in a police state. However, these too invited severe backlash.

In 1976, the All Blacks toured South Africa. In response, 31 countries withdrew from the Montreal Olympics, protesting the presence of New Zealand in the land of apartheid. Hence, the country was responsible for the first major boycott of the Modern Olympics.

The following year, the Commonwealth heads of states adopted the Gleneagles Agreement, discouraging contact and competition between their sportsmen and sporting organisations, teams, or individuals from South Africa.

In 1978, Nigeria withdrew from the Commonwealth Games because of the refusal of New Zealand to comply with the Gleneagles Agreement.

The White nations nevertheless continued to tour South Africa. The British Lions visited in 1974 and 1980, France in 1975 and 1980, and two England sides in 1972 and 1984. However, eventually, the increasing pressure from the anti-apartheid movements stopped official tours to South Africa completely.

Peter Pollock found solace in God, following the cricketing-religious footsteps of Rev David Sheppard and, later, Trevor Goddard.

Graeme Pollock maintained that it was a greater cause for which their careers had to be suspended. He acknowledged that at the very beginning of their careers, in White South Africa, "we didn't give enough thought to the people who weren't given opportunities. In hindsight, we certainly could have done a lot more in trying to get change in South Africa."

Mike Procter and Ali Bacher worked furiously to level the playing fields, to ensure that South Africa re-emerged in the international scene in a manner acceptable to the world.

However, not everyone in the last group of fantastic South African cricketers managed the same level of equanimity.

Some persist in being petulant angry old men of cricket, still not quite at peace with their curtailed careers. The bitterness spills out in their views and analysis of modern cricket.

Not all the measures taken towards recall from isolation and thereafter have been ideal ones either. There are problems aplenty in South African cricket and South African sport even as the book is being written, and a lot of them stem from the long history of discrimination. It is not an easy history to balance. It never is.

In 1982, Nelson Mandela was moved from Robben Island to the Pollsmoor Prison near Cape Town.

In 1986, he was visited in the prison by former Australian Prime Minister Malcolm Fraser. His first question was, "Tell me Mr Fraser, is Don Bradman still alive?"

When Mandela was released from prison in 1990, Fraser presented him with an autographed bat. The inscription read: "To Nelson Mandela in recognition of a great unfinished innings—Don Bradman"

In 1994, the country held its first election in which all races participated with universal adult suffrage. Conducted under the direction of the Independent Electoral Commission (IEC), it marked the culmination of the four-year process that ended apartheid. ANC won in a landslide and Mandela was elected President.

That same year, the Australian cricket team visited South Africa for the first time after isolation. President Nelson Mandela welcomed the visitors with warmth and enthusiasm, recalling his experience of watching Neil Harvey bat in the segregated days.

In the aftermath of the STST movement, Peter Hain was slapped with a private prosecution suit for criminal conspiracy by an eccentric English barrister. The South African Bureau of Secret Service (BOSS) took a leading role in setting him up. The instructions were supposedly to "pin that political butterfly to the wall."

In early 1972, he was delivered a letter that proved to be a bomb that luckily did not explode. The BOSS had carried out several assassinations using the letter-bomb method.

The trial against Peter took place in August 1972, fortunately during his university vacation. The prosecution was funded by pro-apartheid South African Whites. The evidence used against him was his own book *Don't play with Apartheid.* He was fined £200 for the Davis Cup protests and acquitted of the other three counts.

In 1976, Peter was targeted again, this time for a supposed bank-theft in 1975. He was acquitted once again. The BOSS took a while to forget.

Peter eventually proceeded to enjoy a glittering career with the Labour Party. He was elected to the House of Commons at the by-election in April 1991 for the Neath constituency. In his years as a Cabinet Minister, he dealt with—among other issues—Iraq, Mugabe, Gibraltar, blood diamonds, MI5 and MI6, Wales, and the historic Northern Ireland settlement. He even graduated to wearing suits.

Peter, who had become South Africa's Public Enemy Number One, had to wait years before returning to the land of his boyhood. When he met Mandela, the 81-year-old President of South Africa, the great man informed him that bulletins of the STST campaign managed to reach the cells of Robben Island in spite of a news blackout. The white warders—rugby fanatics to a man—were absolutely infuriated and kept talking about the protesters and 'that bastard Hain'.

Basil D'Oliveira ended his Test career in 1972, having played 44 Tests, scoring 2,484 runs at 40.06 with five centuries and 15 fifties. His 47 Test wickets came at 39.55. Quite an achievement for a man for whom international cricket looked a futile dream across infinite impediments.

He carried on playing regularly for Worcestershire till 1978, till the age of 47, often turning in scintillating performances. He appeared even after that, scoring a half-century inclusive of a hooked six off Joel Garner in 1979, and turned out in one match against Middlesex in 1980. The man who should have played much of his cricket facing Jim Laker was dismissed by John Emburey in his final two first-class innings.

He ended up enjoying a long first-class career, with 367 matches, 19,490 runs and 551 wickets. That he did all that after playing his first ever first-class match after 30, first county game at 33, and first Test match at 34, is nothing less than the most wondrous of miracles.

D'Oliveira remained a cricketer and then a coach. Though he was against apartheid, he never became a radical or an activist. This led him to rub many a radical activist in SAN-ROC,

SACBOC and other organisations the wrong way. He frequently clashed with Hassan Howa, and did not see eye to eye with Dennis Brutus.

However, in England and among his people in South Africa, he remained a beacon, a pioneer, a household name.

In the sixth episode of *Fawlty Towers*, Major Gowen tells Basil Fawlty that when he went to a Test match at The Oval, a woman kept referring to the Indians as niggers. "'No, no, no,' I said, 'the niggers are the West Indians. These people are wogs.'"

It is a rather clever way of satirising the English upper-class bigot.

At the same time, in the very first episode of the series, *Touch of Class,* the same uninhibitedly racist Major Gowen reads his paper, and after all the depressing news about the strikes he is delighted to find that D'Oliveira has scored another hundred. John Cleese as Fawlty responds saying, "Good old Dolly!"

Touch of Class, the first episode of *Fawlty Towers* was aired in September 1975. It underlines the enduring appeal of D'Oliveira the cricketer.

Other than that, it also brings out the changes in society that were set off by the phenomenon of D'Oliveira and the subsequent long-hair aided movements he triggered.

The biggest of the culprits had to stand back, admire, applaud, and accept.

APPENDIX

TEST AND 'TEST' SERIES COVERED IN THE BOOK

Tests of South African White side

Season	Opponent	Venue	Matches	Result
1938–39	England	South Africa	5	Eng 1 SA 0
1947	England	England	5	Eng 3 SA 0
1948–49	England	South Africa	5	Eng 2 SA 0
1950–51	Australia	South Africa	5	Aus 4 SA 0
1951	England	England	5	Eng 3 SA 1
1952–53	Australia	Australia	5	Aus 2 SA 2
1953–54	New Zealand	South Africa	5	SA 4 NZ 0
1955	England	England	5	Eng 3 SA 2
1956–57	England	South Africa	5	Eng 2 SA 2
1957–58	Australia	South Africa	5	Aus 3 SA 0
1960	England	England	5	Eng 3 SA 0
1961–62	New Zealand	South Africa	5	SA 2 NZ 2
1963–64	Australia	Australia	5	Aus 1 SA 1
1963–64	New Zealand	New Zealand	3	SA 0 NZ 0
1964–65	England	South Africa	5	Eng 1 SA 0
1965	England	England	3	SA 1 Eng 0
1966–67	Australia	South Africa	5	SA 3 Aus 1
1969–70	Australia	South Africa	4	SA 4 Aus 0

'Tests' of South African non-White team

Season	Opponent	Venue	Matches	Result
1956–57	Kenyan Asians	South Africa	3*	SA 2 KA 0
1958–59	Kenya	East Africa	2*	SA 2 KEN 0
	Uganda	East Africa	1*	SA 1 UGA 0
	East Africa	East Africa	1*	SA 1 EA 0

Tests and 'Tests' of England

Season	Opponent	Venue	Matches	Result
1966	West Indies	England	5	WI 3 Eng 1
1967	India	England	3	Eng 3 Ind 0
1967	Pakistan	England	3	Eng 2 Pak 0
1967–68	West Indies	West Indies	5	Eng 1 WI 0
1968	Australia	England	5	Aus 1 Eng 1
1968–69	Pakistan	Pakistan	3	Pak 0 Eng 0
1969	West Indies	England	3	Eng 2 WI 0
1969	New Zealand	England	3	Eng 2 NZ 0
1970	Rest of the World	England	5*	RoW 4 Eng 1

* unofficial 'Tests'

Basil D'Oliveira in cricket:

- Unofficial 'Tests' for SACBOC/South African non-Whites
- Official Tests for England
- Unofficial non-White matches (for SACBOC in 'Tests' and Tour matches and for SACCA in the Dadabhay Inter-Race Series)
- Official First-Class Matches

'Tests': Age 25–27

Span	Matches	Runs	Ave	100	50	Wkts	Ave
1956–1959	5	447	55.87	1	3	7	15.86

Tests: Age 34–40

Span	Matches	Runs	Ave	100	50	Wkts	Ave
1966–1972	44	2484	40.06	5	15	47	39.55

SACBOC matches of the 1950s not deemed First-Class Age 22–27
(for SACBOC/SA non-Europeans in 'Tests' and Tour matches. and for SACCA in the Dadabhay Inter-Race Series)

Span	Matches	Runs	Ave	100	50	Wkts	Ave
1953–1959	23	1379	49.25	3	11	31	12.77

First-Class: Age 30–48
(includes matches for Eastern Province in the Dadabhay Trophy 1971–72 and 1972–73 and one match for The Rest against Western Province in 1972–73—which were granted first-class status)

Span	Matches	Runs	Ave	100	50	Wkts	Ave
1961–1980	367	19,490	40.26	45	98	548	27.41

BIBLIOGRAPHY

Allen, David Rayvern, *Arlott: The Authorised Biography*, (Harper Collins, 1996)
Allen, David Rayvern, *Sir Aubrey*, (JW McKenzie, 2005)
Allen, Dean, *Empire, War and Cricket in South Africa*, (Zebra Press, 2015)
Angelou, Maya, *I Know Why the Caged Bird Sings*, (Random House, 1969)
Arlott, John, *Gone to the Cricket*, (Longman's Green and Co, 1948)
Arsenault, Raymond, *Arthur Ashe: A Life*, (Simon & Schuster, 2018)
Barker, JS, *In the Main: West Indies versus MCC 1968*, (Pelham Books, 1968)
Barlow, Eddie, *Eddie Barlow: The Autobiography*, (Tafelberg, 2006)
Bassano, Brian and Smith, Rick, *The Visit of Mr WW Read's 1891–92 English Cricket Team to South Africa*, (JW McKenzie, 2007)
Bassano, Brian and Smith, Rick, *Vic's Boys in South Africa 1935–36*, (Apple Books, 1993)
Bassano, Brian, *Mann's Men: The MCC in South Africa 1922–23*, (JW McKenzie, 2004)
Bassano Brian, *MCC in South Africa 1938–39*, (JW McKenzie, 1997)
Bassano, Brian, *South African Cricket 1947–1960*, (Cricket Connections International, 1996)
Bowen, Rowland, *Cricket: A History of its Growth and Development throughout the World*, (Eyre and Spottiswoode, 1970)
Bossenbroek, Martin, *De Boerenoorlog*, (Singel Uitgeverijen, 2014)
Branch, Taylor, *At Canaan's Edge: America in the King Years 1965–68*, (Simon and Schuster, 2006)
Branch, Taylor, *Parting the Waters: America in the King Years 1954–63*, (Touchstone, 1988)
Branch, Taylor, *Pillar of Fire: America in the King Years 1963–65* (Simon and Schuster, 1998)
Brasher, Christopher, *Mexico 1968*, (Stanley Paul, 1968)
Brittenden, RT, *Silver Fern on the Veld*, (Howard B Timmins, 1954)
Brittenden, RT, *Great Days in New Zealand Cricket*, (Bailey Bros and Swinten, 1958)
Burns, Michael, *Endean: A South African Sportsman in the Apartheid Era*, (Nightwatchman Books, 2017)
Buskes, JJ, *Zuid-Afrika's Apartheidsbeleid: Onaanvaardbaar*, (Bert Bakker, Daamen NV, 1955)
Cazenove, Susan, *An Unwitting Assassin*, (Rainbird, 2017)
Chalke, Stephen, *At the Heart of English Cricket: The Life and Memories of Geoffrey Howard*, (Fairfield Books, 2001)
Chalke, Stephen, *Summer's Crown: The Story of Cricket's County Championship* (Fairfield Books, 2015)
Chalke, Stephen, *Tom Cartwright: The Flame Still Burns*, (Fairfield Books, 2007)
Cheetham, Jack, *Caught by the Springboks*, (Hodder and Stoughton, 1953)
Cheetham, Jack, *I Declare*, (Hodder and Stoughton, 1955)
Clarke, John and Scovell, Brian, *Everything that's Cricket: The West Indies Tour 1966*, (Stanley Paul, 1966)
Close, Brian, *The MCC Tour of West Indies, 1968*, (Stanley Paul, 1968)
Cooper, Stephen, *After the Final Whistle*, (The History Press, 2016)
Cowdrey, MC, *MCC*, (Hodder and Stoughton, 1976)

Cox, Charles (ed), *The Cricketing Record of Major Warton's Tour 1888–89*, (John McKenzie, 1987)
Crowley, Brian, *A Cavalcade of International Cricketers,* (Pan Macmillan, 1988)

Crowley, Brian, *Currie Cup Story*, (Don Nelson, 1973)
de Groot, Gerard, *The Sixties Unplugged*, (Pan Books, 2008)
D'Oliveira, Basil, *D'Oliveira: An Autobiography*, (Collins, 1968)
D'Oliveira, Basil, *The Basil D'Oliveira Affair*, (Collins, 1969)
D'Oliveira, Basil, *Time to Declare: An Autobiography*, (JM Dent & Sons, 1980)
D'Oliveira, John, *Vorster-the Man*, (Ernest Stanton, 1977)
Duffus, Louis, *Play Abandoned: An Autobiography*, (Howard Timmins, 1969)
Duffus, Louis, *South African Cricket 1927–1947*, (South African Cricket Association, 1947)
Duffus, Louis, *Springbok Glory*, (Longmans, Green and Co., 1955)
Fisher, John, *Paul Kruger His Life and Times*, (Secker & Warburg, 1974)
Foot, David, *Wally Hammond: The Reasons Why,* (Robson Books, 1996)
Fortune, Charles, *Cricket Overthrown*, (Howard Timmins, 1960)
Fortune, Charles, *MCC in South Africa 1964–5*, (Robert Hale, 1965)
Fortune, Charles, *The MCC Tour of South Africa 1956–1957,* (George G Harrap & Co., 1957)
Frith, David, *England versus Australia: A Pictorial History of the Test Matches Since 1877*, (Willow Books, 1984)
Frith, David, *Silence of the Heart*, (Mainstream Publishing, 2001)
Fry, CB, *Life Worth Living*, (Eyre & Spottiswoode, 1939)
Gassert, Philipp and Klimke, Martin (eds.), *1968 On the Edge of Revolution*, (Black Rose Books, 2018)
Gemmell, John, *The Politics of South African Cricket*, (Routledge, 2004)
Ghosh, Mayukh, *In a League of their Own*, (Cricketmash, 2019)
Giliomee, Hermann, *The Afrikaners: Biography of a People,* (Hurst and Company, 2011)
Goddard, Trevor, *Caught in the Deep*, (Vision Media, 1988)
Gosselink, Martine; Holtrop, Maria and Ross, Robert (eds), *Goed Hoop: Zuid Afrika en Nederland vanaf 1600*, (Rijksmuseum, 2017)
Grundling, Albert; Odendaal, André and Burridge, Spies, *Beyond the Tryline: Rugby and South African Society*, (Ravan Press, 1995)
Haigh, Gideon and Frith, David, *Inside Story: Unlocking Australian Cricket's Archives*, (News Custom Publishing, 2007)
Haigh, Gideon, *The Summer Game: Cricket and Australia in the 50s and 60s*, (ABC Books, 2006)
Hain, Peter, *Ad & Wal: Values, duty, sacrifice in apartheid South Africa*, (Biteback, 2014)
Hain, Peter, *Don't Play with Apartheid*, (George Allen & Unwin Ltd, 1971)
Hain, Peter, *Mandela: His Essential Life*, (Rowman & Littlefield, 2018)
Hain, Peter, *Outsider In*, (Biteback, 2012)
Hilmes, Oliver, *Berlin 1936,* (Vintage, 2016)
Hochschild, Adam, *King Leopold's Ghost*, (Mariner Books, 1998)
Illingworth, Ray, *Yorkshire and Back*, (Queen Anne Press, 1980)
Ingham, Kenneth, *Jan Christian Smuts: The Conscience of a South African*, (Weidenfeld and Nicholson, 1986)
Jaggard, Ed, *Garth: The Story of Graham McKenzie*, (Freemantle Arts Centre Press, 1993)
Jenkinson, Neil, *CB Llewellyn: A Study in Equivocation*, (ACS Publications, 2012)
Joffe, Joel, *The Rivonia Story*, (Mayibuye, 1995)

Joffe, Joel, *The State vs Nelson Mandela*, (Oneworld, 2007)
Keable, Ken (ed), *London Recruits: The Secret War Against Apartheid*, (Merlin Press, 2012)
Kenney, Henry, *Verwoerd: Architect of Apartheid*, (Jonathan Ball, 2016)
Laband, John and Thompson, Paul, *The Illustrated Guide to the Anglo-Zulu War*, (University of Natal Press, 2000)
Laker, Jim, *Cricket Contrasts,* (Stanley Paul, 1985)
Laker, Jim, *Over to Me*, (Frederick Muller, 1960)
Lazenby, John, *Edging Towards Darkness: The Story of the Last Timeless Test,* (Bloomsbury, 2017)
Lindfors, Bernth ed., *The Dennis Brutus Tapes: Essays at Autobiography*, (James Currey, 2001)
Litchfield, Eric, *Cricket Grand Slam*, (AH & AW Reed, 1970)
Luckin, MW, *South African Cricket 1919–1927*, (MW Luckin, 1927)
Luckin, MW, *The History of South African Cricket*, (WE Hortor & Co, 1915)
May, Peter, *The Rebel Tours*, (Sports Books, 2009)
McGlew, Jackie and Litchfield, Eric, *Six for Glory*, (AH & AW Reed, 1967)
McGlew, Jackie, *Cricket Crisis: The MCC visit to South Africa 1964–5*, (Hodder and Stoughton, 1965)
McGlew, Jackie, *Cricket for South Africa*, (Hodder and Stoughton, 1961)
McLean, Roy, *Pitch and Toss*, (Hodder and Stoughton, 1957)
McLean, Roy, *Sackcloth without Ashes*, (Hodder and Stoughton, 1958)
Medworth, CO, *Noursemen in England*, (Werner Laurie, 1952)
Meintjes, Johannes, *President Paul Kruger*, (Cassel, 1974)
Meredith, Martin, *Diamonds Gold and War The Making of South Africa*, (Simon and Schuster, 2007)
Morris, Michael, *Apartheid*, (Jonathan Ball, 2004)
Moyes, AG, *The South Africans in Australia 1952–53*, (George G Harrap & Co., 1953)
Mukherjee, Abhishek, *The Locust Scare*, http://cricmash.com/anecdotes/the-locust-scare
Murray, Bruce and Merrett, Christopher, *Caught Behind: Race and Politics in Springbok Cricket*, (Wits University Press, 2004)
Murray, Bruce; Parry, Richard and Winch, Jonty (ed), *Cricket and Society in South Africa 1910–1971*, (Palgrave, MacMillan, 2018)
Nicholson, Christopher, *Papwa Sewgolum: From Pariah to Legend*, Wits University Press, 2005
Nicol, Mike, *A Good Looking Corpse*, (Secker & Warburg, 1991)
Nourse, Dudley, *Cricket in the Blood*, (Hodder and Stoughton, 1949)
Oborne, Peter, *Basil D'Oliveira Cricket and Conspiracy: The Untold Story*, (Little, Brown, 2004)
Oborne, Peter, *Wounded Tiger*, (Simon and Schuster, 2014)
Odendaal, André; Reddy, Krish and Merrett, Christopher, *Divided Country The History of South African Cricket Retold 1914–1950s*, (BestRed, 2018)
Odendaal, André; Reddy Krish; Merrett, Christopher and Winch, Jonty, *Cricket and Conquest The History of South African Cricket Retold 1795–1914*, (BestRed, 2016)
Odendaal, André, *The Story of an African Game*, (David Phillip, 2003)
Packenham, Thomas, *The Boer War*, (Abacus, 1979)
Pakenham, Thomas, *The Scramble for Africa*, (Abacus, 1991)
Parker, AC, *The Springboks 1891–1970*, (Cassell, 1970)
Peart-Binns, John S., *Archbishop Joost de Blank: Scourge of Apartheid*, (Mulller, Blond and White, 1987)

Peel, Mark, *The Noblest Roman*, (Andre Deutsch, 1999)
Player, Gary, *Grand Slam Golf*, (Cassel, 1966)
Pollock, Peter, *Clean Bowled*, (Vision Media, 1985)
Pollock, Peter, *God's Fast Bowler*, (Christian Art Publishers, 2001)
Ransford, Oliver, *The Great Trek*, (Cardinal, 1974)
Reid, John, *A Million Miles of Cricket*, (AH & AW Reed, 1966)
Reid, John, *Sword of Willow*, (Herbert Jenkins, 1962)
Reyburn, Wallace, *There was also Some Rugby: The Sixth Springboks in Britain*, (Stanley Paul, 1970)
Richards, Huw, *A Game for Hooligans: The History of Rugby Union*, (Mainstream, 2007)
Richards, Trevor, *Dancing on our Bones: New Zealand, South Africa, Rugby and Racism*, (Bridget Williams Books, 1999)
Rijks, Miranda, *The Eccentric Entrepreneur*, (The History Press, 2008)
Ross, Alan, *Cape Summer and The Australians in England*, (Constable, 1986)
Sandbrook, Dominic, *Never Had It So Good: A History of Britain from the Suez to the Beatles*, (Abacus, 2005)
Sandbrook, Dominic, *White Heat: A History of Britain in the Swinging Sixties*, (Abacus, 2006)
Sengupta, Arunabha and Maha, *This Thing Can Be Done: A Comic Strip History of The Ashes*, (unpublished)
Short, Graham, *The Trevor Goddard Story*, (Purfleet Productions, 1965)
Simpson, Bobby, *The Australians in England 1968*, (Stanley Paul, 1968)
Singer, Daniel, *Prelude to Revolution: France in May, 1968*, (Haymarket Books, 1970)
Swanton, EW, *Gubby Allen: Man of Cricket*, (Hutchinson/Stanley Paul, 1985)
Thomas, JBG, *Springbok Invasion*, (Pelham Books, 1970)
Thompson, Leonard, *A History of South Africa*, (Yale University Press, 1990)
Tygiel, Jules, *Baseball's Great Experiment: Jackie Robinson and his Legacy*, (Oxford University Press, 1997)
van der Bijl, Vincent, *Cricket in the Shadows*, (Shuter and Shooter, 1984)
van Ryneveld, Clive, *20th Century All-rounder*, (Pretext, 2011)
van Woerden, Henk, *The Assassin: A Story of Race and Rage in the Land of Apartheid*, (Metropolitan Books, 2001)
Vinen, Richard, *The Long '68*, (Allen Lane, 2018)
Wagg, Stephen (ed), *Cricket and Nationality in the Postcolonial Age*, (Routledge, 2005)
Waite, John, *Perchance to Bowl*, (Nicholas Kaye, 1961)
Warner, PF, *The MCC in South Africa*, (Chapman and Hall, 1906)
Welsh, David, *The Rise and Fall of Apartheid*, (Jonathan Ball, 2009)
Welsh, Frank, *A History of South Africa*, (Harper Collins, 2000)
Whitington, RS, *Simpson's Safari*, (William Heineman Ltd, 1967)
Wigggins, David K and Miller, Patrick B, *The Uneven Playing Field*, (University of Illinois, 2005)
Wilkins, Ivor and Strydom, Hans, *The Broederbond … the most powerful secret society in the world*, (Paddington Press, 1979)
Winter, Gordon, *Inside Boss: South Africa's Secret Police*, (Penguin, 1981)
Witherspoon, Kevin, *Before the Eyes of the World: Mexico and the 1968 Olympic Games*, (Northern Illinois University Press, 2014)
Writer, Larry, *Pitched Battle*, (Scribe, 2016)

VISUAL MATERIAL

The visual material for the book has been collected from various sources including:

The Advertiser
The Age
The Argus
The Australian
Cape Argus
Cape Times
Die Beeld
Die Burger
Diamond Field Advertiser
Drum
Eastern Province Herald
East London Dispatch
Herald Sun
Imwo Zabantsundu
Johannesburg Star
Lovedale Missionary Institution, South Africa: Fifty views from photographs
The Natal Mercury
National Library of South Africa
Peter Hain's personal collection
Pretoria News
Private Eye
Rand Daily Mail
Rijksmuseum, Amsterdam
sahistory.org.za
South African Cricket Annual
South African Golf Association
Sunday Times
Sussex County Cricket Club Museum
Sydney Morning Herald
Volksblad
Wikipedia

(Due care has been taken to ensure that the images are in Public Domain, else the requisite permission has been obtained)

INDEX

ABOUT THE AUTHOR

Arunabha Sengupta is a historian and cricket writer based in Amsterdam. He has worked as a freelance cricket correspondent and columnist for various print and online publications. He is also the author of the cricket-based mystery pastiche *Sherlock Holmes and the Birth of The Ashes.*

Arunabha Sengupta with Peter Hain at the House of Lords, London

Made in the USA
Las Vegas, NV
21 November 2021